DATE DUE

GAYLORD			PRINTED IN U.S.A

Explorations in Role Analysis

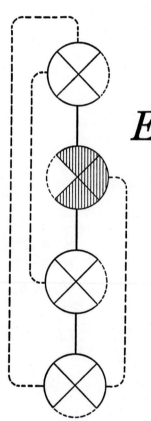

Explorations

STUDIES OF THE

n Role Analysis:

CHOOL SUPERINTENDENCY ROLE

Neal Gross
Harvard University

Ward S. Mason
U. S. Office of Education

Alexander W. McEachern
John Tracy Clinic

OHN WILEY & SONS, INC.

New York · London · Sydney

BOOKS BY GROSS (N), MASON (N. S.)

and McEACHERN (A. W.)—Explorations

in Role Analysis

—Who Runs Our Schools?

FOURTH PRINTING, OCTOBER, 1966

Copyright © 1958, by John Wiley & Sons, Inc.

Library of Congress Catalog Card Number: 57-13443

Printed in the United States of America

To Samuel A. Stouffer
and Francis Keppel

Foreword to the School Executive Studies

This book is one of several publications that have reported or will report the findings of the School Executive Studies, a research program initiated at Harvard University in 1952. Since it is the first book length publication stemming from the Studies, it is appropriate for me, as director, to make certain comments about the research program and to express my indebtedness to staff members and others who have made contributions to the Studies.

The research had two major objectives. The first was to examine certain problem areas of central interest to students of social behavior. Two of these areas were role and role-conflict analysis, and this book reports our theoretical and empirical findings concerning these problem areas. Earlier social science publications have reported the results of our analyses of methodological problems of long interviews* and the analysis of intraoccupational prestige.† Another volume now in preparation will focus on problems of interest to students of the sociology of occupations, the sociology of education, and educational administration. Its major purpose is to present an empirical analysis of the job of the school superintendent in terms of the social structures in which it is involved.

The second major objective of the Studies was to analyze a series of questions of special interest to public school administrators, school board members, and citizens who are interested in public education.

* Neal Gross and Ward S. Mason, "Some Methodological Problems of Eight Hour Interviews," *American Journal of Sociology*, LIX (1953), pp. 197–204.

† Ward S. Mason and Neal Gross, "Intra-Occupational Prestige Differentiation: The School Superintendency," *American Sociological Review*, XX (1955), pp. 326–331.

Our analyses of these applied social science questions have been reported* or will be reported elsewhere.

The doubled-barreled objective of the research reflects a basic assumption underpinning the School Executive Studies: that a research program, if carefully designed, can use the conceptual and methodological tools of the behavioral sciences to analyze strategic public policy problems and at the same time make a contribution to the social sciences. It is no accident that the Studies were co-sponsored by the Laboratory of Social Relations and the Graduate School of Education of Harvard University.

The general design of the Studies was developed by April 1952, and the proposed research program was discussed individually and jointly with Professor Samuel A. Stouffer, Director of the Laboratory of Social Relations, and Dean Francis Keppel of the Graduate School of Education at Harvard University. Primarily through their efforts, financial support was obtained from the Laboratory of Social Relations and the Graduate School of Education to explore the possibilities and pitfalls of such a set of inquiries. Without their encouragement and support it would not have been possible to launch what subsequently turned out to be a fairly substantial research program. In addition, they have given generously of their time and their wisdom throughout the course of the research program. It is with great pleasure that I acknowledge my personal indebtedness to them.

During the summer of 1952 the co-authors of this book were invited to serve as my senior staff associates. They participated in the development of the detailed research designs of the Studies and were centrally involved in the decisions concerning the major theoretical and empirical problems of the research.

I also wish to acknowledge the contribution of other staff members. In addition to Alexander W. McEachern who supervised the school board interviewing program, the school board interviews were conducted by James M. Coffee, Harold J. Greenwald, Donald G. McKinley, and John E. Tirrell. They also served as coders of the interview data and carried out bibliographic assignments. The interviews with the superintendents were conducted by Ward S. Mason and myself. Ralph W. Osborne and Carl J. Freudenreich served as interviewers for the first set of trial interviews.

Aune Heino, Pauline Hemenway, Teresa Kovich, and Gertrude

---

* Neal Gross, *The Pressures on and the Dilemmas of the School Superintendent* (Cambridge: New England School Development Council, 1954); Neal Gross, *The Schools and the Press* (Cambridge: New England School Development Council, 1955).

Tourtellet performed important clerical, computational, or secretarial tasks. Dean K. Whitla supervised one phase of the coding operation and certain preliminary analyses of the data. Robert Dreeben, Donald R. Fagg, and Ruben Santos-Cuyugan provided library assistance. Shirley Atkinson and Dorothy Johnson handled the financial administration of the Studies.

Three other people deserve special recognition for their contributions to the Studies. Especially in the early phases of the project, David V. Tiedeman was generous of his time and his talents in advising on certain statistical problems relating to the research-design and preliminary analysis activities. A special debt of gratitude is owed W. Douglas Brooks who rendered valuable service as the mathematical statistician and supervisor of statistical computations during most of the analysis phase of the research. Marion L. Crowley served as secretary of the Studies, and I am indebted to her for her many contributions to the research program.

Informal discussions on the substantive problems treated in this volume with Jerome S. Bruner, Bernard P. Cohen, Leonard S. Cottrell, Jr., Leland DeVinney, Daniel J. Levinson, David McClelland, Robert K. Merton, Theodore M. Newcomb, Talcott Parsons, Robert R. Sears, Samuel A. Stouffer, Renato Tagiuri and Donald Young proved to be especially rewarding.

It is also a privilege to express my indebtedness to the following individuals who have influenced my thinking about and orientation to the "culture" and problems of public education: Eugene L. Belisle, William H. Burton, Dana M. Cotton, Frank S. Chase, Morris Cogan, John B. Davis, Matthew P. Gaffney, Harold B. Gores, Calvin G. Gross, Herold C. Hunt, Francis Keppel, James Lewis, Cyril G. Sargent, Judson Shaplin, the late Alfred Simpson, Archie L. Threlkeld, David V. Tiedeman, and Robert Ulich.

To the 105 Massachusetts superintendents and 508 school board members whose excellent cooperation made the research possible and who gave so generously of their time, I am especially indebted. Thanks also are due to the Massachusetts Association of School Committees and the New England School Development Council whose sponsorship of the Studies proved to be an extremely important factor in its acceptance by nearly all superintendents and school board members who were involved in the Studies.

The major financial support for the Studies came from a grant from the Rockefeller Foundation. Additional support was received from the W. K. Kellogg Foundation, the Milton Fund of Harvard University, and the American Philosophical Society. The final phase of the Studies devoted to the applied social science problems of the research is being supported by the Russell Sage Foundation. Their encouragement and financial support is acknowledged with gratitude.

It is a distinct pleasure for me to record here my appreciation to all the individuals and organizations that have made a contribution to the Studies.

NEAL GROSS

Preface

The analyses reported in this book explore the problems of consensus on role definition, conformity to expectations, and role-conflict resolution. To deal with these central problems of role analysis we found it necessary to reexamine the conceptualizations of role in the social science literature and certain postulates embedded in them. The family of role concepts at which we arrived posed a number of largely unrecognized operational problems. In this book, in addition to reporting our empirical research, we have examined these theoretical and operational complexities.

Although first drafts of certain sections of this book were assigned to one or another of the authors, each section went through several stages of major revision and detailed editing by all three authors with the consequence that the book may be viewed as a full collaborative effort. Without the assistance, however, of Marion L. Crowley, who contributed to nearly every phase of the research and the preparation of the manuscript, and of W. Douglas Brooks, whose advice was invaluable in many important methodological decisions, who supervised most of our statistical computations and in addition prepared Appendixes C and D, it is doubtful if the authors would have found their tasks as pleasant as they have been.

We are also especially indebted to Samuel A. Stouffer and M. Brewster Smith for their critical reading of an earlier draft of this volume. We also wish to express our appreciation to the following people who offered suggestions after reading sections of the book or individual chapters: Robert F. Bales, Leonard S. Cottrell, Jr., Donald R. Fagg, Francis Keppel, Clyde Kluckhohn, Theodore M. Newcomb, Talcott Parsons, Bryce Ryan, Israel Scheffler, David V. Tiedeman, and John W. M. Whiting.

For their patience and understanding we owe a sincere debt of gratitude to Pan Gross, Ursula Mason, and Elisabeth McEachern.

We are indebted to Robert Dreeben for his aid in the preparation of the index and for checking the quotations and footnotes that appear in this book.

While acknowledging the help of others, the authors accept full responsibility for the analyses and interpretations of findings.

For permission to quote from their publications we acknowledge our thanks to: Addison-Wesley Publishing Co., Appleton-Century-Crofts, Columbia University Press, The Dryden Press, The Free Press, Harcourt, Brace and Company, Harper and Brothers, Harvard University Press, The Macmillan Company, Princeton University Press, University of Chicago Press, *Administrative Science Quarterly, American Anthropologist, American Journal of Sociology, American Sociological Review, Journal of Social Issues, Public Opinion Quarterly,* and *Social Forces.*

NEAL GROSS
WARD S. MASON
ALEXANDER W. MCEACHERN

Cambridge, Massachusetts
November 1957

Contents

Appendix

Explorations in Role Analysis

one

Introduction

This book is an attempt to forge a closer link between theoretical and empirical analyses concerned with the study of roles. It reports the outcome of an empirical inquiry whose major focus was the role of the school superintendent. The essential purpose of the research was to test theoretically derived hypotheses involving expectations for and the behavior of incumbents of positions in social systems.

The concept of role has assumed a key position in the fields of sociology, social psychology, and cultural anthropology. Students of the social sciences frequently make use of it as a central term in conceptual schemes for the analysis of the structure and functioning of social systems and for the explanation of individual behavior. The role concept is pivotal in Parsons' theoretical framework for the analysis of social systems.[1] It is a crucial element in the central problems of social psychology as defined by Newcomb[2] and Sarbin.[3] Through the role concept Linton provided American social anthropology with a link between culture and social structure.[4] It is an essential element in Mead's theory of the development of the self.[5] Cameron[6] has used it as a strategic concept for the analysis of pathological behavior.

Yet, despite its frequent use and presumed heuristic utility, one finds in the literature statements like: "More adequate operational definitions of role are needed; our present poverty in this respect is paralleled by the paucity of systematic role research."[7] After an extensive review of the conceptualization of role Neiman and Hughes concluded:

> Hypotheses involving the concept role are extremely rare in the literature. This raises the question of the utility of the concept. If a concept is useful in the field, is it not logical to assume that one would find varying hypotheses in the reasearch literature putting the concept to the test of empirical research? This is not true of the concept role.[8]

They also observed that:

> The concept role is at present still rather vague, nebulous, and non-definitive. Frequently in the literature, the concept is used without any attempt on the part of the writer to define or delimit the concept, the assumption being that both writer and reader will achieve an immediate compatible consensus.[9]

In our attempts to develop hypotheses and specific research designs we ran headlong into the nominal and operational definitional problems cited by Newcomb and Neiman and Hughes. We also came to realize that many existent conceptualizations of role and role conflict precluded or placed limitations on the examination of the degree of role consensus and the resolution of role conflict, problem areas which we proposed to investigate.

Our examination of the social science literature revealed that role consensus had only recently begun to receive recognition as a significant problem. Not only had there been little systematic research on this problem, but slight attention had been directed to the theoretical implications of differential degrees of consensus on role definition for the functioning of social systems, the behavior of individuals, or the cultural organization of a society. It became apparent that the postulate of role consensus, involved in many formulations of the role concept, was one of the reasons these problems had been neglected.

One of the tasks role theorists set themselves is to account for the variability of the *behavior* of incumbents of the same position. All mothers, for example, do not behave in the same manner, and an adequate theory must allow and account for this variability. One model, which is often followed, posits, either implicitly or explicitly, consensus on expectations and tries to account for the differential behavior of position incumbents by the variability in their attitudes, values, personality characteristics, or some other phenomenon which can be said to intervene between the positional expectation and the role behavior. In its application this model is unquestionably not simple; the suggestion that the expectations held for and perceived by actors may be variable makes it much more complex.

How can we say that an expectation is variable? When, for example, it is said that something "should be done" by a position incumbent there seems to be little scope for variability, but when one asks who defines the obligation, the answer is implicit. In the literature it is ordinarily said that "society" or the "group" defines the obligations attached to a particular position. However, "society" and "group" are abstractions which are open to empirical investigation only through their members. In order to demonstrate what "society" or a "group" expects, we must ask its members what they expect. Asking many different individuals the same question seldom results in a single answer. Thus, by seeking an empirical demonstration of the expectations held for an incumbent of a specified position by a population of role definers, we are led to expect not a single expectation, but a number of expectations that may or may not be the same. In this sense the degree of consensus on any expectation may be viewed as empirically problematic. To paraphrase an observation of Merton's, in this research the process of empirical inquiry raised conceptual issues which had been largely ignored in theoretic inquiry.

It was our assumption that the extent to which there is consensus on role definition may be an important dimension affecting the functioning of social systems, whether they are total societies or subsystems within them. In addition, the degree of consensus among significant role definers as perceived by an actor may be an important variable affecting his behavior. To investigate the problem of role consensus we could not use the formulations of those social scientists who beg the question of consensus in their definitions of role. Furthermore, to engage in theoretical and empirical analysis of role consensus it was necessary to identify the reference of consensus with much greater precision: consensus on what and among whom? Whereas some social scientists view role as the behaviors expected of the incumbent of a social position, they ignore the problem of who the definers of the expected behaviors are, or simply state that they are defined "by society." Again, if role has as its referent behaviors expected of the occupant of a social position, what classification of expected behaviors can an investigator use? The research could not proceed until answers were developed for these and a series of related questions.

Our exploratory activities in the analysis of role conflicts to which superintendents were exposed also suggested certain possible inadequacies in the existing conceptualizations of role conflict. Many formulations of role conflict view it as an actor's exposure to conflicting obligations stemming from his simultaneous occupancy of two positions. Our trial interviews revealed that in addition to this source of conflicting expectations, actors frequently were exposed to incongruent expectations as incumbents of single positions. Different school board members had different expectations for their superintendent, *as a superintendent,* in the same situation. In other cases the teachers and the school board held conflicting expectations for his behavior *as a superintendent.* These observations led to the conclusion that single as well as multiple position incumbency may result in exposure to conflicting expectations, a possibility ignored by many students of role conflict analysis. This had an important theoretical consequence. We were forced to shift our thinking about the resolution of role conflict from a concern with why an actor selects *one position over another,* to why an actor conforms to *one rather than another expectation* for his behavior.

In Part 1 of this volume an attempt is made to examine and deal with a number of theoretical and operational problems with which we were confronted in developing research designs for our empirical analyses. We suspect that some of these theoretical problems have constituted stumbling blocks to the development of a systematic body of role theory and research.

Chapter Two examines certain definitions of the role concept. It attempts to account for differences among them and to isolate the common phenomena with which they are concerned. Chapter Three is an examination of the degree to which the "postulate of role consensus" is embedded in the social science literature. Chapter Four presents a suggested language for role research that attempts to conceptualize the common elements in earlier formulations and which allows for the investigation of consensus on role definition. The concepts have been defined in such a way that they may be applied to individual, social, or cultural phenomena. They constitute the basic language for most of the empirical studies to be reported later. Chapter Five examines certain operational complexities involved in an empirical analysis of the definition of a role.

Part 2 considers the problem areas of role analysis with which our empirical studies were concerned. The first chapter of this section, Chapter Six, presents the research methods used of relevance to the several studies presented later. It describes our research activities prior to the interviewing program, the population and sampling procedures, the superintendent and school board interviews, and data processing and scaling procedures.

The theoretical propositions we propose to examine in this section of the book are concerned with three problem areas of role analysis. The first is consensus on role definition among incumbents of positions in formal organizations and small social systems. What patterns of consensus emerge when a large sample of Massachusetts superintendents and school board members are asked to define the roles of the superintendent and school board? Does there tend to be greater consensus on certain types of expectations than on others? Will there tend to be greater consensus within one of these sets of role definers than within the other? What factors differentiate small social systems that are characterized by more or less consensus on role expectations? Chapters Seven through Thirteen consider and test a series of hypotheses which attempt to provide answers to these and other questions of role consensus.

The second problem area, explored in Chapter Fourteen, is conformity to role expectations. The central question we shall examine is: What differentiates school boards that tend to conform more or less to "professional standards" of superintendents?

The third focus of interest is the area of role conflict analysis. We will test the utility of a simple theoretical model for predicting how an actor will behave when he perceives his exposure to role conflict. We shall also examine some of the major role conflicts with which school superintendents are confronted and their consequences for incumbents of this position. Chapters Fifteen, Sixteen, and Seventeen deal with this problem area.

Chapter Eighteen examines possible implications of this research inquiry for future work concerned with role analysis and role theory.

To sum up: This book has two independent but related objectives. The first is to examine certain theoretical and operational problems of role analysis. The second is to report the findings of several empirical studies that have been influenced by our examination of these theoretical blocks to systematic role research. For some of them we think reasonably satisfactory solutions can be suggested, but for others we remain dissatisfied with our efforts to cope with them. Still others were recognized after field work activity had ceased, and only some of these can be given any consideration at all. It is for these reasons that this book is called *Explorations in Role Analysis*. We have tried to explore a series of problem areas that we are convinced are of importance to the development of the social sciences, but we have little doubt that subsequent theoretical formulations and empirical inquiries will make sharper and deeper penetrations.

Notes and References for Chapter One

[1] Talcott Parsons, *The Social System* (Glencoe: The Free Press, 1951). See also Talcott Parsons and Edward A. Shils, with the assistance of James Olds, "Values, Motives, and Systems of Action," in Talcott Parsons and Edward A. Shils (Editors), *Toward a General Theory of Action* (Cambridge: Harvard University Press, 1951), pp. 47–275.

[2] Theodore M. Newcomb, *Social Psychology* (New York: The Dryden Press, 1951).

See also Theodore M. Newcomb, "Sociology and Psychology," John Gillin (Editor), *For a Science of Social Man* (New York: The Macmillan Company, 1954), pp. 227–256.

[3] Theodore R. Sarbin, "Role Theory," in Gardner Lindzey (Editor), *Handbook of Social Psychology*, Vol. I (Cambridge: Addison-Wesley Publishing Company, 1954), pp. 223–258.

[4] For Murdock's comments on the impact of Linton's formulation, see George Peter Murdock, "Sociology and Anthropology," in Gillin, *op. cit.,* pp. 14–31.

[5] George H. Mead, *Mind, Self & Society* (Chicago: University of Chicago Press, 1934).

[6] Norman Cameron, "Role Concepts in Behavior Pathology," *American Journal of Sociology*, LV (1950), pp. 464–467.

[7] Newcomb, "Sociology and Psychology," in Gillin, *op. cit.,* p. 255.

[8] Lionel J. Neiman and James W. Hughes, "The Problem of the Concept of Role—A Re-Survey of the Literature," *Social Forces*, XXX (1951), p. 149.

[9] *Ibid.,* p. 149.

part 1

Conceptual, Theoretical,
and Operational Problems

two

The Definitional Problem

Many definitions of the term role have been presented in the social science literature, representing different disciplines, different points of view within a single discipline, and, in some cases, different formulations of an individual author. In this chapter we will consider certain of these definitions and try to account for some of their differences. We will also try to identify their common elements in order to provide a basis and a background for Chapter Four, in which a set of concepts for role analyses is presented.

Of several possible categories into which definitions of the term role might be placed, we have selected and will examine three, which, if not exhaustive, are at least representative of the major role formulations in the social science literature. Although many of the authors considered have introduced the role concept as one among an elaborate system of concepts, it is impossible for us to give an adequate appraisal of their systems, and to these authors we do less than justice. In fact, this cursory survey of only a selected part of the literature on role theory can do little more than suggest some of the semantic problems confronting the student of "role" analysis.[1]

Definitions of role[2] which either equate it with or define it to include *normative culture patterns* have been placed in the first category, which includes, among others, Ralph Linton's often-quoted definition. His treatments of the concepts of status and role in the two volumes *The Study of Man*[3] and *The Cultural Background of Personality*[4] have done much to stimulate interest in the area, and the "cultural element" in many subsequent formulations can be traced to his work.

As a basis for the introduction of the status and role concepts Linton says that three separate elements are prerequisites for the existence of a society: ". . . an aggregate of individuals, an organized system of patterns by which the interrelations and activities of these individuals are controlled, and the *esprit de corps* which provides motive power for the expression of these patterns."[5] For Linton a social system is a cultural phenomenon, a set of blueprints for behavior. It is: "The sum total of the ideal patterns which control the reciprocal behavior between individuals and between the individual and society. . . ."[6]

Status and role represent a conceptual elaboration of the "ideal patterns which control reciprocal behavior." Statuses are "the polar positions in . . . patterns of reciprocal behavior. . . . A status, as distinct from the individual who may occupy it, is simply a collection of rights and duties."[7] "A *rôle* represents the dynamic aspect of status. . . . When [the individual] puts the rights and duties which constitute the status into effect, he is performing a rôle."[8]

It is through the occupancy of statuses by individuals and their performance of roles that the "business" of a society is accomplished. It is carried out in a patterned and organized way through the members of the society occupying statuses and performing roles. From the viewpoint of the individual ". . . *the combined status and role* [serve as guides for his conduct, specifying] the minimum of attitudes and behavior which he must assume if he is to participate in the overt expression of the pattern."[9]

The use of the phrase "the combined status and role" indicates that except for the locational function assigned to status which is not assigned to role, there is little to distinguish the two concepts. The former refers to the ideal pattern, the latter to behavior which expresses the pattern. Linton says that the distinction between the two is "of only academic interest."[10] This interpretation is further strengthened by what might otherwise be inferred to be a shift in the definition of role between *The Study of Man* and *The Cultural Background of Personality*. In the latter work role designates ". . . the sum total of culture patterns associated with a particular status."[11] In this treatment role is also viewed as the dynamic aspect of status and this phrase refers to the behavior an individual must engage in "to validate" incumbency of the status. In short, role apparently has reference not to actual behavior of an occupant of a position but to behavioral standards. It consists of ". . . attitudes, values and behavior *ascribed by the society* to any and all persons occupying this status."[12] (Italics ours.)

The definitions of a number of other authors would fall in this same "normative culture pattern" category. In his conceptual scheme Newcomb says that "the ways of behaving which are expected of any individual who occupies a certain position constitute the *role* . . .

associated with that position." [13] Znaniecki says that "there is obviously a fundamental and universal, though unreflective, culture pattern in accordance with which all kinds of lasting relationships between individuals and their social milieus are normatively organized and which we denote by the term 'social role.'" [14] Bennett and Tumin define a role as ". . . what the society expects of an individual occupying a given status. This implies that any status is *functionally* defined by *the role attached to it.*" [15] In one paper Parsons[16] viewed a role in approximately this manner, as have Rose[17] and Komarovsky.[18]

In some definitions, a role is treated as *an individual's definition of his situation with reference to his and others' social positions,* and these deserve a separate categorization. Sargent, for example, says, *"a person's role is a pattern or type of social behavior which seems situationally appropriate to him in terms of the demands and expectations of those in his group."* [19] He goes on to point out that, in this sense, roles "have ingredients of cultural, of personal, and of situational determination. But never is a role *wholly* cultural, *wholly* personal, or *wholly* situational." [20]

Parsons' major formulation is a more elaborate example of a definition in this second category. Its meaning is best understood against the background of the action frame of reference. For Parsons and Shils, action is behavior which is oriented to the attainment of ends or goals or other anticipated states of affairs, takes place in situations, is normatively regulated, and involves expenditure of energy or effort.[21]

> Each action is the action of an actor, and it takes place in a situation consisting of objects. The objects may be other actors or physical or cultural objects. Each actor has a system of relations-to-objects; this is called his 'system of orientations.' The objects may be goal objects, resources, means, conditions, obstacles, or symbols. They may become cathected (wanted or not wanted), and they may have different significances attached to them (that is, they may mean different things to different people). Objects, by the significances and cathexes attached to them, become organized into the actor's system of orientations.[22]

In this context, a role is a mode of organization of the actor's orientation to the situation.

> A role . . . is a sector of the total orientation system of an individual actor which is organized about expectations in relation to a particular interaction context, that is integrated with a particular set of value-standards which govern interaction with one or more alters in the appropriate complementary roles.[23]

It could be argued that the integration with value-standards corresponds to Sargent's cultural element; the actor's orientation includes a motivational orientation, which corresponds to the personal element; and both formulations are based on an actor's orientation to a situation. In the final phrase in his definition, "alters in the appropriate complementary roles," Parsons uses the term role in a different sense, with what appears to be a purely locational connotation. At one point he introduced the concept of status to serve this function,[24] but later dropped it in favor of distinguishing between orientation-role and object-role as analytic aspects of concrete roles.[25] In an interaction situation each actor has an orientation to the other and is himself an object of orientation; both are part of his role.

In a third category we would place definitions which deal with role as *the behavior of actors occupying social positions.* A role defined in this way does not refer to normative patterns for what actors *should do,* nor to an actor's orientation to his situation, but to what actors *actually do* as position occupants.

Davis' definition falls in this category:

> How an individual *actually performs* in a given position, as distinct from how he is supposed to perform, we call his *role.* The role, then, is the manner in which a person actually carries out the requirements of his position. It is the dynamic aspect of status or office and as such is always influenced by factors other than the stipulations of the position itself.[26] (First italics ours.)

The meaning Davis imputes to the phrase, "the dynamic aspect of status," is quite different from Linton's usage: ". . . what the individual *has to do* in order to validate the occupation of the status." [27] (Italics ours.) For Davis the concept of role is virtually equivalent to Newcomb's concept of role behavior[28] and similar to Sarbin's concept of role enactment.[29]

There are two other kinds of formulations which can be included in this behavioral category. The first emphasizes the functional implications of behaviors, either in terms of group process or the attainment of group ends. This approach is illustrated in the work of some small group analysts. Although Benne and Sheats do not present a definition of the term, they present a classification of roles which includes group task roles (for example, opinion seeker, coordinator), group building and maintenance roles (for example, encourager, harmonizer), and individual roles (for example, aggressor, blocker).[30] It could be said that these categories classify individual acts as roles, even though an attempt is made to point to the functional significance of the acts.

Slater has a similar conception of role:

> We might define role as a more or less coherent and unified system of items of interpersonal behavior. With even this minimal definition it becomes apparent that role performance in the small group situation will have both consequences which are important to the functioning of the group in which the role is performed, and personal consequences of importance to the individual who performs it.[31]

In this formulation, operational definitions of role are either in terms of the interaction profiles of group participants or in terms of postsession ratings by participants of each other. Under the latter procedure some of the roles investigated are "best liked," "guidance," "best ideas," and "leader." [32] These ratings are not based on differentiated expectations but rather on molar categorizations of actors dependent on perceptions of their performances. They are not based on expectations for incumbents of differentiated positions but rather on standards which each actor applies to all members of the group. Furthermore, they are not studied directly, and, as Bales and Slater say, "the degree to which differentiated roles in the fully structural sense appear in these small decision-making groups is perhaps a moot point." [33]

Another of Parsons' definitions would fall in this category. A role is ". . . what the actor does in his relations with others seen in the context of its functional significance for the social system." [34]

Another group of definitions, which still link role and behavior, emphasize the "self-other" context in which the behavior occurs, focusing on the reciprocal nature of behavior, or action as *interaction*. Cottrell in one paper says:

> I shall be using the term role to refer to an internally consistent series of conditioned responses by one member of a social situation which represents the stimulus pattern for a similarly internally consistent series of conditioned responses of the other(s) in that situation. Dealing with human behavior in terms of roles, therefore, requires that any given item of behavior must always be placed in some specified self-other context.[35]

Sarbin defines a role as ". . . a patterned sequence of learned *actions* or deeds performed by a person in an interaction situation." [36] Besides the emphasis on interaction, both of these definitions refer to patterns of acts rather than individual acts; and while some authors who have a behavioral definition of role have another concept for norms applying to position incumbents (for example, Davis), Cottrell and Sarbin[37] do not. Both deal with non-normative stimuli and responses: The action of one actor is a stimulus for another actor, whose response becomes a stimulus for the first actor, and so on.

A number of possibilities present themselves to account for some of these differences. One of the most obvious is that the definitions are influenced by the particular disciplines of the definers and the special problems in which they are interested. Linton as an anthropologist stresses cultural patterns and Sargent as a psychologist emphasizes individual perceptions. Parsons develops his conception of role to fit into a theoretical model for social systems as part of a general theory of action while other sociologists emphasize group processes.

As an anthropologist, Linton gives primary emphasis to the normative patterns influencing the behavior of occupants of positions in the social structure, and at one point says, "the anthropological conventions have required that cultures should be described in terms of norms of behavior without reference to either deviations or individuals." [38] Consequently he ignores the concrete behavior of actors in social positions in his formal conceptualization. Although he was aware that behavior is not uniform and does not necessarily correspond to norms for behavior, and even offered possible reasons for nonconformity, he does not make use of a concept for the actual behavior of occupants of social positions.

The starting point for Parsons and Davis, as sociologists, is the interaction situation. Interaction implies behavior and requires a concept to represent how individuals *do* behave in addition to how they *should* behave as incumbents of positions, which Davis and Parsons both have. Davis defined a role as the actual behavior of an incumbent of a position while Parsons uses the term *performances.* As a social psychologist concerned with the impact of culture and social structure on the behavior of individuals, Newcomb also makes use of a concept to represent the actual behavior of position incumbents. He distinguishes between *role behavior* or the actual behavior of position incumbents, and *role,* the ways of behaving expected of position incumbents.

An interest in different problems also implies a difference in the frame of reference within which different authors place their role concept. Linton is concerned with positions in a total society. Cottrell's concepts describe a subsocial system comprised of an ego and alter in actual interaction. Sargent's frame of reference is restricted to that of an individual's perception of a single interaction situation.

Although Linton's starting point is that ". . . the functioning of societies depends upon the presence of patterns for reciprocal behavior between individuals or groups of individuals," [39] he is not primarily concerned with behavior patterns governing the relations between individuals, but rather with the relation of individuals to culture. After pointing out that individuals in a society may be categorized in various ways simultaneously, he says that each of these systems (of categorization) has its own function in *relating the individual to culture.* Consequently, when Linton is specifying the content of a role, he says that it is "the sum total of the culture patterns associated with a particular status. It thus includes the attitudes, values, and behavior ascribed by the society to any and all persons occupying this status." [40]

Because a total society is his primary frame of reference in the consideration of role phenomena, the expectations actors in reciprocal positions hold for each other are of much less importance to Linton than they are to Cottrell and Parsons, for example, and he gives virtually no consideration to the individual's perception of expectations, which is Sargent's primary focus of interest.

Another reason for some of these differences in definition is simply semantic; the same phenomena are frequently given different names. Thus, what Linton and Newcomb define as a role, Davis defines as a status. What Davis defines as a role, Newcomb calls role behavior and Sarbin role enactment.

Still another reason may lie in the fact that almost all of the authors whose definitions have been presented acknowledge indebtedness to Linton. Some of them, however, start from his conception in *The Study of Man,* while others start from *The Cultural Background of Personality.* Some of the differences in Linton's own conceptions in these two volumes continue in this way to be perpetuated among different authors.

Although their formulations have some fundamental differences most of the authors whose definitions have been presented are concerned with the same phenomena. Three basic ideas which appear in most of the conceptualizations considered, if not in the definitions of role themselves, are that individuals: (1) in *social locations* (2) *behave* (3) with reference to *expectations.*

Almost all of the authors have used the role concept to embrace the normative element of social behavior. People do not behave in a random manner; their behavior is influenced to some extent by their own expectations and those of others in the group or society in which they are participants. Some authors have included this idea in the concept of status or position, others in role, but nearly all include it somewhere. For example, Newcomb defines a role as "the ways of behaving which are expected of any individual who occupies a certain position. . . ." [41] Sargent speaks of ". . . *the demands and expectations of those in the group,"* [42] and the notion of expectations is central to the formulations of Linton, Parsons, and Davis. Sometimes, the expectations referred to are "ascribed by society"; in other formulations they are held by members of the group in which the actor participates. Regardless of their derivation, expectations are presumed by most role theorists to be an essential ingredient in any formula for predicting social behavior. Human conduct is in part a function of expectations.

But some expectations apply to certain individuals and not to others. Whether a particular expectation is assigned to an individual depends upon his identity. Whether a person is identified as male or female, as a policeman or a teacher, a salesclerk or a janitor, a member of one social system or of another, makes a difference in the expectations others hold for him or that he holds for himself. It is necessary to specify an individual's locations in social relationship systems or his "relational identities" in order to determine what expectations are held for him. This component is also involved in most, although not all, role conceptualizations. Expectations are assigned to individuals on the basis of their locations or positions in social systems.

We feel that theoretical formulations concerned with role analysis must include these three elements—social locations, behavior, and expectations—which are common to most of the definitions of role which have been considered. The ways in which these ideas have been used in theoretical schemes, the terms used to represent them, and, perhaps most important, the problems for which they provide adequate theoretical tools are far more variable than common. As we suggested earlier, one of the problems whose investigation is essential to role analysis, but which is to a large extent precluded by many definitions of role, is the problem of role consensus. Before we present and elaborate the terms by means of which we will identify these elements of role analysis, we will examine how social scientists have treated the phenomenon of "role consensus" both theoretically and empirically. Since we think the conceptual tools developed should allow rather than preclude analyses of role consensus, it is necessary to review the treatment this problem has been accorded in the past in order to take into account its possible complexities in developing the "language of research" on which our empirical analyses will be based.

Notes and References for Chapter Two

[1] For a general review of definitions of role in the social science literature see Lionel J. Neiman and James W. Hughes, "The Problem of the Concept of Role— A Re-Survey of the Literature," *Social Forces*, XXX (1951), pp. 141–149. A paper by Sarbin on role theory contains an extensive coverage of the psychological literature on role analysis. See Theodore R. Sarbin, "Role Theory," in Gardner Lindzey (Editor), *Handbook of Social Psychology*, Vol. I (Cambridge: Addison-Wesley Publishing Company, 1954), pp. 223–258.

[2] Since the concept of status or position is frequently presented as a prior concept in many role formulations it will be necessary to consider it in the examination of certain definitions of role.

[3] Ralph Linton, *The Study of Man* (New York: D. Appleton-Century Co., 1936).

[4] Ralph Linton, *The Cultural Background of Personality* (New York: D. Appleton-Century Co., 1945).

[5] Linton, *Study of Man*, p. 107.

[6] *Ibid.*, p. 105.

[7] *Ibid.*, p. 113.

[8] *Ibid.*, p. 114.

[9] *Ibid.*, p. 114.

[10] *Ibid.*, p. 114.

[11] Linton, *Cultural Background*, p. 77.

[12] *Ibid.*, p. 77.

[13] Theodore M. Newcomb, *Social Psychology* (New York: The Dryden Press, 1951), p. 280.

[14] Florian Znaniecki, *The Social Role of the Man of Knowledge* (New York: Columbia University Press, 1940), p. 19.

[15] John W. Bennett and Melvin M. Tumin, *Social Life, Structure and Function* (New York: Alfred A. Knopf, 1948), p. 96.

[16] Talcott Parsons, "Age and Sex in the Social Structure of the United States," *American Sociological Review*, VII (1942), pp. 604–616, reprinted in Clyde Kluckhohn and Henry A. Murray (Editors), *Personality in Nature, Society, and Culture* (New York: Alfred A. Knopf, 1948), pp. 269–281.

[17] Arnold M. Rose, "The Adequacy of Women's Expectations for Adult Roles," *Social Forces*, XXX (1951), pp. 69–77.

[18] Mirra Komarovsky, "Cultural Contradictions and Sex Roles," *American Journal of Sociology*, LII (1946), pp. 184–189.

[19] Stansfeld Sargent, "Concepts of Role and Ego in Contemporary Psychology," in John H. Rohrer and Muzafer Sherif (Editors), *Social Psychology at the Crossroads* (New York: Harper and Brothers, 1951), p. 360.

[20] *Ibid.*, p. 359.

[21] Talcott Parsons and Edward A. Shils, with the assistance of James Olds, "Values, Motives, and Systems of Action," in Talcott Parsons and Edward A. Shils (Editors), *Toward a General Theory of Action* (Cambridge: Harvard University Press, 1951), p. 53.

[22] *Ibid.,* p. 54.

[23] Talcott Parsons, *The Social System* (Glencoe: The Free Press, 1951), pp. 38–39.

[24] *Ibid.,* p. 25.

[25] *Ibid.,* pp. 139–140.

[26] Kingsley Davis, *Human Society* (New York: The Macmillan Company, 1948 and 1949), p. 90.

[27] Linton, *Cultural Background,* p. 77.

[28] "Role behavior . . . does refer to the actual behavior of specific individuals as they take roles." Newcomb, *op. cit.,* p. 330.

[29] ". . . role enactments are the overt performances of persons; these performances validate (or invalidate) the expectations of the other person or persons in a social situation." Sarbin, *op. cit.,* p. 232.

[30] K. D. Benne and P. Sheats, "Functional Roles of Group Members," *Journal of Social Issues,* IV, 2 (1948), pp. 41–49.

[31] Philip E. Slater, "Role Differentiation in Small Groups," in A. Paul Hare, Edgar F. Borgatta, Robert F. Bales (Editors), *Small Groups* (New York: Alfred A. Knopf, 1955), p. 498.

[32] *Ibid.,* pp. 499–500.

[33] Robert F. Bales and Philip E. Slater, "Role Differentiation in Small Decision-Making Groups," in Talcott Parsons and Robert F. Bales (Editors), *Family, Socialization and Interaction Process* (Glencoe: The Free Press, 1955), p. 260.

[34] Parsons, *Social System,* p. 25; also, "Suggestions for a Sociological Approach to the Theory of Organizations—I," *Administrative Science Quarterly,* I (1956), pp. 63–85.

[35] Leonard S. Cottrell, Jr., "The Adjustment of the Individual to His Age and Sex Roles," *American Sociological Review,* VII (1942), p. 617. Reprinted in Theodore M. Newcomb and Eugene L. Hartley (Editors), *Readings in Social Psychology* (New York: Henry Holt and Co., 1947).

[36] Sarbin, *op. cit.,* p. 225.

[37] The fact that Sarbin also uses the concept of role expectation might seem to contradict this statement, but closer examination reveals that this concept refers to anticipations, not standards. See Sarbin, *op. cit.,* p. 226.

[38] Ralph Linton, "Foreword," in Abram Kardiner, *The Psychological Frontiers of Society* (New York: Columbia University Press, 1945), p. x.

[39] Linton, *Study of Man,* p. 113.

[40] Linton, *Cultural Background,* p. 77.

[41] Newcomb, *Social Psychology,* p. 280.

[42] Sargent, *op. cit.,* p. 360.

three

The Postulate of Role Consensus

Involved in many, but not all, formulations of the role concept in the social science literature is the assumption that consensus exists on the expectations applied to the incumbents of particular social positions. It is this postulate that we now propose to examine in the fields of cultural anthropology, social psychology, and sociology.

The interest anthropologists have in "roles" and "role expectations" is to a large extent dependent on their interest in "cultures." Since their treatment of the concepts of "culture" and "role" are similarly interdependent, it is necessary in examining the postulate of role consensus to consider initially some aspects of the treatment anthropologists have given the culture concept. "Culture" has been a central conceptual tool of anthropologists in their description and analysis of ethnographic data. Some have been concerned primarily with the dynamics of culture, an interest which is evidenced by the nineteenth century theories of unilinear cultural and social evolution and by the current interest in such problems as innovation in culture,[1] difficulties involved in introducing cultural change,[2] and the analysis of changing values.[3]

A growing emphasis in recent anthropological work, however, tends to be on culture as a variable exerting an impact on other phenomena such as personality, national character, motivation, perception, cognition, language, sexual behavior, and abnormal behavior.[4] Culture is most frequently viewed as an independent variable whereas the other listed phenomena are treated as dependent. These problems suggest the increasing liaison between cultural anthropology and psychology. especially psychoanalytic psychology.

In addition to being central in these special problem areas, culture is the key construct overlying the continuing descriptive ethnological work of anthropologists. As Murdock says:

. . . whatever special problems he may go to the field to investigate, [the anthropologist] is expected to bring back and publish, not only an answer to his special problem, but also a descriptive account, as complete as he can make it, of the entire culture of the people studied.[5]

It can be said that the concept of culture is embedded in nearly every major problem that has attracted the attention of cultural anthropologists since Klemm.

Cultural anthropology, like sociology and psychology, has its semantic problems. Just as sociologists disagree among themselves about the meanings of such terms as "group" and "institution," and just as psychologists engage in semantic disputes over the denotation of "personality," so have anthropologists quarreled among themselves over the definition of culture. Kluckhohn, in quoting from his and Kroeber's extensive and critical review of the concept of culture says that:

. . . most social scientists now formulate the concept of culture approximately as follows: Culture consists of patterns, explicit and implicit, of and for behavior acquired and transmitted by symbols, constituting the distinctive achievement of human groups, including their embodiments in artifacts; the essential core of culture consists of traditional (i.e., historically derived and selected) ideas and especially their attached values; culture systems may, on the one hand, be considered as products of action, on the other hand as conditioning elements of further action.[6]

In elaborating on this formulation Kluckhohn notes that anthropologists are concerned with pattern analysis, ". . . the interrelation of parts and of their relation to the whole" in addition to a listing of cultural traits. It is emphasized that "culture is not behavior . . ." but that it emerges from and returns to behavior. He distinguishes two related but different ways in which anthropologists use "culture."

On the one hand, "culture" denotes a logical construct, the network of abstracted patterns generalized by the anthropologist to represent the regularities distinctive of the group in question. On the other hand, "culture" designates these patterns or "norms" as internalized by the individuals making up the group.[7]

Kluckhohn also describes three parts or aspects of culture:

Part of culture consists in norms for and modalities in behavior. Another part consists in ideologies justifying or rationalizing certain ways of behaving. Finally, every culture includes broad general principles of selectivity and ordering ("highest common factors") in terms of which patterns *of* and *for* behavior are reducible to parsimonious generalizations.[8]

Smith, from the viewpoint of psychology, has also noted certain consistencies in the anthropologist's usage of culture:

"Culture" in the abstract is a generalization from "cultures," while a culture is itself an abstract concept ascribed to some identified social group. The important components of current usage would seem to include (a) a conception of shared ways of behaving, predispositions to behavior, and (perhaps) products of behavior, and (b) the restriction that if something is a part of culture, it is learned—transmitted socially rather than biologically.[9]

According to Smith, culture is not a theory, but simply a concept.

The term itself [culture] embodies no articulated propositions from which consequences can be drawn and put to test. It asserts nothing about reality. The psychologist who turns to anthropology after studying his lessons in the logic of science may therefore show some surprise when he encounters statements about the importance of the concept as an anthropological contribution.[10]

Why has the construct of culture, then, had an impact on the sciences concerned with social man? Smith's observation on its influence in psychology is cogent:

With the *concept* of culture goes an *orientation,* if not a theory, that a very wide range of human phenomena is cultural in nature. The importance of the concept rests, then, in the host of assertions in which it occurs, to the effect that phenomena *x, y, z,* etc. are cultural in origin, or are influenced in specific ways by culture.[11]

The concept of culture has forced psychologists to broaden their frame of reference to include extrapersonal, in addition to intrapersonal forces, in explanations of personality and individual behavior. Although Murdock has observed that the concept of culture is as indigenous to sociology as to anthropology, as seen, for example, in Sumner's concepts of *folkways* and *mores,*[12] certain ideas in anthropology such as cultural relativism have had considerable impact through their destruction of many social science ethnocentric and monolithic theories. The anthropologist's emphasis on variability in cultures in different societies has also resulted in a growing recognition among sociologists that, usually, their generalizations may be limited to, at most, a single culture.

Deeply embedded in the "culture" or ideology of anthropologists is the belief that one of their major tasks, if not their primary one, is to uncover the covert behavior patterns or "blueprints for behavior" of the society they study. Just as a detective feels he must find the motive if he is to resolve a crime, so the anthropologist feels he must isolate culture patterns if he is to make sense out of the myriad bits of behavior he observes in a particular society. It is for these regularities in social behavior that he searches. To state that anthropologists are concerned with isolating the culture or behavior patterns for a society is not, however, to present an unequivocal description of what a specific anthropologist does.

That "culture" is frequently used by anthropologists in ambiguous ways is pointed out by Linton in his warning to psychologists about the pitfalls to be avoided in using the concept. He says:

> In their attempts to use this concept [culture] as a tool for research even the anthropologists sometimes become confused. Thus they frequently fail to distinguish even in their descriptive studies between cultures as they exist through time and cultures as they exist at a particular point in time, although these two aspects of the concept present different problems and call for somewhat different methods of approach. . . . Of much greater importance to the psychologist is the anthropologist's almost constant failure to distinguish clearly between the *reality of a culture as a configuration of behaviors,* and so on, and *the construct which he develops on the basis of this reality* and uses as a tool for the description and manipulation of cultural data. The lack of a terminology which will serve to distinguish clearly between these two aspects of the culture concept has been a source of endless trouble not only to psychologists and anthropologists but also to those logicians and philosophers who have attempted to deal with the culture concept.[13] (Italics ours.)

To distinguish among these ideas Linton introduced the terms *real culture, real culture patterns, culture construct,* and *total culture construct.* The real culture of a society ". . . consists of the actual behavior, and so on, of its members. It includes a vast number of elements, no two of which are identical." [14]

Despite this uniqueness, however, Linton suggests that there is a patterning among the multitude of behavioral items that constitute the real culture of a society. They can be initially categorized by the situations in which they usually occur, and they fall within a definable range:

> Moreover, the variations in such a series will ordinarily be found to fall within certain easily recognizable limits. . . . Behaviors which fall within the effective range [bring the desired results] will be considered normal, while those which fall outside of it will be regarded as queer and, frequently, as reprehensible.[15]

These ranges of normal behaviors to given situations he designates as "patterns within the real culture." A real culture ". . . may be conceived of as a configuration composed of a great number of such patterns all of which are, in greater or less degree, mutually adjusted and functionally interrelated." [16] Linton then makes a statement which has been unfortunately overlooked by many students who have been concerned with culture patterning in a society:

> The important thing to remember is that each of the *real culture patterns* is not a single item of behavior but a series of behaviors varying within certain limits.[17]

After observing that it would be impossible to list or describe all the behavioral items which make up the real culture and pointing out that anthropology needs some type of summary device for descriptive and analytic purposes, he introduces the concepts of *culture construct* and *total culture construct*. The former

> establishes the *mode* of the finite series of variations which are included within each of the real culture patterns and then uses this mode as a symbol for the real cultural patterns. . . . The *total culture construct* is developed by combining all the culture construct patterns which have been developed in this way. . . . Although the culture construct may not be in exact correspondence with the real culture at any point, it provides a brief and convenient approximation of the conditions existing within the real culture.[18] (Italics ours.)

Cultural constructs are modal behaviors and a total culture construct is a series of *modes* abstracted from a series of real culture patterns. Both ignore the variance in the distribution of behaviors found in particular situations.

Linton, then, was certainly aware, as are most anthropologists, that in any given situation the observer will probably find a range of behaviors. He apparently assumed, however, that the distribution of behaviors for a specific situation in a society usually has a single mode, and this assumed mode he defined as a cultural construct. For many situations this assumption of unimodality is undoubtedly reasonable, but to maintain, as Linton apparently does, that most real culture patterns are unimodal is to state a tenuous assumption. It minimizes the importance of the possibility that for some situations there may be bimodal, trimodal, or multimodal behavioral distributions. In a society with clearly differentiated social strata such as castes, classes, ethnic or religious social categorizations, one might expect to find with some regularity multimodal distributions. In a society undergoing rapid social change unimodal tendencies might not be expected in many real culture patterns. In one characterized by sharp internal cleavages bimodalities might be anticipated. These hypotheses are clearly as tenable on a priori grounds as the unimodal one.

The emphasis on unimodality also tends to dismiss variable behavior surrounding the modal category or categories, assuming they exist, as simply deviant behavior. Such behavior *may* represent evidence for the existence of subcultures. It may be indicative of the existence or the emergence of cleavages, strains, or conflicts in the social structure. It may provide clues for the prediction of social and cultural change in the society. As Inkeles and Levinson suggest for national character studies, it may reveal that a particular society contains multimodal personalities or no modal personalities at all, in contrast to a single modal personality.[19]

The postulate of unimodal behavioral distributions is a hypothesis that can be and should be empirically examined, not a "given" to be taken for granted. Perhaps major advances in anthropological theory may result from a shift in focus from "central tendencies" in behavior to variability in behavior *within* a single society.

Deriving from the basic conception of "culture" is the anthropological treatment of consensus on evaluative standards in a society. Although Linton, for example, recognized variability in the behavior of position incumbents he assumed that there was consensus among the members of a society on the behavior *expected* for at least some position incumbents. These he termed *ideal patterns*. Whereas *real culture patterns* refers to a distribution of behaviors of the members of a society in a particular situation and a *culture construct* has reference to the mode of that distribution, *ideal culture patterns*

> . . . are abstractions which have been developed by the members of a society themselves. They represent the consensus of opinion on the part of the society's members as to how people should behave in particular situations. . . . The extent to which such ideal patterns have been developed will vary greatly in different societies. . . . However, no group ever develops ideal patterns of behavior corresponding to all situations. . . . *In general, ideal patterns appear to be developed most frequently with respect to those situations which a society regards as of primary importance and particularly with respect to those involving the interaction of individuals in different positions in the social system.*[20]   (Italics ours.)

Culture, then, could be said to include the patterning of actual behavior and the patterning of evaluative standards for behavior. In Kluckhohn's words:

> *"Patterns of* and *for* behavior" means that both what people do and what they say they do or should do are taken into account. Culture encompasses both "designs for living" and the abstracted patterns of regularities in actual living.[21]

For Murdock, however, patterned behavior apparently refers only to ideal behavior patterns. In discussing what an outside observer in a foreign culture must do to understand the behavior of the people, he says:

> . . . His first task is to make those norms explicit. The inevitable result has been that anthropologists have devoted their primary attention to *patterned behavior*, i.e. *to those norms which are verbalized as the ideals to which behavior should conform*, are taught to each oncoming generation, and are enforced by the formal and the informal punishment of deviation.[22]   (Italics ours.)

How do anthropologists go about isolating these "ideal patterns" (Linton), or "patterned behavior" (Murdock), or "patterns for behavior" (Kluckhohn)? Whereas the real culture constructs or the modes of behavioral distributions are found by observing actual behavior, these "ideal patterns," since they are presumed to be in people's heads, are isolated by asking people what they are. According to Murdock,

> Any member of the society knows a large proportion of these norms, whether or not they govern his own behavior, for the norms incumbent upon persons in other statuses constitute an aspect of his expectations in his social interaction with them. To gain an accurate account of patterned behavior, therefore, an ethnographer needs only a few competent informants, selected judiciously but not necessarily in accordance with any standard sampling technique.[23]

That there are difficulties in such interviews is suggested by Linton's observation on operational procedures:

> Even in the most analytically minded and culture conscious societies the investigator finds again and again that informants are quite unable to tell what the proper behavior in a particular situation would be and have to fall back on relating what happened on various occasions when this situation arose.[24]

Kluckhohn's comments on the methods used to isolate implicit patterns suggest that the anthropologist engage in "inference" to invoke them.

> Here the anthropologist *infers* least common denominators which seem, as it were, to underlie a multiplicity of culture content. Only in the most sophisticated and self-conscious of cultures will his attention be called directly to these by the carriers of the culture, and then only in part.[25]   (Italics ours.)

A statistically oriented social scientist might be upset by Murdock's description of his procedure, especially in view of the following comment by Linton on the anthropologist's problems in psychological testing and recording covert culture:

The problem of establishing the covert patterns within a culture is much the same as that of ascertaining the content and organization of an individual's personality, and investigations are subject to the same sources of error. . . . It is almost impossible to make this a true random sample. The individuals with whom the field worker is brought into contact are not mere units in a statistical table but *actual people whose reactions to the investigator will be as varied as those of persons in our own society.* . . . There is thus a very real, if unconscious, selection of subjects which introduces a margin of error when one attempts to refer the test results to the society as a whole.[26]   (Italics ours.)

Some interesting consequences are suggested by considering the conceptualization of ideal culture patterns in conjunction with the operations used to isolate them.   In the first place, the concept of ideal culture patterns implies that the members of a society have in actuality developed a "consensus of opinion" in regard to some situations "involving the interaction of individuals in different positions in the social system."[27]   This is simply accepted as a postulate by many anthropologists and, since they assume that there is a "consensus" they invariably isolate "agreed upon" ideal culture patterns.   But the idea of consensus on the evaluative standards for the incumbents of a position is clearly subject to empirical examination.   Whether or not there is consensus on the behavior expected of position incumbents, or how much consensus there is, are evidently empirical questions, since "consensus" describes an empirical condition of agreement among a number of people.

Linton indicates that age, sex, and family positions of a society are those on which we can typically expect to find agreement.   But the few empirical studies on the degree of agreement on the evaluative standards applicable to the female position in American society all conclude that there is a high degree of disagreement among the role definers used.[28]   If it is argued that the demonstrated lack of consensus on this position is a function of a complicated industrialized society, then we might consider anthropological studies of less complicated societies.   Lewis in his study of Tepoztlan concludes that

> The picture of village life which emerges from our material is therefore quite different from the idealized, almost Rousseauan version of Tepoztlan conveyed by the earlier study of the village by Robert Redfield and later elaborated by Stuart Chase.[29]

Lewis interprets his data as revealing a wide disparity between actual and ideal behavior.   It is suggested that an equally if not more acceptable interpretation of Lewis' data is that there is a lack of consensus on ideal patterns on the role definition of husband and wife among older and younger women and between women and men in the village. Murdock, assuming consensus, makes the following statement:

> The situation is quite otherwise when a scientist is studying his own society and is writing up his results for other members of the same society. He and his readers, as participants, already *know* the major norms of the culture, and it would be trite to detail them.[30]   (Italics ours.)

This is a remarkable assertion in view of the manifold "subcultures" in American society, its high divorce rate, union-management conflict, North-South differences concerning desegregation in schools and housing, and the conflicting views found in most "readers' columns" in newspapers on the roles of the husband, wife, and child in American society. Perhaps these differences are incidental to the "major norms" to which Murdock was referring, but they can hardly be considered incidental to American society.

Just as the concept of the "culture construct" has tended to focus attention on modal behavior with the result that nonmodal behaviors are ignored, so has the postulate of consensus on ideal culture patterns tended to result in the ignoring of the possible complexities in the evaluative standards that the members of a society have internalized. The result has been lack of concern for the possibility of pluralistic ideal patterns and for those situations which position incumbents face that are characterized by incompatible standards. The possible reality of subcultural patterning has been overshadowed by the assumed actuality of a unicultural patterning. The concept of ideal pattern has similarly tended to block the use of "normative data" to penetrate dynamic problems of cultures—their inconsistencies, their cleavages, and their internal strains.

Smith has observed that the usual anthropological analysis of an entire culture is conducted by one or two field workers who live in the society a relatively short period of time and that, in consequence, ". . . the field worker is forced into bold extrapolations if he aspires to any synthetic characterization of the culture as a whole."[31]   We referred earlier to the differences between Lewis' and Redfield's description of the culture of Tepoztlan. Mead observes, concerning the anthropologist's interviewing skills, "Each informant is evaluated individually against a wide knowledge (on the part of the interviewer) of the culture of the informant, the social structure of which the informant is a part, and the particular subject about which the informant is being interviewed."[32]

Mead's comments suggest a possible compounding of the bias of initial nonrandom selection of respondents through the addition of the bias of prejudgment of their responses. Waller tells us that if we ask teachers and mothers how a teacher should behave toward a child we will obtain different responses.[33] If we ask principals and teachers the same question, we probably would obtain more similar responses. The population of role definers may be a significant factor in the degree of consensus on evaluative standards an investigator finds.

In view of these methodological difficulties it is not surprising that intuitively plausible accounts of the ideal patterns of a society by anthropologists are sometimes viewed as artistic rather than scientific formulations. If ideal patterns are internalized norms then it is reasonable to expect that investigators will use as their basic source of data the responses of the individuals who have presumably internalized them. But Linton and Kluckhohn suggest that respondents frequently cannot verbalize them even though the investigator can. Although intuition and reconstruction have their place in science, they are acceptable only when consistent with reliable and valid empirical evidence. It is frequently difficult to accept inferred ideal patterns as valid. Plausible findings and valid findings deserve to be distinguished from one another.

If these critical observations are reasonable, they imply the need for systematic research on the degree of consensus on evaluative standards in a society—especially for the examination of consensus on role definition. Linton's formulation of the role concept blocks such inquiries because built into its definition is the postulate that there is role consensus. It will be recalled that he defines a role as ". . . the sum total of the culture patterns associated with a particular status. It thus includes the attitudes, values and behavior ascribed by the society to any and all persons occupying this status."[34] It is the phrase "ascribed by society" that contains the postulate of consensus. The untested assumption is that the members of a society hold the same expectations for incumbents of the same position.

This conceptualization of role does not allow for the investigation of the impact of variant and dominant orientations on role definition which Florence Kluckhohn suggests operate in any society.[35] If individuals hold variant orientations this should be expressed in variant definitions of a role as well as in different behavior. This implies that one of the factors accounting for different role behavior may be variant role definitions, a possibility completely ignored by the postulate of role consensus. Nor is this postulate compatible with some of Roberts' empirical findings:

It can be concluded that, insofar as this survey of three closely similar Ramah Navaho households is concerned, the hypothesis that every small group defines an independent and unique group-ordered culture has been supported.[36]

For certain types of anthropological problems purposive sampling procedures are, of course, appropriate. However, for the isolation of the ideal culture patterns of a society it is suggested that random samples of the members of a society may be needed to investigate the degree of consensus on the evaluative standards applied by the *members* of the society to the behavior of position incumbents.

The concept of ideal cultural patterns implies a hypothesis which, like all hypotheses, deserves testing, not the manipulation of operational procedures to insure that it cannot be rejected. Perhaps organism-centered as well as culture-centered conceptual schemes are needed in cultural anthropology which embrace the role definitions of particular individuals rather than, or as well as, the assumed consensus of a population of individuals.[37]

Such an orientation to the problem of role consensus suggests a series of theoretical questions that anthropologists have tended to ignore: How much consensus on what behaviors is required for a society to maintain itself? How much disagreement can a society tolerate in what areas? To what extent do different sets of role definers hold the same role definitions of key positions in a society? On what aspects of role definition do members of different "subcultures" in a society agree and disagree? To what extent is deviant behavior a function of deviant role definitions? Why do members of a society differ in their role definitions? Each of these questions suggests that systematic research on role consensus may be of importance for the development of cultural anthropology.

Acceptance of the postulate of consensus on role definition has not been restricted to the discipline of cultural anthropology but may also be found in the writings of social psychologists and sociologists, especially those who have been influenced by Linton. An examination of its involvement in the work of certain social psychologists and the background from which it developed is instructive. We shall consider two psychologists who have made substantial contributions to the area of social psychology.

The development of "psychological" social psychology was largely a consequence of a recognition that the inclusion of only intrapersonal variables in the analysis of personality and individual behavior limited the phenomena for which adequate theories could be developed.

Although there were numerous obstacles to the diffusion of sociological and anthropological insights, theoretical ideas, and empirical findings to psychology, gradually some of them permeated the frameworks of certain influential psychologists.[38] The most important general contribution of sociology was perhaps, as Newcomb has suggested, ". . . nothing less than the necessity of coming to terms with the ineluctable fact of groups." [39]

That human behavior is in part a function of the actions and reactions of other members of the multiple social systems in which the individual lives and behaves and that it is influenced by normative or evaluative standards are basic notions of sociology and anthropology. The diffusion of these ideas, found in the writings of such men as Cooley,[40] G. H. Mead,[41] Thomas and Znaniecki,[42] Sapir,[43] and Linton,[44] into psychology was greatly facilitated by the research and writings of such psychologists as Lewin,[45] Piaget,[46] Sherif,[47] and Newcomb.[48] The formulations they proposed for examining the phenomena of personality and individual behavior included, explicitly or implicitly, the ideas of social structure and culture. They recognized that extrapersonal influences had to be taken into account. These psychologists were influential in pointing out the importance for many problems of treating the actions of an individual as *interactions,* that the "social self" was largely derivative of the history of interactions of the individual, and that human behavior is influenced by the "norms" of the society and the groups of which the individual is a member.

From the standpoint of the postulate of role consensus perhaps one of the most significant aspects of this diffusion process was that with it went the acceptance by some psychologists of the notion of ideal cultural patterns in the conceptual scheme of Linton, and especially of his concepts of status and role. The reason for the acceptance of Linton's concepts is not surprising. As Murdock has said, Linton clearly and concisely articulated the key idea of the "functional" school in anthropology ". . . that cultures and subcultures are organically related to the structured social groups and subgroups that carry them, which has been axiomatic in sociology at least since the days of Sumner." [49]

Murdock also makes the point that: "Utterly incredible as it must seem to the psychologist and sociologist, it is nevertheless almost literally true that no work by an American anthropologist recognized this fact until the appearance of Linton's *Study of Man* in 1936." [50] In addition, in his collaboration with Kardiner[51] and in his analysis of the relationship between culture and personality,[52] Linton demonstrated that his concepts were useful for the study of personality.

In short, Linton's conceptualization of status and role related the basic ideas of social structure and culture in a form in which they could be readily assimilated into existing social-psychological conceptual schemes. It brought culture and social structure down to the individual level, to the level of analysis at which the psychologist feels most comfortable in developing theory and treating data. The relevance of the broad, and to many psychologists the vague, ideas of culture and social organization to their problems became more evident.

One of the psychologists who has clearly recognized the potential contributions of sociology and anthropology to the analysis of an individual's values, attitudes, and behavior is Newcomb. He views social psychology as a quasi-separate discipline focusing on the individual and his behavior in a socio-cultural matrix. Although he recognizes that for some problems it is relevant for the psychologist to study human behaviors as "functions of persons" [53] without regard to interpersonal and cultural influences, and that for others it is meaningful to study individual behavior without regard to intrapersonal influences, it is his position that many human behavior problems demand a frame of reference containing both sets of factors. For him, this is the special province of social psychology. In developing a framework for this synthetic point of view, Newcomb thinks of the term role as a central concept. Since he has developed one of the most carefully designed sets of "role" concepts in social psychology and since his constructs are based on Linton's conceptualization, it is instructive to examine how role consensus is treated in his work.

That Newcomb's conceptual formulation is based on Linton's definitions of status and role is clear:

> The ways of behaving which are expected of any individual who occupies a certain position constitute the *role* (or, as many writers use the term, social role) associated with that position. . . . A position, as Linton's term "status" implies, is something static; it is a place in a structure, recognized by members of the society and accorded by them to one or more individuals. A role, on the other hand, is something dynamic; it refers to the *behavior* of the occupants of a position—not to all their behavior, as persons, but to what they do *as occupants of the position.*[54]

It is of parenthetical interest to observe that in this quotation from Newcomb there is an example of the ambiguity frequently found in the literature over the differentiation between expected behavior and actual behavior of position incumbents.[55] In the first sentence "role" is defined as "expected ways of behaving." In the last one it is defined as actual behavior of position incumbents, "to what they do *as occupants of the position.*"

Newcomb's treatment of the consensus problem in his *Social Psychology* might best be described as one of ambivalence toward the postulate of role consensus. At one point he says: "Both behavior standards and norms for perceiving people are shared by *all* members of any group, but they apply in distinctive ways to different members of the group, depending upon how these members are classified." [56] (Italics ours.) This would seem to imply that he assumes consensus on role definition. A similar implication might be taken from his discussion of Merton's analysis of the bureaucratic structure:

> . . . each position carries with it *definite prescriptions* toward behaving toward other persons in related positions. Thus, the position of mother carries with it the implication of *certain ways of behaving* toward children, just as the position of store clerk carries with it certain ways of behaving toward customers, toward employers, and toward other clerks. Such ways of behaving toward others, which are *defined* for different positions, are called *roles.* . . .[57] (Italics ours, except for last.)

Yet, on the other hand, at certain points in Newcomb's discussion he appears to be aware of the possibility of lack of consensus on positional expectations. In introducing the concept of role prescription ("a limited set of behaviors, 'tied together' by a common understanding of the functions of a position.")[58] he says, "Roles thus represent ways of carrying out the functions for which positions exist—ways which are *generally agreed upon* within whatever group recognizes any particular position and role." [59] In this statement there would seem to be at least some room for disagreement among group members, and therefore, one could infer, recognition of the possibility of imperfect consensus.

In his discussion of possible operational definitions of a prescribed role, Newcomb most clearly gives recognition to the possibility of lack of consensus among role definers:

> For example, determining what is included in a mother's prescribed role in a specific society would involve obtaining the following kinds of information from a representative sample of all the people in that society who recognize that particular position: (1) a list of behaviors which are expected of mothers—such as nursing infants, protecting children from danger, or teaching them table manners; (2) information as to whether each behavior on the list is demanded or is merely permitted of mothers. A criterion of 50 percent agreement that any given behavior is demanded

of all mothers . . . might be set up. In that case, the prescribed role would consist of all the behaviors which were considered by at least half of the respondents to be demanded of all mothers.[60]

Although this is only an illustration of an operational definition of a prescribed role, one could maintain that fifty percent is as good a criterion of disagreement as agreement. It would also seem reasonable to at least consider what the other fifty percent felt before defining a role according to the fifty percent of respondents who agree.

On the next page of his discussion, however, he says that roles are "ready made." The following quotation suggests the postulate of consensus.

Very few young men in any society have to use an encyclopedia to learn about either their future roles as husbands or those of their future wives. Their brides are similarly familiar, long before marriage, with most aspects of their roles as wives, as well as those of their husbands. If the marriage of any particular couple "fails," it is not likely to be merely because of the strangeness of their prescribed roles. It is apt to be, as Burgess and Cottrell have shown (1939), because the personality of one or both of them is such that special demands, not necessarily included in the prescribed role are made which the other spouse is unable or unwilling to meet.[61]

In this statement we see an example of the reasoning that is likely to follow the assumption of consensus. The assumption is that there is consensus among the members in the society who recognize the positions of husband and wife. The reason a marriage breaks up is "apt to be" that one or both of the position incumbents because of "personality reasons" have "inappropriate" expectations for the other's behavior to which the marriage partner will not conform.

But another explanation of the "break-up" might be that there is a lack of consensus between the position incumbents as to what constitutes the "prescribed roles" of wife or husband. The position incumbents themselves are part of "the population" of the definers of the position. Furthermore, one of the reasons for this lack of consensus could be that the husband comes from a religious-ethnic segment in the society in which there is consensus on the expectation that a husband should be the only breadwinner in the family, regardless of the size of the loaf. On the other hand, his wife's religious-ethnic "group" might be one in which a wife is expected to work the first few years of marriage. In short, there may be a lack of consensus on the expectations attached to the positions of husband and wife between different segments of a population of role definers.

It is interesting that the postulate of consensus seems to enter into

Newcomb's discussion primarily when he is considering the phenomena of social structure and culture at a fairly abstract level. In his consideration of possible operations to delineate a role or a prescribed role the postulate of consensus appears to assume lesser importance.

It should be emphasized that we have examined Newcomb's formulation of role in his *Social Psychology* only from the viewpoint of his treatment of role consensus. It is only fair to state that from other vantage points his formulation represents a clear advance over earlier schemes. For example, his concepts of *prescribed role* and *role behavior* distinguish clearly between the expected and the actual behavior of a position incumbent. He also emphasized that to divorce a position from other positions with which it is related is to lose much of the potential heuristic value of the concept.

One other example of the treatment of role consensus by a psychologist is worthy of consideration in illustrating the more or less uncritical acceptance of the postulate of role consensus. Sherif, under the influence of Sapir, Kroeber, and Rivers, was one of the first psychologists to argue for the inclusion of the concept of norms in psychological theory. His research on the influence of social interaction on perception and on the development of social norms was of considerable importance in diffusing sociocultural ideas in psychology. Sherif appears not only to have accepted the postulate of consensus in role definition but also to have gone a long way beyond most anthropologists in assuming absolute conformity. In discussing the individual's "role" in society, he says:

> Every kind of *status* places the individual in definite relationship to other individuals, whereby his duties, responsibilities, and privileges are prescribed within that social order. Once he is *there*, in a particular status, he has no choice, but fulfills the requirements demanded of the status. And he may (this is the general case) fulfill the requirements with the good natured complacency typical of many a bourgeois gentleman, even with an air of originality, as if he were the first one to accomplish those things.[62]

There are signs, however, that there is growing recognition that the analysis of role consensus is an important theoretical area of inquiry for social psychology. In a statement on research that is needed to achieve better articulation between sociology and psychology, Newcomb recently emphasized the need for "conceptual and operational refinement" of the concept "consensus" in role and communication research.[63] In their review of "psychological aspects of social structure," Riecken and Homans consider certain hypotheses in which consensus on norms is and is *not* assumed. For example, in discussing factors possibly related to the development of group consensus they observe: "The norms of members probably become more similar with time, but there seem to be no empirical studies of this relationship." [64] The different role definitions of stewards held by workers, foremen, and shop stewards, and the implications of these differences for strains in occupational positions have been investigated by Jacobson, Charters, and Lieberman.[65]

Considering consensus on role definition as an empirical problem, not a "given," raises serious questions with respect to Sullivan's concept of the "consensually validated" [66] and Cameron's concept of "public verification" [67] and suggests the potential theoretical importance of introducing role consensus as a variable in studies of psychopathology. Of perhaps even more potential utility for the study of pathological behavior is the notion of perceived role consensus. For example, how does an actor's perception of the degree of consensus on expectations held by "significant others" on evaluative standards applicable to his position affect his role behavior?

Although there is not now a systematic body of literature concerned with the determinants and consequences of consensus on role definition for individual behavior and group functioning, these and other recent developments suggest that such a body of literature will probably emerge.

An examination of role formulations in the sociological literature reveals that the postulate of role consensus has been as embedded in sociology as in anthropology and social psychology. Recently, however, some writers have recognized the theoretical importance of consensus as a problem and have suggested the need for systematic research in this area. In the sociological formulations in which the postulate of consensus is involved, it is usually implied, just as in anthropology and psychology, by the way in which the term role is defined.

A number of formulations of this kind lean heavily on Linton's definition. Bennett and Tumin, for example, say: "By role, then, we have reference to what the society expects of an individual occupying a given status. This implies that any status is *functionally* defined by *the role attached to it*." [68] Linton's influence is also apparent in Wilson and Kolb's formulation:

Culture generally organizes these expectations regarding behavior into an articulated whole, composed of the interrelated *norms* (social rules) defining the basic *social positions* in the group. . . . As indicated, it is the function of the person occupying the position to carry out the rights and obligations associated with it. This collection of rights and duties is a social *status* . . . and in carrying them out the person is playing a social *role.* A *role* is defined as a pattern of behavior corresponding to a system of rights and duties and associated with a particular position in a social group. Since we have already spoken of these patterns as being articulated with one another, it is only necessary to add that such organization of social roles makes it possible for the group to function as a unit and the members to realize their individual and collective goals.[69]

These definitions illustrate the kind most frequently found in the sociological literature. Another formulation of role, found primarily in the writings of the "sociological" social psychologists, is usually derived from G. H. Mead,[70] who used the term role with considerably less precision than the social scientists whose definitions were considered in Chapter Two. Mead was not attempting to develop a set of concepts to embrace social structural and cultural elements, but was primarily interested in a description of the developmental sequence through which a child moves in the process of socialization.

For Mead, to take the role of another is to "put one's self in place of the other," adopting attitudes appropriate to the other's "role," thereby providing one's self with the appropriate stimuli (attitudes) for the particular responses associated with another's role.

It is generally recognized that the specifically social expressions of intelligence, or the exercise of what is often called 'social intelligence,' depend upon the given individual's ability to take the roles of, or 'put himself in place of,' the other individuals implicated with him in given social situations; and upon his consequent sensitivity to their attitudes toward himself and toward one another.[71]

And again: "When a child does assume a role he has in himself the stimuli which call out that particular response or group of responses." [72]

Cottrell's emphasis on the interactional and self-other basis of role in one of his formulations[73] may be thought of as a lineal descendant of Mead's interpretation of the concept. In this definition, the postulate of consensus is not involved, since roles are considered to be elements of concrete interaction situations, and its referent, as we suggested earlier, could be considered non-normative stimuli and responses.

Other "descendants" of Mead in their attempts, apparently, to link his with Linton's definition, seem to accept the postulate of consensus. Cameron's definition illustrates the result of this fusion: "[A role is] . . . a comprehensive and coherent organization in behavior of functionally related, interlocking attitudes and responses . . . a product of social learning which has been *culturally defined* by the behavior of others. . . ." [74] Lindesmith and Strauss have an essentially similar definition in which the postulate of consensus seems to be involved. They say: "The concept of role refers to the most intricately organized patterns of response of which the human organism is capable, i.e., to verbally organized systems of response to an organized, subdivided, and patterned environment." And in elaboration they add:

> In the enactment of roles the following are essential:
> 1. an identification of self;
> 2. behavior in given situations which is appropriate to this identification;
> 3. a background of related acts by others (counter-roles) which serve as cues to guide specific performance;
> 4. an evaluation by the individual, and by others, of the role enactment.[75]

The postulate of consensus may be inferred from the phrase, "behavior, in given situations, which is appropriate to this identification."

In contrast to these formulations are another of Cottrell's and those of Parsons and Stouffer. Cottrell was one of the first sociologists who recognized the theoretical utility of treating role consensus as a variable. In a paper concerned with an individual's adjustment to age and sex roles[76] he presented a series of hypotheses concerning the degree of adjustment to these roles. Several of them are concerned with "role" adjustment as a function of such variables as "the clarity with which such roles are defined," [77] and "the consistency with which others in the individual's life situations exhibit to him the response called for by his role." [78] Here, then, is a clear recognition of role consensus as a useful variable in the analysis of social behavior. Similarly, in suggesting a series of hypotheses concerning social disorganization and "cultural roles," Warren distinguishes among cultural, social, and personal roles and one of his hypotheses is: "Social disorganization varies inversely with the clarity of definition of cultural roles." [79]

From an examination of Parsons' definition of a social system one might infer that he assumes consensus on the evaluative standards applicable to group members. He says that,

> . . . a social system consists in a plurality of individual actors interacting with each other in a situation which has at least a physical or environmental aspect, actors who are motivated in terms of a tendency to the "optimization of gratification" and *whose relation to their situations, including each other, is defined and mediated in terms of a system of culturally structured and shared symbols.*[80] (Italics ours.)

The italicized part of the quotation with its reference to the "culture" or symbolic interaction in a social system might suggest the consensus postulate.

In his elaboration of the elements of a social system, however, it becomes clear that consensus on evaluative standards is assumed only for *stable* interaction systems. After noting that an actor's orientation to another includes evaluative standards, he says,

> *Stability of interaction* in turn depends on the condition that the particular acts of evaluation on both sides should be oriented to *common standards* since only in terms of such standards is "order" in either the communication or the motivational contexts possible.[81]   (Italics ours.)

Although Parsons defines an institution as "a complex of patterned elements in role-expectations which may apply to an indefinite number of collectivities," [82] (collectivities are viewed as systems "of concretely interactive specific roles") he recognizes that, empirically, the degree of agreement on evaluative standards is problematic, falling on a continuum ranging from "full institutionalization" to "anomie."

> The institutionalization of a set of role expectations and of the corresponding sanctions is clearly a matter of degree. This degree is a function of two sets of variables; on the one hand those affecting the actual sharedness of the value orientation patterns, on the other those determining the motivational orientation or commitment to the fulfillment of the relevant expectations. . . . The polar antithesis of full institutionalization is, however, *anomie,* the absence of structured complementarity of the interaction process or, what is the same thing, the complete breakdown of normative order in both senses.[83]

These passages from Parsons indicate not only his recognition of role consensus as a variable but also his recognition of the importance of the theoretical linkage between the "evaluative standards" of groups, of larger systems in which they are involved, and the degree of their internalization in the individual.

Stouffer, in an analysis of conflicting social norms, has demonstrated that college students may perceive that authorities and students hold variant or incongruent expectations. In addition, his analysis makes clear that the *"range* of approved or permissible behavior" [84] must be taken into account in describing social norms and that this range may be necessary for continuing social behavior. His concluding comments are:

> From the theoretical standpoint, the most important implication of this paper may stem from its stress on variability. In essay writing in this field it is common and convenient to think of a social norm as a point, or at least as a very narrow band on either side of a point. This probably is quite unrealistic as to most of our social behavior. And it may be precisely the ranges of permissible behavior which most need examination,

if we are to make progress in this realm which is so central in social science. For it may be the very existence of some flexibility or social slippage—but not too much—which makes behavior in groups possible.[85]

Cottrell and Parsons suggest that consensus on role definition would be related in a positive and linear manner to the stability of social system and to personal gratification, whereas the inference might be drawn from Stouffer's conclusions that it may be curvilinear.

Homans, in *The Human Group,* is also aware that the degree of consensus among group members on positional expectations may vary. After defining a role as norms that state ". . . the expected relationship of a person in a certain position to others he comes into contact with . . ." [86] in his discussion of norms, he says, "No doubt the norms accepted in a group vary somewhat from one person to another . . ." and ". . . the more frequently men interact with one another, *the more nearly alike they become in the norms they hold,* as they do in their sentiments and activities." [87] (Italics ours.)

His proposition that ". . . *the members of the group are more often more alike in the norms they hold than in their overt behavior"* [88] presents degree of consensus as a variable. Homans' suggested explanation of this proposition is that since an individual's perception of a norm is subject to a "less immediate influence than his social activity, itself," it will vary "less than his social activity." [89] On an a priori basis, reasoning leading to the opposite conclusion can easily be developed: since overt behavior is visible and therefore more amenable to social sanctions than norms, individuals will be more alike in their behavior than in their norms.

Despite Homans' awareness of the possibility of imperfect role consensus, he tends to think of consensus on norms among group members in *The Human Group* as a *given* "in social systems" and in consequence explores only conformity to norms, not their variability, as a factor affecting the interaction, sentiments, activities, or rankings of group members.

In the small group research of Bales and his associates consensus on rankings of group members is sometimes treated as a variable, although consensus on role definition is not. This is the case partly because Bales is usually working with contrived groups at a "prenormative stage" and with those that do not contain differentiated positions.[90]

Recently, there has been a handful of empirical studies in which differential role definitions by sets of role definers have been investigated. Davis has attempted to test certain hypotheses originally suggested by Cottrell concerning clarity of role definition and adjustment in "official leader" military "roles." [91] Hall investigated the relationships between "cohesiveness" and role consensus, and between "cohesiveness" and the role behavior of incumbents of the position of aircraft commander.[92]

Borgatta's finding that incumbents of different military positions held different attitudes in a number of different scalable areas[93] and Henry and Borgatta's report of incongruent attitudes of commissioned and enlisted air force personnel toward the punitiveness of sanctions for deviant military behavior[94] both suggest that there are empirical disparities in the evaluative standards applicable to incumbents of the same position.

Several investigations of the existence or correlates of types of marriage "roles" have been concerned with the degree of consensus on role definition among some population of role definers. The hypothesis of lack of consensus is involved in, or may be inferred from, several studies of sex roles, for example, those of Komarovsky,[95] Rose,[96] and Wallin.[97] The studies of Wardwell,[98] Wilson,[99] and Chartier[100] of the "roles" of the chiropractor, the poet, and the "literary elite," respectively, and Reismann's differentiations of four subtypes of the bureaucratic role[101] suggest directly or indirectly the importance of different expectations for occupants of the same position.

Finally, mention must be made of Williams' incisive analysis of institutional variation and "cultural fictions" in a society.[102] In summarizing his consideration of these problems he says:

> It has been repeatedly stressed in this chapter that social norms vary considerably in the way individuals conceive of and conform to them. In addition, we suggested the crucial point, in connection with cultural fictions, that shared assumptions and expectations can play an essential part in behavior, even when regarded by the actors as fictional or when so described. . . .[103]

In attempting to place the problem of role consensus in its social science setting we observed that the postulate of consensus is still enmeshed in the analyses of many students of social behavior. Since their analyses assume consensus on role definitions among members of a group or "society," they have ignored its possible significance as a variable for social science inquiry. We also observed, however, that during the past decade there has been an increasing tendency to consider role consensus an important variable for the study of individual social behavior, the functioning of social systems, and cultural organization.

That the members of a social system, whether a dyad or a total society, must agree among themselves to *some extent* on values or expectations is a matter of definition. The point we have been trying to underscore is that the degree of consensus on expectations associated with positions is an empirical variable, whose theoretical possibilities until recently have remained relatively untapped.

In our examination of the anthropological definitions of culture we suggested a number of questions that deserve investigation. If cultural anthropologists follow Murdock's suggestion and give greater emphasis to variations in normative patterns, they will be forced to deal directly with the theoretical implications of differential role definitions by members of a society.

From the standpoint of individual behavior, research on role consensus is required in order to investigate, for example, the propositions suggested by Cottrell regarding individual adjustment or the utility of Sullivan's and Cameron's notions concerning the therapist-client relationship and the etiology of pathological behavior.

In sociological inquiry a number of questions deserves systematic investigation. For example, what are the determinants of high and low consensus on role definition in social systems? What types of interaction tend to facilitate or block the development of consensus in different kinds of social systems? What impact does differential consensus have on the functioning of social systems, on group effectiveness, group equilibrium, and on the gratification of it members?

This is a very small sample of questions that are open to examination when the postulate of consensus is abandoned. In contrast to the holistic approach so frequently found in social science literature, that is, that a role is an indivisible *unit* of rights and duties ascribed by a group or society, theoretically grounded empirical inquiries are needed to determine how much agreement there is on the expectations for the behavior of position incumbents. Conceptual schemes for role analysis that preclude the investigation of the basic question of role consensus are distinctly limited. In the next chapter a set of concepts will be proposed which may facilitate such research.

Notes and References for Chapter Three

[1] H. G. Barnett, *Innovation: The Basis of Cultural Change* (New York: McGraw-Hill Book Co., 1953).

[2] Edward H. Spicer (Editor), *Human Problems in Technological Change* (New York: Russell Sage Foundation, 1952).

[3] Evon Z. Vogt, "Navaho Veterans: A Study of Changing Values" *Papers of the*

Peabody Museum of American Archeology and Ethnology, Harvard University, Vol. XLI, No. 1 (Cambridge: Peabody Museum, 1951).

[4] For a review of each of these research areas see Clyde Kluckhohn, "Culture and Behavior," in Gardner Lindzey (Editor), *Handbook of Social Psychology,* Vol. II (Cambridge: Addison-Wesley Publishing Company, 1954), pp. 921–976.

[5] George P. Murdock, "Sociology and Anthropology," in John Gillin (Editor), *For a Science of Social Man* (New York: The Macmillan Company, 1954), p. 21.

[6] Kluckhohn, *op. cit.,* p. 923.

[7] *Ibid.,* p. 924.

[8] *Ibid.,* p. 925.

[9] M. Brewster Smith, "Anthropology and Psychology," in John Gillin (Editor), *For a Science of Social Man* (New York: The Macmillan Company, 1954), p. 40.

[10] *Ibid.,* p. 40.

[11] *Ibid.,* pp. 40–41.

[12] William G. Sumner, *Folkways* (Boston: Ginn and Company, 1906).

[13] Ralph Linton, *The Cultural Background of Personality* (New York: D. Appleton-Century Co., 1945), pp. 42–43.

[14] *Ibid.,* p. 43.

[15] *Ibid.,* pp. 44–45.

[16] *Ibid.,* p. 45

[17] *Ibid.,* p. 45.

[18] *Ibid.,* pp. 45–46.

[19] Alex Inkeles and Daniel J. Levinson, "National Character: The Study of Modal Personality and Sociocultural Systems," in Gardner Lindzey (Editor), *Handbook of Social Psychology,* Vol. II (Cambridge: Addison-Wesley Publishing Company, 1954), p. 1015.

[20] Linton, *op. cit.,* pp. 52–53.

[21] Kluckhohn, *op. cit.,* p. 924.

[22] Murdock, *op. cit.,* p. 22.

[23] *Ibid.,* p. 22.

[24] Linton, *op. cit.,* p. 52.

[25] Kluckhohn, *op. cit.,* p. 924.

[26] Linton, *op. cit.,* pp. 39–40.

[27] *Ibid.,* p. 53.

[28] The relevant studies are: Arnold M. Rose, "The Adequacy of Women's Expectations for Adult Roles," *Social Forces,* XXX (1951), pp. 69–77; Mirra Komarovsky, "Cultural Contradictions and Sex Roles," *American Journal of Sociology,* LII (1946), pp. 184–189; Paul Wallin, "Cultural Contradictions and Sex Roles: A Repeat Study," *American Sociological Review,* XV (1950), pp. 288–293.

[29] Oscar Lewis, "Husbands and Wives in a Mexican Village: A Study of Role Conflict," *American Anthropologist,* LI (1949), p. 610.

[30] Murdock, *op. cit.,* p. 22.

[31] Smith, *op. cit.,* p. 37.

[32] From Margaret Mead's Introduction to *Studies in Soviet Communication*

(Cambridge: Center for International Studies, Massachusetts Institute of Technology, 1952), as quoted in Kluckhohn, *op. cit.,* p. 965.

[33] Willard Waller, *The Sociology of Teaching* (New York: John Wiley and Sons, 1932).

[34] Linton, *op. cit.,* p. 77.

[35] Florence R. Kluckhohn, "Dominant and Variant Value Orientations," in Clyde Kluckhohn and Henry A. Murray (Editors), *Personality in Nature, Society and Culture* (New York: Alfred A. Knopf, 1953), pp. 342–357.

[36] John M. Roberts, "Three Navaho Households: A Comparative Study in Small Group Culture," *Papers of the Peabody Museum of American Archeology and Ethnology,* Vol. XL, No. 3 (Cambridge: Peabody Museum, 1951), p. 77.

[37] See John W. M. Whiting and Irving Child, *Child Training and Personality* (New Haven: Yale University Press, 1953), for a conceptual scheme that attempts to bring culture "down to" the individual level. For the implication of the analysis of consensus on culture patterns for personality and culture studies, see Inkeles and Levinson, *op. cit.* It is of further interest to note that Clyde Kluckhohn raised the sampling and variability in culture pattern problems as early as 1939. See Clyde Kluckhohn, "Theoretical Bases for an Empirical Method of Studying the Acquisition of Culture by Individuals," *Man,* XXXIX (1939), pp. 1–6.

[38] See Theodore M. Newcomb, "Sociology and Psychology" in John Gillin (Editor), *For a Science of Social Man* (New York: The Macmillan Company, 1954), pp. 230–240.

[39] *Ibid.,* p. 233.

[40] Charles H. Cooley, *Human Nature and the Social Order* (New York: Charles Scribner and Sons, 1922).

[41] George H. Mead, *Mind, Self & Society* (Chicago: University of Chicago Press, 1934).

[42] William I. Thomas and Florian Znaniecki, *The Polish Peasant in Europe and America,* Volumes I and II (New York: Badger, 1918).

[43] In David G. Mandelbaum (Editor), *Selected Writings of Edward Sapir in Language, Culture and Personality* (Berkeley: University of California Press, 1949).

[44] Ralph Linton, *The Study of Man* (New York: D. Appleton-Century Co., 1936); also see *Cultural Background.*

[45] Kurt Lewin, *A Dynamic Theory of Personality* (New York: McGraw-Hill Book Co., 1935), and Kurt Lewin, *Field Theory in Social Science* (New York: Harper and Brothers, 1951).

[46] Jean Piaget, *The Moral Judgement of the Child* (New York: Harcourt, Brace and Co., 1932).

[47] Muzafer Sherif, *The Psychology of Social Norms* (New York: Harper and Brothers, 1936).

[48] Theodore M. Newcomb, *Personality and Social Change* (New York: Dryden Press, 1943).

[49] Murdock, *op. cit.,* p. 19.

[50] *Ibid.,* pp. 19–20.

[51] See Ralph Linton, "Foreword," in Abram Kardiner, *The Individual and His Society* (New York: Columbia University Press, 1939).

[52] Linton, *Cultural Background.*

[53] Newcomb, "Sociology and Psychology," in Gillin, *op. cit.*, pp. 227–256.

[54] Theodore M. Newcomb, *Social Psychology* (New York: Dryden Press, 1950), p. 280.

[55] See Chapter Two, pp. 11–15.

[56] Newcomb, *Social Psychology*, p. 276.

[57] *Ibid.*, p. 278.

[58] *Ibid.*, p. 282.

[59] *Ibid.*, p. 281.

[60] *Ibid.*, p. 282.

[61] *Ibid.*, p. 283.

[62] Sherif, *op. cit.*, pp. 187–188.

[63] Newcomb, "Sociology and Psychology," in Gillin, *op. cit.*, p. 255.

[64] Henry W. Riecken and George C. Homans, "Psychological Aspects of Social Structure," in Gardner Lindzey (Editor), *Handbook of Social Psychology*, Vol. II (Cambridge: Addison-Wesley Publishing Company, 1954), p. 788.

[65] Eugene Jacobson, W. W. Charters, Jr. and S. Lieberman, "The Use of the Role Concept in the Study of Complex Organization," *Journal of Social Issues*, VII, 3 (1951), pp. 18–27.

[66] See Nelson N. Foote and Leonard S. Cottrell, Jr., *The Contributions of H. S. Sullivan* (New York: Hermitage House, 1952).

[67] Cf. Norman Cameron, *Psychology and the Behavior Disorders* (New York: Houghton Mifflin Co., 1947).

[68] John W. Bennett and Melvin M. Tumin, *Social Life, Structure and Function* (New York: Alfred A. Knopf, 1948), p. 96.

[69] Logan Wilson and William L. Kolb (Editors), *Sociological Analysis* (New York: Harcourt, Brace and Co., 1949), p. 208.

[70] George H. Mead, *op. cit.*

[71] *Ibid.*, p. 141.

[72] *Ibid.*, p. 150.

[73] See Chapter Two, p. 15.

[74] Norman Cameron, *The Psychology of Behavior Disorders* (New York: The Macmillan Company, 1947), p. 90.

[75] A. R. Lindesmith and Anselm L. Strauss, *Social Psychology*, Revised edition (New York: Dryden Press, 1956), pp. 383–384 and 385. In the first edition of this book, 1949, Lindesmith and Strauss view "behavior, in prescribed situations, *which is appropriate to this identification*" as a basic feature of role behavior (pp. 165–166).

[76] Leonard S. Cottrell, "The Adjustment of the Individual to His Age and Sex Roles," *American Sociological Review*, VII (1942), pp. 617–620.

[77] *Ibid.*, p. 618.

[78] *Ibid.*, p. 619.

[79] Roland L. Warren, "Social Disorganization and the Interrelationship of Cultural Roles," *American Sociological Review*, XIV (1949), p. 84.

[80] Talcott Parsons, *The Social System* (Glencoe: The Free Press, 1951), pp. 5–6.

[81] *Ibid.*, p. 37.

[82] *Ibid.*, p. 39.

[83] *Ibid.*, p. 39.

[84] Samuel A. Stouffer, "An Analysis of Conflicting Social Norms," *American Sociological Review*, XIV (1949), p. 708.

[65] *Ibid.*, p. 717.

[86] George C. Homans, *The Human Group* (New York: Harcourt, Brace and Co., 1950), p. 124.

[87] *Ibid.*, p. 126.

[88] *Ibid.*, p. 126.

[89] *Ibid.*, p. 127.

[90] See Chapter Two, p. 15.

[91] F. James Davis, "Conception of Official Leaders Roles in the Air Force," *Social Forces*, XXXII (1954), pp. 253–258.

[92] Robert L. Hall, "Social Influence on the Aircraft Commander's Role," *American Sociological Reveiw*, XX (1955), pp. 292–299.

[93] Edgar F. Borgatta, "Attitudinal Concomitants to Military Statuses," *Social Forces*, XXXIII (1955), pp. 342–347.

[94] Andrew F. Henry and Edgar F. Borgatta, "A Comparison of Attitudes of Enlisted and Commissioned Air Force Personnel," *American Sociological Review*, XVIII (1953), pp. 669–671.

[95] Komarovsky, *op. cit.*

[96] Rose, *op. cit.*

[97] Wallin, *op. cit.*

[98] Walter Wardwell, "A Marginal Professional Role: The Chiropractor," *Social Forces*, XXX (1952), pp. 339–348.

[99] Robert Neal Wilson, "The American Poet: A Role Investigation" (Unpublished Ph.D. Dissertation, Harvard University, 1952).

[100] Barbara Chartier, "The Social Role of the Literary Elite," *Social Forces*, XXIX (1950), pp. 179–186.

[101] Leonard Reismann, "A Study of Role Conception in Bureaucracy," *Social Forces*, XXVII (1949), pp. 305–310.

[102] Robin M. Williams, Jr., *American Society* (New York: Alfred A. Knopf, 1951), pp. 347–371.

[103] *Ibid.*, p. 370.

four

A Language for Role Analysis

The purposes of this chapter are to present a body of concepts that may be useful for students of role analysis and to consider some of their implications for empirical inquiry. Our objective has been to develop a "role" language that may be applied to individual, cultural, or social phenomena and one that makes possible the investigation of the problem of role consensus. We have attempted to introduce the minimum number of concepts and, as much as possible, to limit consideration to those concepts which are capable of operational definition. Some special terms used only in the discussion of role conflict are not considered here.[1] Those which are considered constitute the basic language of the research to be reported in this book. They are presented under four main headings: Position; Expectations; Role, Role Behavior, and Role Attributes; and Sanctions.

POSITION

The term *position* will be used to refer to *the location of an actor or class of actors in a system of social relationships.* The general idea of social location has been represented by some authors with the term status, and by others with position. The two terms have about equal precedent. We have chosen position for this purpose because status connotes the idea of differential ranking among a set of persons or social locations, whereas the more neutral term, position, does not.

The meaning of location in a system of social relationships is not, however, entirely self-evident. It is difficult to separate the idea of location from the relationships which define it. Just as in geometry a point cannot be located without describing its relationships to other points, so persons cannot be located without describing their relations to other individuals; the points imply the relationships and the relationships imply the points. In a system of social relationships, however, the points acquire labels or identities which may come to have an almost autonomous significance. People may recognize that some indentities are located in a relationship system, but have only a rudimentary conception of what those relationships are. For example, many people who recognize that there is such an occupation as school superintendent may understand only that it is found in the school system and has a higher rank than the occupation of teacher or principal.

People do not get sorted out into different locations in systems of social relationships at random. Certain characteristics of actors come to have relationship patterns associated with them. In his analysis of the social system Parsons has developed an elaborate classification of the "modalities of objects as foci of role expectations," the principal differentiation being that between the performances and qualities of actors.[2] Linton speaks of four "reference points for the ascription of status": age, sex, family (biological) relationships, and birth into a particular socially established group.[3] Similarly, Bennett and Tumin list the "raw materials of status" as (1) the wide variety of biologically determined kinship relations, (2) the biological attributes of man, (3) the great number of human and personality traits, and (4) the literally infinite number of situations of interaction possible between human beings.[4]

Of course not all characteristics of actors have social relationships associated with them. Whereas the sex of individuals constitutes the basis for certain relationship patterns, eye color, at least in American society, does not. The labels assigned to positions, as distinguished from the bases for these positions, serve the cognitive function of differentiating among them. In the case of ascribed [5] positions, the labels which refer to them are generally derived from the "presocial system" characteristics on which the patterns are based. We speak directly of such positions as child or male, for example. Achieved positions are entered through performance and competition, and the labels chosen for them usually have a different derivation. They may refer to what the incumbent does either apart from the relationship system (for example, carpenter), or in terms of social relationships (for example, employer); they may refer primarily to rank in a hierarchic system (for example, lieutenant); or possibly to a combination of these. Whatever the source of the labels which allow cognitive discriminations among actors, identities do not become positions until they are placed in a relationship system.

Since positions have been defined as locations of actors in systems of social relationships, they can be completely described only by an examination of the content of their interrelationships. However, before investigating *how* positions are interrelated, we must go a step further in designating the position to be studied. Clarity in this respect is necessary for the selection of appropriate research procedures and for the statement of the universe of phenomena to which research findings may be generalized.

When an investigator uses a sampling procedure in his research, it is necessary that he specify precisely the population from which he is sampling and to which his findings may be generalized. Public opinion poll findings, for example, may be considered meaningless without this specification. However, in addition to specifying the population of respondents, for many types of social science inquiry it is just as necessary to specify the phenomena to which they are responding; it is necessary to specify not only a *subject* population but also an *object* population.

Similarly, in the analysis of a particular position certain specifications are necessary in order that the object of analysis will be clear. We propose to examine two aspects of position specification, the relational and the situational.

The Relational Specification of Positions. Nearly every role theorist, regardless of the frame of reference in which his analysis is couched, adopts the view that a position is an element or a part of a network or system of positions. In *The Study of Man* Linton says that statuses are the "polar positions" in reciprocal behavior patterns.[6] In *The Cultural Background of Personality* he says: "The place in a particular system which a certain individual occupies at a particular time will be referred to as his *status* with respect to that system." [7] For Parsons a status is a ". . . place in the relationship system considered as a structure, that is a patterned system of *parts*." [8] In Newcomb's scheme this point is given especial emphasis:

> Thus the positions, which are the smallest element—the construction blocks—of societies and organized groups, are interrelated and consistent because they are organized to common ends. From one point of view, then, societies and organized groups are structures of positions which are organized to reach certain goals. Since every position is a part of an inclusive system of positions, no one position has any meaning apart from the other positions to which it is related.[9]

The last sentence in the statement from Newcomb suggests the nature of the present problem. If a particular position has no meaning apart from other positions, it is necessary for an investigator, in focusing on one position, to specify the other positions with which his analysis will be concerned. Some positions in our society seem at first glance to be associated with only one other position, for example, the positions of mother or employer. The terms themselves seems to imply only one "opposite number" or reciprocal position, which are for these examples child and employee, respectively. Some theorists, moreover, define their terms to refer only to dyadic relations of this sort.[10] Closer inspection will usually reveal that such positions are related to more than one other position. When a mother consults a teacher about her son's progress in school she is still acting in the

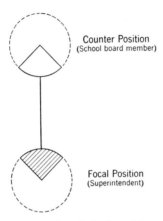

Counter Position
(School board member)

Focal Position
(Superintendent)

Figure 4–1. A dyad model.

mother position, and when the employer deals with the labor union's business manager he is still acting in the position of employer. Other positions, such as college president, may not have implications for any dyadic relationships.

Whatever the implications of the label, a position cannot be completely described until all the other positions to which it is related have been specified. Of course a complete relational specification is a limiting case with which it would be impossible to deal empirically. For a given research problem it may be necessary to take into account only a limited set of counter positions.

In studying a particular position (a *focal* position), it may for some purposes be adequate to consider its relationship to only one other position (a *counter* position). This could be termed a *dyad* model, and is represented by Figure 4–1.

A more complete specification of the focal position of superintendent might include its relationships to teachers and principals as well as school board members, as in Figure 4–2.

In Figure 4–2, which shows what might be termed *a position-centric model,* the focal position is specified by its relationships to three counter positions. In the dyad model a position is specified by its relationship to only one counter position. In the position-centric model the position is specified by its relationships to a number of counter positions. The elements of this more complex specification are the relationships of the focal position to the different counter positions. In referring to these *elements of relational specification,* we will use the concept of positional sectors. A *positional sector* is

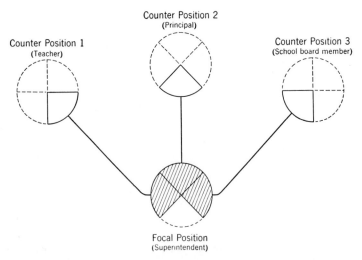

Figure 4–2. A position-centric model.

specified by the relationship of a focal position to a *single* counter position and is defined as an element of the relational specification of a position. Studying the superintendency in its relationship to the school board member position is quite a different unit of analysis from the superintendency in its relation to the principal position.

Some authors would treat each sector of the focal position as a different position. To some extent this may be a matter of arbitrary usage, but those who view each sector as a separate position generally fail to consider the problems of anything more complicated than a dyadic relationship. For certain analysis problems the more meaningful unit of analysis may be the position as defined by multiple relationships. In the first place, the identities of actors can refer to their positions in all relevant relationships, not to just selected ones. This is obviously the case with such identities as school superintendent which implies relationships with many other positions, such as, school board member, principal, teacher, parent, local government official, and so on. It is also the case, though less obviously so, with positions like mother and employer as we tried to show earlier. In the second place, the relationship between the sectors of the total position may be of prime importance. That is, to understand the relationship of position X to Y, it may be necessary to know about the relationship of X to Z; to understand a superintendent's relationship to teachers it

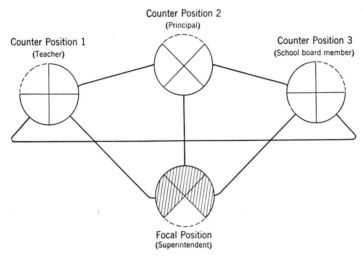

Figure 4–3. A system model.

may be necessary to have some understanding of his relationship to his school board.

The position-centric model provides a framework for focusing on one position and examining its relationships to a series of counter positions. This model does not consider the relationships among the counter positions. If these relationships are added, we have what might be termed a *system model*. By including the relationships among the counter positions an important addition has been made. The object of study which Figure 4–3 represents may be viewed as a system in the scientific sense, that is, as a series of interdependent parts. A position can be completely described only by describing the total system of positions and relationships of which it is a part. In other words, in a system of interdependent parts, a change in any relationship will have an effect on all other relationships, and the positions can be described only by the relationships.

Usually, it is only possible to deal with partial systems. In Figures 4-1, 4-2, and 4-3 one sector of the focal position was left blank to show that only a limited set of positions selected from all possible related positions have been considered. If we add another position, like student, the system, and consequently the specification of each position, will be more complete.

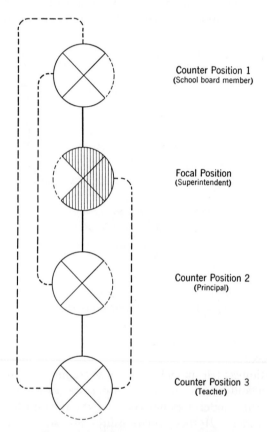

Counter Position 1
(School board member)

Focal Position
(Superintendent)

Counter Position 2
(Principal)

Counter Position 3
(Teacher)

Figure 4-4. A hierarchic system model.

It may be possible to simplify this partial system model if the relationships place the positions in a hierarchical series, as in Figure 4-4. Even in this situation the relationships between nonadjacent positions in the series, although not necessarily of prime importance, are essential to the full understanding of this series of positions as a system. In addition, other positions, like supervisor, may not fit neatly into the series.

A final elaboration might be described. A focal position may be involved in several different systems of positions, as in Figure 4–5. Using the superintendency as a focal position, the system of educational positions which we have been considering can be thought of as one system among a number of systems. Superintendents are involved in

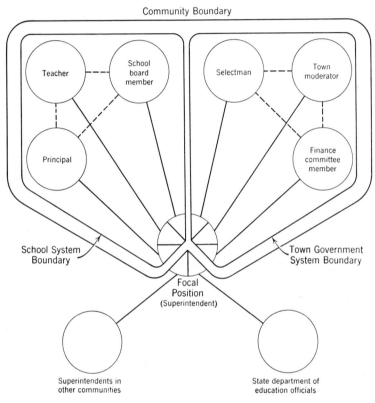

Figure 4–5. A multiple systems model.

many systems, such as, professional organizations and local and state government. Some of these systems are within the local community and some are not. When we observe the relationships between a superintendent and superintendents in other communities, the boundary between the local community and a larger social system has been crossed.

These superintendent-superintendent relationships suggest that relationships among the incumbents of the same position may be investigated. Teachers interact with other teachers, and doctors interact with other doctors. This type of relationship has been largely ignored in the literature.

The difference among these models might better be viewed as one of degree than of kind. In any of them we may pick one position to focus on, and all of these models, including the dyad, can be analyzed as a system. The differentiation is chiefly in terms of the completeness with which we wish to or can make an analysis. No matter how complete the analysis, there are always some things which must be left out; we must always select and abstract. How simple or how complex a relational system must be depends on the given problem. In general, the more complete the relationship system studied, the more completely can a given position be described.

The Situational Specification of Positions. In the preceding sections we have tried to show that a particular position has relationships with a set of positions and that clarity of analysis demands a precise specification of the positional sector or sectors which will be treated in a particular inquiry. A second specification which is required concerns the situational context in which the position will be examined.

The first type of situational specification required is almost geographical in nature. It describes the *scope of the social system* in which the position is to be studied. For example, shall we study the superintendency position in a specific community, in the state of Massachusetts, or in the United States? Positions may be studied at various levels of situational inclusiveness, but it is necessary to specify at which level one intends to work.

The specification of the scope of the social system designates the boundaries of the situation within which the position is being studied. Within these boundaries, however, the situation may include a number of different elements. If we choose a specific community in which to study a given position a complex set of situational factors is implied, for example, the size of the community, the resources available to it, and so on. If we were to study the superintendency in the Commonwealth of Massachusetts this would imply, for example, a study of the status of education in the General Laws of Massachusetts, how the State Department of Education is run, and the structure of town and city government in the Commonwealth. Within a state these factors would be constant. As we enlarge the scope of the system the situational specification of the position becomes more general, for fewer of the situational elements are constant within a larger system. For example, certain types of local government organization in Massachusetts do not exist in other parts of the United States.

At times it may be desirable to study positions in terms of a situational element which cuts across the scope of the system specification. For example we might wish to compare the superintendency in the suburbs of metropolitan areas with the superintendency in central cities.[11] Just what situational elements modify given positions will, of course, vary a great deal with the type of position. Although no attempt will be made here to present a general classification of them, it is necessary for an investigator to specify what situational elements he has used in describing the position which is his focus of interest.

One of the concepts in the literature which might be placed under the general rubric of situational specification is that of *office* as a type of position. For example, Kingsley Davis states:

> The term status would then designate a position in the general institutional system, recognized and supported by the entire society, spontaneously evolved rather than deliberately created, rooted in the folkways and mores. Office, on the other hand, would designate a position in a deliberately created organization, governed by specific and limited rules in a limited group, more generally achieved than ascribed.
>
> .   .   .   .
>
> Occupational position, for instance, is often a status and office both, the first when viewed from the standpoint of the general public, the second when viewed from the standpoint of the particular business or agency.[12]

As an example of status (position) Davis uses "professor" and of a corresponding office, "professor of government at the University of Arizona." The concept of office makes a special kind of situational specification of the position; it implies that the position is to be viewed in the context of all the special situational features of a given organization. Davis' distinction between status and office makes it clear that the same position can be studied at more than one level of situational specificity.

We have considered two aspects of the specification of positions: the relational and the situational. It should be pointed out that the two kinds of specification crosscut each other. A position with a certain relational specification may be studied in several situational contexts, and a position in a certain situational context may be viewed with several different relational specifications. For example, we might study the superintendency as specified relationally with the school board member and teacher counter positions at the community, state, or national level of situational specificity; or, given a level of situational specificity, such as the superintendency in Massachusetts, we might study the position under a variety of relational specifications, for example, in dyadic relation to the school board member position, or as part of a more complete system of educational positions.

EXPECTATIONS

We have defined position as the location of an actor or class of actors in a system of social relationships. The concept refers only to the location itself and not to the expectations and behaviors by means of which the position is described. This distinction is made for analytic purposes since concretely we never have a position without expectations and behaviors. We point this out because some authors have combined the idea of location with at least the normative aspect of the relationship structure. Thus for Linton a status is "simply a collection of rights and duties," [13] and for Sarbin a position is equivalent to "a system of rights and duties." [14] In our scheme "position" is simply a social location.

Networks of positions can be analyzed with respect to either how the incumbents of the positions *should* interact with each other or how they actually *do* interact with each other. We shall consider the behavioral analysis problem later. If the analysis is concerned with how actors should behave, it will deal with *expectations*. An expectation will be defined as an *evaluative standard applied to an incumbent of a position*.

Before elaborating on certain aspects of this definition, two special points deserve emphasis. The first is that the term expectation has been used in role formulations in at least two different senses. In one, it refers to a prediction as in the case of the statement, "My expectation is that he *will* arrive at nine o'clock." In the other, it refers to a normative criterion or standard of evaluation: "My expectation is that he *should* arrive at nine o'clock." When Newcomb views a role as "the ways of behaving which are expected of any individual who occupies a certain position" [15] he is using the word "expected" in its normative sense. Similarly, Parsons and Shils view role-expectations as "patterns of evaluations." [16]

Sarbin uses expectation in its predictive sense when he says, ". . . a position in a social structure [is] a set of expectations or acquired anticipatory reactions. That is to say, the person learns (*a*) to expect or anticipate certain actions from other persons, and (*b*) that others have expectations of him." [17] That stability in the prediction of behavior may be of importance in the development of evaluative standards is probably a correct assumption. Analytically, however, the two ideas are quite distinct. A man may predict that small boys will steal apples from his orchard, but he does not necessarily condone it. What will happen and what should happen in a situation are quite different ideas. The meaning of expectations in our definition is normative rather than predictive. For the predictive sense in which the term "expectation" is used, we would suggest the more general and precise term *anticipation* which would denote statements or feelings with respect to the probability of future events.

Another special point is that an expectation, as we have defined it, may be applied to all incumbents or to a particular incumbent of a specified position. Whether an expectation applies to all incumbents or to a particular incumbent is dependent on how the position has been specified. For example, a position, such as superintendent, could be specified to include only one incumbent, such as the superintendency in New York City. It could also be specified to include all the superintendents in the United States. We have tried to define the concept of expectation so that it could be used in studies dealing with either of these problems.

From the standpoint of actors in social situations, the same distinction can be made. For example, school board members can evaluate their superintendent on the standards they would apply to all superintendents in the United States, general standards modified to fit the local situation, or standards they would hold only for the superintendent in their own community. In concrete interaction situations the expectations that one actor holds for a specific incumbent of a position are in part a function of his relational and situational specifications of this position. In addition, they may be partly a function of his perception of the other positions the incumbent occupies. For example, one actor may see another as the incumbent of only the position of teacher. Another actor may see the same person as an incumbent of the positions of teacher and female. These different perceptions may result in different expectations. Another set of conditions that may influence the expectations one actor holds for a position incumbent is the incumbent's personal characteristics: a teacher may have somewhat different standards for "bright" and "dull" pupils.

Our definition of expectations refers to evaluative standards, not to anticipations. Whereas it is commonly accepted that the behavior of position incumbents is affected by the complex set of conditions in which it takes place, the point we have been trying to make is that expectations held for position incumbents in concrete situations may be similarly a function of many conditions.[18]

Dimensions of a Single Expectation. If we ask individuals to tell us whether they feel that a particular behavior is expected of a position incumbent (for example, a school superintendent), we may find some respondents who reply that it is required whereas another might say that it is prohibited. Two other respondents may agree that a superintendent should engage in a certain behavior, but one may say he *absolutely must* do it and the other may give a more permissive response such as he *preferably should*. These responses suggest two dimensions of a single expectation: direction and intensity.[19]

One question that may be asked about an expectation, then, is about its *direction*. Every expectation can be reduced to a statement for or against something. Whether a particular expectation is a prescription or a proscription is an operational rather than a theoretical problem. The empirical reference of the expectation must be introduced before its direction can be specified.

The second dimension of an expectation is its intensity. Any expectation can be placed somewhere on a continuum which ranges from the completely permissive, through the preferential, to the mandatory. For example, a school board might hold the expectation that its superintendent *absolutely must* attend school board meetings, that he *preferably should* attend meetings of the local teachers' association, and that he *may or may not* attend the meetings of the state superintendency association.

ROLE, ROLE BEHAVIOR, AND ROLE ATTRIBUTES

In the second chapter we considered some of the different definitions of the term role which have been presented in the social science literature. It was pointed out that there was a certain amount of unity within the diversity. Most authors, in discussing roles, consider the ideas of social location, expectations, and behavior. These notions are integral to our own research problems, and we have so far given considerable attention to the concepts of position and expectation in this chapter. We propose to restrict our definition of role to a set of expectations: *A role is a set of expectations,* or in terms of our definition of expectations, it is *a set of evaluative standards applied to an incumbent of a particular position.*

This definition of role depends on the previous definition of position as a location of an actor or class of actors in a system of social relationships. We have defined role so that it can be used as a concept at any of the various levels of relational and situational specificity which can be applied to positions. Defined in this way, the role concept may be used in studies of dyadic or more complicated relational systems, formal and informal organizations, as well as of the structure of a total society. This means that the concept is not restricted to the situations or relationships which are of interest to a particular set of investigators but can be used in the analyses of problems at different levels.

In addition, no restrictions are placed by this definition on the definers of the expectations. The concept may consequently be used in analyses in which the incumbents of the position as well as non-incumbents of the position are the definers of the role or, in general, in analyses of a role as defined by any population an investigator wishes to specify.

In studying a particular role an investigator would presumably try to elicit from the members of a specified population the expectations which they hold for incumbents of a specified position. While it would be possible to proceed simply on this basis, it would seem to be helpful to have some way of organizing or differentiating among these expectations. A collection of expectations, while providing substantive information, would not allow any more detailed analysis of a role than its simple description. If we assume that the expectations applied to a position are not simply a random collection but are themselves organized, the role may be said to have an "internal organization." Consequently, the problem of *role segmentation,* or categorizing the expectations, becomes relevant to role analysis.

It may be helpful to distinguish role segmentation from a problem treated earlier, the distinction between dimensions of a single expectation. Our consideration of the dimensions of a single expectation was an attempt to point out certain questions that could be asked about a single expectation. It was suggested that a particular expectation includes the dimensions of direction and intensity. The focus was on the categorization of a *single* expectation along these two dimensions.

Role segmentation, however, is concerned with the classification of a group or *set* of expectations that individuals may hold for an incumbent of a specified position. Whereas the dimensions were components of expectations, segments are parts of roles. *Multiple* expectations are involved and we wish to consider how they may be categorized on socially relevant criteria. Three categorizations of expectations will be presented which can be applied in the analysis of any role. Each of these categorizations has received consideration by one or another of the social scientists whose definitions of role we examined earlier, and they may be implicit in the formulations of every one of them. It is important to make them explicit. The first categorization differentiates among *role sectors,* the second between *rights and obligations,* and the third between *behaviors and attributes.*

Role Sectors. In our examination of the problem of the relational specification of a position, we pointed out that to study one position it is necessary to consider one or more related positions. An empirical study concerned with the expectations applied to a particular position can focus on the expectations which are involved in any one or all of the relationships by means of which the position has been specified. This implies that the question "What expectations are attached to the position?" cannot be answered until the position has been relationally specified.

The concept of positional sector was introduced to refer to the elements of the relational specification. To correspond to these "parts" of the position, the concept of role sector will be introduced. *A role sector is defined as a set of expectations applied to the relationship of a focal position to a single counter position.*

To categorize expectations on the basis of role sectors is one basis of role segmentation. In an empirical inquiry the analysis may be concerned with one or more role sectors. The variety of possible relationships in which a specific position may be involved requires, therefore, that in the analysis of the set of expectations associated with it the investigator needs to specify precisely what role sectors will be examined.

The concept of role sector suggests certain interesting research questions. For example, for the study of role consensus, we may ask: Is there more consensus among a set of role definers on one role sector than another? Is there more consensus among one set of role definers than among another on a particular role sector?

Rights and Obligations. If the expectations applied to a position are classified according to its relationship with specific counter positions, then we may ask, for each expectation, if it is applied to the incumbent of the focal position or to the incumbent of the counter position. *Rights of the incumbent of a focal position are defined as expectations which are applied to an incumbent of a counter position. Obligations of the incumbent of a focal position are defined as expectations which are applied to the incumbent of the focal position.*

The distinction between rights and obligations implies that the description of the expectations associated with a position in its relationship with another position must include "what is due" the incumbent of the focal position from the incumbent of the counter position (rights) and what the incumbent of the focal position "owes" the occupant of the counter position (obligations). For a given role sector, the question of which expectations are called rights, and which are called obligations, depends, of course, on which position is "focal" for any analysis.

This distinction is clearly implicit in many role formulations and explicit in a number of them. That it is not central to all of them, however, can be seen from Linton's reference to "rights" in his volume, *The Cultural Background of Personality.* After stating that a role "includes the attitudes, values, and behavior ascribed by the society to any and all persons occupying the status," he adds, "It *can even be extended* to include the legitimate expectations of such persons with respect to the behavior toward them of persons in other statuses within the same system." (Italics ours.) [20]

This segmentation of a role into rights and obligations suggests certain additional problems pertaining to role consensus. For example, using incumbents of a focal position as role definers the following questions might be raised: Will the incumbents of a position have more consensus on their rights in one role sector than on their rights in another role sector? Will there be more consensus on some obligations than on others in a single role sector?

Expectations for Behaviors and Attributes. This basis of role segmentation provides concepts by means of which an investigator can distinguish between what incumbents of positions *should do* and what incumbents of positions *should be,* or the characteristics they should have. A role can be segmented into *expectations for behaviors* and *expectations for attributes.*

Most authors have restricted their treatment of expectations to those in the first category, for behavior. Parsons, however, does make exactly this distinction when he says, "In orienting to an actor as object . . . primacy may be given . . . to his attributes or qualities, independently of specific expected performances, or . . . to his performances, completed, in process, or expected in the future." [21] Linton and those who derive directly from him, on the other hand, seem to neglect the possibility that one person may hold expectations for another's attributes. One reason why Parsons appears to be almost alone in making this distinction may be that he is one of the few authors for whom "role expectation" is an elemental concept.

In considering problems that arise in the use of the concept of position in empirical inquiries, we maintained that both relational and situational specifications of the position are required. Since a role analysis is concerned with a set of expectations applicable to incumbents of a particular position, these same specifications are necessary. That is, in specifying the position, we are also specifying the role. However, the expectations which describe the role can be categorized into role segments, and in empirical analysis it is also necessary to say what segments are under examination. The role segments which have been differentiated imply that it is necessary to say, first, what role sectors will be analyzed, second, whether rights, obligations, or both will be included in the analysis, and third, whether the expectations considered will include those for attributes or behaviors, or both. Only some of the phenomena to which these specifications of positions and of role segments apply would probably be considered in any role analysis, but it is our suggestion that the specifications themselves must be made.

We have suggested that one of the ways of segmenting a role, or categorizing the expectations which comprise a role, is into expectations for behavior and expectations for attributes. So far, however, we have not presented concepts for the actual behaviors or attributes, as distinguished from the expectations for them. Although it is possible to conduct role analyses without reference to *actual* behavior or attributes, for some problems concepts to describe them are necessary. The problems of conformity-deviance, for example, imply a comparison of expectations and the behaviors and attributes to which they refer.

In addition to the definitions of role behavior and role attributes, terms parallel to "role sector" will be presented for both behavior and attributes.

A *role behavior* is an actual performance of an incumbent of a position which can be referred to an expectation for an incumbent of that position.[22]

A *role attribute* is an actual quality of an incumbent of a position which can be referred to an expectation for an incumbent of that position.

A *role behavior sector* is a set of actual behaviors which can be referred to a set of expectations for behaviors applied to the relationship of a focal position to a single counter position.

A *role attribute sector* is a set of actual attributes which can be referred to a set of expectations for attributes applied to the relationship of a focal position to a single counter position.

SANCTIONS

In the previous sections we have been concerned with two aspects of social relationships, the normative and the behavioral: what the actor is *supposed to do* and what he *actually does.* The dimension of conformity-deviance is inherent in such a scheme. In studying interactional systems an important question is whether or to what degree the actors are conforming to the roles for their positions. This in turn raises the problem of social control: Is there anything in the system which tends to maintain conformity? We will introduce the concept of sanctions to deal with this problem: *A sanction is a role behavior the primary significance of which is gratificational-deprivational.*

It is useful to differentiate between two "modes of significance" which either expectations or behavior may have, namely, instrumental significance and gratificational significance. The instrumental significance of an act refers to its consequences for some end or goal. The gratificational significance of an act refers to its consequences for some actor's gratification or deprivation. Similarly, expectations can be categorized according to the instrumental and gratificational significance of the behaviors to which they refer.

Any act has both types of significance (or can be analyzed in terms of each), and for certain purposes the relative importance of the two modes might be crucial. Some acts may be almost purely gratificational in significance, as when an actor responds by saying "I think it is wrong for you to do that." Other acts may appear to have only instrumental significance, as when each man operating a two-man saw responds to or follows the other's pull with a pull of his own. However, it could be argued that no act has only one type of significance. In the first example the expression of the negative attitude may also be seen as an interruption of an instrumental sequence; in the two-man saw example, the fact that the interaction continues in orderly fashion means that there is some kind of tacit approval implicit in the interaction. It was for these reasons that in defining the term *sanction* we said its *primary* significance was gratificational. An *instrumental act* is one in which the *primary* significance is instrumental. Corresponding terms on the normative side would be *expectations for sanctions* and *expectations for instrumental acts.* Since a sanction is a role behavior whose primary significance is gratificational, it can be viewed as falling along a positive-negative or reward-punishment dimension.

This treatment of sanctions is similar to that of Parsons, but differs in several important respects. In Parsons' terms, sanctions are reciprocal to role-expectations:

> On the one hand there are the expectations which concern and in part set standards for the behavior of the actor, ego, who is taken as the point of reference; these are his "role-expectations." On the other hand, from

his point of view there is a set of expectations relative to the contingently probable *re*actions of others (alters)—these will be called "sanctions," which in turn may be subdivided into positive and negative according to whether they are felt by ego to be gratification-promoting or depriving. The relation between role-expectations and sanctions then is clearly reciprocal. What are sanctions to ego are role-expectations to alter and vice versa.[23]

At first, Parsons seems to define sanctions independently of the approval-disapproval dimension; the criterion is merely that they concern alter's reactions to ego. This definition would appear to make sanctions identical to the concept of rights, but it employs a word with an approval-disapproval connotation. However, he adds that sanctions may be categorized as positive or negative according to their gratificational significance. This adds the missing approval-disapproval dimension but implies that this is the only significance of alter's reaction. If so, the sanctions would seem to be less inclusive than rights. Alter's reactions have a significance as instrumental acts in addition to significance as gratification-deprivation "agents." For example, if a husband closes his wife's charge account this act can be analyzed in a reward-punishment context relative to the wife's previous buying habits. However, this act has significance quite apart from any consideration of punishment: It will entail a new set of arrangements for purchasing articles and paying for them, for example. Furthermore, it is quite possible that this act has virtually no significance as punishment. The husband may have taken this step because his wages were reduced, not because he was critical of his wife's buying habits.[24]

The definition presented here has a number of advantages. In the first place, sanctions and expectations for sanctions are concepts in their own right. The difference between expectations for sanctions and other expectations is not dependent upon an arbitrary point of reference. Second, in Parsons' treatment, obligations to respond in approving or disapproving ways are always "left on the other side" of the relationship; they are always alter's responsibility, not ego's. The present definition allows us to view the expectations and behavior of *both* ego and alter in terms of their gratificational significance. It emphasizes that all social actions can be analyzed as *reac*tions to some prior event. Third, although we have defined sanctions in terms of the primacy of gratificational significance, we have not excluded instrumental significance.

Another consequence of our definition of sanctions might be noted. There may be considerable difference in the way in which different actors in the system perceive the gratificational significance of given acts and expectations. What is intended as a punishment, for example, may not be perceived as such by the recipient. The question of intent is left open for empirical examination.[25]

To provide both a summary of and a convenient reference to the concepts which have been presented, they are listed with their definitions here. This list represents the basic language for the empirical analyses to be presented in this volume.[26]

A *position* is the location of an actor or class of actors in a system of social relationships.

A *positional sector* is an element of the relational specification of a position, and is specified by the relationship of a focal position to a single counter position.

An *expectation* is an evaluative standard applied to an incumbent of a position.

A *role* is a set of expectations applied to an incumbent of a particular position.

A *role sector* is a set of expectations applied to the relationship of a focal position to a single counter position.

A *right* of an incumbent of a focal position is an expectation applied to the incumbent of a counter position.

An *obligation* of an incumbent of a focal position is an expectation applied to the incumbent of a focal position.

A *role behavior* is an actual performance of an incumbent of a position which can be referred to an expectation for an incumbent of that position.

A *role attribute* is an actual quality of an incumbent of a position which can be referred to an expectation for an incumbent of that position.

A *role behavior sector* is a set of actual behaviors which can be referred to a set of expectations for behaviors applicable to the relationship of a focal position to a single counter position.

A *role attribute sector* is a set of actual attributes which can be referred to a set of expectations for attributes applicable to the relationship of a focal position to a single counter position.

A *sanction* is a role behavior the primary significance of which is gratificational-deprivational.

Notes and References for Chapter Four

[1] See Chapter Fifteen.

[2] Talcott Parsons, *The Social System* (Glencoe: The Free Press, 1951), pp. 88–96.

[3] Ralph Linton, *The Study of Man* (New York: D. Appleton-Century Co., 1936), pp. 115–116.

[4] John W. Bennett and Melvin M. Tumin, *Social Life, Structure and Function* (New York: Alfred A. Knopf, 1948), p. 87.

[5] Linton defines ascribed statuses as ". . . those which are assigned to individuals without reference to their innate differences or abilities." Achieved statuses on the other hand ". . . are left open to be filled through competition and individual effort." (Linton, *op. cit.*, p. 115.) Although Parsons claims indebtedness to Linton he uses the term with a somewhat different meaning: "Achievement-oriented roles are those which place the accent on the performances of the incumbent, ascribed roles, on his qualities or attributes independently of specific expected performances." (Parsons, *op. cit.*, p. 64.) We are following Parsons' usage.

[6] Linton, *op. cit.*, p. 113.

[7] Ralph Linton, *The Cultural Background of Personality* (New York: D. Appleton-Century Co., 1945), p. 76.

[8] Parsons, *op. cit.*, p. 25.

[9] Theodore M. Newcomb, *Social Psychology* (New York: Dryden Press, 1951), p. 277.

[10] E. T. Hiller, *Social Relations and Social Structures: A Study in Principles of Sociology* (New York: Harper and Brothers, 1947).

[11] We are still talking about the superintendency as an *object* of study. We might ask superintendents in both suburbs and central cities to consider both types of superintendency positions.

[12] Kingsley Davis, *Human Society* (New York: The Macmillan Company, 1948 and 1949), pp. 88–89. See also Everett Cherrington Hughes, "Institutional Office and the Person," *American Journal of Sociology*, XLIII (1937), pp. 404–413.

[13] Linton, *Study of Man*, p. 113.

[14] Theodore R. Sarbin, "Role Theory," in Gardner Lindzey (Editor), *Handbook of Social Psychology*, Vol. I (Cambridge: Addison-Wesley Publishing Company, 1954), p. 225.

[15] Newcomb, *op. cit.*, p. 280.

[16] Talcott Parsons and Edward A. Shils with the assistance of James Olds, "Values, Motives, and Systems of Action," in Talcott Parsons and Edward A. Shils (Editors), *Toward A General Theory of Action* (Cambridge: Harvard University Press, 1951), p. 190.

[17] Sarbin, *op. cit.*, p. 225.

[18] Davis seems to be making a similar point when he says, "The essence of any social situation lies in the mutual expectations of the participants. These expectations rest to a great extent on the norms applicable in the situation." (Davis, *op. cit.*, p. 83.) However, later paragraphs indicate that he is using "expectations" in a predictive as well as a normative sense.

[19] Other dimensions of single expectations are suggested by several treatments of related concepts. See Clyde Kluckhohn, "Values and Value-Orientations in the Theory of Action," in Parsons and Shils, *op. cit.*, pp. 412–421; Robin M. Williams, Jr., *American Society* (New York: Alfred A. Knopf, 1952), pp. 24–29; Louis Guttman, "The Principal Components of Scalable Attitudes," in Paul F. Lazarsfeld

(Editor), *Mathematical Thinking in the Social Sciences* (Glencoe: The Free Press, 1954), pp. 216–257.

[20] Linton, *Cultural Background*, p. 77.

[21] Parsons, *Social System*, p. 88. See also Sarbin, *op. cit.*, p. 227 for a similar distinction.

[22] It should be noted that this definition of *a role behavior*, as well as the definitions of *role attribute, role behavior sector*, and *role attribute sector*, does not specify who holds the expectation to which the actual performance of the position is referred. For different research problems variant role definers may be employed, for example, the incumbent of the focal position or incumbents of counter positions. This is an operational question, one that will be considered in the next chapter. The special point to be noted is that in the proposed conceptual scheme these terms refer to actual performances or qualities to which evaluative standards held by some role definer(s) for incumbent(s) of the position may be applied.

[23] Parsons, *Social System*, p. 38.

[24] Parsons seems to be closer to our usage in the following passage: "The most fundamental distinction relative to sanctions which we have made is that between the specific, discrete acts of alter which influence ego's situation of action on the one hand, and alter's attitudes toward ego and his actions on the other. Attitudes as sanctions imply either attachment to alter as an object of cathexis or internalization of the normative pattern alter is 'enforcing' or both. They constitute the central core of the sanction system of a role complex and organize it into a system. Through them specific sanction-acts acquire, in addition to their 'intrinsic' significance the 'meaning' of expressions of these attitudes." Parsons, *Socal System*, p. 272.

[25] Another important set of factors affecting behavior are the "sanctions" internal to the actors in question, that is, feelings of guilt, shame, self-approbation, and so on. It would seem best to continue to refer to these phenomena in terms of psychological categories rather than modify the definition of sanctions so as to include them, although the close relationship of these psychological states to the internalization of expectations in interaction with other actors is recognized.

[26] For another set of concepts that embrace somewhat theoretically similar ideas see Robert K. Merton, *Social Theory and Social Structure* (Glencoe: The Free Press, 1956), pp. 368–370. For other recent efforts to develop a language for role analysis see Frederick L. Bates, "Position, Role, and Status: A Reformulation of Concepts," *Social Forces*, XXXIV (1956), pp. 313–321 and W. B. Brookover, "Research on Teacher and Administrator Roles," *Journal of Educational Sociology*, XXIX (1955), pp. 2–13.

five

The Empirical Study
of Role Definitions

In developing a conceptual scheme for role analyses a special point was made of defining concepts without specifying whether they applied to individual, social, or cultural phenomena   An expectation, for example, was defined as "an evaluative standard applied to an incumbent of a position" with no specification of the position or of the person by whom the expectation is held.   Whether an investigator is interested in studying the expectations held by an individual, by a series of individuals, or those held by a group of interacting individuals, it is possible for him to use the same basic concept, although it is necessary for him to specify in what way he is using it in his inquiry.   In research concerned with problems at the individual level he would ask, for example, how the individual defines a role, or in other words, what expectations the individual holds for an incumbent of a position; if he were interested in problems at the group level, he would ask what expectations are held by group members for an incumbent of a position; or his research problem might require his asking an incumbent of a focal position what expectations he thinks are held for him by incumbents of counter positions.   For the second and third questions the problem of role consensus is relevant, and for the third, the problem of perceived role conflict too.

To investigate the problem of role consensus it is necessary to obtain data on the role definitions held by some population.   In this chapter we shall briefly consider some of the operational problems with which it is necessary to deal in an empirical examination of role definition.   There are two general problems which will be considered, each of which implies that an investigator must make certain specifications.   The first is the *role definers problem,* for which an investigator must specify his subject population. The second is a problem of the focus of the analysis, or the object of study. An investigator may be concerned with *particular expectations*, or with expectations that are appropriate in *particular situations*. These concerns may be illustrated by the questions: Should this behavior be performed by this position incumbent? (the answers to which are all expectations which refer to the *same* behavior) and What should a position incumbent do in this situation? (the answers to which may be expectations which refer to quite *different* behaviors). Another aspect of this same problem is one of the reference of the expectations: It is possible to study expectations at many *levels of generality*, general functions and microscopic acts perhaps illustrating two extremes. In addition to a consideration of these two general problems of role definition, another objective of this chapter is to point out some of the complexities implied in treating role consensus as a variable.

Many writers, as we have already pointed out, speak of roles as defined "by society" or by "the group." This implies that although roles are differentiated in that different sets of expectations are held for incumbents of different positions, the same definitions of each role are held by all the members of the group or society. In other words the *objects* to which the expectations are applied (that is, incumbents of positions) have been differentiated; the *subjects* who hold the expectations (that is, the members of the group or society) have been left undifferentiated. This may be adequate for broad descriptions of modal patterns of role definition, but when the question of variability in role definition is raised it is necessary to distinguish types of role definers and their relationship to the position which is the focus of interest.

Three required specifications of the role definers may be suggested: (1) the number of different positions they occupy, (2) the number of incumbents of each position, (3) the relationships among the positions. To these can be added the distinction between the focal position as a point of reference (in this case the position for which the role definition is being studied) and the counter positions as other positions in the group.

Consider the problem of the role definition of the position of mother. Of the innumerable populations of role definers an investigator might specify, some examples are: incumbents of the focal position (mothers), incumbents of counter positions in the same social systems (fathers, sons, daughters), incumbents of positions in "external" social systems (for example, ministers or teachers), or incumbents of all the positions in the social system in which it is most centrally involved (for example, a mother, a father, a son, a daughter), or the population of role definers might include various combinations of these examples.

The particular population or populations of role definers that an investigator would use depends, of course, on the problem he is interested in examining. An anthropologist, for example, interested in understanding the "culture" of a particular society, might specify as his role definers a sample drawn from all members of that society. At another level of analysis, an interest in the functioning of a less inclusive social system, for example a factory, might lead an investigator to specify all of the members of that social system as his role definers. Still another investigator, concerned with understanding the pathological behavior of one individual, might specify that individual as the only role definer of relevance to the problems in which the investigator is interested. Unless the problem is specified it is impossible to specify the appropriate set of role definers. The main point here is that unless the role definers have been clearly specified, interpretation of research findings will remain ambiguous.

We have previously emphasized the need to specify the object of study in role analysis, that is, the position, both relationally and situationally, and in Chapter Seven we will do so for this study. It is necessary, however, to make an additional distinction with regard to the object of study. Although expectations are always held for position incumbents in situations, for research purposes, it may be convenient to focus on a particular *expectation* (in a situation) or to focus on a *situation* and ask what expectations are held for the position incumbent in that situation. Whether or not there is consensus may be questioned with either focus.

The problem of consensus presents itself, when, in focusing on a particular expectation, an investigator attempts to describe *what* the "norm" is for any specified group of role definers. To describe what the "norm" is, under these conditions, one might resort to some measure of central tendency, such as the mean, the median, or the mode of the distribution. But the use of a measure of central tendency with no indication of the shape of the distribution or of its degree of variability might be misleading. If the distribution is bimodal, for example, no simple description of the norm could be made. For a group of respondents, the study of role consensus is consequently necessary for the description of role content.

Although the same statement, that a consideration of consensus is necessary for description, can be made of the focus on a situation, this second focus presents different problems for the study of consensus on role definition. Presumably each role definer would have an expectation with regard to each of the possible alternatives. We may raise the following questions for a specified set of role definers: Is there agreement, for example, as to which of the alternatives are acceptable? Is there an agreed upon order of preference among the alternatives? The alternatives for the situation can be of two types: they may fall along a continuum, or they may be qualitatively different.

In a suggestive study of conflicting social norms Stouffer dealt with a case of the first type.[1] He studied the expectations which a group of college students perceived to be held by other students and authorities regarding the action a proctor should take upon finding a student cheating. The possible actions ranged along a continuum of punitiveness, from "take away his notes and exam book, dismiss him and report him for cheating" at one end to "act as if nothing had happened and not report him for cheating" at the other.[2] Not only were the alternatives felt to be ordered in this way from a logical point of view, but evidence is presented that they were so perceived by the respondents. The degree of consensus on the expectation for each alternative can be inferred from the percentage who felt that the action would be approved by the students or authorities. One of Stouffer's main points is that expectations should be described as having range rather than described as points. By range, Stouffer is referring to the number of different actions which would be approved in a given situation. Thus in addition to the idea of range as a distribution of responses of a set of role definers on a single expectation, there is the idea of range on a continuum of different actions which would be approved in a particular situation.

The second type, in which the alternatives are qualitatively different rather than ranging along a continuum, has been dealt with by Kluckhohn.[3] Her scheme of value-orientations has three alternatives for each orientation. For example, the "relational orientation" has lineal, collateral, and individualistic alternatives, which can be studied at the level of expectations. In a study of values in five cultures of the Southwest, Strodtbeck, using this scheme, worked out a methodology for measuring the consensus within groups on the *rank ordering* of three alternatives.[4] Kluckhohn's scheme is noteworthy in its emphasis on the existence of variant ways of doing things in cultures, ways which are not deviant but permitted alternatives. This represents a departure from the more monolithic views traditional in an-

thropology, and suggests the desirability of investigating the existence
and ordering of permissible behavioral alternatives.

A related problem of role definition is that of the level of generality
on which the expectations are studied: whether, for example, roles
are studied in terms of expectations for functions or expectations for
detailed behaviors, expectations for ends or means, or if they are
studied with different degrees of situational specificity. There might
be consensus on the definition of a role among a population of role
definers at one level of generality and not at another; for example,
there might be consensus on functions but not on the ways of fulfill-
ing them. Different degrees of consensus at one level might have
consequences different from those found at other levels. Lack of
consensus on functions, for example, might be more disruptive to a
social system than lack of consensus on detailed behaviors.

A final point that should be emphasized is that consensus may be
more fully exploited as a factor influencing social behavior if it is
treated as a variable rather than as an attribute. The complete presence and complete absence of consensus are limiting cases. It is
easily demonstrated with our (or perhaps any other) data that absolute consensus among a group of people on almost anything—expectations, opinions, attitudes, values, etc.—is seldom, if ever, found
empirically. On the other hand it is equally true that social data
frequently, but not invariably, reveal some kind of central tendency
or "strain toward consistency."

When consensus on role definition is considered to be a variable,
a whole new range of questions may be asked. How much consensus
is essential to the effective functioning of a group, and on what aspects of group functioning? Are extreme degrees of consensus dysfunctional? Are there "optimum" degrees of consensus? How little
consensus can there be without the group disintegrating? When these
questions are combined with some of the specifications made previously, a complex set of problems emerges: For example, we might
investigate (1) degrees of consensus (2) among certain populations
of role definers (3) on certain segments of a role (4) at given levels
of generality (5) under given relational and situational specifications
of the position.

Notes and References for Chapter Five

[1] Samuel A. Stouffer, "An Analysis of Conflicting Social Norms," *American
Sociological Review* XIV (1949), pp. 707–717.

[2] *Ibid.,* p. 709.

[3] Florence Kluckhohn, "Dominant and Variant Value Orientations," in Clyde Kluckhohn and Henry A. Murray (Editors), *Personality in Nature, Society and Culture* (New York: Alfred A. Knopf, 1953), pp. 342–357.

[4] Fred L. Strodtbeck, "Value Consensus Real and Perceived in Five Cultures," a paper prepared for the Thirty-first Annual Meeting of the Society for Social Research and the Annual Meeting of the Illinois Council on Family Relations. See also Fred L. Strodtbeck, "Husband-Wife Interaction Over Revealed Differences," *American Sociological Review* XVI (1951), pp. 468–473.

part 2

The Empirical Studies

six

Research Procedures

We have completed our examination of certain theoretical and operational problems of role analysis which emerged in the course of an attempt to develop research designs for the analysis of role consensus, conformity to expectations, and role conflict. The empirical inquiries that stimulated and were influenced by the examination of these problems are reported in this section of the book.

We would like, first of all, to say why the position of school superintendent was selected as the focus of our research activities. This position, as well as having advantages relevant to other objectives of the School Executive Studies which are not considered in this volume, had a number of characteristics which made it particularly suitable for the kinds of problems and hypotheses we proposed to examine. There is a statutory basis for its existence which entails a formal specification of certain of its general relations to other positions such as school board member and teacher. Superintendents tend to view their occupation as a "profession" with the consequence that there is an extensive body of literature describing the behavior expected of superintendents and the kinds of relationships which should exist between them and incumbents of positions to which theirs is related. Both of these conditions provided us with a fairly comprehensive "formal" or "accepted" set of expectations on which to base our investigation of the definition of the superintendent's role. For the investigation of "role conflicts," the literature on educational administration and preliminary contacts with superintendents themselves suggested that theirs was a position in which conflicting expectations were endemic and probably magnified to a degree that would ensure obtaining sufficient data to test propositions regarding the resolution of conflicts to which they had been exposed. And finally, the superintendency is a position which is involved in a number of relationship systems, some of which are in part formally defined, for example the school system itself and the state department of education, some of which are professionally necessary, such as professional associations, and some of which, while perhaps neither formally defined nor professionally necessary, are unavoidable, such as the community.

This chapter describes the methods employed to secure the data for the examination of the major questions of this research, and is concerned with methodological considerations of general relevance to all of the studies reported in this volume. The technical procedures of special relevance to a single problem area, for example, consensus on role definition, will be described in the methodological section of the appropriate chapter.

Preliminary Research Activities. After the general objectives of the School Executive Studies were established, six months were devoted to the following activities: (1) gaining additional knowledge about the superintendency and its relation to other positions; (2) securing acceptance and sponsorship of the study; (3) developing the final research design; and (4) training the interviewing staff.

During this time numerous conferences and meetings were held with educators in New England and other regions. These activities increased our understanding of the issues and problems confronting school administrators and policy-makers, and introduced us to the special language of educators and to the kinds of social environment in which they function. These preliminary contacts with the "culture" of educational administrators and school board members proved to be of considerable value in the interview situation and later, in data analysis activities. In addition, they were invaluable in establishing personal relationships with educational leaders whose interest in and support of the research was an important factor in its acceptance by the Massachusetts superintendents and school board members. Also, during this period the literature in the field of educational administration was examined, and conferences held with colleagues and graduate students in the Graduate School of Education and other faculties at Harvard.

Previous research experience suggested that sponsorship of the study by important educational organizations might tend to create a favorable climate for its acceptance by the superintendents and their school boards. Accordingly, at meetings with the executive committees of the New England School Development Council and the Massachusetts Association of School Committees the purposes and planned procedures of the Studies were described. Both these associations voted to endorse the Studies and serve as sponsors.

Preliminary schedules were developed and the first trial interviews were held with superintendents and school board members in New England states other than Massachusetts in order to avoid interference with the Massachusetts sample, at that time unselected. These preliminary interviews revealed a number of problems to which the interviewers would be exposed if the interviews were held in the superintendent's office. They also led to the conclusion that some of our a priori notions regarding interviewing methods, derived from the literature and previous research activities, were inapplicable in this particular research situation.[1]

The following period was devoted to the analysis and resolution of a number of research design problems and to the development of the instruments and schedules to be used in the superintendency and school board interviews. A second series of trial interviews was undertaken which simulated the conditions under which the interviews were actually held. They resulted in numerous changes in the final schedule, especially in question wording and the sequence in which the questions were asked.

All the interviewers took part in these trial interviews not only to familiarize themselves with the development and content of the schedules, but also to develop a "feel" for the particular kind of situation in which the study interviews would be held. Discussions of the experiences and problems encountered in both the school board and superintendent interviews resulted in a set of procedures for interviewer behavior which will be described later.

The Population and Sampling Procedure. Consideration was at first given to using all the school superintendents in New England as the population. This idea was discarded when we discovered that there was considerable variability among the several states in the legal provisions for the positions of school superintendent and school board member. In Connecticut, for example, the chief local school official in towns with a population less than 3500 is appointed by the State Department of Education, whereas in Massachusetts, the superintendent is always appointed by the local school board. It was felt advisable to control such "state variables" since they might confound the substantive conclusions of the research. Since the number of superintendency positions in Massachusetts was considerably larger than in any other New England state, it was decided to specify all Massachusetts school superintendencies as the population. At one point consideration was given to the possibility of interviewing all 217 superintendents in Massachusetts. A later decision to conduct lengthy interviews precluded this more expansive and more expensive plan. But in view of the relatively small size of the population of superintendents in Massachusetts, and in order to secure an adequate number of cases for purposes of analysis, the sample size was set at half the total number of superintendencies.

To obtain the sample the following procedure was used. A list of all superintendency positions was obtained from the Massachusetts State Department of Education.[2] These 217 superintendencies were categorized on the basis of four geographical areas[3] in order to eliminate any geographical bias in selecting the sample. The problem then was to obtain a 50 percent random sample within each geographical area. Three stratification criteria were used in drawing subsamples from each of the geographical areas:

1. Whether it was a union or nonunion superintendency (a union superintendency is one in which the superintendent is in charge of two or more school systems).[4]

2. The population of the community or communities for which the superintendent administered the local public education program.[5]

3. The extent to which the community or communities gave financial support to the public schools relative to their ability to pay for it. To measure this, a ratio was computed for each school system or set of school systems which was the average school expenditure per child divided by the per capita assessed valuation of the total school area.[6]

The superintendencies in each geographic area were then paired according to their similarity with respect to these three criteria. Since there were 7 superintendencies which could not be paired by this process, 105 pairs, or 210 superintendencies, were left in the population. A coin was flipped to select the superintendency from each pair to be included in the sample. The resulting 105 superintendencies constitute the sample of the School Executive Studies.

We were able to interview 102 of the superintendents in the sample. The 3 superintendents with whom interviews could not be arranged were replaced by their "duplicates" in the matched sample, bringing the total number of superintendent interviews to 105.

Table 6–A shows the extent to which the study sample is representative of the population of *all* superintendencies in Massachusetts on the criteria of geographical location and the number of school systems for which the superintendent was responsible, that is, whether it was a union or nonunion superintendency. The last column of the table shows that at least 45 percent of the superintendencies in each geographical area were included in the sample and that 48 percent of all the superintendencies in the Commonwealth fell within the total sample. The totals of columns 1 and 2 show that the sample includes 49 percent of all the nonunion and 46 percent of the union superintendencies, respectively. With the exception of the union superintendencies in geographical area II (a sample of 5 from a population of 13 cases), each of the geographical area union and nonunion subsamples includes approximately half of the superintendencies.

TABLE 6–A. THE REPRESENTATIVENESS OF THE SAMPLE ON THE CRITERIA OF GEOGRAPHICAL AREA AND WHETHER THE SUPERINTENDENCY IS A UNION OR NONUNION TYPE

Percentage of the Population of Superintendencies Included in the Study Sample

Geographical Area	(1) Nonunion	(N)	(2) Union	(N)	(3) Total	(N)
I	50%	(24)	50%	(22)	50%	(46)
II	50	(20)	34	(13)	45	(33)
III	49	(80)	47	(15)	48	(95)
IV	50	(30)	46	(13)	48	(43)
Total	49	(154)	46	(63)	48	(217)

To test the representativeness of the sample on a variable not used as a stratification criterion, the salaries[7] of administrators in the sample were compared to those in the matched sample.[8] The results are summarized in Table 6–B.

TABLE 6–B. THE PERCENTAGE OF SUPERINTENDENTS AT DIFFERENT SALARY LEVELS IN THE STUDY SAMPLE AND THE MATCHED SAMPLE

Salary Level, $	Study Sample ($N = 105$)	Matched Sample ($N = 105$)
Under 6,000	29.5%	28.5%
6,000–7,499	40.0	42.0
7,500–8,999	21.9	20.0
9,000 and over	8.6	9.5
	100.0%	100.0%

$\chi^2 = 0.02$; $1 > p > 0.99$

Median Salary

Study Sample	$6,486
Matched Sample	$6,511

The degree of equivalence between the two matched samples is quite remarkable when we consider that a chi-square of 0.02 with three degrees of freedom will be exceeded by chance 99 percent of the time. Also, the difference between the two medians is only $25, a result which further strengthens the contention that our sample is representative of the population.

The research design required individual interviews with the school board members associated with each of the superintendents who fell in the sample. This was complicated in the union superintendencies by the fact that each superintendent was associated with more than one board. In these cases, one town from the union was selected at random (using different sets of random numbers depending upon the number of communities in the superintendency union), and an attempt was made to interview all the members of its school board. Since the number of members on different school boards ranges from 3 to 10, the 105 superintendencies provided samples of 105 superintendents, 105 school boards, and 517 school board members. Interviews were completed with 98 percent or 508 of the 517 school board members. At least six attempts were made to arrange interviews with the 9 school board members in the sample whom we were unable to interview.

The *subject* population to which the findings may be generalized, within the limits of sampling error, is therefore nearly all (97 percent) of the superintendents ιin Massachusetts during 1952–1953 and their school board members. There is no statistical basis to claim that the findings apply to any other *respondent* population.

Two consequences of this sampling procedure deserve mention. First, despite the heavy sampling ratio, the total number of cases (105) is relatively small. This places restrictions on the number of controls that can be used in the analysis of qualitative data. Second, although it is realized that in sampling from a *finite* universe the standard error formulas need to be modified, this was not done in our study for two reasons. The first is that the correction that should be applied is available for only a few statistical measures, such as the mean, and the second is that even though the corrections are not made, the errors in generalization will always be on the conservative side. That is, we will be less likely to reject the null hypothesis when it is in fact true. With this in mind we can have more confidence in our findings than that implied by the stated probability level. This is another reason, in addition to the logic of incorporating direction in the stated hypothesis, why we did not hesitate to use one-tailed tests of significance whenever they were appropriate. A third reason is that it may be of interest to consider the *generaliz-*

ability of many of the relationships for which statistical tests have been made to some *infinite* population.

The Superintendency Interview.[9] In designing the superintendency interviews four special considerations had to be taken into account. First, the interviews had to provide data for a series of specific research problems. In addition to the role analysis problems considered in this volume, the School Executive Studies dealt with a number of other questions such as differential levels of aspiration, and job and career satisfaction. Other objectives were to examine the utility of a model for the analysis of social power, and to explore the problem of social sensitivity. Such a multipurpose inquiry demanded a great deal of attention to the length and continuity of the interviews.

Second, since school superintendents are extremely busy and frequently overworked, it was necessary to give special consideration to the problem of obtaining their cooperation in order to complete interviews of any length.

Third, some of the data we required concerned delicate matters, such as, the superintendent's evaluation of his school board members, his perceptions of their motivations in seeking election, his power referents in decision-making, and his behavior when exposed to conflicting expectations. This consideration had implications for our decisions about the place of the interview, the structuring of the respondent's perception of the interviewer, and for the choice of interviewing techniques to maximize rapport in the interview situation.

Fourth, in view of the decision to conduct relatively long interviews it was necessary to make arrangements to deal with potential fatigue problems.

Two aspects of the interviews with the superintendents that are somewhat unusual in sociological investigations are a direct consequence of these considerations. First, the interviews averaged eight hours in length, with a range of from seven to ten hours.[10] Not only did the data requirements necessitate an interview of such length, but it was felt that to obtain certain types of information, a relatively long "build up" period was necessary. The trial interviews suggested that one or two hours would ordinarily not be enough to develop the kind of rapport we felt was needed to encourage uninhibited discussion of topics such as power referents or their behavior when exposed to contradictory expectations. To uncover such material requires a high degree of rapport between interviewer and respondent, and one of the elements in its achievement is time. Questions dealing with power referents and conflicting expectations were not raised until the fifth and sixth hours of the interview.

The second unique aspect of the interview was its location. Instead of interviewing the superintendents in their home communities, they were invited to the research staff offices. This was done for a number of reasons. First, the trial interviews revealed that it was impossible to secure adequate rapport and continuity when the interviews were held in the superintendent's office.[11] Second, interviewing the superintendents in the staff offices provided a more anonymous environment. Third, by holding the interviews in their own offices, the interviewers had much greater control over the interviewing situation. When the trial interviews were conducted in a superintendent's office the interviewer had to accommodate himself continually to a variety of interruptions which did not enhance rapport. Because of the distance, field headquarters, under comparable conditions, were established in the western parts of the state for the convenience of superintendents in those areas.

The interviews were carried out over a nine-month period. Appointments were made by telephone, at which time the superintendent was invited to spend a complete day at Harvard to participate in the study. We told him that it was sponsored by two important New England educational associations and financed by a major foundation, and laid great stress on the anonymous and confidential nature of the interview. It was also explained that the research was similar to studies which have been made of industrial executives, who are apparently important status referents for many superintendents. We appealed to his professional values by pointing out that the research findings could exert an impact on training programs in educational administration.

Each superintendent was interviewed individually by a senior staff member. The superintendent usually arrived at our offices at or before nine o'clock in the morning and left around five in the afternoon, although some of them did not leave until much later. Before beginning the interview the points which had been made in our earlier telephone conversation were reviewed. Special emphasis was given to the anonymous nature of the interview and the importance the research might have for his profession. We encouraged the superintendents to ask any questions they had about the studies, and did not begin the "formal" interview until we judged that they had been answered to their satisfaction.

The first part of the interview was concerned with personal and vocational background information.[12] The interviewer secured a detailed job history, and the superintendent was asked a series of questions about his motivation for entering the field of education and the superintendency, his training, how he secured his positions, how he allocated his time, and about such additional matters as the major problems confronting his school system. The second part of the interview was concerned primarily with a detailed examination of his definition of the superintendent and school board member roles and with his perception of his and the board's behavior. The third part dealt with the following topics: the superintendent's level of aspiration, his job and career satisfaction, his self-evaluation, and the actual and ideal division of labor with his school board. During this period, he was asked to complete instruments designed to tap dimensions such as the degree to which he worried and the degree of freedom of action he felt in his relations with the board.

These early parts of the interviews normally consumed a period of three hours. During the afternoon session the interview turned to more confidential data. The fourth part of the interview dealt with the superintendent's evaluation of his individual school board members and their performance as a board. Several questions concerning his perceptions of the type of community in which he worked were also asked. The fifth part centered on a detailed consideration of the superintendent's influence and power referents who exerted an impact on his decisions. The sixth part was concerned with an examination of his exposure to incongruent expectations or role conflicts. The final part dealt with his social sensitivity. Each superintendent was asked to predict the responses of his school board members to questions about their evaluation of him and to predict their responses to items from the role definition instruments.

To minimize respondent fatigue and to maintain interest, a change of pace was used to provide variety and breathing spells for the respondent. Within the limits of the data requirements and time restrictions an attempt was made to introduce the maximum amount of procedural variety into the interview. Numerous techniques were used, including self-administered questionnaires, interviewer-administered schedules, and closed and open-ended questions. It was found that interest was more easily maintained and fatigue apparently decreased by changing from one type of questioning to another within relatively short periods of time. In a series of trial interviews greater reliance had been placed on self-administered questionnaires; even though these interviews were shorter than those emphasizing open-ended questions, evidence of greater fatigue was apparent.

An important problem that was faced was whether the interview situation should be structured so that the superintendent would view the interviewer as a learner or sophisticate in the problems of public education. We attempted to follow a middle path between these extremes. Each respondent was at the top of the hierarchy of the educational system in his community, whereas the interviewers were sociologists who had affiliations with the Department of Social Relations and the Graduate School of Education at Harvard University.

How an interviewer is perceived depends in large part on the inherent possibilities of the situation as well as the expectations of the interviewee. If, of necessity, the interviewer is defined as a complete outsider (for example, the anthropologist in a foreign culture) there is scarcely any alternative except to occupy the position of the learner. In such a situation the respondent can be highly selective about what he "teaches" the investigator. In the trial interviews it readily became apparent that the respondents perceived the interviewers as representatives of the Graduate School of Education and in consequence as having some degree of sophistication in educational administration. This was felt to be desirable because in these same interviews it was found that superintendents were unwilling to "open up" to an "outsider" on such matters as role referents, problems with school board members, the pressures faced, and the power system of the community.

Four things were done that tended to result in the superintendent's perception of the interviewer as that of the sophisticate. (1) Although the data were to be treated primarily in a sociological and social psychological framework, the substantive material in much of the interview was heavily educationally oriented. The "jargon" of educators was used in the schedule material, and many topics that are controversial among superintendents were mentioned. (2) The interviewer introduced himself to the superintendent in his first contact (usually a telephone call) as a member of the faculty of the Graduate School of Education and used this same identification in the actual preliminaries of the interviewing situation. (3) It was emphasized that the project had been endorsed by the executive committee of two highly respected educational associations in New England.[13] (4) Finally, the interviewer attempted to avoid involvement in discussions of technical educational problems.

On the other hand, in explaining the purposes of the study, the interviewer assumed the learner position. The interviewer told the superintendent that he and the other research staff members had gone through most of the textbooks in educational administration and found them of slight help in understanding what the staff felt to be a crucial problem for the administrator, namely, how to work with and through people. The phrase "human relations" apparently was as attractive to superintendents as it is to business executives. It was explained that his help was needed to determine the problems that the men "on the firing line" actually face, not what the textbook writers talk about. This, apparently, hit a communicative chord. In general, this procedure seemed to be a highly satisfactory resolution of the problem of the interviewer's identity in this lengthy interview situation.[14]

The superintendency occupation, itself, has several features that tended to maximize rapport and minimize fatigue in this interview situation. A superintendent finds it difficult to talk over his problems with people in his own community; as a consequence he seems to derive great cathartic value from being able to talk with a "colleague interviewer." These men are important individuals in their communities. It would seem to be a reasonable hypothesis that one may share confidences with equals but not subordinates. The isolation of the top man in formal organizations has frequently been commented upon by students of industrial sociology. In the case of the school superintendent this isolation applies not only to his relations with his staff but also frequently to his relationships within the community. Nearly everyone in the community is involved in the school system in one way or another and therefore can possibly affect his job and career. Most of his time is spent in his own community, where he must watch his step, but he can "let his hair down" when he leaves his community and when he talks to professional colleagues who "understand these things." These phenomena, plus the fact that great effort had been expended to make them comfortable and feel important, may explain why after eight hours of interviewing, which were actually physically tiring, it very frequently occurred that these men thanked the interviewer for a very enjoyable and profitable day. In addition, by obtaining appointments for him with other faculty members in the School of Education, and promising to inform him of the research findings, an attempt was made to reciprocate for the service he rendered.

The schedules were designed so that the interviewer could directly code many of the superintendent's replies. When the respondent was completing instruments himself, the interviewer used the time to document remarks offered spontaneously during the preceding stage of the interview, to clarify ambiguous responses for the coders, and to review previously completed self-administered instruments. Probes were extensively used, especially in the later phases of the interview. In the portion of the interview concerned with social power referents, the initial questions were indirect and quite general but later were gradually narrowed down until finally questions were asked about relationships with specific individuals. At another point a "reverse funnel" technique was used to obtain the role conflict data.[15]   In general, the interviewing method was eclectic; the procedures used depended upon the nature and the presumed difficulty of securing adequate responses.

The School Board Member Interviews.   In contrast to the interviews with the superintendents, those with the school board members were held in their home communities. They were also much shorter, ranging from one and a half to six hours and averaging two hours.

At the close of each superintendency interview permission was requested to contact his board members. If we had not asked his permission we would have been open to the charge of having told the superintendent only half the story regarding our procedures. Furthermore, since the interviewing program was to cover a period of nine months we felt this procedure would maintain good public relations with other educators, some of whom would be included in the sample. Every superintendent agreed to the request, and in only three cases did we have to convince them to give this permission. The justification presented to the superintendent for the school board interviews was that without them we would have information from only one side of the superintendent-school board relationship. We assured him again of the confidential treatment to be given all interview materials.

The first contact with each board member was by means of a personal letter from the Dean of the Harvard Graduate School of Education. The letter described the general purposes of the Studies and said that within a week a member of the research staff would contact him by telephone to arrange an appointment. As reported earlier, 98 percent of the 517 board members agreed to be, and were, interviewed.

In the telephone conversation, the respondent was told that the interview would require about two hours. He was asked to suggest a place where a confidential interview could be held. They were conducted in the homes of respondents, in restaurants, in automobiles, in offices, factories, hospitals, schools, hotels, and places of business. The lag between the superintendent's and his school board members' interviews averaged two weeks.

The content of the school board member interview to a large extent paralleled the superintendent's since the research design required that a number of the same instruments be administered to both samples. In general, however, the school board interviews were not only shorter, but much more structured than the superintendents'.

Processing of the Data and Scaling Procedures. Each completed superintendency schedule was edited within a day of the interview. The time lag between the school board interviews and the schedule editing averaged about a week.

A large amount of data was either precoded or required only a simple transformation to code. Procedures were set up whereby a 10 percent check was made on all coding. Coding was not acceptable unless it met the standard of 99 percent accuracy. In a few cases where new coders were being broken in and the initial 10 percent check revealed an accuracy several points below 99 percent, the material was completely recoded. After the codes for the open-ended questions were developed, a series of practice coding sessions were held until there was unanimity among the coders on the meaning of the categories. All of the coding of the open-ended questions was done twice, once by an interviewer who was familiar with the material though not with the particular schedule.

Both the superintendent and school board member schedules included a number of instruments on the basis of which attempts were made to develop scales. For the problems investigated we were able to use only one set of scales which had been previously standardized: a set of scales developed by Levinson.[16] All five of these were included in the superintendent schedule, but only one, "Political-Economic Conservatism," was included in the school board member schedule. In the case of other variables it was necessary to devise sets of items and test them for scalability.

In choosing a method of scaling three considerations had to be taken into account. First, there were many variables we wished to measure, and since it was obvious that the interview schedule would be quite long, it was necessary to choose a method which could rely on a relatively small number of items; second, in this research it was not practicable to develop scales in advance; and third, the superintendency sample was relatively small. These conditions suggested the choice of Guttman scaling or scalogram analysis as a measurement procedure.[17]

A Guttman scale is "cumulative": anyone who answers the most "difficult" question positively should answer all less "difficult" questions positively. It was felt to be meaningful to apply a cumulative scaling model to a number of the variables in the research.

There are two features of our use of the Guttman technique which will be described. The first concerns the use of contrived items in the H technique,[18] and the second concerns the samples on which the scales were derived.

Previous work suggested that when attempting to scale ten or twelve items measuring a more broadly defined variable than those on which the technique seems most successful,[19] it is usually possible to find only four or five items which together meet the minimum standards of acceptability.[20] With such variables too much error develops from items having similar marginals. But to use only a few of the original items is to run the risk of capitalizing on chance. In order to avoid this problem the H technique of scalogram analysis was employed. Instead of trying to put all the original items, many of which would have similar marginals, into a scale individually, this method combines the original items into a smaller number of "contrived items." The effect is to increase the reproducibility of the scale and the reliability of the cutting points while reducing the number of rank groups.

Many of the scales which we derived in this way are based on only three contrived items (usually on nine original items). One of Guttman's original requirements for scalability was that the scale have a reproducibility of ninety.[21] However, this figure was based on the assumption that the scale would have about ten items. When there are only three items in the scale it is possible to obtain a reproducibility as high as ninety by chance, and it was consequently necessary to set a higher standard for the reproducibility of these scales. For the three-item scales this figure was arbitrarily set at ninety-five.[22] Since the probability distribution of the coefficient of reproducibility has not been worked out, it is impossible to say whether the obtained coefficients are significantly greater than those expected by chance.

The second special point is concerned with the samples on which the scales were derived. For variables on which measures of both superintendents and school board members were needed, an attempt was made to derive the scales for the combined samples, since meaningful comparisons between the samples would not be possible unless the scales were based on the same items and cutting points. Since the school board sample was nearly five times as large as the superintendent's, these scales would be based primarily on school board data. It frequently happened that there was so much difference between the two samples on their mean rank on the scales (for example, on the Ideal Division of Labor and Educational Progressivism scales) that the smaller superintendent's sample has a very skewed distribution of scale scores. Such skewed distributions may be of little value in relating to other variables, but they are still useful in providing a comparison between the samples. When it was necessary to relate one of these skewed scales to some other variable within the separate samples a new scale for each sample was derived. Although this means that the variable has a different definition in each sample, the fact that it was possible to derive a scale on the combined samples gives us some confidence in judging that this difference is minimal. In each sample the items tended to have the same rank on their marginals, but the marginals for one sample were all much higher than those for the other. It would seem to be a fair interpretation that in such cases the scales for the two samples are measuring the same variable but at different places on the continuum.[23]

Notes and References for Chapter Six

[1] See Neal Gross and Ward S. Mason, "Some Methodological Problems of Eight-Hour Interviews," *American Journal of Sociology*, LIX (1953), pp. 197–204, and see also Chapter Fifteen.

[2] The Commonwealth of Massachusetts, *Annual Report of the Department of Education*, Part II (Public Document No. 2, Boston, 1951).

[3] The four areas were defined as follows: Western Massachusetts (Berkshire, Franklin, Hampshire, and Hampden Counties); Central Massachusetts (Worcester County); Northeastern Massachusetts (Essex, Middlesex, Suffolk, and Norfolk Counties); and Southeastern Massachusetts (Bristol, Plymouth, Barnstable, Dukes and Nantucket Counties).

[4] Information was obtained from the Massachusetts State Department of Education.

[5] These data were secured from United States Bureau of the Census, *United States Census of Population: 1950*, Vol. I, "Number of Inhabitants," Chapter 21: Massachusetts (Washington, D. C., U. S. Government Printing Office, 1951).

[6] Data on expenditures per pupil were obtained from The Commonwealth of Massachusetts, *op. cit.*, data on the equalized valuations of towns and cities were obtained from Massachusetts Teachers Federation, *Equalized Valuations of Towns and Cities,* 1951–52 Series, No. J5, mimeographed. Data on the population of communities from U. S. Bureau of the Census, *op. cit.*

[7] Massachusetts Teachers Federation, *Salaries, Travel Allowances, and Years of Experience of School Superintendents,* 1951–1952 Series, No. J44, mimeographed.

[8] The usual procedure in determining whether any differences between two distributions may be attributed to chance is the chi-square technique, but since chi-square assumes independence of the two distributions it was not appropriate to compare the sample with the total population. Our comparison, therefore, was between the sample and the remainder of the population.

[9] Some of the materials considered in this section were reported in Gross and Mason, *op. cit.*

[10] These interviews were of much longer duration than those employed in most sociological investigations. Their length and "one-shot" nature also differentiate them from most interviewing procedures reported in the behavioral science literature. See the following for studies involving interviews of relatively long duration: Margaret Mead, *The Mountain Arapesh: The Record of Unabelin with Rorschach Analysis*, "Anthropological Papers of the American Museum of Natural History," Vol. XLI, Part III, New York, 1949; Henry A. Murray, *Explorations in Personality* (New York: Oxford University Press, 1938); Henry A. Murray, *Assessment of Men* (New York: Rinehart and Company, 1948); M. Brewster Smith, Jerome Bruner, and Robert White, *Opinion and Personality* (New York: John Wiley and Sons, 1956).

[11] For the rationale behind the choice of the place of the interview in another research situation see John Dollard, *Caste and Class in a Southern Town*, Second Edition (New York: Harper and Brothers, 1949), pp. 23–25.

[12] Although this review of the sequence in which particular problem areas were examined covers the entire interview, it is not practicable to present the interview schedules in this book because the superintendency schedules were fifty-seven pages and the school board member schedules twenty-five pages in length. It should also be noted that this volume is concerned with findings based on only certain parts of the schedules. Appendices A and B contain the instruments and scales used in the analysis of problems treated in this book.

[13] See William K. Sewell, "Field Techniques in Social Psychological Study in a Rural Community," *American Sociological Review*, XIV (1949), pp. 718–719, for a discussion of the "sponsorship" problem.

[14] On the other hand it was found advisable to take the learner position when interviewing school board members. Many school board members are uneasy and "anxious to please" if they feel they are talking to a professional educator, whereas they are glad to propound their own ideas in the presence of a learner.

[15] To be discussed in detail in Chapter Fifteen.

[16] The three scales for which results are reported here, the F, E and PEC scales, are short forms developed by Levinson based on scales persented in T. W. Adorno, Else Frenkel-Brunswik, Daniel J. Levinson, and R. Nevitt Sanford, *The Authoritarian Personality*, (New York: Harper and Brothers, 1950).

[17] See Samuel A. Stouffer, et al., *Measurement and Prediction* (Princeton: Princeton University Press, 1950).

[18] Samuel A. Stouffer, et al., "A Technique for Improving Cumulative Scales," *Public Opinion Quarterly*, XVI (1952), pp. 273–291.

[19] See Stouffer, et al., *Measurement and Prediction*.

[20] Ward S. Mason, "A Method of Scaling Cultural Orientations" (Unpublished Ph.D. dissertation, Harvard University, 1953).

[21] See Louis Guttman, "The Basis for Scalogram Analysis," in Stouffer, et al., *op. cit.*, p. 77.

[22] The actual and chance reproducibilities for each scale are presented in Appendix B. For the method of computing this figure see Matilda W. Riley, John W. Riley, Jr., and Jackson Toby, *Sociological Studies in Scale Analysis* (New Brunswick: Rutgers University Press, 1954), pp. 317–320.

[23] The scales used and the items on which they are based are presented in Appendix B.

seven

Macroscopic Role Consensus Analysis: Objectives and Methodology

Only some of the data which were obtained by the methods described in the preceding chapter will serve as the basis for the studies which comprise the remainder of this volume. The expectations which superintendents and school board members expressed for their own and the other position serve as the starting point for our consideration of consensus on role definition, and in a later chapter, conformity to role expectations. The expectations superintendents perceived as held for them serve as the starting point for our analysis of role conflicts. In each of these problem areas the idea of consensus on expectations is either explicit or implicit; it is explicitly the focus of two of the major sections of the volume, those concerned with "macroscopic" and "microscopic" consensus, and is implicit in both the conformity analysis and the analysis of role conflict.

We have maintained that the phenomenon of role consensus requires both theoretical and empirical examination, and deserves exploitation as a variable in propositions concerned with cultural organization, the functioning of social systems and individual social behavior. In this first empirical section of the volume the focus is on role consensus in a *macroscopic* framework. It is necessary to make clear what we mean by macroscopic role analysis and to distinguish it from microscopic role analysis, the central problem of the second empirical section. In this chapter we will also describe the major problems of the macroscopic consensus analysis, present the specifications of the *object* positions to be examined, and describe the methods used to measure this kind of consensus.

Macroscopic versus Microscopic Analyses. In discussing our proposed conceptual scheme we stressed the importance of a clear specification of the object and subject populations to be investigated. Unless there is clarity on the questions, "Consensus on what?" and "Consensus among whom?" research procedures and findings in studies of role consensus will be characterized by ambiguity. The specifications of the object population of our inquiries will be presented later in this chapter. Since the distinction between macroscopic and microscopic analyses is based on different categorizations of the subject population, or the role definers, it is appropriate to specify now the *subject* population to be used.

For the role analyses presented in this volume, the subject population will consist of *occupants* of the positions to be investigated. We were interested in examining the degree of consensus on the expectations for the behavior and attributes of incumbents of the school superintendent and school board member positions held by individuals who actually occupy these positions. Our data for this purpose consist of the evaluative standards applied to these positions by a stratified random sample of nearly half the superintendents in Massachusetts ($N = 105$) and their school board members ($N = 508$). The same data will be used to investigate two sets of problems which we shall designate as *macroscopic* and *microscopic* role consensus analyses.

The *microscopic* problems, which will be examined in Chapters Ten through Thirteen, are concerned with the variable of role consensus as it relates to the functioning of small social systems comparable to those analyzed by students of small group research. The subjects of these microscopic analyses will be either members of small groups composed of a superintendent and *his* school board or just the members of a single school board. That is, the analysis will be centered on consensus among members of a small group who are responsible for the functioning of one school system. Although there are other possibilities, the microscopic analyses will be restricted to a consideration of consensus *within a school board* and consensus *between school board members and their superintendent*.

In the analysis of *macroscopic* consensus the focus of interest is on the role definitions of the 105 superintendents, of the 508 school board members, or on the consensus between these two samples on their role definitions. In this case the role definers are the *total samples* of superintendents and school board members. Consensus analyses concerned with all the superintendents or all the school board members in our samples, or analyses concerned with consensus between these two samples is macroscopic consensus, whereas consensus among members of a school board in a particular community, or between a school board and its superintendent is microscopic consensus. Although the identical data will be used in both the macroscopic and microscopic analyses, they will be used in different ways.

It is perhaps worth emphasizing that these analyses of consensus will be limited to a restricted set of problems. Consensus may be meaningfully investigated among and between position incumbents in aggregates or social systems ranging in magnitude from a dyad to an entire society. Obviously, the two kinds of consensus, within and between positions at both the microscopic and macroscopic levels of analysis, are only four examples of many possibilities that might be examined. For the particular problems in cultural organization and small group analysis which will be examined in this and the next sections of this book, these four kinds of consensus were considered to be of most relevance.

Macroscopic Analysis Objectives. Our primary objectives will be to describe and investigate degrees of consensus among superintendents, among school board members, and consensus between these two sets of role definers on the expectations they hold for incumbents of their positions. Each respondent was asked to express expectations for the behavior and attributes of occupants of the superintendent and school board member positions. In view of our earlier examination of the postulate of role consensus, our basic working hypotheses are that there will be different amounts of consensus on different expectations within both samples, and between the two samples.

We will try to account for different expectations of the incumbents of two positions. Superintendents and school board members occupy different positions in the social structures of the school systems in which they participate, and we will not only predict that there will be differences between the two samples, but we shall also test a series of hypotheses concerning what those differences will be.

In addition, an attempt will be made to predict differences in the expectations held by incumbents of the same position. Incumbents of the same position may be differentiated according to a number of criteria, some of which, we will argue, ought to have some effect on the expectations they hold. One has been selected for an exploratory analysis: the size of the system in which the positions occur.

We will also examine different degrees of consensus on different role segments. Expectations for position incumbents can be segmented according to the substance of the expectation, and we will ask whether or not there are different degrees of consensus on the different segments, and, if there are, try to explain these differences.

And finally, a general objective of the entire macroscopic analysis is to investigate the utility of a method of studying the expectations held by a specified population of role definers. As Newcomb has suggested, "More adequate operational definitions of role are needed; our present poverty in this respect is paralleled by the paucity of systematic role research." [1]

Specifications of the Position. In Part 1 of this book we discussed positions and roles in fairly general terms. This was done in order to demonstrate the relevance of the proposed conceptual scheme and the theoretical and operational complexities considered for problems with which the *several* social sciences are concerned. In distinguishing between role analyses at the macroscopic and microscopic level we presented the specifications for the role definers, or the *subject* population, which will be used in our empirical analyses. It is relevant now to introduce the relational and situational specifications of the position, or of the *object* population, on which our role consensus analyses will be based.

It was our initial objective to study the "total position" of the school superintendent in the sense that we were interested in examining all of its positional sectors, that is, its relationships to all relevant counter positions. This was an overly ambitious undertaking which could be only approximated in the research. In addition, it is necessary to emphasize that for each positional sector treated, only a relatively small number of expectations could be studied.

Although some consideration will be given to expectations for incumbents of the school board member position, the central focus of our analysis is on certain sectors of the superintendency position. The expectations to be examined deal with a superintendent's relationships to his superordinates, the school board, his subordinates on the school staff, community members in general (some of whom occupy specific positions), and professional educators, such as other superintendents. It can be said, therefore, that we have used the "position-centric model" described in Chapter Four.[2]

To determine their role definitions, we asked the superintendents and school board members to respond to a series of expectation statements preceded in most instances by the question: "As a superintendent (school board member), what obligation do you feel you have (a superintendent has) to do or not to do, the following . . . ?" [3] Although there is little situational specificity in this question, given the information that all of our respondents were informed that the study dealt with superintendents and school board members in Massachusetts, and that they were all themselves occupants of positions in Massachusetts, it may be inferred that the situation for which respondents answered the expectations items was Massachusetts. We say, in consequence, the object of study situationally specified is the superintendency position in Massachusetts. An exception to this specification is the one required for the role attributes instrument (Appendix Table A–2), in which respondents were asked to answer questions according to the requirements of their own communities. For this instrument the object of study is the superintendency position in particular communities.

In considering the specifications of the object population, it is pertinent to make certain observations about the kind of system of social relationships in which the positions of school superintendent and school board member are involved. These observations are also relevant in another way. Since in our inquiry the incumbents of these positions will be used as the role definers, the kind of social system in which they function and their relationships within it may have a direct bearing on the extent to which superintendents and their superordinates agree on their role definitions.

There are five observations concerning the kind of relationship network in which these positions occur which will be discussed. The first is that the superintendency and school board member positions are embedded in a set of relationships like those that Barnard has termed *formal organizations*. As the formal executive administrator and policy makers of local public school systems the superintendent and school board members are involved in ". . . a system of consciously coordinated activities or forces of two or more persons." [4] This implies that a school system viewed as a formal organization has what Barnard has termed an "organizational purpose" or objective(s) which it is attempting to accomplish. The goal of a public school system may be said to be "to educate" children to participate effectively as members of their society.

From Barnard's analysis and those of other students of formal organization[5] we may also say that a school system is a formal organization in that it must deal with "economic" problems, those concerned with the efficient and effective allocation of its material and human resources, and with adaptation problems. For example, it must cope with problems deriving from the "informal organization" that invariably arises within it and that may be a crucial element in the achievement of its formal organizational purpose.

A second related observation is that the positions of school board member and superintendent are locations in a form of organization that has *most* of the characteristics of the type of organization to which Weber has applied the term, *bureaucracy*.[6] The regular activities of a bureaucracy, according to Weber, "are distributed in a fixed way as official duties." In addition to being a social structure characterized by a definite division of labor and having its officials subject to social constraints, a bureaucracy is a social structure governed by a system of abstract rules. It contains a definite social hierarchy of positions. Its members are subjected ". . . to authority only with respect to their impersonal official. obligations . . . ," and selection procedures are established on the basis of technical qualifications. Jobs are obtained through appointment, not election. Personnel is promoted on the basis of accomplishment or length of service.[7] Bureaucracy is an organizational model that appears to be relevant in describing major aspects of the social system of which the positions of school board member and school superintendent are a part.

A third point that deserves emphasis is that these positions are established by state law. By legal definition the school board is the formal policy-making organ of a public school system and the superintendent is its executive officer. The board is superordinate to the superintendent. It hires and fires the superintendent, not vice versa. These two positions are located at the top of the formal social hierarchy of a school system. Through the deliberations and actions of their incumbents, decisions are reached that clearly affect the organizational purpose and the manipulation of its human and material resources. The authority and responsibility to make major policy, allocative, and coordinative decisions for the school systems are vested in these positions.[8]

Fourth, a school system, like any formal organization, must adapt itself to its external environment. Homans would term its adaptation to the environment its "external system." [9] In Parsons' formulation an organization must come to terms with systems in its external situation since its "output" normally is a function of the "input" from the external system.[10]

Public education in the United States is a function of state governments, but the control of public education is largely in the hands of the local community. Although there are exceptions,[11] the general practice is that school boards are elected by residents of the local community and public education is supported in large part by local property taxes. In Massachusetts, all school boards are elected and the greatest share of the expenditures for public education is paid by the local community. The importance of its "external" relations for its existence and functioning must, in consequence, not be minimized.

The final point that deserves consideration is that school systems, like most other governmental bureaucracies and in contrast to most "private" ones, have as their official policy makers *representatives* of the external system with which they must deal. School boards in Massachusetts are comprised of elected representatives of the community which pays for and "buys," in a sense, the "output" of the schools. In the typical corporation in American society the board of directors represents stockholders of the corporation, not customers. In this sense, school board members represent the larger system, the community, of which the school system is a subsystem. The contrast between this structural setting of the position of school board member and that of the superintendency position will later be used as a basis for making certain predictions regarding differences on role definitions between the incumbents of these two positions.

Methodology. To investigate empirically the problem of role consensus it is necessary, first, to specify the object and subject populations to be treated in the analysis, second, to obtain data on the expectations held for incumbents of the specified position(s) by the selected population of role definers, and third, to obtain measures of the degree of consensus on their role definitions.

In our earlier descriptions of the object and subject populations we attempted to meet the first requirement. The purpose of this section is to describe our procedures in meeting the other two.

In Chapter Five it was suggested that there are at least two procedures that can be used to secure data for the analysis of consensus on role definitions.[12] The first is to focus on the degree of agreement among role definers on which one, or which range of alternatives, among a set of available alternatives the incumbent of a position should adopt in a particular situation. The second is to focus on their consensus on a single evaluative standard that might be applied to him. In this research the second alternative was chosen. The reason for this decision was operational. It allowed first, for the investigation of consensus on a greater number of role segments. Second, for the investigation of conformity to expectations, the problem area examined in Chapter Fourteen, the same instruments could be used to obtain data on a wide range of role behaviors as well as on behavioral expectations.

In using this methodological approach we followed the general procedure of asking each respondent whether and to what extent he felt a superintendent (or school board member, where appropriate) was obligated to do (or be like) what was specified in the particular expectation item. The available response categories for each item in the role definition instruments with this design were:

> *A.* Absolutely must
> *B.* Preferably should
> *C.* May or may not
> *D.* Preferably should not
> *E.* Absolutely must not

Five of the six instruments of which greatest use is made in this analysis are of this kind. Their general content will be briefly described here, and the actual items and the form in which they were presented may be seen in Appendix A. For the school board members all responses were elicited verbally, the respondent having a card with the response categories before him, while the interviewer read off the expectation items. The superintendents in some cases gave verbal responses, and in others wrote them. The different treatment of the two samples was due to the different interview situations which have been described in Chapter Four. This difference does not seem great enough to invalidate comparisons of the responses of the two samples.

The first four of the five role definition instruments to be presented contain items which are potential obligations for superintendents, and the fifth contains items which are potential obligations for school board members. The instruments are:

1. *Superintendent's Performances Instrument* (Appendix Table A–1) contains 37 items, each of which describes a behavior in which the superintendent may or may not be expected to engage as the administrator of the public schools. They were designed to cover a sample of the major types of activities in which a superintendent engages when carrying out his job. Some of the items tend to be general statements about a superintendent's behavior (for example, "Make recommendations for the appointment, promotion, or dismissal of subordinates on the basis of merit alone."), whereas others are much more specific (for example, "Speak to all major civic groups at least once a year."). They all deal, however, with things a superintendent may do *as a superintendent*.

2. *Superintendent's Attributes Instrument* (Appendix Table A–2) contains 54 items, each of which is a quality or characteristic. These range from items which deal with marital status, age, and religion

through others which deal with educational qualifications, to some which are descriptive of general personality characteristics or interpersonal skills. The presentation of these items was different from that of the others, in that school board members were asked how they would feel about a person they were about to hire as superintendent having these characteristics, whereas superintendents were asked to respond according to how they would feel about recommending a person for their superintendency position, assuming they had moved to another position themselves, who had these characteristics. Although they were asked as expectations for position prerequisites there seems to be little reason to doubt that obligations for applicants should apply with equal validity to incumbents. At least we feel it is justifiable to make this inference and to compare these attributive obligations with the behavioral obligations of the other instruments.

3. *Superintendent's Participations Instrument* (Appendix Table A–3) contains 11 items, each of which specifies some type of participation in community groups or activities, such as, "Take an active part in local politics." Most of these items are probably peripheral to the superintendent's function of administering the public schools, but they are nearly all concerned with his relationships to other systems in the environment in which a public school system functions. The question to which they are directed is essentially, "To what extent should a school superintendent be expected to relate to specified groups in the community?"

4. *Superintendent's Friendships Instrument* (Appendix Table A–4) contains 15 items, each of which describes an individual highly visible in the community, such as, "a religious leader," "a leader of a veterans' organization," or "a leader of the local taxpayers' association." Like the participations items, these are probably peripheral to the superintendent's major function, and like them again, of possible relevance to his functioning as the administrator of the public schools. The question to which they are directed is "To what extent should a superintendent's intimate friendships be influenced by his public position?"

5. *School Board Performances Instrument* (Appendix Table A–5) contains 20 items, each of which describes a behavior in which the school board may or may not be expected to engage. Like the items of the Superintendent's Performances Instrument, they were designed to cover a sample of the major kinds of activities in which school boards engage in order to carry out their jobs. The items of this obligations instrument may also be considered to be "superintendent's

rights" just as the items from the Superintendent's Performances Instrument may be viewed as school board members' rights.

A sixth set of items of which considerable use will be made in this analysis is the Division of Labor Instrument (Appendix Table A–6). It contains 13 items which were of a different design from that of the other role definition instruments. Each of its items describes a general function which must be carried out in the school system and presents four alternatives for which the respondents could express a preference. The alternatives, although slightly different for different items (according to their content), may be paraphrased as:

1. Should be entirely the responsibility of the School Board.
2. Should be largely the responsibility of the School Board.
3. Should be largely the responsibility of the Superintendent.
4. Should be entirely the responsibility of the Superintendent.

Respondents were asked to answer according to what they felt the division of labor *should be ideally*. The responses to these items are considered to be expectations in the role consensus analysis in the same sense as the items used in the "obligations" type instruments. They apply, however, directly to the relationship between the positions rather than to only one of the positions.

These six instruments and the separate items of which they are comprised form the major part of the data on which the following consensus analysis is based. For some purposes we will be concerned with an examination of responses to the items grouped as they are in the instruments. For others we will be concerned with an examination of responses to the items grouped in ways which will be described in detail when they are first presented. Other variables and classifications are used, and these will also be described when they first arise in the analysis. Since these six role definition instruments will be used extensively, it is suggested that the reader turn to Appendix A and examine the items used, their form of presentation, and the response distributions of the superintendent and school board samples.

Basic to our analysis of macroscopic consensus is the distinction between intraposition consensus, that is, consensus *among* all the superintendents or *among* all the school board members, and interposition consensus, or consensus *between* the two samples of role definers. Since these two kinds of macroscopic consensus pose quite different operational problems, we will discuss their measures separately, considering intraposition consensus first.

In terms of the operational procedures which were used to obtain role definitions from the respondents, the intraposition measurement problem reduces itself to the following question: Given a series of distributions, each of which is comprised of the set of responses of a sample to a single expectation item with five response categories ranging from "absolutely must" to "absolutely must not," how can scores be obtained which will rank the items on a continuum of consensus?

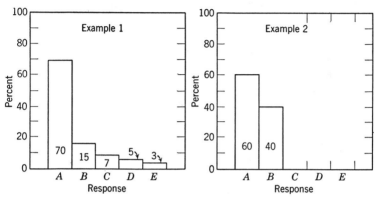

Figure 7–1. Hypothetical examples of percentage frequency distributions of responses to two expectation items.

It is clear that if all the responses for an item fall in one category, there is perfect consensus. This recognition does not take us very far toward a measure of consensus, however, since in our data there is only one item for which the responses come near this extreme. Most of the items used do not even approach this degree of consensus. Two hypothetical examples of distributions of responses suggest one problem with which it is necessary to deal. It could be argued that Examples 1 and 2 of Figure 7–1 both show some consensus, but what criteria can be used to decide which shows more? There is a larger modal category in Example 1 than in 2; that is, there are more people who agree on a single response for Example 1. But Example 1 has responses which are distributed over the entire possible range, whereas Example 2 has responses in only two categories which are, in addition, adjacent. Common sense criteria when applied to these examples seem to lead only to a greater indecision as which shows the most and which the least consensus. The examples suggest that in the measurement of consensus at least two elements need to be considered: central tendencies and variability of the distribution. To take only one of these into account would be to ignore important information.

Another complicating factor is that there are two types of distributions which might indicate a complete lack of consensus among the respondents. These two types are illustrated in Figure 7–2. In Example 3 there is no consensus because each response occurs with equal frequency. In Example 4 the lack of consensus for the total sample would appear to stem from the existence of two completely contradictory evaluative standards applied to the same behavior. These are, of course, extreme cases of lack of consensus and they suggest the need

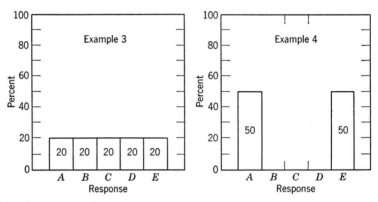

Figure 7–2. Hypothetical examples of percentage frequency distributions of responses to two expectation items.

for caution in interpreting whatever statistical measure is used to represent response variability.

Given this setting of the problem, how can a consensus score be obtained which will take account of both the height and the range of the distribution? If only a classification into a few ordered categories were desired, some scheme like taking the minimum number of response categories required to include 90 percent of the cases might be used. However, for our purposes a continuous series of scores with which to rank the items was needed. This required some sort of score involving deviations about a point of central tendency, and this in turn required assumptions with respect to the distance between the response categories. Several possibilities suggested themselves. When each response category is given a numerical weight, ranging from 1, for the "absolutely must" category, to 5, for the "absolutely must not" category, some kind of average deviation or average squared deviation might be used, based on the mean, the mode, or the median. Several of these scoring methods were examined on a sample of items and found to give very similar results.[13]   It was decided to use the variance of the distribution as the measure of intrasample consensus.[14]

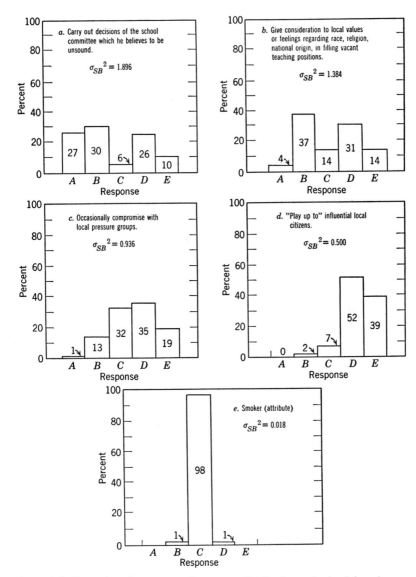

Figure 7–3. Examples of percentage frequency distributions of school board member responses to five expectation items.

Two consensus scores were calculated for each item of the role definition instruments, one for each sample. The variance score obtained for each sample on each item is given in Appendix Tables A–1 through A–6. The distributions of these scores for the six role definition instruments are presented and discussed in Chapter Eight. Some examples of response distributions for particular items and the variance scores obtained for them will be presented here in order to illustrate the problems of interpreting this measure of intraposition consensus.

In Figure 7–3 are presented percentage histograms of the responses of school board members to five items selected from the role definition instruments with variance scores ranging from 0.018 (high consensus) to 1.896 (low consensus). Although there is high consensus on the attribute expectation item, whether or not a superintendent should be a "smoker," the response distribution reveals that this consensus is on the C ("may or may not") category. There is almost perfect agreement among school board members that whether or not a superintendent smokes is quite irrelevant to his role or is at least a conditional matter. On the item with the next highest consensus, "play up to influential local citizens," there is apparently fair agreement that superintendents should not do this, but some disagreement exists about whether this is a preferential proscription ("preferably should not") or a mandatory proscription ("absolutely must not"). Items a, b, and c of Figure 7–3 reveal even more striking disagreement among school board members; in all three there is a sizable number of respondents whose answers reflect a positive and a sizable number whose responses indicate a negative evaluation of the activities in question.

This is an appropriate place to comment on the disagreement which is represented by the variance scores of a great many of the expectation items, namely, a disagreement on intensity rather than on direction. Item d of Figure 7–3 may serve as an illustration. The disagreement among the responses to this item might appear to be negligible insofar as both response categories reveal a negative evaluation of the action in question. Almost all school board members say that a superintendent should not play up to influential local citizens, but some feel he "preferably should not" while others feel he "absolutely must not." Should this be interpreted as only a slight difference? Consider the following cases that suggest the importance of such a difference. Suppose it is accepted by some group that one "preferably should not" dress conspicuously in public places. To change this expectation to "absolutely must not" seems to be a quite drastic restriction of freedom. And on the other side, suppose it is commonly accepted that one "absolutely must not" break windows of public buildings. To change this expectation to "preferably should not" is at least as drastic an extension of license. In these instances we would argue that the difference is clearly of great importance. There would seem to be no reason why it should not be of equal importance in the case of expectations held for school superintendents. The "absolute" categories imply inescapable negative sanctions, while the "preferable" categories imply possibilities of their evasion.

In addition, when a subordinate and superordinate are the role definers, a "preferable" rather than an "absolute" standard may be interpreted as "an escape clause" in role definition. This interpretation is suggested by the following comment of one superintendent, typical of those made by a number of them in discussing the expectations their board members hold.

> They expect you to act like a professional educator when they have no personal interest in the matter. But if one of their friends wants a job or a contract then they kind of forget about professional standards. They don't see why an exception shouldn't be made. After all some of them give a lot of time to school business and feel they ought to get some return for their efforts.

Particular expectations may reflect other positions a role definer occupies. The other positions a school board member occupies may affect expectations he holds for his superintendent. If he is "to take care of a friend" in school matters he cannot hold immutable expectations for his superintendent. "Loopholes" which derive from multiple position occupancy of role definers suggest a major source of strain for incumbents of positions who must resolve the dilemma implied by the simultaneous requirements of maintaining "professional" standards and "keeping the boss happy." In our consideration of the superintendent's exposure to incompatible expectations in Chapter Sixteen we shall examine this problem in greater detail.

The basic problem for the measurement of *interposition* consensus was to find a technique by means of which to determine whether a comparison of the responses of the 105 superintendents and those of the 508 school board members indicated agreement or disagreement on each of the items contained in the six role definition instruments.

Two statistical techniques for testing the significance of the difference between two distributions are the "*t* test" for the difference between means and chi-square, for testing the difference between distributions of frequencies in qualitative categories. We used the *t* test when we were concerned with the substance as well as the presence of disagreement between the two samples. When we wished only to distinguish between items on which there was and was not a significant difference between the distributions of the superintendents' and the

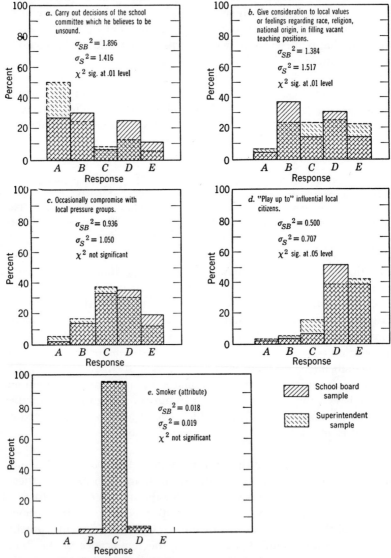

Figure 7–4. Examples of percentage frequency distributions of school board member and superintendent responses to five expectation items.

school board members' responses, we used chi-square. The 5-percent level was accepted as indicating a lack of consensus between the two samples. This will allow us to say whether the differences between the two distributions for a single expectation item are chance differences or not.

Here we would like to present examples of items on which there is disagreement according to the chi-square criterion, and items on which there is not disagreement, in order to discuss some of the complexities that arise in the interpretation of this measure. The same items which were used to illustrate the measure of intraposition consensus will be used. In Figure 7–4 are presented the superimposed percentage histograms of superintendent and school board member responses to these five items.

On three of the items in Figure 7–4 the chi-square between the two distributions is significant, and on two it is not. Of the two items on which there is not a significant chi-square, on one there is high consensus within both samples (item *e*) and on another, relatively low consensus within both samples, (item *c*). Item *c* is a good illustration of the kind of item which will require us to speak of "no disagreement" rather than agreement. Although there is no significant difference between the two distributions, it could hardly be said that there is agreement between superintendents and school board members on whether or not a superintendent should compromise with local pressure groups. There is simply little consensus within either sample and no significant difference between the distributions of responses which reveal this lack of consensus. On the other hand, it can be said that there is agreement between the two samples on the appropriate expectation for the "smoker" item. Both samples agree that a superintendent "may or may not" be a smoker.

Item *d*, on which the chi-square is significant at the .05 level and on which there is approximately average (for our data) consensus within both samples, exemplifies another kind of disagreement between the two samples. There appears to be a greater tendency for superintendents to respond permissively ("may or may not") and for school board members to respond in the "preferably should not" category, whereas in both samples there is a generally negative evaluation of "playing up to influential local citizens." The difference between the samples in this instance seems to be one of degree rather than kind, or intensity rather than direction. We would argue for the importance of this difference on the same reasoning we used in interpreting the significance of the difference between the "preferable" and "absolute" responses for the intrasample analyses.

Items *a* and *b* show quite different discrepancies between the two distributions. On item *b* there seems to be a shift to the negative end of the response categories by the superintendent sample. It is impossible to describe this discrepancy between the two samples as one simply of intensity or simply of direction. There is a greater proportion of school board members who respond permissively, but also a greater proportion of superintendents who say "absolutely must not." The difference may be best described as one in which there are two distinct groups of school board members, one of which evaluates it negatively ("preferably should not"). In contrast to this, the superintendents' responses are distributed nearly equally over four of the five response categories. It is difficult to describe the discrepancy between the two distributions on this item without describing the entire distributions, rather than just those parts which do not overlap.

The difference revealed on item *a* of Figure 7–4 is one which can be described as a difference primarily in direction. A much greater proportion of superintendents evaluate the action of this item positively, and a greater proportion of school board members evaluate it negatively. Although the concentration of superintendents who respond positively is in the absolute category, and of school board members who respond negatively in the preferable category, the discrepancy is primarily one of direction rather than of intensity. It is interesting to note also that superintendents can be said to feel more strongly about this item than do school board members.

From another vantage point these response distributions are illustrations of the heterogeneous patterns that emerge when the role definitions of a subject population are examined empirically. They suggest that caution needs to be exercised in the interpretation of propositions which assert or imply that there are unimodal evaluative standards for position incumbents when incomplete or no empirical evidence is presented.

Two final methodological points need to be discussed before proceeding with the analysis of macroscopic role definition. First, how were the expectation items obtained? They were devised and selected after an examination of the hortative, periodical, and textbook literature in the field of educational administration, after informal discussions with faculty members in the field of education administration in the universities and after our participation in conferences, both formal and informal, with school administrators and school board members. As a consequence of the pretests, the first set of role definition instruments were refined considerably.

This raises the second and final methodological point: the "sampling of items" problem. Throughout the macroscopic analyses we shall be concerned with two primary foci of attention. For some problems we shall compare groups of *people* on given sets of role expectations, whereas for others we shall compare different role expectation *items*. So long as we are concerned with the first of these foci, the analysis is straightforward. We will be dealing with two stratified random samples which have been drawn according to conventional procedures, and we can make tests of significance in order to generalize from our samples to the populations from which they were drawn— the superintendents and school board members of Massachusetts.

At other times, however, we shall focus attention on items rather than on people. We have argued earlier that the holistic conception of role should be abandoned in favor of a "role segments" conception. Within the context of our present interest in macroscopic consensus one of the problems is to determine whether there is more consensus on some segments of a role than on others. To generalize our findings from the analysis of this problem to a larger population of expectation items would imply that the items used were a random sample from a larger universe of expectations. This would be, of course, very difficult to demonstrate even if no known bias entered into the selection of the items and they appeared to be representative of specified "functions" of the position. This is the case because, as Louis Guttman says in his discussion of the problem of sampling items,

> Questions are *constructed* by the research worker. He selects a particular wording of the question, a particular aspect of the content to emphasize, etc., etc. It is not as if there were available a list of all possible questions and their variations from which those used in the study were drawn at random.[16]

If we ask, for example, whether superintendents have more consensus on their performances or on their attributes, it is necessary to consider the possibility that the performance items were worded ambiguously, whereas the attributes items were very clear, or one segment might contain more items that turn out to be clichés within the profession. Any or all of the items might have been phrased differently which could change the degree of consensus on any item as well as its relative position among a group of items. Therefore, when we *compare* groups of items we cannot generalize beyond our own expectation items.

Some of the problems which we have set ourselves are ones for which there are few precedents in sociological research, and consequently the methods we have adopted may strike some readers as arbitrary. Our intention is to explore certain problem areas which seem of first importance to the development of role theory. We have used whatever tools were at hand and, in cases where they were lacking, invented some of our own. Wherever it seemed reasonable we have attempted to present our analyses deductively, but where this did not appear to be a profitable procedure we did not avoid induction. The analyses which are presented have little similarity to "crucial experiments," based as they are on data gathered in diverse interview situations (although they were as uniform as possible) and on schedules designed to elicit as much information as possible about as many different facets of role definition and role behavior in as little time as possible. They should, however, provide some foundation for further research in the same general problem areas, and as well, some insights into the complexities of social relations in social systems.

Notes and References for Chapter Seven

[1] Theodore M. Newcomb, "Sociology and Psychology," in John Gillin (Editor), For a Science of Social Man (New York: The Macmillan Company, 1954), p. 255.

[2] See p. 52.

[3] See Appendix A for the instruments and items utilized to determine superintendent and school board member role definitions.

[4] Chester I. Barnard, The Functions of the Executive (Cambridge: Harvard University Press, 1938), p. 73.

[5] Cf. Talcott Parsons, "Suggestions for a Sociological Approach to the Theory of Organizations—I," Administrative Science Quarterly, I (1956), pp. 63–85; Philip Selznick, "Foundations of the Theory of Organization," Americal Sociological Review, XIII (1948), pp. 25–26; Max Weber, The Theory of Social and Economic Organization (New York: Oxford University Press, 1947); Herbert A. Simon, Administrative Behavior (New York: The Macmillan Company, 1945).

[6] Weber, op. cit.

[7] Ibid., p. 196, and pp. 330–334.

[8] See Parsons' treatment of decision making in formal organizations, Parsons, op. cit., pp. 74–80.

[9] George C. Homans, The Human Group (New York: Harcourt, Brace and Co., 1950).

[10] Parsons, op. cit.

[11] In some communities, for example, New York City and Chicago, school board members are appointed by the mayor.

[12] See pp. 72–73.

[13] It was found that similar results were obtained when using different measures of dispersion. For example, the correlation between the average deviation about the mode and the average deviation about the mean for the 137 items is .91 for the superintendent's sample and .90 for the school board member sample.

[14] The variance has a number of advantages: (1) The variance employs squared deviations, and it was felt to be desirable to magnify extreme deviations, particularly in view of the fact that the check list included variations in intensity. Differences between adjacent categories such as "absolutely must" and "preferably should" measure differences in the degree to which the role obligation is felt to be obligatory, whereas differences between nonadjacent categories appear to measure far more important conflicts of viewpoint. (2) The variance could be computed relatively easily. By using the formula $\dfrac{N(\Sigma X^2) - (\Sigma X)^2}{N^2}$ it was possible to compute the variances without actually finding the deviation scores and the sums required by the formula could be accumulated rather easily on I.B.M. equipment. (3) The variance is a statistic which lends itself easily to a variety of statistical computations and manipulations. For example, the difference in the amount of consensus on a given item for the superintendent and school board samples could be quickly determined by the F test or variance ratio, which simply utilizes the ratio of our two consensus scores. (4) The variance lends itself equally well to the measurement of macro- and microconsensus. This was not true of measures utilizing deviations about the mode, for example, for the mode is not very meaningful for very small samples.

[15] The variance scores for the Division of Labor items, which have four response categories, were adjusted to make them comparable with items in the other instruments, all of which had five response categories.

[16] Samuel A. Stouffer, et al., *Measurement and Prediction* (Princeton: Princeton University Press, 1950), p. 286.

eight

The Analysis
of Interposition Consensus

The major focus of interest in this chapter is the agreement and disagreement *between* two sets of role definers, incumbents of the superintendency position and incumbents of the school board member position. First, we shall investigate the proportion of items in each of the role definition instruments for which there are statistically significant differences between the response distributions of these two sets of role definers. These data will then be used to test a series of hypotheses which are concerned with the explanation of disagreement on role definition between incumbents of the administrator and policy-maker positions in the formal organization of the school system.

The percentage of items in each of the role definition instruments on which there is disagreement between the superintendent and school board member samples according to the chi-square criterion is presented in Table 8–A. On over one third (37 percent) of the expecta-

TABLE 8–A. PERCENTAGE OF ITEMS YIELDING SIGNIFICANT CHI-SQUARES FOR THE COMPARISON OF THE SUPERINTENDENT AND SCHOOL BOARD SAMPLES ON INDIVIDUAL ROLE DEFINITION ITEMS

		Percentage of Items for Which the Chi-Square Was Significant:		
Instrument	N	At Less than .01	Between .01 and .05	Total Less than .05
Division of Labor	13	100%	0%	100%
Superintendent Performances	37	59	11	70
Superintendent Attributes	54	54	9	63
School Board Performances	20	60	0	60
Superintendent Participations	11	27	18	45
Superintendent Friendships	15	13	13	26
All Instruments	150	54	9	63

tions items there is no significant difference. This suggests some strain toward consistency between the two samples. However, the fact that on 63 percent of the expectation items there is a significant difference between the two distributions (significant at least at the .05 level) indicates that there is a marked tendency toward disagreement between the two samples of position incumbents.

In view of the complexities, noted in Chapter Seven, that arise in the interpretation of disagreements between the samples according to the chi-square criterion, these findings require a more detailed examination. In appraising them it is relevant to ask to what extent the differences found between the superintendent sample and the school board sample reflect differences in role definition on items on which there is relatively high agreement *within* one or both of the samples. Similarly, we may question the extent to which the "strain toward consistency" (suggested by the fact that on 37 percent of the items there were no significant differences between the samples) occurs because there is high agreement *within* either or both of the samples. To answer these questions, the role definition items were classified according to the degree of consensus *within* each of the two samples. The cutting point selected was the median variance score (.395) of the distribution of variance scores obtained for all items in both samples. In Table 8–B, the role definition items have been categorized according to whether there is high or low consensus *within* each of the two samples, as well as according to whether or not there is agreement between the two samples.

TABLE 8–B. CLASSIFICATION OF ALL (150) ROLE DEFINITION ITEMS ACCORDING TO CONSENSUS WITHIN EACH OF THE SAMPLES AND ACCORDING TO WHETHER OR NOT THERE IS A SIGNIFICANT DEGREE OF DISAGREEMENT BETWEEN THE TWO SAMPLES

Disagreement *between* the Two Samples	High (H) or Low (L) Consensus *within* Each Sample				
	$H_S H_{SB}$	$H_S L_{SB}$	$L_S H_{SB}$	$L_S L_{SB}$	Total
Nonsignificant	32	9	2	16	59
Significant	26	20	3	42	91
Total	58	29	5	58	150

On sixteen of the items on which the chi-square between the two distributions is insignificant there is low consensus within both samples, suggesting that for these items, the findings can more reasonably be interpreted as indicating "lack of disagreement" rather than "agreement," and to some extent suggesting that the "strain toward consistency" interpretation is in error. Reference to Example *c* of Figure 7–4 (p. 110) will perhaps clarify this interpretation. For neither sample can it be said that there is agreement on whether or not a superintendent should "occasionally compromise with local pressure groups." To say that the insignificant chi-square obtained for this item represents agreement between the two samples would ignore the relatively low consensus within both samples. We consequently interpret the findings for this item as representing "lack of disagreement."

On another 32 items in Table 8–B on which the chi-square between the two distributions is insignificant, there is high consensus within both samples. It is perhaps only with respect to these items, comprising only 21 percent of the role definition items used in this analysis, that it would be reasonable to suggest that there is a "strain toward consistency" in the role definitions of the two samples. There are 87 items on which the superintendent's sample has relatively high consensus (columns 1 and 2), but of these, there are 46 on which there is a significant difference between the two samples. Similarly, of the 63 items on which school board members agree among themselves (columns 1 and 3), there are 29 on which they disagree with superintendents. The distribution of items in this table makes salient the suggestion that there are important differences in the way the two samples define their roles. It is consequently relevant to determine whether these disagreements on role definition represent differences in the *intensity* (or mandatoriness) with which the expectations are held, or differences in the *direction* of the expectations, that is, whether they are positive or negative.

It will be recalled that the respondents were given a choice between "absolutely must" and "preferably should" or between "absolutely must not" and "preferably should not," or the neutral category, "may or may not," for each expectation item. Do the findings which have been presented represent disagreements between the superintendent and school board member samples on the *direction* of the evaluative standards applied to position incumbents, or do they represent differences only with respect to whether the expectations are mandatory or preferential?

To investigate this problem at least two approaches were possible,[1] one of which was to combine the "absolutely" and "preferably" categories at each end of the check list and split the neutral category, "may or may not," between the two. This approach assumes that there are only two directions to the expectation, positive and negative. We chose a second approach, which was to leave the neutral category separate. In effect we took the position that there were three directions to an expectation: positive, negative, and neutral. From one point of view the response "may or may not" is not an expectation but a lack of an expectation. On the other hand it can be thought of as a midpoint between the positive and negative poles. Both approaches appear reasonable but each requires that in interpreting findings, one must constantly bear in mind the procedure used. In the accompanying analysis we have computed chi-squares for "direction only" by leaving the "may or may not" response cate-

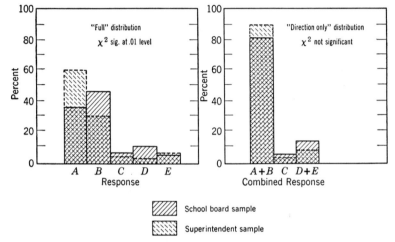

Figure 8–1. "Full" and "direction only" percentage frequency distributions of school board member and superintendent responses to the item, "refuse to recommend the dismissal of a teacher the public wants dismissed if he feels that the public complaint is invalid."

gory separate.[2] This means that a significant chi-square on direction may represent a difference between a positive or negative evaluation of the behavior or attribute, or a difference between its positive-neutral or a negative-neutral evaluation. An inspection of the response distributions in Appendix Tables A–1 through A–6 will reveal that the latter differences have a considerably greater frequency than the former.

Figure 8–1 illustrates for one item the procedure employed. In this case although the original "full distribution" chi-square was significant at the one percent level the recomputed chi-square when the effect of intensity is removed was not significant at the 5 percent level.

A comparison of the chi-squares obtained for the "full distributions" with those computed for "direction only" is found in Table 8–C. Whereas 63 percent of all the expectation items show significant

TABLE 8–C. PERCENTAGE OF ITEMS YIELDING SIGNIFICANT CHI-SQUARES FOR THE COMPARISON OF THE SUPERINTENDENT AND SCHOOL BOARD SAMPLES ON INDIVIDUAL ROLE DEFINITION ITEMS, BY "FULL DISTRIBUTION" AND BY "DIRECTION ONLY"

Instrument	N	Percentage of Items for Which the Chi-Square Was Significant at Less than .05, for:		Difference between the Percentages for "Full Distribution" and "Direction Only," %
		Full Distribution, %	Direction Only, %	
Superintendent Performances	37	70	49	21
Superintendent Attributes	54	63	46	17
Superintendent Participations	11	45	36	9
Superintendent Friendships	15	36	36	0
School Board Performances	20	60	35	25
Division of Labor*	13	100	85	15
All Instruments	150	63	46	17

* For this instrument the "Direction Only" chi-square was computed by combining category 1 with 2, and 3 with 4 (in Appendix Table A–6).

differences in the original analysis, 46 percent do so after the "absolutely" and "preferably" categories have been combined, a drop of 17 percent. This shows that to some extent differences between the two samples represent differences in intensity or mandatoriness but it also demonstrates that a majority of the differences are of a perhaps more "serious" nature.

In the last column of Table 8–C it will be seen that there are relatively fewer significant relationships lost by eliminating intensity from the Participations and Friendships Instruments than for other groups of role definition items. The responses to these items for both samples were most frequently permissive, which means that few responses tend to be in the extreme categories. Consequently for these items combining A with B and E with D has little effect. Eliminating intensity has less effect on highly permissive items and considerably more on preferential and mandatory items.

From this part of the interposition macroscopic consensus analysis the following conclusions may be drawn:

1. For 37 percent of the items, using the chi-square criterion, no differences were found between the distributions of superintendents' and school board members' responses.

2. On a large proportion of items (63 percent), however, there was a significant difference between the distributions of their responses.

3. On some of the items the difference demonstrated may be considered to be due to different degrees of intensity with which the position incumbents express their expectations, that is, the disagreement is on whether the expectation is mandatory or preferred.

4. On other items the demonstrated differences may be considered to be due to different directions of expectations, that is, the disagreement is on whether the expectation is positive, neutral, or negative.

These preliminary analyses have been concerned with the extent to which there is disagreement between two samples of role definers. In the following section, hypotheses which in part account for this disagreement will be presented and tested. The hypotheses will be concerned with the explanation of differences in the *substance* of the the expectations held by incumbents of the positions of superintendent and school board member. Having shown that there are different degrees of consensus among samples of position incumbents, our objective now is to present and empirically test explanations of why this disagreement on role definition occurs.

We have chosen to base our theoretical formulations of the problems to be considered on assumptions about formal organizations from which hypotheses may be derived concerning disagreements in role definition between incumbents of a superordinate and a subordinate position. While this may place a theoretical restriction on the generalizability of our findings, it will serve the purpose of illustrating the utility of the role concepts presented in Chapter Four for analyses in different problem areas, in this case, problems of formal organizations.

The data by means of which we will test the hypotheses were obtained from respondents who were incumbents of positions in school systems, which, we have argued, can be viewed as formal organizations. The available data can consequently provide relatively clear tests of theoretical reasoning and hypotheses concerned with formal organizations. It may be that some of the hypotheses derived are capable of generalization to incumbents of *any* position in *any* social system, but since we do not have the data by means of which to test it, we have not made this generalization. Furthermore, in the case of certain hypotheses it would have been possible to derive them on the basis of other (and perhaps simpler) assumptions, for example, with respect to psychological processes. Since there are, however, other hypotheses which are perhaps specific to formal organizations, placing this restriction on the theoretical and empirical analysis allows us to adopt and test a consistent theoretical framework for the explanation of con-

ditions leading to disagreements on role definition in both the inter-
and intraposition macroscopic consensus analyses.

In Chapter Seven we made five observations regarding the system
of social relationships in which the positions of superintendent and
school board member are involved. These were, briefly, that a school
system is a formal organization, that it has many of the characteristics
of a bureaucracy, that the school board is superordinate to the superintendent, that school systems must deal with their external environment, and that the school board represents the external system with
which the school system must deal. Given social systems with these
characteristics, what can be inferred about differences in the expectations held by incumbents of the superintendent and school board
member positions?

We shall argue that in formal organizations like public school systems there are inherent forces which tend to create disagreements
between policy makers and their administrators. Each of the hypotheses which will be presented and tested is based on certain definitions and assumptions. It is relevant to make these definitions and a
number of these assumptions explicit at the outset.

1. A formal organization is defined as a social system with "*a
primacy of orientation to the attainment of a specific goal.*" [3]

2. To achieve this goal, formal provisions must be made to break it
down into specific tasks whose achievement is delegated to incumbents
of formally established positions.

3. The achievement of the goal of the organization is contingent
on the achievement of tasks by position incumbents.

4. The general function of a position incumbent who has authority
over incumbents of other positions is to see that the particular set of
tasks for which his subordinates are responsible is accomplished and
that they contribute to the achievement of the "higher" order task (s)
for which he is himself responsible.

5. In order to achieve the task(s) for which his position has been
formally created, the incumbent of any position must make decisions
or choices among possible alternative courses of action.

6. Any decision of an incumbent of a position in a formal organization will have an effect not only on the achievement of the task(s) of
that position, but also on the achievement of "higher" and "lower"
order tasks for which incumbents of other positions are held accountable, and ultimately, on the achievement of the goal of the organization.

7. From the viewpoint of the incumbent of a particular position,
his primacy of orientation is not to the organizational goal but to the

achievement of the task(s) for which his position has been created and for which he is held accountable.

8. In order to carry out the task(s) of a position, an incumbent will feel that it is necessary to have as complete control as possible over the factors and conditions impinging on decisions for which he will be held accountable.

9. An overriding assumption which it is necessary to make in order to deduce hypotheses from these eight propositions is that incumbents of positions in formal organizations are motivated to achieve the tasks for which they are held accountable.

Definition of Superordinate-Subordinate Responsibilities in the Division of Labor. What implications can be drawn from this series of definitions and certain of these assumptions about how superordinates and subordinates will define their respective responsibilities in relationships involving the tasks for which they are each held accountable?

If the decisions of a position incumbent have an effect on the attainment of the formal task(s) of his position and the formal task(s) of his superordinate (Proposition 6) and if the superordinate and subordinate both feel it necessary to have as complete control as possible over decisions affecting their respective tasks (Proposition 8), and if both are motivated to achieve their formal tasks (Proposition 9), then it follows that:

Hypothesis 8–1: In specifying the division of responsibility between a subordinate and superordinate, incumbents of each of these positions will assign more responsibility to their own position than incumbents of the other position will assign to it.

The following characteristics of school systems relevant to the propositions from which this hypothesis has been deduced, make it possible for us to test it for the superordinate and subordinate positions of school board member and superintendent. First, the formal organizational goal of the public schools is to provide public education for children so that they may participate effectively as members of society. Second, by law the tasks of the school board are to establish the policies under which the school system will be administered and to see that the type of educational program desired by the community, of which the board members are the elected representatives, is provided in the schools. Third, the tasks of the superintendent are to administer and supervise the physical and human resources involved in the internal functioning of the school system as the chief administrative officer of the board. And fourth, decisions affecting the accomplishment of their respective tasks must be made concerning the hiring, firing, and promotion of personnel, the fiscal support to be requested of the community, textbook selection, and so on.

The responses of superintendents and school board members to the Division of Labor Instrument comprise the data with which Hypothesis 8–1 can be tested. The hypothesis would lead to the prediction that for each item in this instrument the superintendent's sample will have a higher mean response than the school board member sample since the four response categories are numbered from one through four, beginning with "this is entirely the responsibility of the school committee" (scored 1) and ending with "this is entirely the responsibility of the superintendent" (scored 4).

TABLE 8–D. DIFFERENCES BETWEEN THE MEAN RESPONSES OF SUPERINTENDENTS AND SCHOOL BOARD MEMBERS TO THE DIVISION OF LABOR ITEMS

Item*	N_{SB}	$\overline{X}_{SB}$	N_S	$\overline{X}_S$	D	C.R.	Probability Less than	Direction Predicted Correctly (+) or Incorrectly (−) According to Hypothesis 8–1
a. When a new teacher is to be hired:	504	2.98	104	3.71	0.73	13.2	.001	+
b. If a new building is needed:	476	2.61	102	3.00	0.39	5.7	.001	+
c. When a new textbook is needed:	506	3.31	103	3.85	0.54	9.8	.001	+
d. On the budget:	506	2.90	104	3.21	0.31	6.0	.001	+
e. On instructional policy:	507	2.91	104	3.10	0.19	3.6	.001	+
f. On public relations:	501	2.83	103	3.13	0.30	5.6	.001	+
g. How are teachers' grievances handled?	504	3.49	103	3.89	0.40	14.3	.001	+
h. Who handles relationships with community groups that wish to use pupils for their own purposes?	500	2.49	104	3.30	0.81	10.0	.001	+
i. When a community organization wishes to use school property, the request:	504	2.35	104	2.95	0.60	9.0	.001	+
j. Who is responsible for and supervises the maintenance necessary to keep the school plant in good operating condition?	497	2.94	104	3.44	0.50	7.0	.001	+
k. Who is responsible for the child attendance regulations?	506	3.38	104	3.71	0.33	4.6	.001	+
l. Who makes recommendations for increases in salaries of school system employees?	503	3.02	104	3.62	0.60	8.5	.001	+
m. Who initiates policy matters?	507	2.69	104	3.06	0.37	5.6	.001	+

Proportion of the items for which the direction of the difference was predicted correctly according to Hypothesis 8–1 = 13/13 = 1.00, which is significant at the 0.01 level.†

* The response categories, which differ for each item, are presented in Notes for Appendix Table A–6.
† The test of whether the number of correct predictions differs significantly from what would be expected by chance used throughout the volume was a sign test, using the table of binomial coefficients.

Table 8–D reports the mean scores for both the superintendents and school board members on each of the items in the Division of Labor Instrument. The evidence provides strong support for the hypothesis as applied to superintendents and school board members. The differences between the school board and superintendent means are consistently in the direction predicted on the basis of the hypothesis. The proportion of items correctly predicted (1.00 or 13/13) is statistically significant at the .01 level by the sign test. Furthermore, the difference between the means of the responses of superintendents and school board members for every item is statistically significant at the .001 level.

Implied in this hypothesis is a single dimension of "dominance in the assignment of responsibility" between two positions, and when it is tested with thirteen individual items, the hypothesis receives support. By deriving a Guttman scale on the basis of the combined sample of superintendents and school board members (see Appendix Table B–3a) it is possible to demonstrate whether or not the difference between superintendents and school board members predicted for individual items is also obtained with a summary measure. In Table 8–E are presented the frequency of scale scores of board members and superintendents on the Ideal Division of Labor Instrument. The difference between

TABLE 8–E. FREQUENCIES OF SCALE SCORES OF SUPERINTENDENTS AND SCHOOL BOARD MEMBERS ON THE IDEAL DIVISION OF LABOR SCALE*

	Frequency	
Scale Score	School Board Members ($N = 467$)	Superintendents ($N = 103$)
3	62	61
2	143	37
1	186	5
0	76	0
Mean Scale Score 1.41		2.54

Critical Ratio = 12.02
Probability less than .001

* This scale is described in Appendix Table B–3a.

the mean scale scores of school board members and superintendents is 1.13 which, for a range of only 4, is sizable and statistically significant at the .001 level. Since this second test is based on the same data (although differently treated), it does not provide additional evidence for Hypothesis 8–1, although it does substantiate the conclusion that superintendents and school board members differ on the dimension of "dominance in the assignment of responsibility" between their positions.

Required Degrees of Technical Competence and the Division of Responsibilities. The reasoning underlying Hypothesis 8–1 led to the conclusion that either a superordinate or subordinate will assign greater responsibility to himself than the other will assign to him.

It allowed us to predict that there would be differences in the responses of superintendents and school board members to the Division of Labor Instrument. If two additional assumptions are made, another hypothesis may be developed which is concerned with the division of responsibility between subordinates and superordinates, but which takes into account the fact that different degrees of technical competence are required for different tasks.

The starting point for deriving this hypothesis consists of the two following assumptions: The decisions made by incumbents of superordinate and subordinate positions have an effect on the achievement of each other's task(s) (Proposition 6), and incumbents of both positions are motivated to achieve their formal tasks (Proposition 9). The two additional assumptions required for this hypothesis are first, that the incumbents of both the superordinate and subordinate positions are aware that for the achievement of different tasks, different degrees of technical competence are required, and second, that incumbents of both positions recognize that although the superordinate has greater authority, he does not need the technical competence required for the achievement of the formally prescribed tasks of his subordinates. Given these two additional assumptions, the hypothesis follows that:

Hypothesis 8–2: Incumbents of both superordinate and subordinate positions will assign relatively greater responsibility to the subordinate for actions requiring greater technical competence than for actions requiring less technical competence.

To test this hypothesis the items from the Division of Labor Instrument were categorized according to an assessment of the degree of technical competence they required. Some of the items may be thought of as purely technical, such as decisions about new textbooks, instructional policy, and the administration of child attendance regulations. Others require a lesser degree of technical competence, for example, the initiation of policies, responsibility for new buildings, and general responsibility for the budget. Another group of items seems to require still less technical competence (that is, these items do not necessarily require technical competence, although this does not imply that there are no established techniques for dealing with them); public relations is one such item, and "relations with community groups who wish to use pupils for their own purposes" is another. The items are arranged in Table 8–F into the three groups of "Most Technical," "Less Technical," and "Least Technical."

With this classification, the prediction based on Hypothesis 8–2 is that each of the items classified as "Most Technical" will obtain from both the superintendent and the school board member samples a mean score larger (closer to the superintendent's end of the response category continuum) than each of the remaining items; "Least Technical" items will obtain mean scores smaller than all other items.[4]

There will be two tests of this hypothesis (one for each sample) for each category of items. There are six "Most Technical" items, each one of which will be compared with the remaining seven items in the instrument, making 42 comparisons in all for each sample. Whether or not the proportion of these comparisons which is predicted correctly is significant will be the operational test; for the "Less Technical" items there are 36 comparisons to be made, and for the "Least

TABLE 8–F. PROPORTION OF COMPARISONS OF "MOST," "LESS," AND "LEAST TECHNICAL" ITEMS FROM THE DIVISION OF LABOR INSTRUMENT FOR WHICH HYPOTHESIS 8–2 LED TO THE CORRECT PREDICTIONS IN THE SCHOOL BOARD MEMBER AND SUPERINTENDENT SAMPLES

Category of Items	School Board Member Sample		Superintendent Sample	
	Proportion	Probability Less than	Proportion	Probability Less than
Most Technical (Items a, c, e, g, j, and k of Table 8–D)	39/42 = .93	.01	37/42 = .88	.01
Less Technical (Items b, d, l, and m of Table 8–D)	31/36 = .86	.01	28/36 = .78	.01
Least Technical (Items f, h, and i of Table 8–D)	28/30 = .93	.01	23/30 = .77	.01

Technical," 30 comparisons. In Table 8–F is presented for each sample and each category of items the proportion of comparisons for which the hypothesis led to the correct prediction. These findings provide significant support for the hypothesis, in the case of each set of comparisons at least at the .01 level.

It is perhaps worth commenting on the fact that we have tested the second hypothesis with six separate (but not independent) tests. It was felt to be necessary to make separate tests for the two samples because of the possibility that the means of one sample would tend to confirm the hypothesis whereas those of the other did not. The same can be said of the categories of items, even though the sign tests for each category are not independent of one another; it would have been possible to confirm the hypothesis for the "Most Technical" items, within a sample, when neither of the other two categories received confirmation, because only one of the two sets of comparisons is common to any two of the tests for the separate categories. Given confirmation on two categories, however, the third will be necessarily confirmed. As it happened, with our data it made little difference, since all of the sign tests are significant.

Obligations to Incumbents of Counter Positions. In carrying out their tasks position incumbents in formal organizations must deal with incumbents, not of all, but of only *certain* counter positions. These counter positions may be involved in the formal organization or not, as for example, customers with whom a salesman must deal directly who are not in the formal organization in which the salesman is employed. Since incumbents of different positions in formal organizations are held accountable for different tasks (Proposition 2) this assumption leads to the conclusion that they will deal directly with incumbents of different counter positions.

Under these conditions, the following reasoning leads to an hypothesis which is concerned with different degrees of expressed obligation to incumbents of different counter positions. If incumbents of two positions deal directly with incumbents of different counter positions, and it is also assumed that in order to carry out their tasks position incumbents must maintain positive relationships with those with whom they deal directly, then, because the primacy of orientation of position incumbents is to the achievement of their own tasks (Proposition 7) and they are motivated to achieve these tasks (Proposition 9), the hypothesis follows that:

Hypothesis 8–3: In specifying the obligations of an incumbent of any position (A) in a formal organization to the incumbents of a counter position (B), incumbents of positions in the organization who deal directly with incumbents of this counter position (B) will specify a greater degree of obligation of A to B than will incumbents of positions who do not deal directly with incumbents of this counter position.

It was pointed out earlier that one of the tasks of the school board is to see that the type of education desired by the community is provided in the school system. The achievement of this task requires that school board members, as their elected representatives, must deal directly with community members. Community member then, may be thought of as a counter position with the incumbents of which school board members must deal directly in carrying out their formally prescribed tasks. The primary tasks of the superintendent are to administer and supervise the physical and human resources involved in the *internal* functioning of the school system, so that he need not deal directly with community members, even though, in carrying out subsidiary functions, such as public relations, he may.

School superintendents must, however, deal directly with the school staff in carrying out their prescribed tasks. Furthermore, since the superintendent intervenes in the line of authority between the teachers and the school board, it can be said that the board need not deal directly with incumbents of the counter position of teacher. These are two counter positions which can be used in a test of this "obligations to different counter positions" hypothesis. School board members are required to deal directly with community members, whereas superintendents are not; superintendents are required to deal directly with teachers, whereas school board members are not.

A third counter position which may be used in a test of Hypothesis 8-3 is that of "professional educator" outside the local school system. In order to carry out their administrative tasks effectively, superintendents must have certain technical skills which are ordinarily acquired through formal training in institutions of higher education, through experience in other administrative positions, and through association with other superintendents in associations of professional educators. Furthermore, in order to maintain their skills at the highest possible level, superintendents must continually associate with their fellow professionals. We will say, consequently, that in order to carry out effectively their formally prescribed tasks, superintendents must deal directly with incumbents of the counter position of "other professional educator." Since school board members are not required to perform technical administrative tasks, they need not deal directly with incumbents of this counter position.

In order to test the hypothesis, items from the Superintendents and School Board Members Performances Instruments were used which could be interpreted as dealing with "obligations" to incumbents of the three counter positions of "Community Member," "Teacher," and "Professional Educator." These items are presented under their appropriate categorization in Table 8–G. The predictions are that superintendents' responses, on the average, will reflect a greater felt obligation to teachers and other professional educators, than do school board members' responses, and that school board members' responses will reflect a greater felt obligation to local community members than do superintendents' responses.

Whether or not a particular response to an item reflects more or less felt obligation to the incumbent of the counter position to which the item refers depends on the phrasing of the item. It will consequently be helpful to illustrate the prediction to which the hypothesis leads for one item from each group. Item 1 in Table 8–G is (should the superintendent) "Favor local firms in awarding school contracts, even though this may increase public expenses somewhat." To select "absolutely must" from the response categories for this item implies the strongest felt obligation to "members of the local community," and consequently, on the basis of our hypothesis we would predict that the school board sample would obtain a lower mean response (that is, closer to the "absolutely must" end of the continuum) than would the superintendents' sample. The superintendents' sample should obtain a lower mean on item 7, "Write articles for professional journals," since the response "absolutely must" implies the strongest degree of felt obligation to "professional educators." Similarly, the superintendents' sample should obtain a lower mean on item 11, "Refuse to recommend the dismissal of a teacher the public wants dismissed, if he feels that the public complaint is invalid," since an "absolutely must" response to this item implies the strongest degree of felt obligation to "teachers."

A sign test was used as the test of the hypothesis, and the results are presented in Table 8–G. The results of this test support the hypothesis; the direction of the difference between the means of the superintendents and the school board members samples was predicted correctly for 13 of the 16 items, and this proportion (.81) is significant at the .05 level.

Task Orientations to Different External Systems. The assumptions and definitions from which the hypotheses we have so far examined were derived, have been restricted to aspects of the *internal* functioning of formal organizations. By introducing the ideas that (1) formal organizations are subsystems within larger systems (for example, a school system is a subsystem within the community) and (2) that position incumbents in one formal organization are also members of other social systems, we may proceed with the development of an hypothesis leading to the prediction of additional differences in role definition between the incumbents of two positions in a formal organization.

If it is assumed that members of two different social systems external to a formal organization interpret its organizational goal differently, and that in order to carry out their assigned tasks incumbents of different positions in a formal organization identify with members of, or are themselves members of, these two external systems, and since the tasks of incumbents of each position in a formal or-

TABLE 8–G. DIFFERENCES BETWEEN THE MEAN RESPONSES OF SUPERINTEND-
ENTS AND SCHOOL BOARD MEMBERS TO ITEMS DESCRIBING OBLIGATIONS TO
INCUMBENTS OF THE COUNTER POSITIONS OF "COMMUNITY MEMBER," "PRO-
FESSIONAL EDUCATOR," AND "TEACHER"

Item and Response Category Reflecting Greatest Obligation to Incumbents of Counter Position*	N_{SB}	$\overline{X}_{SB}$	N_S	$\overline{X}_S$	D	C.R.	Probability Less than	Direction Predicted Correctly (+) or Incorrectly (−) According to Hypothesis 8–3
Community Member Counter Position								
1. Favor local firms in the awarding of school contracts even though this may increase school expenses somewhat. (A)	494	3.59	105	3.66	.07	0.7	not sig.	+
2. Give consideration to local values or feelings regarding race, religion, national origin, in filling vacant teaching positions. (A)	507	3.14	105	3.33	.19	1.4	not sig.	+
3. Fight continuously against any local attacks on educational principles or methods which he knows are sound. (E)	507	1.60	105	1.23	.32	4.7	.001	+
4. Occasionally compromise with local pressure groups. (A)	505	3.58	105	3.30	.28	2.6	.01	−
5. Take a definite stand against any unreasonable demands which may come from local taxpayers. (E)	507	2.02	105	1.36	.66	9.3	.001	+
6. A committee not afraid to take stands regarding education in advance of community thinking. (E)	506	1.54	105	1.63	.09	1.3	not sig.	−
Professional Educator Counter Position								
7. Write articles for professional journals which will be of benefit to others in the profession. (A)	507	2.36	105	2.28	.08	1.4	not sig.	+
8. Read most of the professional journals. (A)	507	1.97	105	1.91	.06	1.1	not sig.	+
9. Work on committees sponsored by the state department of education and professional organizations. (A)	507	2.33	105	1.95	.38	7.5	.001	+
10. Cooperate willingly with researchers who are attempting to advance knowledge in his field. (A)	507	1.68	105	1.69	.01	0.2	not sig.	−
Teacher Counter Position								
11. Refuse to recommend the dismissal of a teacher the public wants dismissed if he feels that the public complaint is invalid. (A)	505	1.98	105	1.61	.37	3.4	.001	+
12. Consult with staff members about filling vacant teaching positions. (A)	507	2.34	105	1.99	.35	4.7	.001	+
13. Defend his teachers from attack when they try to present the pros and cons of various controversial social and political issues. (A)	505	2.03	105	1.44	.59	6.7	.001	+
14. Help his teachers to get higher salaries. (A)	506	2.36	105	1.60	.76	11.3	.001	+
15. Make curriculum changes without consulting the teaching staff. (E)	506	3.97	105	4.37	.40	5.0	.001	+
16. Help the school committee resist demands by teachers for higher salaries. (E)	502	3.11	105	3.85	.74	8.3	.001	+

Proportion of the items for which the direction of the difference was predicted correctly according to Hypothesis 8–3 = 13/16 = 0.81, which is significant at the .05 level.

---

* The response categories and their numerical equivalents used in computing means were:
    A = Absolutely must = 1   D = Preferably should not = 4
    B = Preferably should = 2   E = Absolutely must not = 5
    C = May or may not = 3

ganization contribute to the organizational goal (Proposition 2) and the primacy of orientation of position incumbents is to the achievement of their own tasks (Proposition 7), and since position incumbents are motivated to achieve their assigned tasks (Proposition 9), then the hypothesis follows that:

Hypothesis 8–4: Incumbents of different positions in a formal organization who identify with members or are themselves members of different external systems which interpret the organizational goal differently will express expectations for incumbents of any position within the formal organization which are influenced by their different identification or membership.

As with the preceding hypotheses, this is a statement of a quite general relationship. In order to test it, it is necessary to identify, in addition to the positions in the formal organization, the external systems to which the formal organization is related. The school system is part of the community, which may be thought of as a system not only external to the school system, but one which includes it. The community has a number of functions or goals in addition to the goal of the school system. In a sense, the organizational goal of the school system, when viewed in the context of the community, becomes a "task" whose achievement contributes to a broader community "goal." We might reasonably conclude that community members would define the goal of the school system as subsidiary to the broader "community goal." In reaching decisions about financial matters, for example, we would infer that community members would consider the *relative* importance of education among the many services for which they are taxed. Since school board members are elected representatives of the community and because of the nature of their formally prescribed tasks, we would also infer that school board members are more likely than superintendents to identify with community members in reaching decisions.

Another system which is external to the school system is one which was mentioned in the discussion of the preceding hypothesis: association(s) of professional educators. It seems reasonable to infer that associations of professional educators would define the organizational goal of a school system differently from community members, if for no other reason than that they are comprised of professional educators whose vocation is education. In financial matters, it could be inferred that professional educators would give less consideration to other goals of a community than community members themselves. Education is of *primary* importance to professional educators, rather than of relative importance among the various functions of a community. Superintendents are not only more likely than school board members to identify with professional educators but are very likely to be members of their associations.

Having identified elements by means of which Hypothesis 8–4 can be tested, we must establish a specific prediction on the basis of them. Superintendents are more likely to identify with professional educators who define the organizational goal of school systems without primary reference to other community objectives, whereas school board members are more likely to identify with community members, who define the organizational goal of the school system as subsidiary to more general community goals. The prediction which is based on this reasoning and which will serve as a test of Hypothesis 8–4, is that superintendents will express expectations which reflect a greater willingness to appropriate money for education than those expressed by school board members.

To test this prediction, four items may be interpreted as measuring the degree of willingness to appropriate money for education. Since there are only four items appropriate for this test, a sign test could not be used. Even four correct predictions cannot be considered significantly different from what would be expected by chance. Consequently we will consider that we have four separate tests of the hypothesis. When the mean of the superintendents' responses is compared with the mean of the school board members' responses, it should be larger or closer to the "absolutely must not" response category (E) in the case of items 1 and 3, and smaller or closer to the "absolutely must" response category (A) for items 2 and 4. The

TABLE 8–H. DIFFERENCES BETWEEN THE MEAN RESPONSES OF SUPERINTENDENTS AND SCHOOL BOARD MEMBERS TO ITEMS REFLECTING DEGREES OF "WILLINGNESS TO APPROPRIATE MONEY"

Item and Response Category Reflecting Greatest "Willingness to Appropriate Money"	N_{SB}	$\overline{X}_{SB}$	N_S	$\overline{X}_S$	D	C.R.	Probability Less than	Direction Predicted Correctly (+) or Incorrectly (−) According to Hypothesis 8–4
1. In drawing up the budget, cost factors are given greater consideration than educational needs. (E)	505	4.04	105	4.19	.15	1.6	.052	+
2. Help his teachers to get higher salaries. (A)	506	2.36	105	1.60	.76	11.3	.001	+
3. Help the school committee resist demands by teachers for higher salaries. (E)	502	3.11	105	3.85	.74	8.3	.001	+
4. Take a definite stand against any unreasonable demands which may come from local taxpayers. (A)	507	2.02	105	1.36	.66	9.3	.001	+

results of this analysis are presented in Table 8–H. On each of the four items the mean of the superintendents' responses reflects a greater willingness to appropriate money for education than does the mean of the school board responses. The difference between the two sample means is statistically significant on the last three items at the .001 level. The first, since the level of significance is so close to the .05 level (.052), will be interpreted, with the last three, as evidence in support of the hypothesis.

Differences in the Definition of the Line of Authority. It is possible to deduce from the original propositions that there will be differences between superordinates and subordinates in their definition of the line of authority among incumbents of their own positions and positions adjacent to them in the hierarchy of the formal organization in which they occur. By definition, a formal organization contains a hierarchy of authority, and therefore, except for incumbents of the position at its apex, every position incumbent is directly responsible to incumbents of a superordinate position. The general function of any superordinate is to see that the tasks for which his subordinates are responsible are accomplished and that they contribute to the higher order task(s) for which he is himself responsible (Proposition 4).

If a position incumbent's primary orientation is to the achievement of his own task(s) (Proposition 7), and he feels it is necessary to have as complete control as possible over the factors and conditions impinging on decisions for which he is held accountable (Proposition 8), and it is assumed that communication between a position incumbent's subordinates and superordinates, or a by-pass of his position, will detract from this control, and he is motivated to achieve his tasks (Proposition 9), then the hypothesis follows that:

Hypothesis 8–5: In defining the line of authority in a formal organization, position incumbents will be less likely to accept or more likely to reject a by-pass of their own position than are position incumbents, whether subordinates or superordinates, who participate in the by-pass.

This hypothesis leads to the predictions that superintendents will be less likely than school board members to accept (or more likely to reject) by-passes in the line of authority involving communication between the school board and the superintendent's subordinates (teachers and other school staff), and that school board members will be less likely to accept than superintendents by-passes which involve communication between the superintendent and the school board's superordinates (the community members).

In order to test this hypothesis nine items were used, each of which is considered to be measuring the degree of approval (or acceptance) of a by-pass of either the superintendent or the school board. Although some of these nine are clearly descriptive of by-passes, that is, communication between nonadjacent positions, others are only implicative of such communication, and for the inclusion of these it is necessary to present an explanation.

The first four items of Table 8–I are used to evaluate superintendents' and school board members' feelings about by-passes of superintendents. The first two would seem quite clearly descriptive of by-passes of the superintendent. The four response categories of the first item (from the Division of Labor Instrument) extend from "Teachers always bring their grievances directly to the school committee members," to "Teachers always bring their grievances to the school committee through the superintendent." The first response category describes a by-pass of the superintendent, and the fourth describes an adherence to the line of authority. The prediction on this item is that superintendents will obtain a mean response closer to the fourth response category than will school board members. The prediction for the second item is that superintendents will obtain a higher mean response, that is, closer to the "absolutely must not," category. It is felt that little defense is needed of these two items.

The third item (should the school board) "Appoint only teachers nominated by the superintendent?" does require defense, since it is only implicative of a possible by-pass. Parenthetically, the responses of both samples are somewhat peculiar since this is a legally prescribed obligation of school board members; it is against the law for them to do anything else. Only 53 out of 105 superintendents said "absolutely must," to this item, and only 113 out of 508 school board members gave this response. There were 112 school board members who said either "preferably should not" or "absolutely must not." This suggests that legal prescriptions do not always completely define obligations with which position incumbents are faced. How is this item implicative of a by-pass of the superintendent? If the school board appoints a teacher whom the superintendent has not nominated this detracts from the control he has over the characteristics or qualities of his staff. Furthermore, in appointing someone whom the superintendent has not nominated, the school board is communicating with a teacher (in a sense) against his advice. Although they may not be actually by-passing the superintendent, they are by-pass-ing his advice and one of his legally prescribed functions. This item is used with the understanding that it does not describe the same kind of by-pass as the others but one for which the same arguments would hold.

The fourth item of the "superintendents' by-pass" items, is (should the superintendent) "Accept full responsibility for the decisions of his subordinates?" We think this question may be interpreted as asking whether or not the superintendent *himself* should do some-thing which could result in a by-pass *of himself*. The item does not describe a by-pass but a situation or action which could lead to a by-pass. If the superintendent does not accept full responsibility for the decisions of his subordinates (presumably responsibility to the board), he is in a sense stepping outside the line of authority and allowing his subordinates to assume this responsibility directly. While the action described in the item is not a by-pass, it seems to imply a possible by-pass and is therefore considered appropriate in a test of the hypothesis.

The last five items in Table 8–I deal with by-passes of the school board. The first of these (item 5), if paraphrased to read "Should the board intervene between the community and the superintendent," can be interpreted as a by-pass item, since a negative response ("pref-erably should not" or "absolutely must not") implies that the board would, like the superintendent in item 4, step outside the line of authority and allow for the possibility of a by-pass.

Item 6 (should the superintendent) "Keep his office open at all times to all community members?" implies a by-pass (rather than describes one), because if the superintendent does this, he allows the community members direct access to him rather than access only through the board. Both items 7 and 8 are "public relations" func-tions which are descriptive of by-passes of the board by the super-intendent since he would be communicating with the community directly rather than through the board. Whether or not this is with the board's approval is irrelevant, just as it would be irrelevant to the interpretation of item 2 whether or not the superintendent ap-proved of the board's giving orders directly to his subordinates. They are both by-passes because they describe communication be-tween nonadjacent positions, not because someone does or does not approve.

Item 9 describes communication between the superintendent and a special category of community members and is considered a by-pass even though it might be strange under some circumstances to expect the superintendent actually to urge people to run for the board by asking the board to do it for him. It is a by-pass, for which, according to the hypothesis, we would predict that school board members will obtain a higher mean (that is, closer to the "absolutely must not" category) than will superintendents.

The test of the predictions for these nine items is a sign test, the results of which are presented in Table 8–I. The probability of

TABLE 8–I. DIFFERENCES BETWEEN THE MEAN RESPONSES OF SUPERINTENDENTS AND SCHOOL BOARD MEMBERS TO "LINE OF AUTHORITY" ITEMS

Item and Response Category Reflecting Greatest Willingness to By-pass the Line of Authority	N_{SB}	$\overline{X}_{SB}$	N_S	$\overline{X}_S$	D	C.R.	Probability Less than	Direction Predicted Correctly (+) or Incorrectly (−) According to Hypothesis 8–5
By-pass of Superintendent								
1. How are teachers' grievances handled? (School board dominance) *	504	3.49	103	3.89	.40	14.3	.001	+
2. Give directions directly to the superintendent's subordinates. (A)	507	4.52	105	4.86	.34	5.5	.001	+
3. Appoint only teachers nominated by the superintendent. (E)	507	2.47	105	1.51	.96	13.5	.001	+
4. Accept full responsibility for the decisions of his subordinates. (E)	507	2.04	105	1.88	.16	1.6	not sig.	+
By-pass of School Board								
5. Protect the superintendent from community pressures. (E)	507	1.75	105	2.00	.25	2.9	.01	+
6. Keep his office open to all community members at all times. (A)	506	1.80	105	1.70	.10	1.0	not sig.	+
7. Establish regular channels of communication with local newspapers. (A)	506	2.08	105	1.59	.49	7.5	.001	+
8. Speak to all major civic groups at least once a year. (A)	506	2.39	105	2.37	.02	0.3	not sig.	+
9. Urge people whom he respects to run for the school committee. (A)	507	3.65	105	3.57	.08	0.7	not sig.	+

Proportion of the items for which the direction of the difference was predicted correctly according to Hypothesis 8–5 = 9/9 = 1.00, which is significant at the 0.01 level.

* The response categories for this item, from the Division of Labor Instrument, are given in Appendix A–6. The "school board dominance" response category is scored 1, and the "superintendent dominance" category scored 4.

predicting all nine items correctly by chance is less than .01, and the evidence can therefore be said to support the hypothesis.

Although only one test of this hypothesis has been made, it should perhaps be remarked that it has been tested for the incumbents of two positions, for which by-passes are considerably different in kind. In general, it can be said that both samples disapprove of by-passes of superintendents, superintendents more strongly than school board members. Of the by-pass of two school board items (5 and 9) both samples disapprove, school board members more strongly than superintendents, whereas on the remaining three (6, 7, and 8) both samples approve of the by-passes, superintendents more strongly than school board members. Despite this variability in the kinds of by-pass (or implied by-pass) and in the general feelings of the respondents (as revealed by the means of both samples), the difference between the two samples is consistently as predicted on the basis of the general hypothesis.

The Direct Relevance of Expectations to the Role Definers' Relationship. The preceding hypotheses were developed in order to explain differences in role definition of incumbents of positions in formal organizations. Another macroscopic problem which was explored was differential agreement on role segments. That is, on what grounds might it be argued that the two samples would tend to have greater agreement on certain sets of expectation items than on others. In searching for possible explanations of some of these differences which are differences between sets of *items,* we decided to proceed inductively. A number of classifications of the items were made, but any subclassification within instruments had to depend on so few items that we felt little confidence could be placed in any conclusions which were suggested. However, one classification of the items of the Superintendent Performances Instrument taken together with the differences among the instruments themselves, suggested a hypothesis similar to one Speier had developed earlier from an examination of data reported in *The American Soldier.*[5] Speier's hypothesis is that ". . . the difference between opinions on the same subject matter expressed by groups high or low in power, privilege, or prestige will increase as the subject matter is more closely and directly related to the status characteristics and relations of the group."[6]

This hypothesis may be rephrased to deal with consensus on expectations rather than differences of opinion and examined with our data: The more direct the relevance of an expectation to the relationship of incumbents of superordinate-subordinate positions, the less consensus there will be on the expectation between incumbents of those positions, or, the relationship relevance of an expectation is inversely related to consensus between incumbents of positions in a subordinate-superordinate relationship.

Table 8–A (page 116) orders the role definition instruments according to the proportion of items on which there is disagreement between the two samples. The Division of Labor Instrument, on which 100 percent of the item chi-squares are significant, is the one instrument which is comprised exclusively of items directly concerned with the *relationship* between the superintendent and the school board; this instrument is concerned with an integral aspect of their relationship—the division of responsibilities between them. At the other extreme is the Friendships Instrument, on which only 26 percent of the items are significant. With the exception of "school board member" the items of this instrument have virtually nothing to do with the superintendent-school board relationship. The items of the Participations Instrument, which has the next fewest significant chi-squares (45 percent) may be considered peripheral to the relationship but not so peripheral as the Friendships Instrument, because participation in community affairs has definite "public relations" implications for the school system and therefore more implications than a superintendent's friendships for the relationship between the school system's administrator and his board of directors. The Attributes and the two Performances Instruments which fall between these extremes on the percentage of significant chi-squares, are clearly much more relevant to the superintendent-school board relationship than either the Participations or Friendships Instruments, and because they are only in part *directly* concerned with that relationship, not so relevant as the Division of Labor Instrument. This ordering of the role definition instruments on the dimension of the degree of relevance to the superintendent-school board relationship supports the hypothesis that the more directly concerned expectations are with relationship between the incumbents of two positions, the less agreement there will be between them.

This same hypothesis can be examined with a subcategorization of items from the Superintendent Performances Instrument. Thirty-one of the thirty-seven items from this instrument may be categorized according to who is the recipient of the behavior specified by the item. The categories are the School Board, the Staff, the Community, and the Profession. In Table 8–J are presented the percentages of items in each of these categories on which there is a significant chi-square between the superintendent and school board member distributions.

There is least agreement on items for which the school board and the staff are the recipients (100 percent in both cases). We may make a direct comparison between the school board as the recipient of the superintendent's behavior and the Division of Labor Instrument: In both of these the relationship between the superintendent and the school board is of direct concern. The staff, which would include all under the aegis of the superintendent and school board, is also a categorization of direct concern to this relationship; the school board is the legal employer of all school staff, and the superintendent is their administrator. What the superintendent does in relation to the staff is of direct importance to the board, and therefore, of direct relevance to the relationship between the board and the superintendent. At the other extreme, the "profession" (that is, the superin-

TABLE 8–J. PERCENTAGE OF ITEMS FROM THE SUPERINTENDENT PERFORMANCES INSTRUMENT YIELDING SIGNIFICANT CHI-SQUARES FOR THE COMPARISON OF THE SUPERINTENDENT AND SCHOOL BOARD SAMPLES ON INDIVIDUAL ITEMS CATEGORIZED ACCORDING TO WHO IS THE "RECIPIENT OF THE BEHAVIOR"

Recipient of the Behavior	N	Percentage of Items for Which the Chi-Square Was Significant at Less than .05
1. School Committee (Items 1, 3, 16, 19, 25, and 35 of Appendix Table A–1.)	6	100%
2. Staff (Items 5, 8, 10, 14, 20, 23, and 30 of Appendix Table A–1.)	7	100
3. Community (Items 4, 6, 11, 12, 15, 17, 22, 24, 27, 28, 29, 31, and 33 of Appendix Table A–1.)	13	77
4. Profession (Items 7, 9, 21, 34, and 37 of Appendix Table A–1.)	5	20

tendent's professional associates) is the category on which there are fewest significant chi-squares, or most agreement. The "profession" is not directly involved in the school system and is related, like the individuals specified by the items from the Friendships Instrument, solely to the superintendent. The category of the "community" as recipient has 77 percent of its items significant and may be considered more relevant to the relationship between the superintendent and school board than the "profession" because the community is directly concerned in the functioning of the particular school system, but less relevant than either the staff or the school board.

These analyses suggest that there tends to be less agreement between incumbents of two positions on items which are of direct relevance to their relationship than there is on items which are only indirectly relevant. It must be noted, however, that these analyses are open to a number of possibly valid criticisms. In the analysis based on the Superintendent Performances Instrument there are relatively few items in each of the "recipient of the behavior" categories. In the analysis involving all the role definition instruments the Division of Labor Instrument is not formally comparable to the others. And in this analysis, too, it can be shown that the relationship depends in part on the frequency with which the neutral category is used as a response category. That is, the finding is inconclusive insofar as positive or negative responses tend to prevail over neutral ones in proportion to relevance.

These limitations clearly indicate that our findings must be viewed as suggestive. Since this hypothesis is, however, one that appears to be contrary to "common sense" and certain important theoretical notions, it is suggested that it be subjected to rigorous theoretical and empirical analysis.

Summary. In this chapter some exploratory steps have been made in the analysis of macroscopic role consensus between incumbents of two positions. The general objectives were to examine consensus between samples of incumbents of the positions of superintendent and school board member and to test certain hypotheses concerning differences in role definition of incumbents of different positions in formal organizations.

On a sizable proportion (37 percent) of the role definition items used in this analysis there were no significant differences between the distributions of expectation responses of school board members and superintendents. On the majority of items (63 percent) there were significant differences between the two samples. On 46 percent, the differences could be attributed to differences in the "direction" with which incumbents of the two positions expressed their expectations. On still another group of items the differences between the two samples could be attributed to the "intensity" with which the expectations were held when the "direction" was eliminated.

In approaching the question of why there is disagreement on role definition between incumbents of two positions in a formal organization, a series of propositions describing characteristics of formal organizations were presented, on the basis of which five hypotheses were derived. The first of these led to the prediction that school board members and superintendents, in defining the division of responsibilities between their two positions, would each assign greater responsibility than the other to his own position. This hypothesis was supported. Another hypothesis concerned with the division of responsibilities which received significant support led to the prediction that superintendents and school board members would assign more responsibility to the superintendent's position for actions requiring greater technical competence, and less for actions requiring less technical competence.

A third hypothesis which was based on these propositions led to the prediction that, because of their different tasks, superintendents and school board members would express expectations which reflected a greater degree of felt obligation to incumbents of different counter positions. This prediction was confirmed for the counter position of "community member" to whom school board members felt more obligated than superintendents, for the counter position of "teacher" to whom superintendents felt more obligated than school board members, and for "professional educator," to whom superintendents also felt more obligated than school board members.

Similar reasoning led to a fourth hypothesis on the basis of which the prediction was made that superintendents would be more willing to appropriate money for education than are school board members. This hypothesis was also supported by the data.

A fifth hypothesis based on these formal propositions was that incumbents of two positions adjacent in the hierarchy of a formal organization would express different expectations about "by-passes" in the line of authority. This led to the prediction that school board members would be more likely than superintendents to accept by-passes of the superintendent, and superintendents more likely than school board members to accept by-passes of the school board. This prediction also received support from the data for by-passes of both kinds, even though certain "by-pass of superintendent" items used in the test of the hypothesis dealt with what may be considered to be "public relations" activities of the superintendent.

A final analysis attempted to account for some of the variability in the degree of consensus between the incumbents of the two positions *on different role segments*. An hypothesis was suggested concerning consensus and different degrees of direct relevance of the segments to the relationship between incumbents of superordinate and subordinate positions.

These hypotheses and analyses have all been concerned with expectations of incumbents of two different positions. A set of problems which will be explored in the next chapter is implicit in the fact of variability in role definition among the incumbents of the same position. The general working hypothesis on the basis of which the analyses of both between position macroscopic consensus and within position macroscopic consensus was predicated is of the variability in the expectations of position incumbents. Having explored between position consensus, our next task is to demonstrate, examine, and in part account for variability in the expectations expressed by incumbents of the *same* position.

Notes and References for Chapter Eight

[1] This discussion does not apply to the items in the Division of Labor Instrument. These have a *four* part check list which ranges, in general terms, from superintendent dominance to school board dominance. For these items intensity was eliminated by combining category 1 with 2, and 3 with 4. (See Notes for Appendix Table A–6).

[2] It should be pointed out that when the chi-squares were computed for the "full distributions" it was sometimes necessary to combine categories because of the small expected frequencies for some of the cells. They are "full distributions" in the sense that maximum use was made of the data. Furthermore, in some of the "direction only" computations category *C* ("may or may not") was combined with *AB* or with *DE* for the same reason.

[3] Talcott Parsons, "Suggestions for a Sociological Approach to the Theory of Organizations–I" *Administrative Science Quarterly,* I (1956), p. 64.

[4] The prediction for the "Less Technical" items is that they will obtain a mean score *larger* than the "Least Technical" and a mean score *smaller* than the "Most Technical" items.

[5] Samuel A. Stouffer et al., *The American Soldier,* I and II (Princeton: Princeton University Press, 1949).

[6] Hans Speier, "The American Soldier and the Sociology of Military Organization," in Robert K. Merton and Paul F. Lazarsfeld (Editors), *Continuities in Social Research* (Glencoe: The Free Press, 1950), p. 124.

nine

The Analysis
of Intraposition Consensus

The extent of variability in the role definitions of incumbents of the same position is a phenomenon that has received slight theoretical or empirical treatment in the social sciences. The purpose of this chapter is to explore this area. Using the method to measure macroscopic intraposition consensus described in Chapter Seven, we shall first present the frequency distributions of the intraposition consensus scores on each of the role definition instruments for the two sets of role definers of this study, the 105 superintendents and the 508 school board members. These data will then be used in the examination of a number of intraposition consensus problems.

Preliminary Observations. The percentage frequency distributions of the intraposition consensus scores (variance scores, high consensus equals low variance) on the six role definition instruments for both the superintendent and school board member samples are presented in Figure 9–1. The seventh distribution includes the variance scores of all items from all six instruments for each of the samples.

Several preliminary observations may be made regarding these distributions. First, they provide support for the basic working hypothesis that there are different amounts of consensus on different expectation items within each sample of role definers. For each role segment and for all role segments combined there is clear indication of variability in the degrees of consensus on different expectation items among each of the two sets of role definers. Second, there is a greater dispersion of variance scores for both samples on the Superintendent and School Board Member Performances Instruments (*b* and *c*) than there is on the Attributes, Participations, and Friendships Instruments (*d*, *e*, and *f*). Third, it may be observed that whereas the distributions of the two sets of variance scores tend to parallel each other closely for five of the six role definition instruments, on the Division of Labor Instrument there is a marked difference between them. A comparison of these two distributions (Figure 9–1, *a*) indicates that for items of the Division of Labor role segment there is in general less consensus among school board mem-

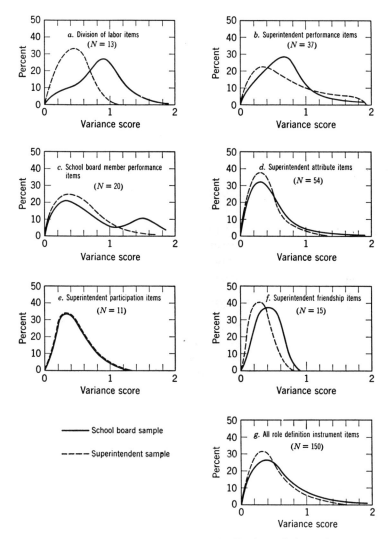

Figure 9–1. Smoothed percentage frequency distributions of the variance scores of the school board and superintendent samples on the items of six role definition instruments.

bers than among superintendents. Fourth, although there are no items on which there is perfect consensus among superintendents or school board members (that is, items with a variance score of zero) neither are there any items on which there is a *complete* absence of agreement.[1]

The objectives of the remainder of this chapter are to present and test hypotheses which will account for the different expectations of incumbents of the same position.

Differences between the Samples on Intraposition Consensus. The first analysis to be undertaken with the intraposition consensus data is directed to the question: Among which of the two sets of role definers, the 105 superintendents or the 508 school board members, will there be greater consensus on their role definitions?

If we make two assumptions, a general hypothesis may be derived which would embrace this specific question. The first concerns the socialization process or type of training required for incumbents of different positions in formal organizations of the same type. In hospitals, both nurses and internes must undergo long and highly similar training programs before they can occupy their respective positions. For the incumbents of certain other positions in the hospital, for example, a member of the board of trustees or an elevator operator, there is usually no formal or systematic training required. In other groups of formal organizations with the same primary organizational goals, for example, business firms or school systems, differences in the socialization prerequisites for becoming an incumbent of different positions are also found. This is the basis for the first assumption: Incumbents of some positions in formal organizations of the same type undergo a more homogeneous process of socialization prior to position incumbency than do incumbents of other positions. The second assumption is that the greater the homogeneity in the training required of incumbents for occupancy of a particular position, the more similar will be the standards on which they evaluate the incumbents of their own or related positions in the organization.

From these two assumptions it follows that:

Hypothesis 9–1: In specifying the expectations applicable to an incumbent of any position in formal organizations of the same type, incumbents of one position in these organizations who have had a more homogeneous preparation for occupancy of their position than incumbents of another position, will have greater consensus than incumbents of the other position.

In order to test this hypothesis with our data it is necessary to establish that incumbents of one of the positions of superintendent or school board member have had a more similar preparation for their position incumbency than have incumbents of the other position. School board members, as elected representatives of the community, undergo no formal preparation before they become incumbents of the school board member position. Superintendents, on the other hand, undergo highly similar training programs before they can assume their occupational position.

For our two samples, the hypothesis can be tested with the prediction that there will be more consensus on role definition among superintendents than among school board members. Operationally we would predict for each item of the six instruments used in this analysis that the superintendency sample will obtain a smaller variance score (higher consensus) than will the school board sample. The results of this operational test are presented in Table 9–A.

TABLE 9–A. THE PROPORTION OF ITEMS FROM SIX ROLE DEFINITION INSTRUMENTS FOR WHICH THE SUPERINTENDENT SAMPLE HAS A SMALLER VARIANCE SCORE THAN THE SCHOOL BOARD MEMBER SAMPLE

Instrument	N	Proportion of Items Predicted Correctly According to Hypothesis 9–1	Probability Less than
Superintendent Friendships	15	1.00	.01
School Board Performances	20	.85	.01
Division of Labor	13	.85	.05
Superintendent Participations	11	.82	.05
Superintendent Performances	37	.73	.01
Superintendent Attributes	54	.67	.05
All Instruments	150	.76	.05

For each instrument and for all items the proportion predicted correctly is significantly greater than would be expected by chance (at least at the .05 level). We may say that the evidence supports the hypothesis.

The Covariation of the Intraposition Consensus Scores. The second problem we will examine is whether or not there is a relationship between the intraposition consensus scores that the two samples obtain on the same expectation items. Although it has been demonstrated that the superintendents tend to have higher consensus in general than do the school board members, it remains problematic whether or not expectation items on which there is a high degree of consensus among superintendents are the same items on which there is a high degree of consensus among school board members. An answer to this question can be obtained by correlating the variance scores for the same items obtained by the two samples. The correlations are presented in Table 9–B. The correlations

TABLE 9–B. CORRELATIONS BETWEEN THE VARIANCE SCORES OBTAINED BY ITEMS OF SIX ROLE DEFINITION INSTRUMENTS IN THE SCHOOL BOARD AND SUPERINTENDENT SAMPLES

Instrument	N	r	Probability Less than*
Superintendent Performances	37	.82	.01
Superintendent Attributes	54	.79	.01
Superintendent Participations	11	.85	.01
Superintendent Friendships	15	.85	.01
School Board Performances	20	.72	.01
Division of Labor	13	.63	.02
All Instruments	150	.78	.01

* Using a two-tailed test.

range from .85 to .63. The correlation of these scores for all 150 expectations items in the six role definition instruments is .78.

One possible explanation of this finding is that the incumbents of each of these positions participate in other "special" social systems. School board members belong to school board associations and superintendents to superintendents' associations, both of which have as one of their purposes the development of common codes of behavior for their members, or, in the terms of our analysis, the establishment of role definitions for their members. Since a primary concern of both school board members and superintendents is the functioning of the public schools, we would infer that both superintendent and school board associations are concerned with the same basic problems. Since the problems considered in their two associations are essentially the same, to the extent that the associations function effectively or influence their members, superintendents and school board members will tend to reach consensus on the same *aspects* of role definition. There is no implication in this reasoning that superintendents and school board members will agree *with one another,* since their associations may very well reach different solutions to the same problem.

The positive correlations actually obtained may be interpreted as indicating that within the two sets of role definers the role segments are consensually structured in highly *similar* ways. This finding, just as the reasoning with which we have tried to explain it, tells us nothing about whether there is agreement between the samples on the *substance* of their responses, which is the interposition consensus question treated earlier. For any given item both samples may have high consensus scores, but in one sample there may be consensus that a superintendent "absolutely must" engage in a behavior, and in the other, consensus that he "absolutely must not."

Different Degrees of Consensus on Role Segments. In discussing the postulate of role consensus in Chapter Three it was suggested that among the questions raised by abandoning it are those concerned with different degrees of consensus on different segments of a role within a particular population of role definers. The next section of this chapter will be concerned with a comparison of the intraposition consensus scores obtained for both the superintendents and school board members on their performances. In this section the role segments of attributes and performances will be compared.

We shall use the intraposition consensus scores on the Superintendent Attributes and the Superintendent Performances Instruments to test an hypothesis concerning different degrees of consensus on expectations *prerequisite* to the occupancy of a position and those applicable to a position incumbent after he occupies it, or *postrequisite* expectations. The question is whether there is greater consensus on prerequisite or on postrequisite expectations for the incumbent of the chief administrative position in a formal organization among incumbents of that position, and among the incumbents of the position superordinate to it, the policy-makers of the formal organization.

Our reasoning leads us to expect greater consensus among both sets of role definers on prerequisite expectations. It is based on the following assumptions.

(1) The evaluative standards that a set of role definers apply to an incumbent of a position (X) of which they are incumbents or to which they are superordinate will be influenced by the unique set of factors in the situation surrounding their positions.

(2) The task(s) of position (X) are common in all situations in which the position occurs but the behaviors employed to carry out the task(s) will be variable because of the unique set of factors in each situation.

(3) In choosing an individual to occupy a vacated position (X), the prerequisite expectations are more frequently tied to the task(s) of the position than to specific behaviors that the occupant might be expected to perform as a consequence of the unique set of factors surrounding the situation in which it occurs.

Given these assumptions the hypothesis follows that:

Hypothesis 9–2: Among incumbents of a position X *or among incumbents of its superordinate position there will be greater consensus on prerequisite expectations for attributes necessary to accomplish the task(s) of the position* X *than on postrequisite expectations for behaviors by means of which the task(s) of the position* X *are carried out.*

With our data this hypothesis leads to the prediction that there will be greater consensus on expectations for the items in the Superintendent Attributes Instrument than for those in the Superintendent Performances Instrument, since the former were asked as prerequisite and the latter as postrequisite expectations.

The difference between the distributions of variance scores for the Superintendent Performances and the Superintendent Attributes Instruments suggests that in general there is more consensus within both samples on expectations for attributes than on expectations for performances. (Compare *b* and *d* of Figure 9–1.) To test the hypothesis, the items from both instruments were divided into those with "high" and those with "low" consensus on the basis of a cutting point which is the median variance (.395) of the distribution of variance scores for all expectation items for both samples. The findings are reported in Table 9–C.

TABLE 9–C. PERCENTAGE OF ITEMS FROM THE SUPERINTENDENT PERFORM-
ANCES AND ATTRIBUTES INSTRUMENTS FALLING IN "HIGH" AND "LOW"
CONSENSUS CATEGORIES FOR THE SUPERINTENDENT AND SCHOOL BOARD
SAMPLES

Superintendent Sample

	Consensus Category, %			
Instrument	High	Low	N	
Attributes	70	30	54	$\chi^2 = 7.93$
Performances	41	59	37	(Probability less than .01)

School Board Sample

	Consensus Category, %			
Instrument	High	Low	N	
Attributes	59	41	54	$\chi^2 = 12.63$
Performances	22	78	37	(Probability less than .001)

For the superintendent sample, 70 percent of the expectations for Superintendent Attributes fall into the high consensus category as compared to 41 percent of their expectations for Superintendent Performances. For the school board sample similar results are obtained. Fifty-nine percent of the Attributes items in contrast to only 22 percent of the Performance items are in the high consensus category. In both instances these differences are statistically significant at the 1 percent level.

Therefore, support may be claimed for the hypothesis. For both sets of role definers there was greater consensus on prerequisite than on postrequisite expectations.

Superintendent and School Board Performances. An hypothesis which will lead to a prediction of whether there is more intraposition consensus on expectations for superintendents' performances than on those for school board performances can be derived from two postulates concerning different degrees of formal codification of expectations for incumbents of different positions. These postulates are:

(1) There are different degrees of formal codification of the obligations of incumbents of different positions in formal organizations.

(2) The greater the codification of the obligations of incumbents of one position in a formal organization, the more similar the standards which the incumbents of any position in the organization will apply to incumbents of that position.

Given these two postulates, the hypothesis follows that:

Hypothesis 9–3: In specifying the obligations of incumbents of two positions in a formal organization, there will be greater consensus among incumbents of any one position in the organization on the obligations of incumbents of the position for which there has been the greater degree of codification.

Since the state law of Massachusetts contains an extensive statement of the obligations of a school board (we would say that school board obligations are to this extent formally codified) and is practically silent on those of a superintendent,[2] the hypothesis leads to the prediction that there will be greater consensus among both sets of role definers on the obligations of school board members than there is on the obligations of superintendents.

In Table 9–D are presented the proportions of items of the Superintendent Performances Instrument and of the School Board Performances Instrument for which there is high and low consensus in each sample. Although for both samples there is a greater proportion of school board than of superintendent performances items in the high consensus category, the differences are not statistically significant at the 5-percent level. Therefore we cannot claim support for the hypothesis.

In the preceding two analyses the problems investigated were concerned with different degrees of consensus within each of the samples of role definers on different *role segments*. Our concern in the following analyses is with the problem of why there are differences in the content of role definitions among incumbents of the same position. Whereas in the interposition consensus analysis of Chapter

TABLE 9–D. PERCENTAGE OF ITEMS FROM THE SUPERINTENDENT PERFORMANCES AND SCHOOL BOARD PERFORMANCES INSTRUMENTS FALLING IN "HIGH" AND "LOW" CONSENSUS CATEGORIES FOR THE SUPERINTENDENT AND SCHOOL BOARD SAMPLES

Superintendent Sample

	Consensus Category, %			
Instrument	High	Low	N	
Superintendent Performances	41	59	37	$\chi^2 = .11$
School Board Performances	45	55	20	(Probability greater than .05)

School Board Sample

	Consensus Category, %			
Instrument	High	Low	N	
Superintendent Performances	22	78	37	$\chi^2 = 2.17$
School Board Performances	40	60	20	(Probability greater than .05)

Eight, several hypotheses were presented which accounted for some of the differences in the expectations held by incumbents of two different positions, superintendent and school board member, in this section of the intraposition analysis hypotheses will be presented and tested which account for some of the differences in the expectations held by different incumbents of the *same* position, for both the superintendent and school board member positions.

From among the numerous factors of theoretical relevance to the explanation of differences in role definition among incumbents of the same position, one has been selected for exploration. This is the size of the formal organization in which the positions occupied by the role definers are involved. The hypotheses to be examined are based in part on the propositions with respect to formal organizations presented in Chapter Eight (pp. 122–123), and in addition, on one or more of the accompanying set of assumptions:

Assumption 1. For formal organizations of the same type, the larger the organization, the greater the financial rewards it can offer its technical and executive personnel.

Assumption 2. The greater the financial rewards a formal organization of a given type can offer, the more competent the technical and executive personnel it will attract and have.

Assumption 3. The more competent the incumbent(s) of a technical or executive position in one organization as compared to the incumbent(s) of the same position in other organizations of the same type, the greater confidence an incumbent of that position will have in himself, and the more incumbents of other positions will have confidence in and give support to him.

Assumption 4. The larger the formal organization, the larger the number of different positions within it, the larger the number of personnel to fill these positions, and therefore, the more complex and extended the line of authority and the more complex the problems of administration and coordination.

Definition of Superordinate-Subordinate Responsibilities in the Division of Labor. What consequences can be derived from this set of assumptions and the propositions of Chapter Eight with respect to differences in the definition of the responsibilities of subordinates and superordinates by incumbents of these positions in large and small formal organizations?

If the general function of a position incumbent who has authority over incumbents of other positions is to see that the particular set of tasks for which his subordinates are responsible are accomplished and that they contribute to the achievement of the "higher" order tasks for which he is himself responsible (Proposition 4, Chapter Eight), and if larger organizations tend to have more competent executive personnel (Assumption 2 of this chapter), and if position incumbents have greater confidence in themselves and their subordinates if they are more competent (Assumption 3), the hypothesis follows that:

Hypothesis 9–4: In specifying the division of responsibility between an executive subordinate and his superordinate, incumbents of either position in large formal organizations will assign more responsibility to the subordinate than will incumbents of the same position in small formal organizations.

This hypothesis leads to the predictions that superintendents from larger school systems will assign greater responsibility to their own positions in the division of responsibilities with the school board than will superintendents from smaller systems, and similarly, that school board members from larger systems will assign greater responsibility to superintendents than will school board members from smaller systems. In the case of both superintendents and school board members, the prediction is that those from larger systems will obtain a higher mean response to each of the division of labor items (that is, a mean response which reflects the assignment of greater responsibility to the superintendent) than will those from smaller systems.

As a measure of the size of the formal organizations the "net average membership" (NAM) of pupils enrolled in the school systems was used. The school systems were dichotomized into "large" and "small," using the median NAM as the cutting point.[3]

The tests of Hypothesis 9–4 are presented in Table 9–E.

For the superintendent sample, on eleven of the thirteen Division of Labor items, the difference between those from large and those from small systems is in the predicted direction, and this proportion (11/13 or .85) is significant at the .05 level. For the school board member sample the direction of the differences was predicted correctly for nine of the thirteen items, but this proportion (9/13 or .69) is not significant at the .05 level, for which 10/13 of the items would have had to be predicted correctly.

Support may be claimed for the hypothesis on the basis of the data obtained from incumbents of the subordinate position with which it was tested (superintendents) but not on the basis of the data obtained from incumbents of the superordinate position (school board members).

Obligations to Incumbents of Positions within Formal Organizations of Different Size. Two of the assumptions regarding differences between large and small formal organizations lead to a very general hypothesis with respect to different degrees of expressed obligation to incumbents of positions *within* formal organizations, which can be tested with our data.

If larger organizations tend to have more competent technical and executive personnel (Assumption 2 of this chapter) and if position incumbents give more support to more competent personnel (Assumption 3), then the hypothesis follows that:

Hypothesis 9–5: For incumbents of a specified technical or executive position in formal organizations of the same type, occupants of any position X *in larger formal organizations will express expectations which reflect a greater degree of support for incumbents of the specified technical or executive position than will occupants of the same position* X *in smaller formal organizations.*

In order to test this hypothesis, items were used from the Superin-

TABLE 9–E. DIFFERENCES BETWEEN THE MEAN RESPONSES OF SUPERINTEND-
ENTS FROM "LARGE" AND "SMALL" SCHOOL SYSTEMS, AND BETWEEN THE
MEAN RESPONSES OF SCHOOL BOARD MEMBERS FROM "LARGE" AND "SMALL"
SCHOOL SYSTEMS TO THE ITEMS OF THE DIVISION OF LABOR INSTRUMENT

Item *	N_L	$\overline{X}_L$	N_S	$\overline{X}_S$	D	C.R.	Probability Less than	Direction Predicted Correctly (+) or Incorrectly (−) According to Hypothesis 9–4
Superintendent Sample								
a. When a new teacher is to be hired.	41	3.73	63	3.70	.03	0.1	not sig.	+
b. If a new building is needed.	41	3.15	61	2.90	.25	2.1	.05	+
c. When a new textbook is needed.	41	3.90	62	3.82	.08	1.0	not sig.	+
d. On the budget.	41	3.37	63	3.11	.26	2.7	.01	+
e. On instructional policy.	41	3.05	63	3.13	.08	0.7	not sig.	−
f. On public relations.	41	3.20	62	3.08	.12	1.2	not sig.	+
g. How are teachers' grievances handled?	41	3.93	62	3.87	.06	1.0	not sig.	+
h. Who handles relationships with community groups that wish to use pupils for their own purposes?	41	3.29	63	3.30	.01	0.1	not sig.	−
i. When a community organization wishes to use school property, the request.	41	3.02	63	2.90	.12	1.1	not sig.	+
j. Who is responsible for and supervises the maintenance necessary to keep the school plant in good operating condition?	41	3.51	63	3.40	.11	0.9	not sig.	+
k. Who is responsible for the child attendance regulations?	41	3.76	63	3.68	.08	1.2	not sig.	+
l. Who makes recommendations for increases in salaries of school system employees?	41	3.68	63	3.59	.09	0.8	not sig.	+
m. Who initiates policy matters?	41	3.17	63	2.98	.19	1.5	not sig.	+

Proportion of the items for which the direction of the difference was predicted correctly according to Hypothesis 9–4 = 11/13 = .85, which is significant at the .05 level.

Item *	N_L	$\overline{X}_L$	N_S	$\overline{X}_S$	D	C.R.	Probability Less than	Direction
School Board Sample								
a. When a new teacher is to be hired.	254	3.02	250	2.94	.08	1.2	not sig.	+
b. If a new building is needed.	244	2.75	232	2.46	.29	4.5	.001	+
c. When a new textbook is needed.	257	3.28	249	3.33	.05	0.8	not sig.	−
d. On the budget.	257	2.97	249	2.84	.13	3.3	.001	+
e. On instructional policy.	258	2.93	249	2.90	.03	0.8	not sig.	+
f. On public relations.	256	2.86	245	2.80	.06	1.1	not sig.	+
g. How are teachers' grievances handled?	256	3.50	248	3.48	.02	0.3	not sig.	+
h. Who handles relationships with community groups that wish to use pupils for their own purposes?	256	2.27	244	2.73	.46	5.5	.001	−
i. When a community organization wishes to use school property, the request.	257	2.41	247	2.28	.13	1.7	.05	+
j. Who is responsible for and supervises the maintenance necessary to keep the school plant in good operating condition?	249	3.09	248	2.79	.30	4.0	.001	+
k. Who is responsible for the child attendance regulations?	258	3.42	248	3.34	.08	1.1	not sig.	+
l. Who makes recommendations for increases in salaries of school system employees?	254	2.98	249	3.07	.09	1.2	not sig.	−
m. Who initiates policy matters?	257	2.68	250	2.70	.02	0.3	not sig.	−

Proportion of the items for which the direction of the difference was predicted correctly according to Hypothesis 9–4 = 9/13 = .69, which is not significant at the .05 level.

* The response categories, which differ for each item, are presented in Notes for Appendix Table A–6.

tendent and School Board Performances Instruments which can be interpreted to be measuring the extent to which expectations reflect support for incumbents of "technical" positions within the school systems. It follows from this hypothesis that the expectations expressed by superintendents from large school systems will reflect a greater degree of support for teachers, who are incumbents of a "technical" position within their school systems, than do the expectations expressed by superintendents from small systems. The same prediction can be made for school board members from large and small systems.

TABLE 9–F. DIFFERENCES BETWEEN THE MEAN RESPONSES OF SUPERINTEND-ENTS FROM "LARGE" AND "SMALL" SCHOOL SYSTEMS, AND BETWEEN THE MEAN RESPONSES OF SCHOOL BOARD MEMBERS FROM "LARGE" AND "SMALL" SYSTEMS TO ITEMS DESCRIBING OBLIGATIONS TO INCUMBENTS OF POSITIONS "WITHIN THE SYSTEM"

Item and Response Category Reflecting Greatest Obligation to Incumbents of Positions "within the System"	N_L	$\overline{X}_L$	N_S	$\overline{X}_S$	D	C.R.	Probability Less than	Direction Predicted Correctly (+) or Incorrectly (−) According to Hypothesis 9–5
Superintendent Sample								
1. Refuse to recommend the dismissal of a teacher the public wants dismissed if he feels that the public complaint is invalid. (A)	42	1.60	63	1.62	0.02	0.1	not sig.	+
2. Consult with staff members about filling vacant teaching positions. (A)	42	1.88	63	2.06	0.18	1.4	not sig.	+
3. Defend his teachers from attack when they try to present the pros and cons of various controversial social and political issues. (A)	42	1.38	63	1.48	0.10	0.6	not sig.	+
4. Help his teachers to get higher salaries. (A)	42	1.55	63	1.63	0.08	0.7	not sig.	+
5. Make curriculum changes without consulting the teaching staff. (E)	42	4.48	63	4.30	0.18	1.3	not sig.	+
6. Favor local firms in the awarding of school contracts even though this may increase school expenses somewhat. (E)	42	3.67	63	3.65	0.02	0.1	not sig.	+
7. Give consideration to local values or feelings regarding race, religion, national origin, in filling vacant teaching positions. (E)	42	3.52	63	3.21	0.31	1.2	not sig.	+
8. Fight continuously against any local attacks on educational principles or methods which he knows are sound. (A)	42	1.12	63	1.38	0.26	2.5	.01	+
9. Occasionally compromise with local pressure groups. (E)	42	3.31	63	3.30	0.01	0.1	not sig.	+
10. Take a definite stand against any unreasonable demands that may come from local taxpayers. (A)	42	1.31	63	1.40	0.09	0.7	not sig.	+
11. A committee not afraid to take stands regarding education in advance of community thinking. (A)	42	1.62	63	1.63	0.01	0.1	not sig.	+

Proportion of items for which the direction of the difference was predicted correctly according to Hypothesis 9–5 = 11/11 = 1.00, which is significant at the .001 level.

TABLE 9–F (continued)

Item and Response Category Reflecting Greatest Obligation to Incumbents of Positions "within the System"	N_L	$\overline{X}_L$	N_S	$\overline{X}_S$	D	C.R.	Probability Less than	Direction Predicted Correctly (+) or Incorrectly (−) According to Hypothesis 9–5
School Board Sample								
1. Refuse to recommend the dismissal of a teacher the public wants dismissed if he feels that the public complaint is invalid. (A)	256	1.91	249	2.05	0.14	1.5	not sig.	+
2. Consult with staff members about filling vacant teaching positions. (A)	257	2.19	250	2.49	0.30	3.9	.001	+
3. Defend his teachers from attack when they try to present the pros and cons of various controversial social and political issues. (A)	257	1.95	248	2.11	0.16	2.0	.05	+
4. Help his teachers to get higher salaries. (A)	256	2.29	250	2.43	0.14	2.2	.05	+
5. Make curriculum changes without consulting the teaching staff. (E)	256	3.99	250	3.95	0.04	0.6	not sig.	+
6. Favor local firms in the awarding of school contracts even though this may increase school expenses somewhat. (E)	247	3.68	247	3.50	0.18	1.8	.05	+
7. Give consideration to local values or feelings regarding race, religion, national origin, in filling vacant teaching positions. (E)	257	3.22	250	3.05	0.17	1.63	.052	+
8. Fight continuously against any local attacks on educational principles or methods which he knows are sound. (A)	257	1.50	250	1.69	0.19	2.9	.01	+
9. Occasionally compromise with local pressure groups. (E)	257	3.57	248	3.60	0.03	0.4	not sig.	−
10. Take a definite stand against any unreasonable demands that may come from local taxpayers. (A)	257	1.91	250	2.14	0.23	2.7	.01	+
11. A committee not afraid to take stands regarding education in advance of community thinking. (A)	257	1.53	249	1.56	0.03	0.6	not sig.	+

Proportion of items for which the direction of the difference was predicted correctly according to Hypothesis 9–5 = 10/11 = .91, which is significant at the .01 level.

These predictions can be tested with five of six items which were used to test the prediction with respect to "Teachers" based on Hypothesis 8–3. Since the sixth item of this set opposes the interests of teachers and the school board, both of which are positions within the system, it is not an appropriate item for a test of this hypothesis.

All six items which were used to test the "community member" prediction based on Hypothesis 8–3 may be used in a test of Hypothesis 9–5. Responses to these items may be interpreted as indicative, either by implication or directly, of the degree of support superintendents and school board members offer incumbents of technical and executive positions within the school system. The prediction in the case of each of the seven items is that the expectations expressed by superintendents from larger systems will reflect a greater degree of support for incumbents of these positions with the system than do the expectations expressed by superintendents from smaller systems. That is, the former will express expectations more protective of themselves or their subordinates when "demands" are made by groups external to the organization. A similar prediction is made for school board members from large and small school systems.

There are consequently eleven items for which predictions based on Hypothesis 9–5 can be tested. The tests for the two samples of role definers are presented in Table 9–F.

For the superintendents' sample, the direction of the difference between the means of those from large and those from small school systems was predicted correctly for all eleven items. This proportion (1.00) is significant at the .001 level, and provides support for the hypothesis. For the school board member sample the direction of the difference between the means of those from large and small systems was predicted correctly for ten of the eleven items, and this proportion (.91) is significant at the .01 level. The hypothesis can consequently be said to have received support from predictions about the responses of both superintendents and school board members from large and small school systems.

The Definition of the Line of Authority in Formal Organizations of Different Size. In Hypothesis 8–5 it was stated that incumbents of positions who are by-passed are less likely to accept the by-pass than are position incumbents who participate in the by-pass. This hypothesis received confirmation when it was tested with items dealing with by-passes of both superintendents and school board members, some of which could be said to be generally approved, and some of which could be said to be generally disapproved. Implicit in this hypothesis was the idea that in formal organizations there is an established line of authority, which, for certain tasks of particular position incumbents, may include by-passes or communications between nonadjacent positions. It is generally agreed, for example, among superintendents and school board members, that a superintendent should "Keep his office open to all community members at all times," according to the mean responses obtained in both samples. (See Appendix Table A–1, item 6.)

If it is assumed that the established line of authority in formal organizations may require certain by-passes by incumbents of particular positions in order for them to carry out their tasks, and that the larger the formal organization the more complex and extended the line of authority (Assumption 4), and additionally assumed that a deviation from the established line of authority (whether a by-pass or a non-by-pass is established) will interfere with a position incumbent's carrying out his task, and that the more complex and extended the line of authority in a formal organization the greater the interference with the task(s) of any position incumbent a deviation from the established line of authority will be, then the hypothesis follows that:

Hypothesis 9–6: In defining the line of authority in a formal organization, incumbents of any position X in large formal organizations will be less likely to accept or more likely to reject a deviation from the established line of authority, whether a by-pass or a non-by-pass is established, than will incumbents of the same position X in small formal organizations.

If we assume that the means obtained by the two samples are a fair index of the *established* line of authority, that is, of what is "generally agreed" by our respondents, then we may use all nine of the "by-pass" items used in the test of Hypothesis 8–5 to test Hypothesis 9–6. A mean which is larger than 3.00 (may or may not) reflects a generally negative evaluation of the item, and a mean smaller than 3.00 reflects a generally positive evaluation of the item according to the weights given the five response categories. The specific prediction for each of the items used in this test will be that large system superintendents and school board members will obtain smaller means on items whose general means are less than 3.00 and larger means on items whose general means are greater than 3.00. Since the means of both samples and of both subgroups (large and small) are consistently on one side or the other of 3.00, there is no operational difficulty in deciding whether a negative or positive evaluation of the item defines the *established* line of authority.

Before presenting our tests of this hypothesis we should comment on one further difference between large and small systems which is relevant to the predictions for the "by-pass of school board" items. Three of these items, which are positively evaluated (items 6, 7, and 8), describe "public relations" activities of the superintendent. We think it is reasonable to assume that in the larger systems an established "public relations program" is necessary in order to have effective public relations. Smaller systems can perhaps operate effectively with fewer formally established procedures because it is possible for them to maximize the intimacy of small communities. The general hypothesis concerning deviations from the established line of authority would lead to the prediction on these items that larger systems will evaluate them more positively than small systems, since they are in general positively evaluated. The public relations reasoning leads to the same prediction: Incumbents of positions in large systems are more likely to favor public relations activities.

In Table 9-G are presented the data for a test of the general hypoth-

TABLE 9-G. DIFFERENCES BETWEEN THE MEAN RESPONSES OF SUPERINTEND-ENTS FROM "LARGE" AND "SMALL" SCHOOL SYSTEMS, AND BETWEEN THE MEAN RESPONSES OF SCHOOL BOARD MEMBERS FROM "LARGE" AND "SMALL" SYSTEMS TO ITEMS DESCRIBING AN "ESTABLISHED LINE OF AUTHORITY"

Item and the "Established Line of Authority" as a Positive (+) or Negative (−) Evaluation of the Item	N_L	$\overline{X}_L$	N_S	$\overline{X}_S$	D	C.R.	Probability Less than	Direction Predicted Correctly (+) or Incorrectly (−) According to Hypothesis 9–6
Superintendent Sample								
1. How are teachers' grievances handled? (Superintendent dominance.)*	41	3.93	62	3.87	.06	1.0	not sig.	+
2. Give directions directly to the superintendent's subordinates. (−)	42	4.86	63	4.87	.01	0.1	not sig.	−
3. Appoint only teachers nominated by the superintendent. (+)	42	1.40	63	1.59	.19	1.8	.05	+
4. Accept full responsibility for the decisions of his subordinates. (+)	42	1.64	63	2.03	.39	2.0	.05	+
5. Protect the superintendent from community pressures. (+)	42	2.12	63	1.92	.20	1.3	not sig.	−
6. Keep his office open to all community members at all times. (+)	42	1.62	63	1.76	.14	0.8	not sig.	+
7. Establish regular channels of communication with local newspapers. (+)	42	1.50	63	1.65	.15	1.3	not sig.	+
8. Speak to all major civic groups at least once a year. (+)	42	2.33	63	2.40	.07	0.6	not sig.	+
9. Urge people whom he respects to run for the school committee. (−)	42	3.60	63	3.56	.04	0.2	not sig.	+

Proportion of the items for which the direction of the difference was predicted correctly according to Hypothesis 9–6 = 7/9 = .78, which is not significant at the .05 level.

	N_L	$\overline{X}_L$	N_S	$\overline{X}_S$	D	C.R.	Probability Less than	Direction
School Board Sample								
1. How are teachers' grievances handled? (Superintendent dominance.)*	256	3.50	248	3.48	.02	0.3	not sig.	+
2. Give directions directly to the superintendent's subordinates. (−)	258	4.58	249	4.46	.12	1.8	.05	+
3. Appoint only teachers nominated by the superintendent. (+)	258	2.26	249	2.69	.43	4.1	.001	+
4. Accept full responsibility for the decisions of his subordinates. (+)	257	1.96	250	2.11	.15	1.9	.05	+
5. Protect the superintendent from community pressures. (+)	258	1.71	249	1.80	.09	1.2	not sig.	+
6. Keep his office open to all community members at all times. (+)	257	1.78	249	1.83	.05	0.8	not sig.	+
7. Establish regular channels of communication with local newspapers. (+)	257	1.98	249	2.18	.20	3.5	.001	+
8. Speak to all major civic groups at least once a year. (+)	257	2.33	249	2.45	.12	2.3	.05	+
9. Urge people whom he respects to run for the school committee. (−)	257	3.65	250	3.66	.01	0.1	not sig.	−

Proportion of the items for which the direction of the difference was predicted correctly according to Hypothesis 9–6 = 8/9 = .89, which is significant at the .05 level.

*The response categories for this item, from the Division of Labor Instrument, are given in Appendix Table A–6. The "superintendent dominance" category is scored 4, and the "school board dominance" category scored 1.

esis for the superintendents' sample and for the school board members' sample.

The data from the superintendents' sample do not provide significant support for the hypothesis, although the number of items correctly predicted is only one short of the number required for significance. These data suggest that the differences in this sample are in general slight, but what differences there are are in the direction predicted on the basis of the hypothesis.

The school board sample data, on the other hand, can be said to provide significant support for the hypothesis. Eight of the nine items were predicted correctly, and this proportion is significant at the .05 level. On the basis of these findings only limited support can be claimed for the general hypothesis.

Summary. In this chapter some exploratory steps have been made in the analysis of macroscopic role consensus among incumbents of the same position. The general objectives were to examine consensus within samples of incumbents of two positions on different segments of role definition and to test certain hypotheses concerning differences in role definition among incumbents of the same position.

First it was shown that there are different degrees of consensus within both samples of role definers, superintendents, and school board members, on different items of each role segment and on different role segments.

An hypothesis based on the assumption of differential homogeneity of socialization required for incumbents of two positions in a formal organization led to the prediction that there would be more consensus within the superintendents' sample, for whose position it was argued relatively homogeneous socialization is required, than within the school board member sample, for whose position relatively heterogeneous socialization could be assumed. This prediction was confirmed. It was also found that there was a positive relationship between the consensus scores obtained in the two samples.

Two hypotheses relating to different degrees of consensus on different role segments were presented and tested. The first of these led to the prediction that there would be more consensus within both the superintendents and the school board samples on expectations for prerequisite attributes than on expectations for postrequisite behaviors. In the case of both samples the prediction was confirmed. The second hypothesis with respect to different degrees of consensus on different role segments led to the prediction that there would be more consensus within both samples on expectations for performances of position incumbents whose obligations have been to a greater extent formally codified than on expectations for performances of position incumbents whose obligations have to a lesser extent been formally codified. It was argued that obligations of school board members are codified in the state laws to a greater extent than are those of superintendents, and that consequently, there would be more consensus within both samples on the items of the School Board Performances Instrument than on the items of the Superintendent Performances Instrument. The differences between the two instruments were not significant for either sample, and consequently support could not be claimed for the hypothesis.

On the basis of a series of propositions describing characteristics of formal organizations, and on the basis of four additional assumptions with respect to differences between large and small formal organizations, three hypotheses were derived which led to predictions that there would be differences between incumbents of the *same* position from large and small formal organizations.

The first of these hypotheses dealt with the definition of the division of labor between a superordinate and his executive subordinate, and the prediction was made that incumbents of both of these positions in larger formal organizations would assign more responsibility to the subordinate than would position incumbents in smaller formal organizations. This prediction was confirmed and interpreted as supporting the hypothesis for the superintendents sample, but not for the school board members sample.

The second hypothesis concerned with differences between incumbents of the same position in large and small formal organizations led to a prediction that those from larger formal organizations would express expectations which reflect a greater degree of support for incumbents of technical and executive positions within their organizations, than would incumbents of the same position in smaller formal organizations. This prediction was confirmed for both the superintendents and the school board samples.

The third hypothesis of this group dealt with different definitions of the line of authority by incumbents of positions in large and small formal organizations. The prediction to which this hypothesis led was that those from large formal organizations would be less likely to accept or more likely to reject a deviation from the *established line of authority* than would those from small formal organizations. This prediction was confirmed for the school board members sample but not for the superintendents sample.

In the exploratory analyses presented in this and the preceding chapters, it has been shown that differences in the expectations position incumbents hold, which are the basis of different degrees of macroscopic consensus on role definition, can be in part accounted for by the fact that they occupy different positions and in part by the fact that they occupy positions in formal organizations of different size. These factors, the position occupied and the kind of formal organization, are only two among many possible determinants of different expectations. In the following chapters some exploratory steps will be made toward accounting for different expectations held by incumbents of the same and of different positions within the *same* formal organization, or microscopic role consensus. Although the focus of analysis in the studies of microscopic role consensus is on position incumbents who interact with one another, the problem which is of central concern is directly comparable to the one with which we have been dealing in these macroscopic studies: to account for different degrees of consensus on role definition.

Notes and References for Chapter Nine

[1] As indicated in Chapter Seven, p. 106 this condition would be represented by a set of responses equally distributed over the five response categories or a set of responses equally divided between the two extreme categories. Although the set of responses for no item completely met these conditions, it should be noted that for each sample there were two items which showed no *statistical* evidence of agreement, i.e., the differences between the distribution of responses for each of these items and a rectangular distribution were only chance differences.

[2] Whereas state laws of Massachusetts contain numerous provisions to the duties of a school committee, the duties of a superintendent of schools are defined in Massachusetts in the following brief statement:

A superintendent . . . shall be the executive officer of the committee, and under its general direction, shall have the care and supervision of the public schools, shall assist it in keeping its records and accounts and in making such reports as are required by law, and shall recommend to the committee teachers, textbooks, and courses of study.

The Commonwealth of Massachusetts, *General Laws Relating to Education*, Bulletin of the Department of Education, 1947, No. 5, p. 60.

[3] Source: The Commonwealth of Massachusetts, *Annual Report of the Department of Education for the Year Ending June 30, 1951*, Public Document No. 2.

Microscopic Role Consensus Analysis: Objectives and Methodology

In the preceding three chapters our concern has been with the analysis of *macroscopic* role consensus. The focus of the analysis was on the agreement and disagreement in role definition of the total samples of incumbents of the superintendent and school board member positions. Several hypotheses were presented and tested which to some extent account for the differences uncovered in role definition within and between the two samples of role definers. The purpose of this and the next three chapters is to explore the correlates of consensus on role definition among position incumbents who participate in the same small social system, or *microscopic role consensus,* and in doing so, to test hypotheses about its determinants and consequences.

Although *macroscopic role consensus* has received little or no theoretical attention, and virtually no empirical consideration,[1] statements from the literature can be readily found which indicate that *microscopic role consensus* among group members is recognized as a problem both by essayists, and by those who are concerned primarily with small group experimentation. According to Davis, for example,

> . . . the interacting situation [is] the meeting ground of all sociological abstractions . . . [and] . . . the essence of any social situation lies in the mutual expectations of the participants. . . . It is through a chain of overt responses (either symbolic or literal) that the process of interchange moves along, each act testing the various mutual expectations and forcing a constant redefinition.[2]

The inference may be made that Davis would agree with the statement that consensus on role expectations is a phenomenon of central importance to an understanding of interaction situations. Bales and his associates[3] have shown empirically that developmental trends in small groups differ according to the degree of consensus on rankings of members as determined at the end of the first meeting, and they assume that consensus on ranking derives from "*consensus* as to the nature of the criterion . . ." which would seem to approximate the concept of expectations or evaluative standards.[4] Although this assumption may be considered empirically problematic (it is a relationship which will be tested), the fact that it is made implies that these authors would also agree that consensus on role expectations may have an impact on group processes.

Despite this recognition of the importance of consensus in group functioning there have been few empirical studies of consensus on the expectations applied to incumbents of particular positions in small groups.[5] One possible reason for this might be that much of the research on small groups deals with groups which are at a prenormative stage of development. As Bales and Slater say of one such study, the aim is ". . . to catch role differentiation 'in the making' from some minimal level. . . ." [6] In the case of the groups we are studying the differentiation between two positions is formally prescribed. In each school system studied there is always a school superintendent and a number of school board members who must interact with one another in the course of carrying out their general function of providing and administering educational facilities in their communities. It is therefore possible for us to study expectations for incumbents of particular positions held by members of the group who occupy those positions.

This difference between the microscopic studies reported here and experimental small group research is attributable to a still more fundamental difference. We are concerned with "natural" groups, not with groups artificially constructed in the laboratory. We are studying the expectations of and for people who occupy clearly designated positions in a group that must deal with an important phase of community life. They are not randomly assembled sets of individuals who have no stake in their group or its functions. Although this had certain advantages, it also raised certain problems.

First, although it may be safely assumed that the group members were involved in the problems faced by their group, it was not possible to exert any control over the problems which were dealt with by different groups. For all school systems these problems can be generally described as "providing educational facilities," but on a more specific level the issues with which they are concerned may vary considerably from community to community. It is necessary for us to assume, and we believe it is a reasonable assumption, that the expectation items which have been used in these analyses are relevant to problems encountered in the school systems in this study. This assumption allows us to consider that the group members have discussed problems to which the expectation items used in these analyses are relevant, and consequently, to think of consensus on these expectations as, in part, *the outcome of group processes*. Without this assumption and line of reasoning it would be necessary to consider the phenomenon under consideration as "convergence of private expectations."

The second problem concerns the kind of controls that could be used. Since we were not working with contrived groups, in examining particular relationships it was not possible to carry out controls by experimental manipulation. In consequence, in drawing conclusions regarding specific relationships (for example, from correlations), it is either necessary to assume that "other things are equal" or to control "other things" statistically. Since it is seldom practicable to effect more than partial controls in this kind of analysis, our intention will be to explore many zero order relationships with consensus, whose results should be suggestive for both future cross sectional studies like this one, and for experimental small group studies in which variables can be systematically controlled and manipulated.

The small groups which serve as the subject population for these microscopic analyses are composed of an incumbent of the superintendency position and incumbents of the school board member position. This situation provides us with an opportunity to study microscopic consensus of two kinds: first, within groups in which all members occupy one position—school board member; and second, within groups in which the members occupy two positions—superintendent and school board member.

The object population being analyzed is the same for the microscopic as it was for the macroscopic analyses, because the same data are used. For much of the reasoning about microscopic consensus it will be necessary to infer that the expectations expressed for "superintendents in Massachusetts" apply to "superintendents in particular communities," so that although the object of study is still the same (that is, superintendents in Massachusetts) the reasoning on which our hypotheses are based applies to consensus on expectations for a superintendent in a particular community. It is necessary to make this inference because expectations and consensus on expectations for the general category of "superintendents in Massachusetts" are not likely to be related to the interaction of a particular group of people unless the expectations apply to the superintendent in their particular situation too.

Since our objective was to examine two types of microscopic consensus among group members, consensus among incumbents of a single position and consensus between incumbents of two positions, two measures of consensus were consequently obtained. The first is of consensus within the school board, and the second is of consensus between a superintendent and his school board members. Since these two kinds of consensus pose different problems of measurement they will be taken up separately.

Microscopic Consensus Among the Incumbents of a Single Position. The problem of measuring consensus among the incumbents of the same position in one group is comparable to the measurement of consensus among the incumbents of the same positions in many groups, the only difference being in the number of individuals whose agreement with one another is under examination. The same solution to this problem has been adopted on the microscopic as on the macroscopic level, that is, the use of the variance as the measure of consensus. One special characteristic of the variance in small groups should be described, however. In small groups the variance is markedly affected by the size of the group, and, in the case of school boards which range in size from two to ten members, we might expect this condition to have an appreciable effect on the variance scores. If chance were the only factor operating, larger boards would have significantly higher variance scores (less consensus) than smaller ones.

Before considering this problem in detail, it should be clearly stated that our objective is to obtain a measure of the amount of agreement among the individuals in a group, and not to estimate the variance of some larger population of which our groups might be viewed as samples. Two formulas for computing the variance have been considered. The first "leaves in size," or represents an estimate of the intragroup variance which is biased by the size of the group. The second "takes out size," or represents an estimate unbiased by the size of the group. The first of these we will call V, and the second V':

$$V = \frac{\sum\limits_{i=1}^{N} (x_i^2)}{N}$$

$$V' = \frac{\sum\limits_{i=1}^{N} (x_i^2)}{N - 1}$$

where X_i is the score assigned the response of individual i, x_i is this score in deviation form, and N is the number in the group.

With very small groups, as those with which we are dealing, which of these two formulas is used makes a definite difference in the variance scores which are obtained. The hypothetical examples presented in Table 10–A illustrate this. Using the V measure (that is, the one

TABLE 10–A. V AND V' SCORES BASED ON THE HYPOTHETICAL RESPONSES OF MEMBERS OF A THREE-MAN GROUP AND OF A SIX-MAN GROUP

Response Category		Frequency of Responses	
Category	Numerical Weight	Three-Man Group	Six-Man Group
A	1	0	0
B	2	1	2
C	3	1	2
D	4	1	2
E	5	0	0
	$V =$	0.667	.667
	$V' =$	1.000	.800

which leaves in size) no difference is obtained between the variance scores of the three- and of the six-man boards. Using V' (which takes out size), there would be less consensus within the three-man board (that is, a higher variance score) than within the six-man board. In the V' scores, the fact that the chance probabilities of the three- and of the six-man boards obtaining the same degree of consensus are different is taken into account: The three-man group is more likely than the six-man group to have a variance as low as 0.667 by chance and the V' estimates for the two boards are weighted to allow for this difference.[7]

Since our interest is not in estimating population variances, but in measuring consensus, the decision as to which of these two measures should be used reduces itself to whether we prefer to keep the effects of size of group in the measure, or if we would prefer to take it out. It seems to be a matter of intuitive preference, and it has been decided to use the measure which "keeps size in," or V, because it is our judgment that the size of a group is inseparably related to the amount of agreement among the group members. We would say that by definition it is more difficult to reach agreement in larger than in smaller groups and will therefore define our measure of consensus to include this relative difficulty as part of the measure.

Certain disadvantages to this decision are immediately apparent. Size of group has been shown to be of considerable importance in studies of other aspects of small group functioning.[8] Using our measure of consensus V creates a problem for examining the relationship between size and consensus because size of board and consensus are related by definition.   The use of V also places restrictions on the interpretation of relationships between consensus and other variables. There is always the possibility that any demonstrated relationship between consensus and some other variable can be accounted for wholly or in part by the relationship between size of board and the other variable.   Since it is quite possible to account for differences in size of board without reference to group processes (for example, almost all small towns have small school boards and larger ones large boards), the conclusions drawn must be tempered by the possibility that the relationships demonstrated have nothing to do with group processes.

The advantages of using V over V' are supplemented by the fact that V is systematically related to our measure of between position consensus, which is described in the next section, whereas V' is not, but the essential reason for its use remains the intuitive argument that size of group may be viewed as a part of the concept of consensus.   The disadvantage cited in the preceding paragraph of using V can be eliminated by using V' as a variable to explore relationships between size of the board and consensus.   Its other major disadvantages can be eliminated by investigating whether the relationship of V to another variable could be attributed entirely or partially to its definition to include size of board.   This is the expedient which has been adopted.   Our operational definition of consensus is the V measure and hypotheses concerning consensus will be tested with V, but to supplement our understanding, each analysis with V will be duplicated with V'.

Microscopic Consensus between the Incumbents of Two Positions. The problem with which we will be concerned here is how to measure for a single expectation item the amount of consensus between the response of one position incumbent and the responses of a number of incumbents of another position.   For our analysis, the problem was how to measure consensus between a superintendent and his school board members.   The first index of this kind of consensus which suggested itself was the difference between the superintendent's response and the mean response of his school board.   An objection to this index is immediately apparent: The superintendent's response and the mean school board response could be the same without a single school board member responding in the same category as the superintendent.   The difference between the superintendent's response and the mean of the school board members' responses ignores variability within the board which would seem to be one of the components of consensus between positions when there are multiple incumbents of one of the positions.

An operational approach which combines these two components (that is, the mean difference and the variance of the board members' responses) into a single score is to use a measure of the dispersion of school board responses about the superintendent's response. In using such a score to represent the two recognized components of between position consensus, the information contained in measures of the components themselves, although not ignored, would be confounded. A solution similar to the one adopted for the V and V' problem suggests itself here too. While the primary concern of analyses of between position consensus will be with the overall or "combined" measure of dispersion about the superintendent's response, the mean difference and variance can be examined too, thus providing a measure which fulfills the requirements intuitively felt to be necessary for an adequate measure of between position consensus, without ignoring the information contained in its two separable components.

It can be shown that the three scores adopted for this purpose are related in the following way: If $V =$ the variance of the school board responses (this is the same V which is used to measure within board consensus) and $M =$ the square of the difference between a superintendent's response and the mean response of the board members, then $D = V + M$. Thus D, the measure of overall between position consensus, is simply the sum of its two components, V and M.[9]

These four scores V, V', M and D, are the basis for the analysis of microscopic role consensus which is undertaken in these chapters. The next problem which must be dealt with is how to obtain summary scores over a number of role definition items which will discriminate among groups on their general level of consensus. Excluding the Division of Labor Instrument whose response categories differ from the others, there are five instruments of role definition containing 137 individual items whose response categories were all of the five-step kind, "absolutely must" to "absolutely must not." (These instruments are Superintendent Performances, Superintendent Attributes, Superintendent Participations, Superintendent Friendships, and School Board Performances.)[10]

One possible solution to the problem of a general score would be to simply add all scores over the 137 items. But it would seem to be of interest to ask first whether microscopic consensus on one segment (or role definition instrument) is related to microscopic consensus on another. In order to answer this question, segment totals were computed for each school system on each of the five consensus measures. Four matrices of correlations (one for each consensus measure) among the instrument totals and between each instrument total and a grand total were computed, and are presented in Table 10–B.

TABLE 10–B. CORRELATIONS BETWEEN CONSENSUS SCORES OBTAINED ON FIVE ROLE DEFINITION INSTRUMENTS*

$(N = 105)$

V': Correlations between V' Scores

	P	F	SP	SBP	Total V'
SA	.35	.43	**.58**	**.36**	.80
P		.32	.40	.15	.51
F			.28	.16	.53
SP				**.50**	.89
SBP					.66

V: Correlations between V Scores

	P	F	SP	SBP	Total V
SA	.44	.52	**.69**	**.51**	.86
P		.37	.49	.27	.65
F			.41	.30	.60
SP				**.59**	.91
SBP					.73

M: Correlations between M Scores

	P	F	SP	SBP	Total M
SA	.09	.10	**.30**	**.17**	.71
P		.12	.08	−.05	.24
F			.03	−.07	.26
SP				**.28**	.77
SBP					.52

D: Correlations between D Scores

	P	F	SP	SBP	Total D
SA	.15	.16	**.28**	**.22**	.70
P		.14	.25	−.02	.37
F			.07	−.08	.32
SP				**.32**	.77
SBP					.54

Total: Correlations between
Total Consensus Scores

	V	M	D
V'	.91	.02	.42
V		−.05	.39
M			.90

* The five role definition instruments are abbreviated as follows:
  SA = Superintendent Attributes Instrument
  P = Superintendent Participations Instrument
  F = Superintendent Friendships Instrument
  SP = Superintendent Performances Instrument
  SBP = School Board Performances Instrument

The similarity between the V and V' matrices and between the M and D matrices can be attributed to the high correlations between V and V' total scores ($r = .905$) and between M and D total scores ($r = .898$). The intercorrelations for the two within position matrices (V and V') are all higher than the corresponding figures of the between position matrices. A conclusion which is suggested by this comparison is that consensus on role definition tends to be more homogeneous when the role definers are all incumbents of the same position (school board member) than when they are incumbents of two different positions (school board member and superintendent). None of the correlations is high enough, however, to allow conclusions to the effect that consensus either between positions or within a single position is a homogeneous phenomenon.

Given the information contained in these matrices, it would appear to be necessary to examine the relationship of other variables to consensus on each role segment separately, since the extent to which the segments are related does not seem sufficient to justify their combination. This is, of course, quite an impracticable proposal, and in addition, can be objected to on the grounds that probably none of the segment totals is sufficiently reliable by itself to justify analyses with it alone because of the small number of items each contains. The problem appears to be one of balancing homogeneity and reliability; to maintain homogeneity it would be desirable to study the segments separately, but to obtain adequate reliability it would be desirable to combine them.

The obvious compromise is to combine the two or three most highly related segments. Participations and Friendships were eliminated from consideration, first, because they have consistently the lowest correlations with the other segments, and second, because they may be viewed as peripheral to the superintendent's role. The intercorrelations among the remaining three instruments (in bold face type in Table 10–B) are all positive, significant, and usually higher than those with Participations and Friendships. Superintendent Performances, as well as being most highly correlated with the grand total score for each measure, is the instrument which seems to be closest to the "core" of the superintendent's role. The corrected split half reliability of the four consensus scores on this instrument are: D, .547; M, .570; V, .765; and V', .667.[11] Assuming that it is desirable to include this instrument in the final measure because it is central to the superintendent's task, how could this apparently inadequate reliability be improved? This question resolves itself into which of the two remaining instruments (Superintendent Attributes or School Board Performances) should be combined with it so that on logical as well as statistical criteria we can obtain the most homogeneous and reliable scores.

Although Role Attributes is consistently better than School Board Performances in its correlations with Superintendent Performances and the Total Scores, several reasons dictate the selection of the School Board Performances Instrument for combination with the Superintendent Performances. The Attributes Instrument deals with qualities rather than performances and was asked in a frame of reference slightly different from that of the others.[12] Further, it contains some items which a priori have little or nothing to do with the superintendent's functions. The School Board Performances Instrument has none of these disqualifications and is at the same time complementary to the Superintendent Performances Instrument in that it contains items which can be considered the superintendent's rights. From a

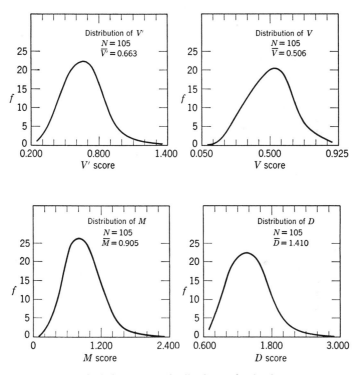

Figure 10–1. Smoothed frequency distributions of school system scores on four consensus variables, *V'*, *V*, *M* and *D*.

theoretical point of view any expectation for the incumbent of one position has a concomitant expectation as to how the incumbents of counter positions should react. In combining these two instruments, therefore, we are focusing on the performance segments of a two position relationship. In addition, a condition which gives us confidence that the combination of these two instruments is justified is that the correlations between them on the four consensus scores (*D*, .323; *M*, .282; *V*, .586; and *V'*, .501) are about as high as the correlations between the split halves of either. For example, the uncorrected correlation between the split halves of Superintendent Performances for

D is .376, as compared with the correlation on D of .323 for the two instruments.

The estimated reliability coefficients for the combined scores of the two performances instruments (based on the 57 items) are: D, .650; M, .671; V, .834; and V', .755. The frequency distributions of the scores obtained in each of the 105 school systems on these four variables are presented in Figure 10–1.

The analyses in the next three chapters are based on these consensus scores which describe the degree of consensus on the definition of the performance segments of two formally related positions. The analyses are organized into those which are concerned with the determinants of consensus and those which are concerned with its consequences. To a considerable extent, the reasoning which applies to one kind of consensus also applies to the other, and consequently, the analyses will be concerned with general relationships between consensus and other variables, each of the consensus variables being considered in turn in each section.

Notes and References for Chapter Ten

[1] See Chapter Three, pp. 36–37 and p. 42 for the few studies in this area.

[2] Kingsley Davis, *Human Society* (New York: The Macmillan Company, 1948 and 1949), pp. 83–84.

[3] Robert F. Bales and Philip E. Slater, "Role Differentiation in Small Decision-Making Groups," in Talcott Parsons and Robert F. Bales (Editors), *Family, Socialization and Interaction Process* (Glencoe: The Free Press, 1955), p. 275. See also C. M. Heinicke and Robert F. Bales, "Developmental Trends in the Structure of Small Groups," *Sociometry*, XVI (1953), pp. 7–38.

[4] Bales and Slater, *loc. cit.*, p. 275.

[5] A valuable recent study concerned with consensus on the aircraft commander's role is Robert L. Hall, "Social Influence on the Aircraft Commander's Role," *American Sociological Review*, XX (1955), pp. 294–299.

[6] Bales and Slater, *op. cit.*, p. 260.

[7] The impact of the size of the school board and the number of response categories on V are considered in greater detail in Appendix C.

[8] Seventy-seven items are listed under "size of group" in the index to the bibliography in A. Paul Hare, Edgar F. Borgatta, and Robert F. Bales, *Small Groups: Studies in Social Interaction* (New York: Alfred A. Knopf, 1955), pp. 665–666.

[9] The proof for this equation is presented in Appendix D.

[10] See Chapter Seven, pp. 101–104 for a general description of these instruments and Appendix A for the question wording and items used.

[11] In the computation of the consensus scores a problem arose in that occasionally a superintendent or school board member failed to answer a question. In order that the several summary consensus scores for one school system would be based

on the same items and the same respondents no consensus scores were computed *for any item* which any respondent failed to answer. The four summary consensus scores (V, V', M, and D) for each school system were therefore always based on the same items but the scores for different school systems were based on slightly different sets of items, standardized for the number of items in the instrument. This method of computing scores created a problem for determining reliability coefficients. The problem was handled in the following manner: Items in a given instrument were assigned to split halves for a particular school system; if an item was omitted a score was inserted based on the average of the other scores in that half.

[12] This matter was considered earlier in Chapter Seven, pp. 98–99.

eleven

Interaction and Homogeneity

In discussing consensus on norms and values in their review of psychological factors involved in group phenomena, Riecken and Homans say:

> The degree of consensus may depend on the members' similarity in cultural and social background, and also on the length of time the members have been in interaction with one another. The norms of members probably become more similar with time, but there seem to be no empirical studies of this relationship.[1]

These two properties of groups, the length of interaction among members and their homogeneity in cultural and social backgrounds, are the variables whose relationship to intra- and interposition microscopic consensus will be examined in this chapter.

THE INTERACTION HYPOTHESIS

The expectations position incumbents hold for one another are psychological events, and as such, they are capable of being affected by social interaction. In the course of interaction, individuals not only act in relation to one another, but they react, express approval and disapproval, communicate their own expectations and gain ideas about the expectations of others. How would such conditions affect the consensus among a group of position incumbents?

When individuals first come together in a group, their expectations may or may not be similar but there is one condition which can be reasonably assumed: They will not know what the expectations of the others are. As they perceive the expectations which are held by those with whom they interact, their own expectations may be modified. Will this modification be in a direction such that the expectations of the group members become more similar, or less similar? In other words, does amount of interaction lead to more or less consensus on expectations among a group of position incumbents?

The hypothesis we shall use in dealing with this question is based on the accompanying set of postulates:

1. The longer a group meets, the more informal the interaction among its group members (for example, it will place less emphasis on parliamentary rules of procedure and members will more frequently call each other by their first names).

2. As the interaction among group members becomes less formal, the "social climate" will become more conducive to the consideration of, and to the development of steps leading to the elimination of dysfunctional elements affecting the achievement of the group's goal(s).

3. Lack of consensus among group members on their role definitions is a major dysfunctional element affecting the achievement of a group's goal(s).

From these three postulates, the hypothesis follows that:

Hypothesis 11–1: The longer the members of a social system have interacted with one another, the more consensus they will have on the expectations they apply to incumbents of positions in that social system.

Hypothesis 11–1 leads to two predictions which it is possible to test with our two measures of consensus, V and D. In the case of one measure V, the prediction will be that the longer school board members have interacted with one another, the more consensus they will have; in the case of the other measure D, the prediction will be that the longer a superintendent has interacted with the members of his board, the more consensus there will be between them.

In order to measure the "amount of interaction" in a school board, the length of time every board member had served had to be compared with that of every other board member, and of each pair, the smaller figure selected. These figures, representing the number of years of interaction of each pair of board members, were then averaged, providing a measure of the "average amount of interaction between pairs of present members of the school board." This is, of course, a very rough index of the amount of interaction, which ignores the number of meetings, the length of the meetings, and attendance at meetings. It might be considered that the amount of informal interaction would be an even more crucial element in an ideal measure of the "amount of interaction" of members of formal organizations, but this would be very difficult to assess. The measure we have, with these recognized limitations, seems adequate for the exploratory analysis for which it is designed.

A consideration which should not be ignored is of the different degrees of "experience" of board members independent of the amount of interaction they have in common with one another. The members of a school board are not all elected at the same time, nor have they all served an equal number of years. Some members may have been on the board much longer than others, which means that they have interacted with board members other than those who comprise the board for purposes of our analysis. That is, some board members have "experience" over and above their interaction with present members of the board. School board members are laymen who must, to some extent, learn what is involved in their position after they have assumed it. Whether or not they do so, members who have been on their boards for a long time have had more opportunity to learn the "professional" norms of their superintendent and the expectations of their fellow board members. It might be that "experience" (independent of interaction) has a great deal to do with the consensus among board members. Experience on a board necessarily implies interaction with *some* board members, even though they are not necessarily the ones considered in the present analysis. A measure of this "experience" phenomenon is the mean number of years of service of school board members. Although the "experience" variable is more inclusive since it measures "interaction" plus something else, the two are correlated $+.81$, which suggests that to a considerable extent they are measuring the same thing.

The hypothesis may be tested by correlating the interaction score of the boards with their V scores. This correlation is $-.19$, which is significantly different from zero at the .05 level. This correlation is interpreted as supporting the hypothesis.

TABLE 11–A. CORRELATIONS BETWEEN THE "AVERAGE INTERACTION" AND "AVERAGE EXPERIENCE" OF SCHOOL BOARDS AND CONSENSUS WITHIN THE BOARDS

$(N = 105)$

Zero Order Correlations

	V	V'
I. Interaction among School Board Members:	$-.19*$	$-.21\dagger$
E. Experience of School Board Members:	$-.22\dagger$	$-.21\dagger$
($r_{IE} = .81$)		

Multiple Correlations

$$R_{V \cdot IE} = .22 \qquad R_{V' \cdot IE} = .22$$

* Significant at the .05 level.
† Significant at the .02 level.

A second question which can be asked, whether or not the measure of "average amount of experience" of board members is correlated with the degree of consensus, can also be answered affirmatively. The correlation between this measure and the V score is $-.22$, which is significant at the .02 level. We can say, consequently, that both the amount of interaction among school board members and the amount of experience of board members are correlated with the amount of consensus among them. Since these two measures are so highly correlated with one another, however, it appears that one relationship, rather than two, has been demonstrated.

The multiple correlation between V and the interaction and experience variables $(R_{V \cdot IE} = .22)$ is insignificant at the .05 level and is practically the same as the zero order correlation between V and the experience variable $(r_{VE} = -.22)$ which is significant at this level. It is difficult to separate these two variables logically. A school board member cannot have had much interaction unless he has had at least as much experience (according to our operational definitions), nor can he have had much experience without an equivalent amount of interaction with *some* other school board members, although not necessarily with those who are involved in this analysis. Since the two variables are so highly correlated, it can be concluded that, on the average, the interaction implied by experience has been with members who are involved in this analysis.

Consequently, although a relationship has been demonstrated between an interaction-experience phenomenon and consensus within school boards, we do not feel that conclusions can be offered with respect to relationships between "interaction" and consensus, and "experience" and consensus, independently of one another, because the two variables in our analysis are operationally similar and with our sample, empirically related.

Had we done this analysis with V', the measure of consensus which does not involve the size of the group in its definition, the results would have been little different. The correlation between Interaction and V' is $-.21$, and between Experience and V', $-.21$. The first is slightly more than the corresponding correlation with V, and the second is slightly less than the corresponding correlation with V. The multiple correlation with V' is .22, which is not significant. The conclusion which is suggested by this elaboration on the analysis of interaction-experience and consensus, is that the relationships are approximately of the same magnitude whether or not our measure of consensus is defined to include size of the group.

To test the second prediction to which the interaction hypothesis leads, that there will be more consensus between superintendents and their boards if they have interacted for a longer period of time, a measure of interaction between them, similar to the one we have described for "within boards," was derived. To do this we compared the length of time the superintendent had been in his present job with the length of service of each of his board members. The smaller of these two figures represents the number of years the superintendent has interacted with that board member, and an average of these smaller figures represents the "average amount of interaction" between a superintendent and each of his board members. The correlation between this measure and D, the measure of consensus between a superintendent and his board, is .07, which is not significant.

TABLE 11–B. CORRELATIONS BETWEEN "INTERACTION" AND "EXPERIENCE" OF SCHOOL BOARDS AND SUPERINTENDENTS AND CONSENSUS BETWEEN THE BOARDS AND THEIR SUPERINTENDENTS
($N = 105$)

	D	M	V
$I.$ Interaction between the Superintendent and School Board Members	.07	.07	.02
$E_S.$ Experience of the Superintendent	.02	−.03	.11
$E_{SB}.$ Experience of the School Board Members	−.06	.04	−.22*

* Significant at the .02 level.

The conclusion must be drawn that there is no relationship between the amount of interaction between a superintendent and his board and the amount of consensus between them. Nor is this interaction measure related to either of the components of D (M and V), with which it is correlated .07 and .02, respectively. From Table 11–B, the following negative conclusions can also be drawn: There is no relationship between the superintendent's "experience in his present job" and the consensus with his board; nor is there a relationship between the "experience of the school board members" (the same experience variable with which we have already dealt) and consensus between the board and the superintendent. The only significant correlation in Table 11–B is that between experience of the board and consensus within the board, which has already been considered. In the evidence, consequently, there seems little to contradict the conclusion that the consensus between a superintendent and his school board is independent of the amount of time they have been together and of the amount of time they have each been in their positions.

One possible reason why this "interaction-consensus" hypothesis

has not received support from the analysis of consensus between superintendents and their school board members is that the superintendent occupies a "professional" position, while school board members
do not. One of the assumptions on which the hypothesis was based is
that in the course of interaction, individuals change their expectations. If the incumbent of one position is a "professional" and holds
what he and his fellow professionals consider to be "professional"
expectations, there would seem little basis for reasoning that he will
change his expectations in the course of interacting with nonprofessionals.

Another possibility is that the insignificant correlation obtained may
be a result of the interaction of two opposite effects: consensus and
interaction between the superintendent and school board may be positively related when the school boards consider their superintendent
to be an effective school administrator and negatively related when
they view him as ineffective. As they interact over time, only if his
actions meet with their approval will school board members tend to
reach consensus on role definition with their superintendent. To the
extent that his school board disapproves of his actions, we might expect longer interaction to result in less consensus. This is a suggestion which may be given an approximate test with our data.
School board members rated their superintendent on how well he
carried out seven functions of school administration. On the basis
of this rating a mean rating score for each school board was computed,
and the boards divided on the basis of the median of this score into
two groups: those who gave their superintendent a relatively high rating, and those who gave their superintendent a relatively low rating.

On the basis of this reasoning we would predict that school boards
which rated their superintendent high would reach more consensus
with him the longer they interact with him. School boards which
gave their superintendent a low rating, would reach less consensus
with him the longer they interacted. Neither of these predictions was
confirmed, so that we are led to conclude that this line of reasoning
does not explain the absence of a relationship between interaction
and consensus between the superintendent and his board.[2]

Still another possible reason for the finding that interaction and
consensus are not related *between* superintendents and their board
members whereas they are *among* board members, could lie in the
different formally defined relationships between superintendents and
their board members, and among board members themselves. The
superintendent is formally the school board's subordinate. There is
no formally prescribed relationship among board members other than

that they should work together. The latter condition would seem more likely to lead to the "informal" interaction assumed as a basis for this hypothesis than would the former one.

THE HOMOGENEITY HYPOTHESIS

Incumbents of particular positions in given social systems (as for example, superintendents and school board members in school systems) are as a rule incumbents of other positions in other social systems and have many different characteristics, qualities, and their own private histories. These differences may predispose them to hold different role definitions of the positions which they assume and those occupied by other group members. The question in which we are interested here is whether position incumbents who are more and less similar in their qualities and characteristics will have more or less consensus on the expectations for their own and other positions. In Chapter Twelve we will consider the question of whether or not the *characteristics* of position incumbents, without regard to their *similarity* on these characteristics, have an effect on their consensus on role definition.

There are two arguments which lead us to a single general hypothesis. The first is that people with similar backgrounds will have been exposed to similar influences and therefore will develop similar role definitions. That is, people with the same background characteristics develop similar constellations of values and expectations, and when they encounter new situations the similarity in background will tend to result in similar definitions of the new situations. The second argument is less direct. From their examination of the literature on the influence of social characteristics of group members on group processes, Riecken and Homans conclude that ". . . persons who are of similar background outside the group being studied—similar in group memberships, rank interests, etc., outside—tend to choose one another highly and interact with one another often *within* the group." [3] This line of reasoning leads back to the interaction hypothesis. It adds another important element, however. Given the similarity in background there is a basis for identification. People who tend to identify with one another, will tend to accept the expectations which the others hold. If the person who is identified with is a more experienced incumbent of the position, the newcomer will learn from him the expectations he already holds. If the person identified with is also a newcomer, the two who identify with one another may "learn together," so to speak, each accepting what the other accepts and rejecting what the other rejects. The general hypothesis to which this reasoning leads is:

Hypothesis 11–2: The greater the homogeneity among or between position incumbents, the more consensus they will have on the expectations for their own and others' positions.

In order to test this hypothesis it is necessary to specify in what respects the position incumbents are similar to one another. In fact, an important research question is what characteristics and past experiences are salient and relevant to feelings of identification in particular social systems. The objective of this analysis is as much to specify in what respects the hypothesis holds (that is, with what characteristics for our position incumbents) as it is to test the general relationship it posits. Some characteristics by means of which people can be differentiated seem irrelevant because they have few or no implications for social behavior; many but not all physical characteristics would be included among these. Others appear to be highly relevant to almost all social situations, such as the sex of the incumbents. The relevance of others is perhaps more problematic, for example, the religion, occupation, or political attitudes of position incumbents.

Five types of characteristics have been chosen for analysis, each of which seems, if not of obvious relevance to the expectations which can be developed for school board members and superintendents, of at least possible relevance. These are: educational and political attitudes, religion, motivation of school board members, sex, and social status characteristics.

In order to test the hypothesis it was necessary to develop measures of homogeneity among school board members and between the school board and the superintendent for the variables and qualities which will be used in the analyses. Measures of homogeneity on quantitative variables are identical methodologically to the measures of consensus which have already been described. For each variable V, M, and D scores were developed.[4] For the qualitative characteristics which are included in the analysis comparable scores were derived.[5]

Educational and Political Attitudes and Consensus. A scale of "Educational Progressivism" was developed which is comprised of items dealing with school practices which are considered by professional educators to be more and less progressive. (See Appendix B–3c.) It might be considered that the attitudinal dimension which is measured by this scale is of immediate relevance to the role definition of school board members and superintendents. But this is not necessarily the case. Whereas the items of this scale deal with specific educational practices which reflect an overall "educational" philosophy, the items of role definition which are the expectations on which the consensus measures are based deal with practices of school "administration." Although they are both concerned with education, they are not so closely related as might at first appear. (See Appendix Table B–3c and Appendix Tables A–1 and A–5 for the original items involved.) Consequently, the attitudes on this dimension may not be crucial to the identification process which has been offered as an intervening variable between the homogeneity of interacting position incumbents and their consensus on role definition.

With this qualification, the two predictions to which the general hypothesis would lead are (1) that there is a positive relationship between similarity in the educational progressivism of the members of a school board and the degree of consensus in their role definitions and (2) that the more similar the educational progressivism of board members is to the educational progressivism of their superintendent, the more consensus there will be between them on their definitions of each other's role.

TABLE 11–C. CORRELATIONS BETWEEN HOMOGENEITY ON THE EDUCATIONAL PROGRESSIVISM AND POLITICAL-ECONOMIC CONSERVATISM OF SUPERINTENDENTS AND SCHOOL BOARDS AND CONSENSUS WITHIN THE BOARDS AND BETWEEN THE BOARDS AND THEIR SUPERINTENDENTS
($N = 105$)

	Consensus Variables			
Educational Progressivism	V	V'	D	M
V. Homogeneity of the board	.11	.06	−.05	−.11
D. Homogeneity of the board and the superintendent	.03	.02	.05	.05
M. Squared mean difference between the board and the superintendent	.01	−.02	.07	.08
Political-Economic Conservatism				
V. Homogeneity of the board	.32†	.25*	.15	.01
D. Homogeneity of the board and the superintendent	.09	.14	.16	.11
M. Squared mean difference between the board and the superintendent	.01	.04	.12	.11

* Significant at the .01 level.
† Significant at the .001 level.

The tests of these predictions are presented in Table 11–C. Neither prediction is confirmed, and the hypothesis does not receive support from these analyses. The correlation of the educational progressivism V with the consensus V is only .11, and with the consensus V' only .06, neither of which is significant. It is necessary to conclude that the homogeneity of a school board on attitudes about educational progressivism has no demonstrable relationship to, and therefore no effect on, the consensus within the board on role definition.

The correlation between the two D measures which tests the second prediction, that between the superintendent and the board, is .05, which is also not significant. Furthermore, neither the V nor M component of D on the homogeneity measure is related to either of the components of D on the consensus measure. There are no relationships which require any qualification to the conclusion that similarity in educational attitudes has no demonstrable relationship to consensus on role definition, either within a school board or between the board and its superintendent.

The other attitudinal dimension which was selected for analysis is the Political-Economic Conservatism (PEC) of the school board members and of the superintendent (Appendix B–4a). Although these attitudes do not seem to have any direct relevance to educational problems, they may be of importance in the identification process which has been suggested as an intervening variable between homogeneity and consensus. The prototype of the PEC scale we used appears in *The Authoritarian Personality*.[6] The predictions are the same with this as with the other attitudinal variable: a positive correlation between the two V measures and between the two D measures.

As can be seen from Table 11–C, the within board prediction is confirmed, $(r_{VV\,(\text{PEC})} = .32)$, but that between the superintendent and the board is not $(r_{DD\,(\text{PEC})} = .156;\ .165$ required with a one-tailed test). Board members who are homogeneous with respect to political-economic attitudes are more likely to reach consensus on role definition than are those who are not; but there is no significant relationship between the similarity of a superintendent and his board on these attitudes and consensus between them on role definition. The first relationship, although reduced when V_{PEC} and V' are related instead of V, is still significant (.25), which suggests the conclusion that, although it may be to some extent dependent on the size of the board, the relationship which has just been demonstrated holds when the measure of consensus which does not include size is used.

Why should this relationship hold within the school board but not between the board and the superintendent? One possible explanation is that the school board members' position is one which is more liable to be affected by the political and economic attitudes of the members. The school superintendent is a "professional" educator, whose conduct in his job, and whose administrative procedures are probably only slightly influenced by his political or even his economic attitudes. To school board members, who are responsible for the broad policies of the school system (and the most important policy decisions resolve themselves into budgetary decisions to expand or not, to improve or not) the economic and political attitudes of their fellow members are more directly relevant when they evaluate one another and when the process of identification is taking place. The policy decisions of school board members can be visibly related to their political-economic conservatism, but the actions of a superintendent are not likely to be.

Analyses with two attitudinal variables provided only very limited support for the homogeneity hypothesis. There were no relationships between homogeneity of any kind on educational progressivism and consensus of any kind. There was one significant relationship between homogeneity on political-economic conservatism and consensus: The more homogeneous boards on this variable have more consensus. These two attitudinal variables provide data which are of importance in pointing out the necessity for caution in suggesting, without specification, such an overriding hypothesis as the general "homogeneity" hypothesis. Under only one set of conditions which have been considered so far, does it appear to hold.

Religion and Consensus. The religion of incumbents of the two positions under examination would seem to be of direct relevance to their consensus for two reasons. First of all, it is an index of a very complex and probably fundamental series of attitudinal variables, habits of thought, conception, and belief, which, although they may be difficult to identify and specify, can be assumed to be significantly different for the two major classes of religious identification we have used: Catholics and non-Catholics.[7] It is also possible to think of these religious designations as bases for positions which have different expectations associated with them. The other reason is that church groups have taken variant stands on matters affecting the public schools.

The two predictions are the same for religion as for the attitudinal variables. It should be pointed out again, that V for religion is pq (the proportion of Catholics multiplied by the proportion of non-Catholics); M is p'^2 (the squared proportion of board members who differ from the superintendent on religion—they are considered the same if they are both non-Catholics); and D is p', because under the definition of D which is used for the consensus measures, $D = V + M$, which, for qualitative dichotomous characteristics can be shown to be equal to p'.[8]

TABLE 11–D. CORRELATIONS BETWEEN HOMOGENEITY ON THE RELIGION OF SUPERINTENDENTS AND SCHOOL BOARDS AND CONSENSUS WITHIN THE BOARDS AND BETWEEN THE BOARDS AND THEIR SUPERINTENDENTS
$(N = 105)$

Religion	Consensus Variables			
	V	V'	D	M
V. Homogeneity of the board	.24*	.15	.01	−.11
D. Homogeneity of the board and the superintendent	.05	.07	.08	.06
M. Squared mean difference between the board and the superintendent	−.03	−.01	.09	.11

* Significant at the .01 level.

In Table 11–D are presented the correlations which test these predictions. The prediction within boards is again confirmed (r_{VV} (religion) = .24), whereas that between the board and the superintendent is not (r_{DD} (religion) = .08). The conclusion which is suggested is that the more homogeneous school boards are with respect to religion, the more consensus they will have, but that religious similarity has no effect on the consensus between a board and its superintendent. The homogeneity measure on religion is not significantly related to V', which suggests that the relationship holds only when consensus is defined so as to include size of group.

Motivation of School Board Members and Consensus. The following prediction would derive directly from the homogeneity hypothesis: The more similar school board members are in the motives they had for seeking election to the board, the more consensus they will have on their role definitions. But since "motivation" is a very ambiguous term, it is necessary to specify what the "motivations" are on which school board members will be considered more and less similar to one another. Each superintendent was asked to describe, for each of his school board members, the motives he thought they had in seeking election. A check list was provided, and three of the response categories (see Appendix B–4c) have been selected for analysis here, one of which is considered to be a commendable motivation (from the point of view of the superintendent and the school system) and the other two of which are considered to be potentially disruptive.

The predictions are that the more homogeneous school boards are with respect to the three motives, "Motivated by civic duty," "Represent some group," and "Obtain political experience," the more consensus they will have. The correlations which test these three predictions are presented in Table 11–E. With the "Civic duty" motive, the

TABLE 11–E. CORRELATIONS BETWEEN THE HOMOGENEITY OF SCHOOL BOARD MEMBERS ON THREE MOTIVATIONS AND CONSENSUS WITHIN THE BOARDS

$(N = 105)$

Motivation	Consensus Variables	
	V	V'
$V.$ "Civic duty"	.10	.09
$V.$ "Represent some group"	.37*	.32*
$V.$ "Political experience"	.32*	.21†

* Significant at the .001 level.
† Significant at the .02 level.

homogeneity hypothesis receives no support ($r_{VV \text{ (motive)}} = .10$). With "Represent some group," and "Obtain political experience," the correlations between the homogeneity measures and consensus V are both significant ($r_{VV \text{ (motive)}}$ is .37 and .32 for the two motives, respectively) and support the homogeneity hypothesis. Both of these demonstrated relationships hold when the homogeneity measures are correlated with consensus V', for which the correlations are .32 and .21, respectively.

One possible explanation of the difference in the findings for the single "commendable" motivation and the two potentially disruptive motivations might be in the salience or visibility of the motivations themselves. To be motivated by civic duty might be to have certain feelings of sincerity and desire for the good of the schools, which are very difficult to translate into action. Superintendents, recognizing the sincerity of their members ascribed this motivation to them without concern for the members' expression of this motivation on the board. The other two motives are fairly specific and fairly easily translatable into action on the board, and in fact, they both imply action of a particular kind. This difference in the salience and visibility of the motives or of their consequences in action, might account in part for the different effects which homogeneity with respect to them has on the consensus of the school boards. In the next chapter we will take up the question of whether the *content* of these motivations may be involved rather than homogeneity.

Sexual Composition and Consensus. Sex is a characteristic which people carry with them all of the time, and, like age, may be considered a position in terms of which social relations are at least partially influenced by expectations. For this reason it is perhaps one of the most obvious characteristics with which the homogeneity hypothesis should be tested. Since sex is a position which may be assumed to bear some influence on nearly all social relations, its effect or lack of effect on the school board members' definition of their own and the superintendent's role deserves exploration. This suggests the more general problem area of the impact of multiple position occupancy on role definitions.

A condition which to some extent modifies the generality of this test, is the fact that superintendents are, in our sample, consistently male. The predictions to which the homogeneity hypothesis would lead are (1) that the more homogeneous school boards are with respect to sex, the more consensus they will have, and (2) the more homogeneous a school board and its superintendent with respect to sex (and since the superintendents are all male, this means the fewer women on the board), the more consensus between them. In all but four cases women are in a minority on the school boards of our sample. Consequently, the predictions based on the homogeneity hypothesis imply that the fewer women there are on the board, the more consensus both within the board and between the board and the superintendent. The tests of these predictions are presented in Table 11–F.

TABLE 11–F. CORRELATIONS BETWEEN HOMOGENEITY ON SEX OF SCHOOL BOARDS AND SUPERINTENDENTS AND CONSENSUS WITHIN THE BOARDS AND BETWEEN THE BOARDS AND THEIR SUPERINTENDENTS

$(N = 105)$*

Sex	Consensus Variables			
	V	V'	D	M
V. Homogeneity of the board	$-.13$	$-.19$	$-.04$	$.02$
D. Homogeneity of the board and the superintendent	$-.18$	$-.19$	$-.07$	$.01$
M. Squared mean difference between the board and the superintendent	$-.19$	$-.16$	$.01$	$-.08$

* Since the correlations in this table are in general not in the predicted direction, it is necessary to use a two-tailed test of significance. A correlation of .196 is required for significance at the .05 level with a two-tailed test.

Neither of the predictions is confirmed. The first, of within board consensus, is *not* in the direction predicted by the homogeneity hypothesis ($r_{VV \ (sex)} = -.13$, and $r_{V'V \ (sex)} = -.19$). Since these correlations are not in the predicted direction it is necessary to use a two-tailed test in determining whether or not they are significantly different from zero. The correlation with V is clearly not significant, but that with V' is almost significant (.196 required at the .05 level). The implication is that the more women there are on the board or the more heterogeneous as measured by pq, the more consensus within the board.

The second prediction leads to completely negative results. There is no evidence that there is a relationship between the proportion of women on the board and consensus between the board and the superintendent ($r_{\text{DD (sex)}} = -.08$).

In the case of one prediction, the homogeneity hypothesis is essentially contradicted (the only instance, incidentally, in which it is contradicted with our data), and in the case of the other prediction, unconfirmed. Whether the sexual *composition* of school boards bears any relationship to consensus, independently of their sexual *homogeneity*, is discussed in Chapter Twelve.

Social Status Characteristics and Consensus. There is considerable evidence that individuals of different "social status" have different values and attitudes.[9] Indexes of social status which are ordinarily used, and which we will use, are highly visible and for this reason are very likely to give rise to the phenomenon of identification, which has been proposed as a variable intervening between homogeneity and consensus. Education is probably a highly visible characteristic in this situation just because this is an educational setting. Income, on the other hand, is visible only in terms of the use to which it is put, or because of either voluntary or formal communication, as in the case of the school board's knowledge of the superintendent's salary (if not income) independent of what he apparently spends or is willing to tell them.

The homogeneity hypothesis could be tested with the education variable only within the school board, because the superintendent's educational level could not be meaningfully compared with that of

TABLE 11–G. CORRELATIONS BETWEEN HOMOGENEITY ON EDUCATION AND INCOME OF SCHOOL BOARD MEMBERS AND SUPERINTENDENTS AND CONSENSUS WITHIN THE BOARDS AND BETWEEN THE BOARDS AND THEIR SUPERINTENDENTS ($N = 105$)

	Consensus Variables			
Education	V	V'	D	M
V. Homogeneity of the board	.18*	.07	.00	−.09
Income				
V. Homogeneity of the board	.02	−.09	−.05	−.07
D. Homogeneity of the board and the superintendent	−.04	−.11	−.03	−.02
M. Squared mean difference between the board and the superintendent	−.11	−.13	−.04	.01

* Significant at the .05 level.

his school board members.[10] Income, on the other hand, as an intrinsically quantitative variable, can provide tests of the homogeneity hypothesis both within the board and between the board and the superintendent. The predictions are, of course, that homogeneity will be positively correlated with consensus in all cases.

The prediction that the more homogeneous the board with respect to education, the more consensus within the board receives confirmation ($r_{VV \text{ (education)}} = .18$). It is necessary to conclude that this relationship is almost entirely due to the effect of size of board, which is common to both V measures, because when homogeneity on education is correlated with V', the correlation reduces to .07. Neither of the predictions in which income is involved is confirmed ($r_{VV \text{ (income)}}$ being .02 and $r_{DD \text{ (income)}}$ being $-.03$). Although the homogeneity hypothesis has been supported by one of the relationships with which it has been tested with these two indexes of social status, this single confirmation can be considered to be due to the fact that homogeneity and consensus as operationally defined are methodologically related.

Discussion of the Homogeneity Hypothesis. The several analyses with which the homogeneity hypothesis has been tested would indicate that it is quite limited and cannot be considered accurately descriptive of any generally effective principle governing the role definitions of interacting position incumbents. Whether or not there is a relationship between the homogeneity of members of a group and their consensus on role expectations is dependent, first, on the characteristics on which the homogeneity measures are obtained, and second, on the positions occupied by the incumbents under examination. There have been no relationships demonstrated between the homogeneity of a superintendent and his board and consensus between them on the expectations for their two positions, so that we must conclude that there is no evidence which would support the homogeneity hypothesis for incumbents of two positions. Within the board, five significant relationships were found, providing support for the hypothesis with respect to groups of incumbents of the same position.

It is interesting to ask, with the significant relationships which we have found, to what extent consensus on role definition (in general) can be accounted for by the homogeneity of the members of a group. Since there were no significant relationships found with the interposition tests of this hypothesis, the answer to this question must be restricted to homogeneity of school board members and their consensus among themselves. Using four of the homogeneity variables which were found to be significantly related to V (consensus), the V measures on Political-Economic Conservatism, Religion, the Group Representation motivation, and the Political Experience motivation, a multiple correlation with V of .54 was obtained ($R = .54$, $R^2 = .29$). We may say, then, that in examining the homogeneity hypothesis we have been considering determinants which account for slightly over one fourth of the variance of consensus. The three homogeneity variables which are significantly related to the V' measure of consensus, PEC, Group Representation, and Political Experience, provide a multiple correlation with V' of .42 ($R = .42$, $R^2 = .18$), accounting for less than one fifth of the variance of V', the measure of consensus which is defined so as not to include size of board.

Notes and References for Chapter Eleven

[1] Henry W. Riecken and George C. Homans, "Psychological Aspects of Social Structure," in Gardner Lindzey (Editor), *Handbook of Social Psychology*, II (Cambridge: Addison-Wesley Publishing Company, 1954), p. 788.

[2] The correlation between length of interaction and consensus D for the high rating group was $+.19$, and for the low rating group, $-.15$. With N's of 52 and 53, respectively, neither of these correlations is significant at the .05 level for which a correlation of at least .23 would have been required. Since a high D score represents low consensus, it can be seen that these correlations, as well as being insignificant, are both in the wrong direction.

[3] Riecken and Homans, *op. cit.*, p. 803.

[4] For the operational procedures used in developing these scores, see Chapter Ten, pp. 167–174.

[5] $V = pq$ (where p is the proportion of those who have the characteristic of interest and q the proportion of those who do not); $M = p'^2$ (where p' is the proportion of board members who are different from the superintendent on the characteristic); and since $D = V + M$, $D = pq + p'^2$. Since p' is equal either to p or to q, then D becomes $p'(1 - p') + p'^2 = p'$ (simply, the proportion of board members who differ on the characteristic from their superintendent).

[6] T. W. Adorno, E. Frenkel-Brunswik, D. J. Levinson, and R. N. Sanford, *The Authoritarian Personality* (New York: Harper and Brothers, 1950). For the scale used see Appendix Table B–4a.

[7] Thirty-seven percent of the 508 school board members were Catholics and 63 percent non-Catholics. The 320 non-Catholic board members included 293 Protestants, 12 Jews, 12 with no religious identification, and 3 with "other" church identifications.

[8] See note 5 above. The relationships among D, V, and M are considered in detail in Appendix D.

[9] See, for example, Richard Centers, *The Psychology of Social Classes* (Princeton: Princeton University Press, 1949).

[10] This happens because of the difficulty of interpreting differences between the educational level of superintendents and school board members with professional occupations. The impact of the average occupational level of the school board on intra- and interposition consensus is treated in Chapter Twelve.

twelve

Other Determinants
of Microscopic Role Consensus

Characteristics of Position Incumbents. In Chapter Eleven we considered two hypotheses about the determinants of microscopic role consensus: the first, that amount of interaction is related to consensus, and the second, that homogeneity of group members on certain characteristics is related to consensus. In this chapter the basic question which will be asked is whether or not groups with different characteristics (for example, groups of different size) and groups composed of people differentiated according to certain characteristics (for example, religion) will have different degrees of consensus. Most of our explorations will be concerned with the impact on role consensus of the same variables and qualitative differentiations used in testing the homogeneity hypothesis.

Whereas in testing the homogeneity hypothesis we examined the relationship between consensus and the degree of *similarity* among group members on these characteristics, in this case our interest is in the relationship between consensus and the *content* of the characteristics. For example, in our consideration of the homogeneity hypothesis we raised the question of whether groups whose members tend to hold more similar political and economic attitudes than the members of other groups, tend to have more consensus on their role definitions. In this chapter we shall ask whether groups whose members tend to be more progressive in their political and economic attitudes than the members of other groups tend to have more consensus on their role definitions.

Educational and Political Attitudes and Consensus. If it is assumed that the superintendent, as a professional educator, represents the "progressive point of view" to his school board members, a prediction may be made with respect to the "educational progressivism" of school boards and their consensus with their superintendent. If the superintendent represents the "progressive point of view" to his school board members and if they themselves hold educationally progressive attitudes, then, it can be argued, they will be motivated to agree with their superintendent on the definition of their roles, to the extent that they *perceive* that their values with respect to education are similar to his. If the superintendent represents the "progressive point of view" to his board members and if they themselves hold educationally conservative attitudes, then, it can be argued, they will not be motivated to agree with their superintendent because they *perceive* that their values with respect to education differ from their superintendent's. These two conditions lead to the prediction that there will be a positive relationship between *school board* "educational progressivism" and consensus between the superintendent and the school board: the more progressive the board, the more consensus they will have with their superintendent.

If it is assumed that from the vantage point of the superintendent, his school board, comprised as it is of laymen, represents the "conservative point of view" with respect to educational values, a contrary prediction can be made for the relationship between a *superintendent's* "educational progressivism" and consensus with his school board. If he considers his school board members "conservative" with respect to educational issues, then the more progressive a superintendent, the less likely he is to be motivated to agree with them, because he perceives that his and their educational views are divergent; the more "conservative" the superintendent, the more likely he is to be motivated to agree with them, because he will perceive that his and their educational views are convergent. The prediction will be of a negative relationship between a *superintendent's* educational progressivism and consensus with his board: the more progressive the superintendent, the less consensus he will have with his board.

By comparing the distributions of scale scores obtained in the two samples on a scale based on the combined responses of superintendents and school board members, some evidence may be claimed in support of the assumptions that the school board represents the "conservative" and the superintendent the "progressive" point of view to each other. (See Appendix B–3c.) On this scale, the scores of the superintendents' sample are negatively skewed, that is, they are concentrated at the progressive end of the continuum. The school board members' scores are distributed fairly evenly over the continuum of progressivism, since, in large part, the scale is based on their responses, but relative to superintendents, it can be said the school board members are more likely to be "conservative."

TABLE 12–A. CORRELATIONS BETWEEN THE EDUCATIONAL PROGRESSIVISM AND POLITICAL-ECONOMIC CONSERVATISM OF SUPERINTENDENTS AND SCHOOL BOARDS AND CONSENSUS WITHIN THE BOARDS AND BETWEEN THE BOARDS AND THEIR SUPERINTENDENTS

$(N = 105)$

Educational Progressivism	Consensus Variables			
	V	V'	D	M
Superintendent's scale score	−.09	−.09	.09	.15
Mean scale score of school board members	.07	−.02	−.19*	−.24‡
Political-Economic Conservatism				
Superintendent's score	−.17*	.06	−.05	.03
Mean score of school board members	−.22†	−.17*	.02	.13

* Significant at the .05 level.
† Significant at the .02 level.
‡ Significant at the .01 level.

The correlations which test these two predictions are presented in Table 12–A. The prediction that school boards whose members are more "educationally progressive" will have more consensus with their superintendents is confirmed. The correlation between the mean educational progressivism score of the school board members and D is −.19, which is significant at the .05 level and in the direction predicted. The correlation with M, the "between" component of D, is −.24, which is significant at the .01 level. The second prediction, that more progressive superintendents will have less consensus with their boards, is not confirmed. The correlation between the superintendent's progressivism and his consensus with his board is .09, which, although it is in the direction predicted, is not significant at the .05 level. With M, the superintendent's progressivism is correlated .15 which is again in the direction predicted, but not significant at the .05 level (.165 required).

The "Political-Economic Conservatism"[1] of superintendents and school board members would seem to have little to do with whether or not they agree with one another and among themselves on the expectations for their positions. We might ask, however, whether this kind of conservatism has implications for "motivation to agree with one's fellow group members." It could be argued that the "progressive" is one who wants change and who is dissatisfied with the status quo. Given a set of expectations, the "progressive" individual is one who will be interested in changing them. We will argue, therefore, that a progressive superintendent or school board member will be less likely to be motivated to agree with a given set of expectations than will one who is conservative.

It is predicted that school boards whose members on the average obtain more progressive scores on the PEC instrument will be less likely to have consensus among themselves (that is, there will be a negative correlation between the school board mean PEC score and V); the more progressive the members, the less likely they are to agree with one another. The same prediction might be made with respect to the superintendent's progressivism and his consensus with his board for approximately the same reasons. The progressive superintendents will not be motivated to establish consensus with their boards, because, it has been argued, progressives seek change. From the correlations presented in Table 12–A it can be seen that the first prediction receives support ($r = -.22$, which is significant at the .05 level); the more progressive boards have less consensus. The second prediction receives no support ($r = -.05$).

One possible explanation of the lack of relationship between the D measure and the progressivism of either the superintendent or of the board, is that consensus or agreement according to this measure is dependent on *both* the board and the superintendent, so that although one may be motivated to seek agreement with the other, no predictions can be made unless the other also seeks agreement, or at least fails to seek disagreement. Interestingly, a significant correlation was obtained between the progressivism of the superintendents and the V score, or consensus within the board. This means that the more progressive superintendents are associated with boards in which there is less consensus. This relationship is not maintained, however, with the measure of within board consensus in which the size of the board is not involved: with V', the r is .06. The relationship between the progressivism of the boards and consensus is maintained with the measure of consensus in which size of board is not involved: with V' the r is $-.17$, which is significant.

Two relatively clear relationships have been demonstrated: Educationally progressive school boards are more likely to have consensus with their superintendents, and politically progressive school boards are less likely to have consensus among themselves. Of just as much importance, perhaps, are the negative findings that the attitudes of superintendents on these two variables are not related to consensus within their boards or between their boards and themselves (with the single exception that was shown to be due to the inclusion of size of board in the definition of consensus V).

Religion and Consensus. Although religion can, in a sense, be considered an index of a complex of attitudes, it would seem to be a much more complicated identification than even that, and it is for this reason treated separately from the preceding two analyses of attitudes. In considering possible theoretical links between religion of group members and microscopic role consensus, the most plausible line of reasoning appeared to be that used in the homogeneity hypothesis; that is, similarity of religion among group members provides a basis for identification which leads to the acceptance of similar role definitions. There appeared to be no a priori basis on which predictions could be made about the influence of the superintendent's religion or of the proportion of board members with the same religion on microscopic role consensus other than the reasoning employed in presenting the homogeneity hypothesis. Accordingly, although we shall consider the empirical findings relating the religion of the superintendent and the religious composition of the board to consensus, no additional hypotheses were developed for this problem.

TABLE 12–B. CORRELATIONS BETWEEN THE RELIGION OF SUPERINTENDENTS AND SCHOOL BOARDS AND CONSENSUS WITHIN THE BOARDS AND BETWEEN THE BOARDS AND THEIR SUPERINTENDENTS

$$(N = 105)$$

Zero Order Correlations

	Consensus Variables			
Religion	V	V'	D	M
Of the superintendent (Catholic = 1; non-Catholic = 0)	.14	.12	.29†	.33‡
p of the school board (p = proportion of Catholics) ($r_{p,pq}$ = .51)	.47‡	.37‡	.00	.20*

Multiple Correlation

$$R_{V \cdot p,pq} = .47$$

Independent and Joint Contributions of p and pq to the Explained Variance in Consensus V

$$\beta_p^2 = .215$$
$$\beta_{pq}^2 = .000$$
$$2\beta_p\beta_{pq}r_{pq} = .002$$

* Significant at the .05 level.
† Significant at the .01 level.
‡ Significant at the .001 level.

In Table 12–B are presented the correlations between religion (Catholic, non-Catholic) and the consensus measures.

Whether or not a superintendent is a Catholic has a significant negative effect on the consensus he has with his board, the correlation[2] with D being $+.29$, and with M, $+.33$. The relationship between the superintendent's religion and V is insignificant, but in the same direction as it is with M. These relationships may be interpreted as meaning that Catholic superintendents tend to have less consensus with their boards than do non-Catholic superintendents. One plausible explanation of such a finding is suggested by the homogeneity hypothesis: that Catholic superintendents are more likely different in religion from their boards and therefore have less consensus with them. The relationship between the homogeneity of the superintendent and school board on religion and consensus, which has already been considered, provides empirical refutation for this explanation. There was no demonstrated relationship between the two. (See Chapter Eleven, page 187.)

Perhaps even more surprising is the finding with respect to the proportion of Catholics on the school board. The higher the proportion of Catholics, the less consensus within the board. This correlation ($+.47$) is high enough to provide a significant correlation between the proportion (p) of Catholics on the board and D, although there is virtually no relationship between p and M. Three plausible explanations of this finding present themselves, two of which can be empirically refuted.

The first possible explanation might be that boards with a higher proportion of Catholics are from large urban communities which have larger boards. Since we know that the size of the group is involved in the V measure of consensus, this factor might account for the finding. That the relationship is maintained with V', in which size of the board is not involved in the measure of consensus, is some refutation of this point. The relationship is not entirely due to the size of the boards which have high proportions of Catholics.

A second possible explanation is of the homogeneity of Catholic boards. The correlation between pq (the measure of homogeneity on religion, where p is the proportion of Catholics) and the V score was .24, which is significant, and the correlation of p (the proportion of Catholics) and pq is .51. The multiple correlation ($r_{V \cdot p, pq}$) is .47, not at all different from the zero order correlation between p and V. The relative contributions of p and pq to the amount of explained variance of V represented by this multiple correlation are revealing. The homogeneity measure, pq, does not add anything to the explanation of V independently of its relationship to p. This finding is confirmed by an examination of the scatter diagram of p and V, in which the relationship which is demonstrated still holds in communities where

Catholics are in the majority on the school board. Whether Catholics are in a majority or minority, the more Catholics on the board, the less consensus among its members.

A third possible explanation might be that Catholic board members have less motivation to agree with other board members than non-Catholics have. This might be the case if Catholic board members are more likely than non-Catholic board members to view their function as one of blocking the achievement of the educational program of the public schools. Since their formally defined function is to facilitate its achievement, if this assumption is valid, Catholic board members would tend to hold evaluative standards at variance with those held by other board members.

This line of reasoning would suggest that the motivations of Catholic board members for seeking election to the board would tend to be potentially more disruptive than those of non-Catholics. That this appears to be the case can be seen from Table 12–C. A significantly

TABLE 12–C. PERCENTAGE OF CATHOLIC AND NON-CATHOLIC SCHOOL BOARD MEMBERS WHOSE SUPERINTENDENTS DESCRIBE THEM AS MOTIVATED BY CIVIC DUTY, TO REPRESENT SOME GROUP, AND TO GAIN POLITICAL EXPERIENCE

	Motivated by Civic Duty			
	Yes	No	N	
Catholic	49.4%	50.6%	188	$\chi^2 = 28.90$
Non-Catholic	73.1%	26.9%	320	(Probability less than .001)

	Motivated to Represent Some Group			
	Yes	No	N	
Catholic	37.8%	62.2%	188	$\chi^2 = 12.45$
Non-Catholic	23.1%	76.9%	320	(Probability less than .001)

	Motivated to Gain Political Experience			
	Yes	No	N	
Catholic	36.2%	63.8%	188	$\chi^2 = 48.16$
Non-Catholic	10.6%	89.4%	320	(Probability less than .001)

larger proportion of Catholic than of non-Catholic board members had potentially disruptive motivations (as perceived by their superintendents) for seeking election to their school boards. Although it cannot be claimed that this explanation accounts for the relationship between the proportion of Catholics on the board and consensus among its members, the empirical evidence supports the intervening variable suggested in presenting this line of reasoning.

Motivations of School Board Members and Consensus. The three "motivations" used in the homogeneity analysis will also be used here. The measure in this case is the proportion of board members who are described by the superintendent as motivated by the motivation in question. In the case of the first, "Civic duty," it will be predicted that the higher the proportion of board members who are so motivated, the more consensus they will have among themselves.

The remaining two motivations, "To represent a particular group," and to "Get political experience," are assumed to be potentially disruptive with respect to the effective functioning of the school board. Members who are motivated to represent a factional group, it is argued, are not so likely to be directly concerned with agreement with their fellows as are those who are not so motivated. That is, their motives are to benefit a factional group, and the more people on a board who are so motivated (unless they are all representing the same factional group), the less consensus the board members will have among themselves. Approximately the same reasoning will be applied to the "political experience" motivation. Board members who are so motivated are assumed to be primarily motivated to benefit themselves (that is, their political careers) or their political faction, rather than the schools. As a potentially disruptive motivation, this one will lead to lack of consensus, because those who are so motivated are less likely to be concerned with the best interests of the schools, which, in turn, can seldom be served by disagreements within the board.

The correlations which test these three predictions are presented in Table 12–D.

The first predicted relationship between consensus within the board and the motivation of its members receives significant support. The correlation between the proportion of members motivated by civic duty and consensus V is $-.48$, which means that the larger the proportion so motivated, the more consensus within the board. The relationship is maintained with the V' measure in which the effect of size of board is reduced. There is also a significant relationship between the p for civic duty motivation and D, $(-.23)$, but since there is virtually no relationship between M and the p of civic duty, this can be considered to be due almost entirely to the relationship with the V score. It will be recalled that there were no relationships between the homogeneity measure (pq) on this motivation and any of the consensus variables. Consequently the relationship demonstrated here cannot be due to the similarity of motivation in boards with a high proportion of members motivated by civic duty, but must be considered due to the proportion (or the extent of this motivation) itself.

TABLE 12–D. CORRELATIONS BETWEEN THE MOTIVATIONS OF SCHOOL BOARD
MEMBERS AND CONSENSUS WITHIN THE BOARDS AND BETWEEN THE BOARDS
AND THEIR SUPERINTENDENTS

$(N = 105)$

Zero Order Correlations

Motivation	Consensus Variables			
	V	V'	D	M
p. Proportion of school board members motivated by civic duty	$-.48\ddagger$	$-.45\ddagger$	$-.227*$	$-.02$
p. Proportion of school board members motivated to represent some group $(r_{p,pq} = .67)$	$.23\dagger$	$.16$	$.03$	$.08$
p. Proportion of school board members motivated for political experience $(r_{p,pq} = .81)$	$.36\ddagger$	$.306\dagger$	$.15$	$-.01$

Multiple Correlations

Represent Some Group	Political Experience
$R_{V \cdot p,pq} = .37$	$R_{V \cdot p,pq} = .37$

Independent and Joint Contributions of p and pq to the
Explained Variance in Consensus V

Represent Some Group	Political Experience
$\beta_p{}^2 = .001$	$\beta_p{}^2 = .091$
$\beta_{pq}{}^2 = .156$	$\beta_{pq}{}^2 = .006$
$2\beta_p\beta_{pq}r_{p,pq} = -.018$	$2\beta_p\beta_{pq}r_{p,pq} = .037$

* Significant at the .02 level.
† Significant at the .01 level ($r = .233$ required).
‡ Significant at the .001 level ($r = .309$ required).

Both predictions about the relationships between the p for the two
remaining motivations and V receive significant support from the data
($r = .23$ in the case of the group representation motivation, and .36
in the case of the political experience motivation): The higher the
proportion of members motivated by either of these, the less the consensus within the board. However, since the homogeneity measures
pq on these two motivations were significantly correlated with the V
score (see Table 11–E, page 188), it is necessary to ask whether either
or both of these relationships could be due to the homogeneity of the
board with respect to these motivations, or if we can, as in the case of
the civic duty motivation, attribute the relationship to the effects of
the proportion (or the extent of the motivation) itself.

The multiple correlation between the V score and the p and pq
measures on the group representation motivation is .37, which is
almost exactly the same as the zero order between V and the pq measure $(+.37)$. The apportioning of the variance of V explained by these
two measures suggests that p (content) explains very little if any of

the variance of V independently of its relationship to pq (homogeneity). Consequently, it is necessary to conclude that the relationship between the proportion of board members motivated to represent some group and consensus within the board is due to the effect of the homogeneity of the board with respect to this motive. Since there is a positive correlation between p and pq (+.67) we may say that the higher the proportion who are motivated to represent groups, the less the similarity on this variable (or the higher the variance, pq). This implies that the "group representers" are usually in a minority. It is interesting to question whether, if they were in a majority, the relationships which have been shown would still hold. When there is a majority of members who are motivated to represent some group, the homogeneity hypothesis would conflict with the one tested here, which is to say, when there is a majority so motivated there would then be more similarity or homogeneity on this motivation. Because the group representers are always in the minority, the homogeneity measure on this variable measures the extent to which the boards do not have group representers. It is suggested that if they were in the majority the homogeneity hypothesis would no longer hold because, then, the more group representers, the more homogeneous.

The multiple correlation between the V score and the p and pq measures on the political experience motivation is .37, which is little different from the zero order between V and p (+.36). As Table 12–D shows, the independent contribution of pq (the homogeneity measure) to the explanation of V is very small, compared with that of p. The conclusion is suggested that the relationship between pq and V is due almost entirely to the relationship between p and pq ($r = +.81$). The meaning of this correlation is similar to the one suggested for that between p and pq on the group representation motivation: The fewer the members who are motivated by a desire for political experience, the more homogeneous the board with respect to this motivation. Thus, those seeking political experience on a board are usually in a minority. If they were in a majority it is suggested here too that the homogeneity hypothesis would no longer hold, because then the homogeneity and the motivation hypotheses would conflict. The meaning of p would be the same, but that of pq (homogeneity) would be reversed with respect to whether or not the politically motivated were in the majority or minority.

Besides remarking on the absence of significant relationships between the proportion of board members described as motivated in certain ways and the consensus between the board and the superintendent (with the exception of the correlation of p (civic duty) and D, which can be accounted for by the relationship between this p and V), the absence of relationships here can be interpreted as evidence supporting the validity of the criterion of motivation used. It will be recalled that the various measures of school board motivation are all based on the superintendent's assessment of the motives of individual school board members. Conceivably, the sequence of the relationships that have been shown to exist could be temporally reversed: Although we posit that the motivations are prior to the consensus, it is possible, considering the index of motivation used, that the consensus, when perceived by the superintendent, would lead him to evaluate school board members' motivations accordingly. He would say a high consensus board was made up of members motivated by civic duty, and a low consensus board of members motivated by political or factional interests.

But it seems reasonable to look for these effects in the relationship between the superintendent's evaluation of motives and *his* consensus with his board members, not their consensus among themselves. The fact that there are no significant relationships between the motivation variables and consensus between the board and the superintendent leads us to reject the reasoning presented above; we think this is evidence which can be interpreted as supporting the validity of the indexes of motivation used and their consideration as *determinants* of consensus.

Proportion of Women on the Board and Consensus. Like religion, the sex of board members may be assumed to be a very important social characteristic. It can also, like religion, be considered another position. The question in which we are interested is how the sexual composition of a group of position incumbents will affect their consensus with one another. Two assumptions concerning the difference between men and women will be used as the basis of a prediction. The first is that women are more likely to be submissive to men than men are to women, particularly in a quasi-political sphere such as the school board is, where women have been legally accepted for only a relatively short time. The second is that in groups, women tend to elicit more courteous behavior from men than do other men. Both of these considerations (or preconceptions) would lead to the prediction that the more women there are on a school board the more consensus there will be among the school board members. Since they tend to be submissive, they tend to submit to the expectations of the men, and since they elicit courteous behavior, the men tend to modify their expectations, so that there is less likelihood of argument and disagreement.

The test of the prediction is the correlation between V and the proportion of women on the school board, which is presented in Table 12–E. This correlation is −.18, which is significant at the .05 level and in the predicted direction. Interestingly, this is one of the few relationships which is increased by using the V' measure of consensus, for which the correlation is −.19. The difference between these two correlations is so slight, however, as to suggest that there is virtually no difference between them.

TABLE 12–E. CORRELATIONS BETWEEN THE PROPORTION OF WOMEN ON SCHOOL BOARDS AND CONSENSUS WITHIN THE BOARDS AND BETWEEN THE BOARDS AND THEIR SUPERINTENDENTS

$(N = 105)$

| | Consensus Variables | | | |
	V	V'	D	M
b. Proportion of women on the school board	−.18*	−.19*	−.07	.01

* Significant at the .05 level.

No relationship appears to exist between the proportion of women and consensus between the board and the superintendent. Perhaps this is what would be expected on the basis of the preceding hypothesis. The assumptions that women are more submissive than men and men more courteous in the presence of women have no implications for the consensus between the superintendent (who is, in our sample, always a man) and the board, because the expectations in the board are still largely dependent on what the male school board members think, and the women, although tending to agree with the superintendent more than the men do, also tend to agree with the men on the board, who ordinarily outnumber the superintendent. These two effects might be assumed to counteract one another, so that there is no relationship.

Social Status Characteristics and Consensus. It is difficult to specify intervening variables between social status characteristics, such as education and income, which would lead those who are differentiated on these variables to have different degrees of consensus without reverting to the homogeneity hypothesis which was examined in the preceding chapter. It is nevertheless important to ask whether boards of "higher" social status composition do have more or less consensus than those of "lower" status composition, first, because of the emphasis given social status concepts in social science in recent years, and second, because of the views prevalent in educational circles concerning the greater effectiveness of better educated and higher income school board members. Education, while it may be thought of as an index of social status, is also an index of training or socialization for more complex functions. A certain amount of education is mandatory for superintendents, and practically mandatory for school board members in order that they can carry out their jobs. While it might seem reasonable to predict that the better-educated board members and superintendents would do better jobs, there would seem to be no connection between this relationship and whether or not there was consensus within the board or between the board and the superintendent.

In Table 12–F are presented the correlations which provide the answers to the questions of whether the education of either the superintendent or the board (average education) is related to consensus between them or within the board, and whether the income of the superintendent or board (average income) is related to either kind of consensus. There are no correlations which are significantly different

TABLE 12–F. CORRELATIONS BETWEEN EDUCATION AND INCOME OF SUPERINTENDENTS AND SCHOOL BOARD MEMBERS AND CONSENSUS WITHIN THE BOARDS AND BETWEEN THE BOARDS AND THEIR SUPERINTENDENTS
$(N = 105)$

| | Consensus Variables | | | |
	V	V'	D	M
Education				
Of the superintendent	.02	−.05	−.01	−.03
Average education of the school board members	.08	.05	−.02	−.06
Income				
Of the superintendent	.07	.05	.11	.09
Average income of the school board members	.01	−.09	.03	.03

from zero in Table 12–F, and we are consequently led to the conclusion that there are no relationships between the two social status variables, income and education, and the consensus variables.

Size of School Board and Mandatoriness of Superintendents. The importance of considering size of group in an analysis of consensus among group members is evident from the finding that V, the measure of consensus among group members, is correlated with size of board .46. When V' and size are correlated, this relationship reduces to .11, which is insignificant. In one sense, the size of the board is a situational condition, but in another, it is a characteristic of the school board with which the superintendent is confronted. Irrespective of how it is regarded, we may ask whether or not the size of the school

TABLE 12–G. CORRELATIONS BETWEEN MANDATORINESS OF SUPERINTEND-
ENTS AND SIZE OF SCHOOL BOARDS AND CONSENSUS WITHIN THE BOARDS
AND BETWEEN THE BOARDS AND THEIR SUPERINTENDENTS
$(N = 105)$

	Consensus Variables			
	V	V'	D	M
Mandatoriness of the superintendent	−.01	−.06	.41*	.46*
Size of the school board	.46*	.11	.02	−.20†

* Significant at the .001 level.
† Significant at the .05 level.

board is related to the consensus *between* the superintendent and the board. The question is whether the amount of consensus between an individual and a small group is different from the amount of consensus between an individual and a larger group. Since D, the measure of between consensus, has as one of its components V, which is by definition highly related to size of board, it is necessary to test this relationship using the correlation between size of board and M, which is unrelated to V, but constitutes only one component of our measure of between position consensus.

It is difficult to present a logical argument for the prediction of such a relationship, but in a study by Hemphill, an empirical observation is made which would suggest a particular direction for such a relationship. Hemphill concluded that the larger the group becomes the more tolerant group members are to leader centered direction.[3] If certain assumptions are made, this generalization would lead us to the prediction that larger boards will have more consensus with their superintendents than do smaller boards. One of the assumptions it is necessary to make is that the superintendent, although he is its legal subordinate, is also the "leader" of the board, in the sense that he is a professional whose job it is to provide the board with professional "leadership." A second necessary assumption is that such leadership will influence the expectations of the school board members. It is possible to tolerate "leadership" without adopting a leader's values or expectations, and it is necessary to assume that this does not happen. The correlation between M and size of board, presented in Table 12–G, is −.20, which is significant at the .05 level, and provides confirmation for the prediction. It is interesting that the opposite relationship obtains between V and size, and M and size, such that the D score, which has as its components the V and M scores, is not significantly related to size of board, even though both of its components are. Although it has been shown that in one sense, there is more consensus between superintendents and large boards than between superintendents and small boards, since this relationship holds only with the measure M, which, it has been argued, is only one part of between consensus, the finding must be qualified by its partial nature. There is no relationship between D, the more complete measure of between consensus, and size of board, because the relations between size and the two components of D balance out one another.

The more mandatory a superintendent in expressing his expectations, the more it is possible for his board members to disagree with him, and consequently, the higher the probability that there will be disagreement or lack of consensus between his board and himself. If, as Stouffer has suggested,[4] a certain amount of "social slippage" is necessary for the maintenance of effective social relationships, a person whose expectations tend to be mandatory, that is, tend to be expressed as points which allow little variability (absolutely must or absolutely must not), will be one with whom it is difficult to maintain effective social relationships. It follows that superintendents who express more mandatory expectations will be likely to have less consensus with their boards than do superintendents who express less mandatory expectations. The correlations between mandatoriness of superintendents and D and mandatoriness and M are .41 and .46 respectively, both of which are significant and in the direction required by this reasoning.[5]

It is interesting to ask whether there is any relationship between the mandatoriness of a superintendent and consensus within his board, which is the other component of D. Apparently there is not, for with V, mandatoriness is correlated $-.01$, and with V', $-.06$, neither of which is significant.

The Relationship of Community Characteristics to Consensus. The question in which we are interested in this section concerns the relationship of certain community characteristics to the degree of microscopic role consensus among school board members and between them and their superintendent. There are three characteristics of communities which will be used in this analysis. These are size as represented by the size of the school system,[6] the form of government,[7] and the economic base,[8] each of which may be thought of as an index of a very complex phenomenon, "urbanism." The larger the community, the more industrial, and the more complex its government, the more urban we will say it is. If we assume that urbanism is associated with the heterogeneity of the population, with the development of special interest and factional groups, and with the growth of political organizations, we might then infer that school boards will be elected in large communities which are more heterogeneous in many respects and whose members are more likely to be politically motivated or motivated to represent certain special interest or factional groups than those elected in smaller communities.

All these characteristics of board members have been shown to be related to lack of consensus on role definition within the board. The reasoning, therefore, leads to the general hypothesis that the more urban the community according to its size, economic base, and form of government, the less consensus on role definition there will be (*a*) within the school board and (*b*) between the school board and the superintendent.

The second part of this hypothesis is perhaps less defensible than the first, because fewer relationships have been demonstrated between the "homogeneity" of boards and superintendents, and consensus between them, or between variables descriptive of superintendents and board members and consensus between them.

The prediction with respect to the size of system variable, net aver-

TABLE 12–H.   CORRELATIONS BETWEEN COMMUNITY CHARACTERISTICS AND CONSENSUS WITHIN THE BOARDS AND BETWEEN THE BOARDS AND THEIR SUPERINTENDENTS

$$(N = 105)$$

Product Moment Correlation Coefficients (r)

		Consensus Variables		
	V	V'	D	M
Size of System (NAM)	.26*	.07	.12	.01

Correlation Ratios (Eta)

	V	V'	D	M
Economic Base	.42*	.24	.31†	.30†
Form of Government	.44*	.20	.21	.21

Mean Consensus Scores

	$\overline{V}$	$\overline{V'}$	$\overline{D}$	$\overline{M}$
Economic Base				
Primarily residential	.47	.62	1.39	.93
Rural-resort-residential	.44	.65	1.39	.95
Composite with industrial	.55	.68	1.28	.74
Primarily industrial	.60	.73	1.59	.99
Form of Government				
Open town meeting (union systems)	.42	.62	1.41	.99
Open town meeting (non-union systems)	.51	.67	1.36	.85
Representative town meeting	.55	.69	1.40	.85
City	.60	.71	1.55	.95

* Significant at the .01 level.
† Significant at the .05 level.

age membership (NAM), is that the larger the system, the less consensus. In Table 12–H are presented the correlations which serve as tests of this prediction. The hypothesis receives significant support with respect to within board consensus (NAM and V are correlated .26) but the correlations of NAM with M and with D are insignificant. When the measure of consensus V' in which size of board is not involved is used, the correlation with NAM reduces to insignificance (.07). We are led to the conclusion that if it were not for the fact that in large communities there are large-sized school boards, our hypothesis would not be supported by the evidence. This conclusion has the implication that the reasoning for the hypothesis has been in error, and that the only reason why there is less consensus in large communities than in small ones is because larger communities have larger school boards.

Communities were classified into those which are "primarily residential," "rural-resort-residential," "composite with industrial," and "primarily industrial." The eta (correlation ratio)[9] of V on this categorization of "economic base" is .42, which is significant at the .01 level. The relative magnitudes of the mean V scores are presented below this eta in Table 12–H. The first two residential categories have lower mean V scores or higher consensus than the two industrial categories, which is in confirmation of the general hypothesis. The economic base is not significantly related to V', having an eta of only .24. The relative magnitudes of the means are, however, still ordered in the same way as they were with the V measure. That the economic base is not significantly related to V' suggests that the significant relationship found with V has been due to the effect of the size of board.

There are also significant relationships between the economic base of a community and the consensus between the superintendent and school board, the eta with D being .31 and that with M being .30, both of which are significant at the .05 level. Whether or not these relationships can be interpreted as supporting the hypothesis is somewhat ambiguous, for, although the "primarily industrial" category obtains the highest mean score on both M and D, thus showing the least consensus, the lowest mean score (or most consensus) is obtained by the composite industrial category. There are significant differences among the mean consensus scores obtained by these four categories, but these do not order themselves according to the prediction based on the hypothesis.

The third index of "urbanism" which has been used is the Form of Government of the community; four categories were used, ranging from "union towns with open town meetings" through "single towns with open town meetings," and "those with representative town meetings," to "cities." The eta of the relationship between Form of Government and V is .44, which is significant at the .01 level. The mean V scores obtained in the categories of Form of Government are ordered in the way in which they were predicted by the general hypothesis: "union and open town meeting" obtaining the smallest mean, "nonunion open town meeting" was the next in order, "representative town meeting" the next, and "cities" the highest mean score or the least consensus. The relationship with the V' measure is not significant, which suggests that the one with V has been due to a large extent to the effects of the size of board. This finding leads to the same conclusion as that drawn for the two preceding indexes of "urbanism": Although the hypothesis has been confirmed, this confirmation is to a large extent dependent on our definition of consensus V to include size of board.

The eta of Form of Government and D is insignificant, as is that with M, so that the second part of the general hypothesis receives no support from its test with this index. It is perhaps interesting to observe that the school boards in the smallest and largest communities (that is, unions with open town meeting and cities) have the least consensus with their superintendents, and the two middle categories the most, on both the D and the M measure.

All three tests of the intraposition aspect of the "urbanism" hypothesis provided significant support for the hypothesis, but in each of them there was evidence which suggested that the reasoning on which this hypothesis was based was erroneous. The relationships demonstrated were, in each case, shown to be largely due to the effect of the size of the board, which is an integral part of consensus, and, at the same time, related to the size of the system, the economic base, and form of government. Larger towns do have larger boards and this is enough to provide confirmation of the hypothesis without the assumption of complex selective effects on the composition of boards in different kinds of communities.

The second part of the hypothesis concerned with interposition consensus received no support from the analyses of the relationships between the three "urbanism" variables and consensus between the superintendent and his board. Although the relationship between the economic base of a commuity and D (and M) was significant, the direction of this relationship was not consistent with the prediction based on the hypothesis.

Notes and References for Chapter Twelve

[1] See Appendix B–4a for the Political-Economic Conservatism Scale used. We are indebted to Dr. Daniel J. Levinson for making this short form of the scale available for the research.

[2] In calculating the Pearsonian correlation coefficient between religion of the superintendent and the consensus variables, a score of 1 was assigned to the Catholic category and 0 to the non-Catholic category. This correlation is sometimes referred to as the point-biserial correlation.

[3] J. K. Hemphill, "Relations Between the Size of the Group and the Behavior of 'Superior' Leaders," *Journal of Social Psychology,* XXXII (1950), pp. 11–22.

[4] Samuel A. Stouffer, "An Analysis of Conflicting Social Norms," *American Sociological Review,* XIV (1949), pp. 707–717.

[5] In connection with the M component there is a problem comparable to the problem of the relationship between V and the size of board. It is that M (which is the square of the difference between the superintendent's response to an item and the mean school board response) is probably related to the intensity or mandatoriness of the superintendent's expectation because of the definition of the measure and the distributions of responses from superintendents and school board members. The intensity scores are obtained by "folding over" the response categories. It will be recalled that the response categories for the expectation items were "absolutely must," "preferably should," "may or may not," "preferably should not," and "absolutely must not," and that they were weighted one through five, respectively. If a superintendent responds "may or may not" (3), the least mandatory response, the most his school board members can disagree is by two steps (they can say either "absolutely must" [1] or "absolutely must not" [5]). If the superintendent gives one of these mandatory responses (1) or (5), the school board members can disagree by four steps (mandatory in the opposite direction). Consequently the correlation between the mandatoriness of a superintendent and the M component of consensus with his board could be anticipated on the basis of a knowledge of the distributions of superintendent and individual school board responses. But since the definition of the mandatoriness measure is independent of the consensus measure and since the relationships between mandatoriness and M and D are dependent on the actual responses of both superintendents and school board members, which are empirically problematic, there is justification for the claim that the empirical findings support the hypothesis.

[6] The net average membership of the school system (NAM) was obtained from The Commonwealth of Massachusetts, *Annual Report of the Department of Education for the Year Ending June 30, 1951,* Public Document No. 2.

[7] The classification used was city, representative town meeting, and open town meeting (union and nonunion).

[8] The economic base categories used were: "primarily residential," "rural-resort-residential," "composite with industrial," and "primarily industrial."

[9] The correlation ratio (eta) was used to examine the relationships between consensus and economic base and form of government because of the qualitative nature of the categories employed for the latter variables.

thirteen

Consequences of Microscopic
Role Consensus

In Chapters Eleven and Twelve an attempt has been made to explore some determinants of two kinds of consensus: consensus among an interacting set of incumbents of the same position, and between a small number of incumbents of one position and a single incumbent of a counter position. In this section an attempt will be made to explore some of the possible consequences of both kinds of consensus. The question in which we are interested here is whether or not agreement on expectations is related to other conditions which can be thought of as consequences of this agreement.

Two major hypotheses will be proposed, each of which can be tested with relationships between the two kinds of consensus and several other variables, dealing, for the first hypothesis, with the *satisfaction* of the position incumbents, and for the second hypothesis, with how the position incumbents *evaluate* one another. The objective of these analyses is as much to specify under what conditions the hypotheses do and do not hold, as it is to provide tests of the hypotheses themselves. It should be kept in mind that, of all the possible consequences of consensus on role expectations, the two classes of variables which have been selected for analysis are very limited in scope; satisfactions and evaluations are both, in a sense, "psychological" consequences of consensus for individuals, consensus being a condition which is descriptive of a social group or the relationship between a group and an individual (according to the operational definitions which consensus has received here). We are thus studying individual outcomes of group conditions.

The Satisfaction Hypothesis. The hypothesis to be examined derives from the following reasoning. If two or more actors agree with one another about what is expected of themselves and others as incumbents of positions in a social system, then they will use common standards to evaluate each other's behavior. If they do not agree on expectations then they will tend to evaluate one another's behavior on the basis of different standards. If it is further assumed that an actor tends to behave in conformity with the expectations he applies to his own position, then insofar as these are common standards, other actors will approve of his behavior and apply positive sanctions. Insofar as they are not common standards other actors will disapprove of his behavior and apply negative sanctions. If it is additionally assumed that the gratification an actor derives from the incumbency of his position is a function of the sanctions to which he is exposed, that is, positive sanctions lead to more and negative sanctions to less gratification, then the hypothesis follows that:

Hypothesis 13–1: The more consensus they have on the expectations for their own and the others' positions, the more gratification members of a group will derive from the occupancy of their positions.

On the basis of this general hypothesis, several specific predictions will be made. The first is that school boards in which there is greater consensus among the members will have members who express more satisfaction with their participation in the group. As an index of the satisfaction of board members an instrument was constructed containing items dealing with satisfaction with the "way your school board functions." The individual members answered these items according to a check list ranging in four categories from "very satisfied," to "very dissatisfied." On the basis of the responses of individual school board members to these items a scale was developed, which measures the extent to which school board members are satisfied with the way their board functions. (See Appendix B–2a.) According to

TABLE 13–A. CORRELATIONS BETWEEN "SATISFACTION" OF SCHOOL BOARDS AND SUPERINTENDENTS AND CONSENSUS WITHIN THE BOARDS AND BETWEEN THE BOARDS AND THEIR SUPERINTENDENT
(N = 105)

| | Consensus Variables | | | |
	V	V'	D	M
Mean School Board Dissatisfaction scale score	.36*	.31*	.05	−.12
Superintendent Job Satisfaction	−.08	−.12	−.14	−.11
Superintendent Career Satisfaction	.01	.00	−.09	−.10
Superintendent Worry	.12	.12	−.08	−.14

* Significant at the .001 level.

the general "satisfaction hypothesis" we would predict that the less consensus within a school board, the more dissatisfied the school board will be, according to the mean scale scores of its members. The correlation which tests this prediction is presented in Table 13–A.

The correlation between School Board Dissatisfaction and V is .36, which confirms the prediction (at the .001 level) and for this relationship provides support for the hypothesis. Among a group of incumbents of the *same* position there is a positive relationship between satisfaction and consensus. From the correlation between School Board Dissatisfaction and V', we may also conclude that the effect of the size of the board which is present in the V measure, has little effect on this particular relationship, since V' and Dissatisfaction are correlated .31, which is not significantly different from the correlation between V and Dissatisfaction.

Two measures of the superintendent's satisfaction with his position, his "Job Satisfaction" and his "Career Satisfaction," may be used in further tests of the general hypothesis (see Appendix B–1b, B–1c). It can be argued that whether or not a superintendent is satisfied with his job will depend to a considerable extent on his relationship to his school board, because the board is the superordinate to whom he is directly responsible. The argument that whether or not a superintendent is satisfied with his career is also affected to some extent by his relations with his present school board may not be so defensible as the other. The scale of Job Satisfaction which was developed contains two of nine items which deal directly with the superintendent's relations to his board and others which can be considered to provide an indirect indication of whether or not he is satisfied with this relationship (see Appendix B–1b). The scale of Career Satisfaction contains no items which deal directly with a superintendent's relations to his board, and we are consequently less inclined to anticipate the success of a prediction about this scale and consensus between a superintendent and his board. In the case of both scales the prediction is that there will be a negative correlation with D (and M and V). But, as can be seen in Table 13–A neither Job Satisfaction nor Career Satisfaction is significantly related to D or to either of its two components. The predictions are unconfirmed, and the hypothesis receives no support.

A final variable which has certain logical implications for the satisfaction of a superintendent with his relations to his board is measured by the superintendent's Worry Scale (see Appendix B–1e). While there is only one item contained in this scale dealing with a superintendent's anxiety over his relations to his board, the other five items are, like the satisfaction items, implicative of satisfaction (or at least lack of worry) with his relations with the school board. The prediction is that there will be a positive correlation between the Worry Scale and D, which is to say, the less consensus a superintendent has with his board, the more worry he will reveal. This prediction is also unconfirmed (the correlation is $-.08$) and provides no support for the general hypothesis.

The evidence which has been presented provides support for only a limited part of the hypothesis, or only one kind of consensus. Support was obtained for the proposition that satisfaction is related to consensus within a group of incumbents of the *same* position, but in three tests of the same proposition with respect to incumbents of two different positions, no support was obtained. One possible explanation of this difference in the findings for the two kinds of consensus is that no direct measures of satisfaction with their relations with one another, to correspond to the measure of consensus between incumbents of the two positions, were available. To some extent this explanation can be considered acceptable, because as we shall show, there is a positive relationship between how a superintendent *evaluates* his board (which is conceivably a more direct index of his satisfaction with the board than is his own job satisfaction) and his consensus with them. But this is only a partial explanation because, as we shall also show, how a school board rates the superintendent is not related to the consensus between them. Consequently, although the negative results concerning the satisfaction hypothesis and between position consensus may be partly due to the inadequacy of the measures with which tests were made, this possible inadequacy can be considered only a partial explanation.

There are certain formal differences between the relations within a school board and the relations between a board and its superintendent which could provide a more satisfactory explanation of the differences in the results for the two kinds of consensus. Formally, a school board can function only as a board. The individual members cannot perform any official actions as individuals. To a certain extent the majority of the board members *must* agree with one another before anything can be done by the board. The functioning of the board is *directly* contingent, we might say, on its members' ability to reach some consensus with one another. This condition does not exist between the superintendent and his board. A superintendent and board could continue to disagree with one another while performing their functions in their own way. It is true that the superintendent is liable to be fired if he ignores the board's expectations, but within limits it is possible for him to do so; and of course, the board can do what it likes whatever the superintendent thinks, again within certain limits. A board cannot do anything unless there is a certain amount of consensus among its members, whereas a superintendent and board can continue to function even though they completely disagree with one another. Practically, neither of these statements may be true, but as theoretical possibilities, they may very well affect the degree of satisfaction they feel about their own behavior and about their relationship.

If we suppose that satisfaction is a direct result of "doing what one likes," it is evident that a superintendent can do what he likes and therefore be satisfied while disagreeing with the board about what ought to be done. A school board can do what the majority of its members like and therefore be satisfied, while disagreeing with the superintendent about what ought to be done. But a school board cannot do what it likes and derive satisfaction from this behavior, unless at least a majority of its members are in agreement about what ought to be done. With this reasoning we would be led to the conclusions which have been demonstrated: that satisfaction and consensus are related *within* an interacting group of incumbents of the same position but not *between* a group and an incumbent of a counter position.

The Evaluation Hypothesis. Although an evaluation of another person and satisfaction with one's relations with him may be closely related, the two concepts of "evaluation" and "satisfaction" can be both logically and operationally distinguished. The difference between satisfaction and evaluation is in the criteria which are implied by the terms. Satisfaction implies affective critera, while evaluation implies cognitive criteria.

The reasoning for a hypothesis relating evaluations and consensus will be approximately the same as it was for the satisfaction hypothesis. Because incumbents of two positions agree on what is expected of one another, their behavior will tend to conform to each other's expectations (assuming that position incumbents tend to conform to their own expectations). If a person *A*, with whom another person *B* interacts, does what *B* expects *A* to do most of the time, it seems reasonable to assume that *B* will in consequence think *A* is performing effectively or doing a good job. This suggests the hypothesis that:

Hypothesis 13–2: The more consensus there is between the incumbents of two positions on their definitions of each other's roles, the more highly they will rate one another's performance.

This hypothesis is directly comparable to the satisfaction hypothesis, and it is presented despite the empirical finding that satisfaction and consensus between the superintendent and school board are *not* related. This evaluation relationship should hold no matter what the relationship between satisfaction and consensus. Whether or not something is pleasing to a person, can be independent of whether or not it fulfills certain cognitive criteria. This reasoning suggests a further hypothesis, which is based on the assumption of the independence of satisfaction and evaluation and on the assumption that school boards within which there is high consensus can perform more effectively than those in which there is low consensus. If all the members of a board usually agree about what should be done, it should be done with more expedition than if they usually disagree. A superintendent interacting with a high consensus board would be likely to think it was an effective board whether or not it behaved according to his expectations. Because there is consensus among the board members, the superintendent would evaluate it as an effective board.

Hypothesis 13–3: The more consensus there is within a group of incumbents of the same position, the more highly will the group's performance be rated by the incumbent of a position counter to that of the group members.

This evaluation hypothesis is a good example of our reason for separating "satisfaction" and "evaluation." Whereas we would not expect to find a relationship between a superintendent's satisfaction and consensus *within* the board, because for his satisfaction the substance of their expectations is crucial as well as their consensus, it does seem reasonable to formulate this second evaluation hypothesis, because a group in which there is consensus will appear to an outside observer (such as the superintendent observing his school board) as a group which can function effectively, even though it fails to provide him with affective satisfaction.

Two predictions will be based on the first hypothesis. The first is that superintendents will rate their school boards more highly if they have more consensus with them than if they have less. With a rating scale ranging through the categories, "excellent, good, fair, poor, very poor," (excellent scored 1, and very poor scored 5), a positive correlation will be predicted with the measure of consensus between the board and the superintendent, D. The correlation which tests this prediction is presented in Table 13–B.

TABLE 13–B. CORRELATIONS BETWEEN "EVALUATION" VARIABLES AND
CONSENSUS WITHIN THE BOARDS AND BETWEEN THE BOARDS AND THEIR
SUPERINTENDENTS
($N = 105$)

	Consensus Variables			
	V	V'	D	M
Superintendent's rating of the school board	.33*	.34*	.32*	.20†
Superintendent's description of school board behavior-conformity	−.28‡	−.27‡	−.24†	−.13
Mean school board rating of the superintendent on job performance	.24‡	.22§	.10	−.01
Mean school board rating of the superintendent on personality characteristics	.02	.01	−.05	−.06

* Significant at the .001 level.
† Significant at the .05 level.
‡ Significant at the .01 level.
§ Significant at the .02 level.

The correlation between the superintendent's rating of the school board and D is .32, which confirms the prediction and allows us to conclude that the hypothesis has to this extent been supported. The correlations between the superintendent's rating of the school board and the two components of D, M and V, are .20 and .33, respectively, which are both significant and in a direction confirming the prediction. The latter correlation, between V and the rating of the school board by the superintendent, is a test of the second hypothesis, and, since it is significant and in the predicted direction, allows us to conclude that superintendents tend to rate their boards highly if there is consensus within the board. Recalling that V and M are independent provides evidence to refute the possible explanation that superintendents evaluate their boards highly when there is consensus among the members because they also agree with them. Although the two hypotheses have been tested with the same relationships, it can be argued that for practical purposes they are independent tests, since V and M are empirically independent of one another, and M is the "between" component of the "between" tests.

As a further exploration of the relationship predicted on the basis of the second hypothesis, another relationship may be considered. Superintendents described the behavior of their boards, and these behaviors were compared with "superintendents norms" to provide a measure of the "conformity" of the school board with norms defined by the superintendent's sample. (The operational procedures used to obtain this conformity measure will be described in Chapter Fourteen, pp. 224–229.) With this variable we may ask whether boards in which there is consensus among the members are also boards which tend to do what superintendents, on the average, consider desirable. The correlation of −.28 between "conformity" and V provides an affirmative answer to this question (high score = low consensus; low score = low conformity). Two statements can be made concerning consensus within the boards: (a) Superintendents tend to evaluate highly boards in which there is consensus, and (b) boards in which there is consensus tend to be conforming boards. There are probably links among consensus, "conformity," and evaluation by the superintendent. Although we have no test of the sequence in which these occur, it can be argued that consensus is prior to conformity (that is, the members hold expectations which agree with one another before they behave), and that conformity is prior to the evaluation of the board by the superintendent. Whether the positive evaluation can be said to be due primarily to the consensus or to the conformity is problematic. Interestingly, all of these relationships hold with the V' measure of consensus. The correlations between the superintendent's evaluation and consensus and between conformity and consensus are virtually the same with V and with V', the measure in which size of school board is not involved.

The second prediction which can be made on the basis of the first evaluation hypothesis is that school boards who have consensus with their superintendents will rate them highly. The correlation between the board's rating of the superintendent on how well he performs the seven functions of a school administrator (see Appendix B–4b) with D is .10, which is insignificant. This leads to the conclusion that there is no demonstrable relationship between a school board's rating of their superintendent and the degree of consensus they have with one another. Nor is there a relationship between the D measure of consensus and the school board's rating of the superintendent on several personality characteristics, (see Appendix B–3b). Surprisingly, there is a significant correlation between V, the consensus within the board, and its rating of the superintendent on his job performance. The more consensus the board has, the more likely they are to rate their superintendent highly. It may be questioned whether the rating of the superintendent can be considered a consequence of the consensus within a board. It would be just as reasonable to argue that a board whose members rated the superintendent highly on how he carries out his job would develop consensus by the members' acceptance of the superintendent's definition of their roles; the consensus in this case would be a consequence of their evaluation of the superintendent.

This chain of reasoning has an empirical flaw which is evident in the insignificant correlation between D and the board's rating. The argument depends on the assumption that the board accepts the superintendent's role definition, in which case there would also be high consensus between the superintendent and the board, which is empirically contradicted. The finding is one whose ambiguity is evident in the following restatement: A board whose members agree among themselves on the expectations for their own and the superintendent's positions, will rate the superintendent highly on how well he performs his job, whether or not they agree with the superintendent on the role definitions for his and their positions. This finding holds with V' to almost the same extent as with V, suggesting that it is not due to the effect of size of board which is present in the V measure.

In summarizing this brief exploration of some of the consequences of consensus among interacting position incumbents, an observation may be made which it was not possible to make while considering either of the two major hypotheses tested separately. It was shown that the satisfaction hypothesis held for satisfaction of the school board and consensus within the board. It held neither for the satisfaction of the superintendent and consensus between him and the board nor for satisfaction of the board and consensus with the superintendent. The evaluation hypothesis held for the rating of the school board (by the superintendent) and consensus between the superintendent and the board. It did not hold for the rating of the superintendent (by the board) and consensus between them. If one ignores the subsidiary relationships which were demonstrated, one conclusion is suggested by these findings: Both the satisfaction and the evaluation hypotheses hold for variables descriptive of the board, but not for variables descriptive of the superintendent. This cannot be accounted for by whose responses were used, because in both cases the position incumbents defined their own satisfaction and rated the incumbents of the other position.

The most immediate explanation that suggests itself is that the school board performs its functions almost exclusively in the presence of the superintendent. The board members' performances take place in the interaction situation which has provided the focus for the definition of consensus. The superintendents, on the other hand, perform most of their functions outside this interaction situation with the board. They deal and interact directly with incumbents of many other positions than the school board and spend much more time doing so than they do in board meetings. Although it cannot be argued that the superintendent's interaction with the board is unimportant (because the board is, after all, his superordinate), it is limited quantitatively in time and for this reason may have a smaller effect on his satisfaction and effectiveness of his performance than it does on the satisfactions of the board and the board's effectiveness in performing its functions.

fourteen

Conformity
to Professional Expectations

Up to this point our analyses have been concerned with consensus on role definition, and although we have so far considered in some detail the *expectations* role definers apply to the incumbents of the superintendent and school board member positions, these analyses have not required an examination of the *actual behavior* of incumbents of these positions. This will be the purpose of this chapter, in which our objective is to examine a set of problems concerned with *conformity* to expectations. This general problem area is concerned with the degree to which role behavior conforms to or deviates from expectations that role definers apply to position incumbents. The research problem which we are interested in exploring is the isolation of factors differentiating position incumbents who conform to expectations from those who do not.

Social scientists who have been concerned with the phenomenon of conformity have directed their attention primarily to two major problems: the processes and mechanisms of social control and the explanation of deviant behavior. We do not propose to attempt a review or summary of the vast literature concerning either of these two complex topics. A point that deserves emphasis, however, and one that is frequently neglected, is that analyses concerned with either of these problems require a clear specification of the set of expectations according to which the investigator is defining conformity or deviance. As Parsons says, "The problem of conformity cannot be dissociated from a consideration of that with which conformity is expected." [1]

Two aspects of this problem deserve elaboration: the specification of the role definers used and the degree of consensus among them on their expectations. Specification of the role definers used in a conformity analysis is essential, because, as we have demonstrated in our role consensus analyses, different role definers may hold different expectations for incumbents of the same position. A behavior which would be considered conforming when referred to the expectations of superintendents might be considered deviant when referred to the expectations of school board members. Students of criminology have frequently pointed out that behaviors which are defined as deviant according to legal standards are often defined as conformist according to the standards of participants in "organized crime." One set of role definers may consider refusal to undergo military service deviant, whereas another set of definers may consider it conformist. These examples point up the necessity for a specification of the role definers used in any conformity analysis.

The second aspect of the problem of specifying the expectations used in a conformity analysis, specifying the degree of consensus among the role definers, is conditioned by what role definers are used. If there is only one role definer, for example, the position incumbent himself, there is, of course, no problem of consensus. If the definitions of two or more role definers are used, however, the question of the degree of consensus between or among them is crucial. In the preceding sections of this volume our analyses have suggested that the postulate of consensus can seldom be accepted even for a set of role definers occupying the same position. Their degree of consensus on any expectation is, we have demonstrated, always empirically problematic. Therefore, in trying to measure the extent of an actor's conformity to a set of expectations it is necessary that the expectations used in the measure be limited to those on which there is a high degree of consensus among the role definers used. Otherwise, the meaning of assigned conformity scores would be as ambiguous as the expectations on which they were based.

In the experimental small group literature concerned with the treatment of deviants by group members, this problem is avoided by defining "group standards" as "given." A group standard is presumed to exist ". . . if the [group agent] communicates to the members the information that along a given dimension a certain range of behavior is expected. In addition, the group member usually will be informed that deviations beyond the expected range are not sanctioned and will be treated in a certain manner." [2] Similar experimental controls can hardly be used in analyses concerned with "natural" groups, nor do we think they can be assumed for any group, whether "experimental" or "natural."

Although conforming behavior may be conceptually defined as behavior which fulfills the expectation to which it is referred, it may be operationally defined according to different expectations or sets of expectations. Any analysis of conformity may be based on the degree of conformity to "agreed upon" standards of a group, to the expectations of actors in given positions, to the expectations of position incumbents for themselves, to legally defined expectations, or to perceived or actual expectations of others. When conformity is defined according to a particular set of expectations, the other sets may become relevant as conditions which can affect the degree of conformity.

It should also be pointed out that conformity may be a matter of degree, depending on the specificity of the expectations to which particular behaviors are referred. An individual's behavior may completely, partly, or not at all conform to a particular expectation if that expectation is fairly general. The more specific the expectation, the less conformity can be a matter of degree; the most specific expectations may admit only of conformity or nonconformity and preclude the possibility of partial conformity. Given a *set* of expectations, however, such as are provided by written laws, we suppose that almost all individuals who are subject to them will conform to some of the expectations in the set and fail to conform to others. Law-abiding citizens not infrequently fail to obey traffic laws and are in this respect nonconformists in relation to the law. On the other hand, delinquents who steal cars are frequently law-abiding on public roads, because conformity in this respect is a necessary expedient if they are to avoid sanctions that are applied for nonconformity with respect to stealing cars. The conclusion we would draw from these examples is that conformity to a *set* of expectations may be viewed as a matter of degree.

In the following analyses conformity will be defined with reference to a set of expectations on which there is a high degree of consensus among a set of role definers who occupy the same position. The role definers will be superintendents and their standards will be applied to the performances of school boards.

The Measurement of Conformity to Professional Expectations. The most frequent reference of conformity in the social science literature is to behavior that conforms to some kind of supra-individual expectation—an expectation held by "society" or an expectation held by some specified group. In some cases the supra-individual expectations used are legal statutes like criminal codes, while in others they are "group standards" on which there is presumed to be consensus.

The operational definition of conformity we shall use in this chapter is of this general kind. Specifically, the conformity measure will represent the degree to which school boards conform to a set of "professional" expectations for their behavior. These expectations will be selected according to the degree of consensus among a group of professional educators, school superintendents.

Before presenting our operational definition of the measure of this kind of conformity, two general observations about it deserve emphasis. The first is that it represents the conformity to professional expectations of a collectivity, the school board, not of individual school board members. The criterion expectations will be standards which are applied to school boards. The reason for this reference of the conformity measure is that according to law, and according to widely accepted beliefs of professional educators, obligations and rights generally apply to school boards, not to individual board members. State laws specify the duties and obligations of school boards, not individual board members. When, during our trial interviews, we asked superintendents to discuss the rights and obligations of a board member, the respondents typically replied that only the board, and not the board member, had rights and obligations.

The second point that deserves emphasis is that this conformity measure will deal with the degree of conformity of the behavior of school boards to common "professional" standards, standards held by professional educators, and not those held in common by some other set of role definers, such as, school board members, citizens, or local government officials.

In Chapter Eight considerable variability was shown in the degree of consensus among superintendents on different expectation items. Furthermore, it was found that on some items there was a high degree of consensus that the expected behavior was mandatory, whereas for others there was consensus that it was preferred or permitted. These observations suggested the two criteria that were used in selecting items from the School Board Performances Instrument for use in this conformity measure. The first was that there must be as much agreement as possible among superintendents on what is expected of school boards. The second criterion was that the modal response of the superintendents should be mandatory, that is, either "absolutely must" (A) or "absolutely must not" (E). With one exception each expectation used as a conformity criterion can be characterized as a behavior in which a school board absolutely must or absolutely must not engage, according to most superintendents. It was found, in application, that this second criterion took care of the first. There were twelve items in the School Board Performances Instrument on which the superintendent's sample obtained a mode in either A or E, and on each of these there was relatively high consensus within the superintendent's sample.[3]

One substitution was made of an item with a mode of B for an item with a mode of A. The reason for the substitution was to obtain greater variation in the substance dealt with by the items. The item eliminated was, "Respect the judgment of the superintendent on strictly educational matters," which had a mode of A and a variance score of .326. The item which was substituted for it is, "A committee not afraid to take stands regarding education in advance of community thinking," which had a mode of B for the superintendent's sample, and a variance score of .462. By examining the list of items which comprise this measure in Table 14–A, page 228, it can be seen that there are six items which deal directly with the superintendent's relationship to the board (items 1, 2, 6, 7, 8, and 9) as did the item eliminated, whereas there are only two (items 3 and 12) which deal directly with the board's relationship to the entire community, including the one which was substituted.

Responses describing the actual behavior of each school board were obtained from superintendents who answered the following question for each of the twelve expectations items: "Does your school committee (board) do this?" The response categories were "yes," "partly," and "no." It is quite clear that if the expectation is "absolutely must not," then the "partly" behavior response does not conform to the expectation. It was also felt that if the expectation were "absolutely must," then the "partly" response would not describe a conforming behavior either. A "partly" response was therefore considered in all cases to be nonconforming.

The conformity score for each school board was obtained in the following way. If a superintendent said "yes" to the behavior question when the superintendent's sample modal response to an item was A, or "no" when the mode was E, then his board was scored 1 on that item; otherwise the board was scored 0. The conformity score of a board can therefore fall within the range of 0–12, since there are twelve items which comprise the measure.

Many of the following analyses in which this score is involved can be considered dependent on the assumption that the superintendent's description of his school board's behavior is a valid one. This assumption might have been avoided by changing the reasoning and hypotheses in which "conformity of school boards" is involved to refer to "conformity of school boards as perceived by their superintendent." We have not felt it necessary to do this for a number of reasons, support for some of which may be claimed from the available evidence.

First of all, it should be kept in mind that these scores do not represent an attempt on the part of the superintendents to evaluate their boards against "professional norms." The superintendents did not have available the information on the basis of which we have defined "professional norms," and indirectly, this conformity measure: they did not know what the distribution of all superintendents' expectation responses would be. Also, although we would not argue that the superintendent is "objective" in the sense of being uninvolved in what the school board does, it does seem reasonable that his description of the *board's* behavior will be more objective and therefore more valid, than would the descriptions of the board members themselves. Furthermore, using the superintendent's response avoids the difficulty that would result from using multiple responses of school board members. And finally, the superintendent is the only individual who is in a position to know what the "school board" does for many of the items. Whether or not "individual school board members give directions directly to the superintendent," is a question only the superintendent and those school board members who do give him directions can answer. It seemed a safe assumption that even those school board members who do give him directions would fail to say so, because it is against the law for them to do so and seemed unlikely (again because it is against the law) that the members who do not give him directions would know that some of their fellows do.

These were, essentially, the arguments which suggested the use of the superintendents' description of their school boards' behavior, rather than school board members' description of this behavior. It is nevertheless interesting to ask how these descriptions compare, and whether, from this comparison, any support may be claimed for the decision as to which of the two would be more valid. In Table 14–A are presented the percentages of school board members who agreed with their superintendent with respect to the behavior of the board on the twelve school board performance items used in the measure of school board conformity.

On some of the items the percentage of school board members who agree with their superintendent is little more than would be expected by chance, which raises a serious question with respect to the accuracy of superintendents, school board members, or both, in describing school board behavior. Both in deriving the conformity score

TABLE 14–A. SCHOOL BOARD PERFORMANCE ITEMS USED IN THE MEASURE OF SCHOOL BOARD CONFORMITY TO PROFESSIONAL EXPECTATIONS

Item *	Superintendents' Modal Response †	Conforming Behavior Response	Percentage of School Board Members who Agree with Their Superintendent on the Behavior of their Board ‡
1. Pay the necessary expenses to allow the superintendent to attend meetings of professional organizations, visit other school systems, and do other things which will keep him up to date on educational developments.	A	Yes	85.4
2. Appoint only teachers nominated by the superintendent.	A	Yes	68.2
3. Help "sell" good education to the community.	A	Yes	64.9
4. Have a clear statement of the policies under which the school system should be operated.	A	Yes	55.4
5. Take full responsibility for its decisions.	A	Yes	69.4
6. Have a clear-cut statement of the division of responsibilities between the school committee and the superintendent.	A	Yes	50.3
7. Individual school committee members give directions to the superintendent.	E	No	65.5
8. Give directions directly to the superintendent's subordinates.	E	No	76.9
9. Keep the superintendent informed of important matters that come to their attention.	A	Yes	81.7
10. In deciding issues the members vote as representatives of important blocs or segments.	E	No	67.9
11. "A board which functions as a unit not as individuals."	A	Yes	65.5
12. A committee not afraid to take stands regarding education in advance of community thinking.	B	Yes	53.8

* For full information about each item, see Appendix Table A–5.
† Response A = absolutely must; B = preferably should; E = absolutely must not.
‡ The behavior reported by each school board member for his board was compared with the behavior reported by his superintendent. The percentages given in this column are defined as the percentage of school board members who agree with their superintendent on whether or not their board conforms according to the criterion behavior specified in the preceding column.

and in comparing the responses of superintendents and school board members, however, a "partly" response was considered a "nonconforming" response. If we assume that a "partly" response to a question of whether or not something is done by a board is more likely to be valid than either an unequivocal "yes" or "no," by examining the original distributions of responses to the behavior questions for these twelve items we can say whether superintendents or school board members gave the more "valid" responses. By examining Appendix Table A–2 it may be seen that superintendents consistently gave more "partly" responses to all twelve of these items. Furthermore, if "partly" responses had been interpreted as "conforming" responses we could say that there would have been much more agreement between the superintendents' and school board members' descriptions of school board behavior. A test was made of this statement by treating the superintendents' "partly" responses as the equivalent of "yes" responses for the three items with the smallest percentage of agreement between the superintendents and school board members, (these were all items for which a "yes" response was a conforming response) and then computing the percentage of board members who agreed with this as well as with the unambiguous responses of their superintendents. Item 6, with an original percentage of 50.3, showed a gain of over 25 to 75.7 percent. The other two items (4 and 12) gained even more. Similar results would be obtained by performing the same operation for the remaining items.

We may say that the major source of disagreement between their responses can be accounted for by superintendents' tendency to say "partly" when his board members describe their board's behavior unambiguously; there would not be a great deal of difference if either group were used to define the measure so long as a "partly" response from the superintendent was treated as symptomatic of the desirable behavior.[4]

In summary, our reasons for accepting the superintendent's description of his board's behavior as more valid than that of his school board members are: first, that the superintendent as an observer is more likely to provide an "objective" appraisal; second, that the superintendent is more likely to have the required knowledge for an accurate description of his board's behavior; and third, that the difference between the superintendents' and board members' descriptions of school board behavior is to a large extent due to the frequency with which superintendents gave "partly" rather than an unambiguously "conforming" response.

In Figure 14–1 is presented the histogram of the conformity scores obtained on the basis of the superintendents' description of their school boards' behavior. The measure results in a negatively skewed distribution of scores. The tendency is for a concentration of scores at the "conforming" end of the continuum. A score of twelve, which was obtained by twenty school boards, means that to every item (see Table 14–A) their superintendents said they did what was prescribed by the superintendents' sample. At the other extreme there is one board which obtained a score of zero, whose superintendent said they did none of the things they were supposed to do according to the superintendents' sample.

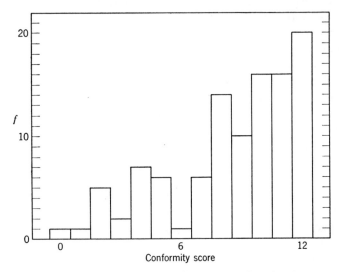

Figure 14–1. Frequency distribution of school board conformity scores.

Before proceeding with an analysis of these data it is interesting to observe that the distribution of conformity scores obtained using this measure approximates what would be expected on the basis of the *J*-curve hypothesis of conforming behavior suggested by Allport.[5] A difference which is perhaps worth commenting on is that Allport's hypothesis was suggested for degrees of conformity to *single* standards for behavior, whereas our measure discriminates among school boards which conform to greater and lesser degrees to a *set* of standards (expectations) for their behavior.

The expectations against which the behaviors of the boards were compared in obtaining this measure of conformity were those of superintendents, who are professional educators. At the same time it is the superintendents who report whether or not their boards do what is described by the items used in the measure, so that not only is there a "professional" expectation with which to compare the boards' behaviors, but also a "professional" description of what those behaviors are.

For purposes of the analyses to be presented, this "professionalism" aspect of our conformity measure cannot be stressed too much. In order to make any predictions at all about differences between conformists and nonconformists it is necessary to know exactly what their conformity implies. For example, the superintendents of Massachusetts, who represent the profession, are pretty well agreed that the school board should "appoint only teachers nominated by the superintendent." In some communities, however, it may be the custom for the school board to take orders from the mayor and for the superintendent to follow the dictates of the board with respect to hiring teachers. It may be accepted in the community that the school system functions as a part of a political machine without regard to "professional" considerations. In such a community, a board member who tried to persuade the board to "appoint only teachers nominated by the superintendent," rather than those nominated by the mayor, would be urging nonconformist behavior on the board from the points of view of the other board members, those involved in the political machine, and possibly the community members at large. Any prediction about "conformists" in this situation, would have to take into account the fact that they are different from conformists according to "professional" criteria.

The analyses to be undertaken with this measure of conformity will deal with some possible consequences for their superintendent of the school board's conformity to professional expectations, with some possible correlates of conformity which are commonly viewed as valid by professional educators, and will provide empirical tests of three hypotheses concerning possible determinants of this kind of conformity.

Consequences of School Board Conformity for Superintendents. Considering the fact that the superintendent as a professional is subordinate to a group of laymen, the school board, its behavior as a board should have an effect on how the superintendent feels about his job. This could perhaps be said of any type of social relationship. Actors in complementary positions provide support for each other, cooperate in a division of labor, and sanction each other's behavior. How one actor behaves in this relationship should therefore have an effect on how the other experiences the relationship.

What particular effects on the superintendent is his board's conformity to professional expectations likely to have? In suggesting particular variables descriptive of the superintendent's reaction to his job it will perhaps be helpful to reconsider briefly the responses of the superintendents to the twelve items on the basis of which the conformity score was obtained. It will be recalled that two of the criteria on the basis of which the items were selected were that (1) there must be a mandatory mode from the superintendents' sample, and (2) there must be a high degree of consensus within the superintendent's sample. Examining the actual response distributions of the superintendent's sample to these items (Appendix Table A–5) will show that as far as agreement on the positive or negative direction of the expectation is concerned, the agreement among superintendents is almost perfect on all twelve items. There were only 18 responses out of a total of 1260 which contradicted the professional expectation as defined by the mode. Among superintendents, almost without exception, it can be said that there is agreement on the professional standards against which the conformity of their school boards has been assessed. There is consequently a basis for the assumption that any given superintendent's expectations and the "professional" expectations used in this analysis are the same.

We propose to examine three possible consequences on the superintendent's reaction to his job that could result from his school board's conformity to professional expectations. These are his job satisfaction, career satisfaction, and the worry he experiences as an incumbent of the superintendency position. In examining the relationship between school board conformity and job satisfaction it is relevant to introduce a conclusion Riecken and Homans came to in their review of small group research:

> In examining research on the relation between sentiment, activity, and norms, we have generalized the findings to one basic hypothesis, which may be stated as follows: a member O of a group chooses or likes a member P to the degree that P's activities realize O's norms and values.[6]

It does not seem unreasonable to add that not only will a member O "choose and like" P, but he will also evaluate P's performance of his job highly to the degree that P's activities realize O's expectations for him. With our data, this additional proposition would lead to the prediction that the more the school board conforms to professional standards, the more highly the superintendent will evaluate the performance of the board. As can be seen in Table 14–B this empirical prediction is confirmed.

The importance of this finding for our analysis is that it provides a possible intervening link between school board conformity and superintendent's job satisfaction. If school board conformity is posi-

TABLE 14–B. RELATIONSHIPS OF SCHOOL BOARD CONFORMITY AND SUPER-
INTENDENT'S JOB SATISFACTION WITH THE EVALUATION OF THE SCHOOL
BOARD BY THE SUPERINTENDENT

1. Percentage of school boards with "Low," "Medium," and "High" conformity
scores who are evaluated as "Excellent," "Good," and "Fair, Poor, or Very
Poor" by their superintendent.

	Superintendent's Evaluation of School Board, %				
School Board Conformity	Excellent	Good	Fair, Poor, Very Poor	Total Percent	N
Low (0– 6)	8.7	21.7	69.6	100	23
Medium (7–10)	50.0	43.5	6.5	100	46
High (11–12)	72.2	27.8	0.0	100	36
All School Boards	48.6	33.3	18.1	100	105

$\chi^2 = 58.0$, with 4 degrees of freedom, significant at the .001 level

2. Percentage of superintendents with different job satisfaction scores who evaluate their school boards as "Excellent," "Good," and "Fair, Poor, or Very
Poor."

	Superintendent's Evaluation of School Board, %				
Superintendent's Job Satisfaction	Excellent	Good	Fair, Poor, Very Poor	Total Percent	N
(Low) 0	26.1	21.7	52.2	100	23
1	41.9	45.2	12.9	100	31
2	57.7	34.6	7.7	100	26
(High) 3	68.0	28.0	4.0	100	25
All Superintendents	48.6	33.3	18.1	100	105

$\chi^2 = 27.0$, with 6 degrees of freedom, significant at the .001 level

tively related to the evaluation of the school board's performance by
the superintendent, and if the positive evaluation of a superordinate
by a subordinate tends to result in high job satisfaction for the subordinate, then the hypothesis follows that:

*Hypothesis 14–1: In social systems in which a subordinate is a mem-
ber of a profession and his superordinate is not, the extent to which
the superordinate conforms to the standards of this profession will
be positively related to the subordinate's job satisfaction.*

Before examining the correlation between conformity and job satisfaction it is worthwhile testing whether the evaluation of the board
by the superintendent, which has been shown to be related to conformity, is also, as the line of reasoning requires, related to the superintendent's job satisfaction. In the second part of Table 14–B
it can be seen that this relationship holds. The more highly the

superintendent evaluates his school board's performance, the higher his job satisfaction. The relationship which tests the hypothesis and which completes the test of the reasoned sequence is between conformity and job satisfaction. A positive correlation is predicted, and,

TABLE 14–C. CORRELATIONS OF SUPERINTENDENT'S JOB SATISFACTION, CAREER SATISFACTION AND WORRY WITH SCHOOL BOARD CONFORMITY ($N = 105$)

	School Board Conformity
Superintendent's Job Satisfaction	.60*
Superintendent's Career Satisfaction	.25†
Superintendent's Worry	−.21‡

* Significant at the .001 level.
† Significant at the .01 level.
‡ Significant at the .02 level.

as can be seen in Table 14–C, obtained. The correlation is $+.60$, which is highly significant, and which provides significant confirmation for the hypothesis.

A corollary of this hypothesis is that there will be a smaller but still positive relationship between a superintendent's career satisfaction and the conformity of his school board. Whether or not a superintendent is satisfied with his career in general, as opposed to his job in particular, would depend on many more factors than the conformity of the school board in the particular school system in which he happens to be employed at the time. The construction of the two scales reflects this difference (see Appendix B–1*b* and B–1*c*). Two items of the job satisfaction scale have direct reference to the school board in the particular job, and others have an implied reference, whereas the items of the career satisfaction instrument do not even mention school boards either directly or by implication. For these reasons, although the direction of the correlation between these two scales and the conformity measure should be the same, there should be a much stronger relation between job satisfaction and conformity than between career satisfaction and conformity.

Table 14–C shows that this prediction is confirmed. Although there is a positive and significant correlation (at the .01 level) between career satisfaction and school board conformity (.25), it is significantly smaller than the correlation between job satisfaction and conformity (.60). The difference between these two correlations of .35 is significant at the .01 level.[7]

A third prediction will be made, which is that superintendents who have conforming boards will experience less worry than those who have nonconforming boards. This can be considered a second corollary to the job satisfaction hypothesis insofar as greater satisfaction implies less anxiety. The worry scale (described in Appendix B–1e) will be used to test this prediction. A negative correlation is predicted, which would describe a relationship in which the greater the conformity of the board, the less the superintendent worries about his job. The correlation presented in Table 14–C is −.21, which is significant at the .05 level and confirms the prediction.

On the basis of these three demonstrated relationships it is felt justifiable to conclude that whether or not a school board conforms to professional expectations has an effect on how the superintendent views and experiences his job.

Determinants of School Board Conformity. What factors can account for the differential conformity of school boards to professional expectations? We raised this question informally with a number of superintendents in trial interviews and with faculty members of institutions with training programs for educational administrators. Before presenting our own analysis of this problem it is of interest to examine some of the factors frequently mentioned by them as concomitants of school board conformity.

One set of factors thought to be associated with "professional behavior" of the board was the type of community. It was felt by some educators that political structure, size of community, or the relative degree of fiscal support for public education provided by the community were some of the most important correlates of school board conformity. Others felt that among the crucial factors were certain characteristics of the school board members, such as their occupation, income, and education. Still others maintained that the basic operative factors were characteristics of the superintendent, such as, the extent of his experiences or his capabilities in educational administration.

With some qualification, this last factor will be involved in our own analysis of the determinants of school board conformity, and an hypothesis presented and tested with respect to it. For the first two classes of factors and the experience of the superintendents, we will simply examine their relationships to the conformity measure.

Measures of four community characteristics, four characteristics of school boards, and three items of superintendents' experience in their jobs were obtained. The following operational definitions of these indexes were used:

1. *Community Characteristics*

Political structure	*a.* City, representative town meeting, open town meeting, union systems (all open town meeting)
Size of community	*b.* 1950 United States census population[8]
Degree of fiscal support	*c.* School support per pupil [9]
	d. School tax as percentage of total local property tax[10]

2. *Characteristics of School Boards*

Occupation	*a.* Occupational level of school board [11]
Income	*b.* Mean income of board members as reported by them
Educational progressivism	*c.* Mean score of school board member progressivism scale (Appendix B-3c)
Education	*d.* Mean educational level of school board members

3. *Experience of the Superintendent*

    a. Number of years in present superintendency

    b. Number of previous superintendencies

    c. Number of years in all superintendency positions

TABLE 14–D. RELATIONSHIPS OF COMMUNITY, SCHOOL BOARD, AND SUPER-INTENDENT CHARACTERISTICS WITH SCHOOL BOARD CONFORMITY

$(N = 105)$

	Relationship with School Board Conformity
1. Community Characteristics	
a. Political structure	$\chi^2 = 7.34$, with 6 degrees of freedom, not significant at the .05 level
b. Size of community	$r = -.11$
c. School support per pupil	$r = -.01$
d. School tax	$r = .09$
2. Characteristics of School Boards	
a. Mean occupational level	$r = .08$
b. Mean income	$r = .07$
c. Mean school board progressivism	$r = -.02$
d. Mean educational level	$r = .19*$
3. Experience of the Superintendent	
a. Number of years in present superintendency	$r = -.09$
b. Number of previous superintendencies	$r = .01$
c. Number of years in all superintendency positions	$r = .01$

* Significant at the .05 level.

The relationships between these indexes and school board conformity are reported in Table 14–D. With the single exception of the average education of the board members $(r = .19)$ none of these factors is significantly correlated with conformity. We are consequently led to the conclusion that, with this exception, these commonly accepted correlates of "professional conformity" of school boards are invalid, and are left with the problem of accounting for different degrees of conformity with other factors.

In examining this problem three hypotheses will be presented and tested. The factors involved in these hypotheses are: (1) the consensus on role definition between the board and its superintendent, (2) the motivation school board members had for seeking election to the board, and (3) the school board's evaluation of its superintendent's performance of his job.

Consensus between the Superintendent and School Board. Since the superintendent in any community is a "professional educator" and in this sense represents to his school board the professional point of view, the relationships between the board and its superintendent should have some bearing on whether or not it conforms to professional expectations. A crucial aspect of this relationship is, as we have argued, whether or not the superintendent and school board have consensus on their definitions of one another's roles.

If the role behaviors of a position incumbent A tend to conform to his own definition of his role and if his role definition is the same as that of another definer B, his role behaviors will tend to conform with B's definition of his role. If their role definitions differ, A's role behaviors will tend not to conform to B's definition of his role. From this line of reasoning it follows that:

Hypothesis 14–2: The greater the consensus on role definition between incumbents of two related positions, one of which is a professional position, the more the role behaviors of the incumbent(s) of the nonprofessional position will conform to the role definition of the incumbent of the professional position.

In Chapter Ten a measure of the degree of consensus between a superintendent and his school board on their definition of one another's roles was presented. This score, the D score, was based on the average squared deviation of the school board members' responses from the superintendent's response. To represent the role definitions of the incumbent of the professional position we may use the "professional" expectation items employed in the conformity measure since we have earlier shown that they constitute expectations held in common by nearly all superintendents. The prediction to which

Hypothesis 14–2 leads is that there will be a negative correlation between the consensus measure D, and the conformity score. This prediction is confirmed; the correlation is −.24 which is significant at the .01 level and provides significant support for the hypothesis.

Motivations of School Board Members in Seeking Election. We have just shown that consensus between the board and its superintendent is positively related to the board's conformity to professional expectations. Now we will examine the relationship between school board motivation and this type of conformity.

One possible line of reasoning establishing a theoretical relationship between board member motivations and their conformity to professional expectations would be to connect these concepts through the intervening variable of consensus. If it could be assumed (1) that the motivations board members had for seeking election were related to consensus, and (2) that consensus was related to conformity, it would follow that motivation is related to conformity.

Unfortunately there is a flaw in this line of reasoning, however. Although the second assumption is a reasonable one in view of the support Hypothesis 14–2 received, the first assumption is not. In Chapter Twelve certain of the empirical analyses did not support the relationship involved in the first assumption. The correlations (D) between the proportions of board members motivated to "get political experience" and of those motivated "to represent some group" and consensus between the board and the superintendent were insignificant (Table 12–D, p. 201). What other reasoning can be used in dealing with this problem? Whether or not school board members are motivated to conform to professional expectations, it will be argued, is dependent on the motivation they had for seeking election to the school board. More generally, if in a social system incumbents of a superordinate position are laymen and their subordinates "professionals," and if the superordinates are differentiable on the degree to which they are motivated to achieve the goals of the system, and if this is related to the extent to which they respect and fulfill "professional" expectations even though they may disagree with them, the hypothesis follows that:

Hypothesis 14–3: In social systems in which incumbents of a nonprofessional superordinate position have professional subordinates, the extent to which the superordinates are motivated to achieve the goals of the system will be positively related to the extent to which they conform to professional expectations.

Three indexes of the "motivation of school boards" were presented in Chapter Twelve (page 200). These were the proportion of board members whom the superintendent described as motivated by civic duty, to represent some group, and to gain political experience. To what predictions would the general hypothesis lead with respect to the relationships between these three indexes of school board motivation and conformity to professional norms?

The interpretation may be made that school boards which are comprised of members who were motivated by "civic duty" in seeking election will be boards whose members are primarily motivated to achieve the goals of their school systems and, therefore, of members who will respect and fulfill professional expectations. The prediction will consequently be made that there will be a positive correlation between the proportion of members so motivated and the degree of conformity of the board to professional expectations. This prediction is confirmed; the correlation between these two variables is +.52, which is significant at the .001 level (Table 14–E).

TABLE 14–E. CORRELATIONS BETWEEN THE MOTIVATIONS OF SCHOOL BOARD MEMBERS AND SCHOOL BOARD CONFORMITY

($N = 105$)

Motivation	School Board Conformity
a. Proportion of school board members motivated by civic duty	.52*
b. Proportion of school board members motivated to represent some group	−.23†
c. Proportion of school board members motivated for political experience	−.33*

* Significant at the .001 level.
† Significant at the .02 level.

Both remaining motivation variables are descriptive of inclinations which are potentially disruptive to the school system. The first deals with the motivation to "represent a particular group," and the second with the personal motivation of a desire for "political experience." The predictions will be made that there will be negative correlations between both of these motivation variables and conformity to professional expectations. In Table 14–E it can be seen that the proportion of board members motivated to "represent some group" is correlated with conformity −.23, and the proportion of board members motivated to obtain "political experience" is correlated with conformity −.33, both of which are significant.

Each of these three correlations between a motivation variable and conformity may be interpreted as supporting the hypothesis. These are relationships which are fairly self-evident but, nevertheless, important. Boards whose members are motivated by a sense of civic duty, behave professionally; other boards whose members are motivated by a desire to serve their own interests or those of special groups do not behave so professionally. No other correlation between a "determinant" and conformity approaches the magnitude of the correlation between "civic duty" and conformity (+.52).

School Board Evaluation of the Superintendent. Still another aspect of the relationship between a school board and its superintendent is their evaluation of the effectiveness with which they carry out their respective tasks. The superintendent as a professional usually advises the school board on its decisions, organizes its meetings, looks after its accounts, and does or can do everything except make its final decisions. It seems reasonable to argue that school board behavior will be influenced by how the board evaluates the superintendent. If school board members evaluate their superintendent highly, they will have confidence in his judgment and will therefore be motivated to respect his definition of their obligations and conform to professional expectations (since the superintendent is a professional) in order not to interfere with the effectiveness with which they think he is carrying out his tasks. From this argument the hypothesis follows that:

Hypothesis 14–4: The evaluation of incumbents of a professional position by incumbents of a nonprofessional position will be positively related to the conformity of the nonprofessionals to professional expectations.

School board members were asked to rate their superintendents on seven functions of school administrators, using the check list "excellent, good, fair, poor." On the basis of this rating by the individual school board members a mean rating for each board was obtained (see Appendix B–4b), which can be interpreted as differentiating among superintendents according to how well their job performance is evaluated by their school board. On the basis of the hypothesis presented above, it will be predicted that there will be a positive correlation between this scale and the conformity score of the school board.

This prediction is confirmed; the correlation between the school board's rating of the superintendent on his seven functions and conformity is +.23 which is significant at the .01 level, and provides support for the hypothesis.

A point which should perhaps be emphasized is that this relationship does not depend on consensus on role definition between the superintendent and school board. In fact, it was shown in Chapter Thirteen that how the school board evaluates the superintendent is not related to consensus between them. An implication of this finding is that whether or not the school board members agree with their superintendent, if he appears to them to be doing a good job, they will tend to conform to his "professional" expectations for them, because, we argued, they *respect* (rather than agree with) these expectations. This in turn suggests that the "tendency to conform to own expectations" which it has been necessary to assume for many of the hypotheses presented, may not be universally valid.

Summary. In this analysis of the conformity of school boards to professional expectations we explored an hypothesis with respect to consequences of this kind of conformity on how the superintendent experiences his job, several commonly accepted concomitants of conformity, and three hypotheses with respect to the determinants of conformity.

It was hypothesized that because the superintendent is a professional, whether or not his board conforms to professional expectations would have an effect on his job satisfaction and, as corollaries to this relationship, on his career satisfaction and the extent to which he worries about his job. Each of these consequent variables was found to be significantly related to conformity.

In exploring correlates of this kind of conformity, those frequently mentioned by professional educators were examined first. Three general classes of factors which were commonly thought by educators to be related to conformity (type of community, characteristics of board members, and experience of superintendents) were correlated with the conformity measure. Of several variables used in each of these classes, only one was found to be significantly related to conformity. This was the average education of school board members. Consequently, in trying to explain why some school boards conform to a greater extent than others to professional standards, it was necessary to base our reasoning on other factors.

In exploring possible determinants of conformity to professional expectations, three hypotheses were developed. The first led to the prediction that school boards which had relatively high consensus with their superintendents would be more likely to conform to professional expectations. The second led to the prediction that boards with a higher proportion of members motivated by "civic duty" were more likely to conform, and boards with a higher proportion of members motivated "to represent some group" and "to get political experience" were less likely to conform. The third hypothesis led to the prediction that boards who tended to evaluate their superintendent highly would tend to conform to professional expectations. All three of these hypotheses received support from the analyses.

From the magnitude of the correlations obtained, we can conclude that the most important single consequence of the conformity of his school board for a superintendent is his job satisfaction ($r = .60$). Although it was found that the average education of the board members, their consensus with their superintendent on role definitions, and their evaluation of their superintendent were all significantly related to conformity, the most important single determinant, on the basis of the magnitude of the correlations obtained, can be said to be the motivation board members had for seeking election.

Notes and References for Chapter Fourteen

[1] Talcott Parsons, *The Social System* (Glencoe: The Free Press, 1951), p. 267.

[2] Harold H. Kelley and John W. Thibaut, "Experimental Studies of Group Problem Solving and Process," in Gardner Lindzey (Editor), *Handbook of Social Psychology*, II (Cambridge: Addison-Wesley Publishing Company, 1954), p. 767.

[3] The variance of the distributions of superintendents' responses to these twelve items ranged from .688 to .171 as compared with the range of variance scores for all School Board Performance items from 1.126 to .171. The means of the variance scores of the twelve selected items·and all items in the School Board Performances Instrument were .368 and .487, respectively.

[4] Conformity scores for each school board were computed on the basis of school board member responses, using the same definition of the measure as was used for the superintendents, that is, with the "partly" responses treated consistently as "nonconforming." Even with this definition there is a significant degree of association between the conformity scores assigned to the school boards by superintendents and those assigned by school board members. The correlation between these two sets of scores (matching the score assigned on the basis of each board member's responses with the score assigned on the basis of his superintendent's responses so that $N = 507$) was .25.

[5] Floyd H. Allport, "The *J*-Curve Hypothesis of Conforming Behavior," *Journal of Social Psychology*, V (1934), pp. 141–183.

[6] Henry W. Riecken and George C. Homans, "Psychological Aspects of Social Structures," in Gardner Lindzey (Editor), *Handbook of Social Psychology*, II (Cambridge: Addison-Wesley Publishing Company, 1954), p. 794.

[7] Since these two correlations were computed on the same population it was necessary in testing the significance of their difference to use Hotelling's solution "of the problem of the significance of the difference between r_{yz} and r_{xz} without making any assumption as to the form of distribution of X and Y in the population." See Helen M. Walker and Joseph Lev, *Statistical Inference* (New York: Henry Holt and Co., 1953), pp. 256–257.

[8] Source: United States Bureau of the Census, *United States Census of Population:*

1950. I, "Number of Inhabitants," Chapter 21: Massachusetts (Washington, D. C., U. S. Government Printing Office, 1951).

[9] Source: The Commonwealth of Massachusetts, *Annual Report of the Department of Education for the Year Ending June 30, 1951,* Public Document No. 2.

[10] Source: Massachusetts Teachers Federation, *Background Data for Comparing Towns in Respect to Payment of Adequate Salaries to Teachers* (1952–1953 Series, No. K5–I, II, III, IV, October 1, 1952).

[11] A mean occupational level was computed for each school board. The categories and the weights assigned them were: Professional (6), businesss proprietors and managers (5), clerks and kindred workers (4), skilled (3), semi-skilled (2), unskilled workers (1). For housewives, the occupation of their husbands was used.

fifteen

Role Conflict: Purposes, Concepts, and Methodology

The general problem area of this and the following two chapters is role conflict. In this chapter some consideration will be given to the literature on this problem, particularly as it is useful for a theory concerned with the resolution of conflicts. Definitions will be presented of the special concepts which will serve as the basis for the analyses undertaken in the remaining chapters. The methodological procedures used to uncover exposure to conflicting expectations will also be presented.

SOME PRIOR FORMULATIONS

In discussing various treatments of the problem of role conflict by social scientists, three bases of differentiating among them will be used. The first differentiates those who define role conflict according to incompatible expectations *perceived by the observer* from those who define role conflict according to incompatible expectations *perceived by the actor*. The second differentiates those who, in defining role conflict, specify that the actor must occupy *two or more* social positions simultaneously in order to be exposed to role conflict from those who do not make this specification. The third differentiation is similarly between those who make a specification and those who fail to do so; in this case, the specification is that an expectation must be *legitimate* for it to be involved in role conflict.

The Observer-Actor Differentiation. Those who use role conflict to refer to cultural contradictions perceived by an observer would use it to include any contradiction to which an actor *may* be exposed. There is no implication that he is necessarily aware of or perceives incompatibilities in the expectations for his behavior. For example, Jacobson, Charters, and Lieberman define role conflict as ". . . the situation in which there are differences between criterion groups with respect to social role." [1] They say that their conception denotes only "cultural discrepancies" as ascertained by the investigator. It is problematic whether the subject cognizes the discrepancies.

A similar conception is used by Seeman. After defining role conflict as ". . . the exposure of the individual in a given position to incompatible behavioral expectations," he says, "The term 'role conflict' may be somewhat misleading, carrying implications of necessary personal conflict. This refers, however, only to situations in which *the observer notes what appear to be* conflicting sets of expectations, —i.e., to *potential* sources of difficulty for the actor." [2] (Italics ours, except for the last.)

Other social scientists mean by role conflict situations in which *the actor perceives* incompatible expectations. For example, Parsons says (after defining role conflict as ". . . the exposure of the actor to conflicting sets of legitimized role expectations such that complete fulfillment of both is realistically impossible."):

> It is necessary to compromise, that is, to sacrifice some at least of both sets of expectations, or to choose one alternative and sacrifice the other. In any case the actor is exposed to negative sanctions and, as far as both sets of values are internalized, to internal conflict. There may, of course, be limited possibilities of transcending the conflict by redefining the situation, as well as of evasion as for example through secrecy, and segregation of occasions. [3]

It is clear, according to Parsons, that the actor must decide on a course of action as a consequence of perceiving his exposure to contradictory expectations. If there were no perception of the incompatible expectations there would be no need to choose among "alternatives." This formulation of role conflict is consistent with Parsons' position that the starting point for the analysis of social action is an actor's "orientation" to the situation.

A similar conception of role conflict is implicit in the work of Stouffer. [4] Like Parsons he is concerned with situations in which the actor must choose between a limited set of incompatible alternatives and in which the actor thinks incompatible expectations for his behavior are involved.

A theoretical model for the problem of how an actor will behave when exposed to incompatible expectations must be based on the assumption that the actor perceives the expectations as incompatible. Incumbents of counter positions may actually hold contradictory expectations for an incumbent of a focal position, but if he is unaware of them, the situation, from our viewpoint, is residual. Superordinates and subordinates, for example, may hold incompatible expectations for the behavior of their superintendent. If he is unaware of this incompatibility, the situation does not require a decision as far as he is concerned. The "obvious" dilemma of foreman and noncommissioned officer deriving from incompatible expectations of their superordinates and subordinates may or may not be obvious to the incumbents of these positions. For these reasons, our focus of interest will be on the perceptions of the position incumbents, rather than of the observer. The operational implications of this specification will be treated later.

Multiple Positions. In some formulations of role conflict it is specified that the actor must occupy simultaneously two or more positions. Others ignore this specification and simply require that an actor be exposed to incompatible expectations, whether deriving from an actor's occupancy of a single position or of multiple positions. Sarbin, for example, says, "Role conflicts occur when a person occupies two or more positions simultaneously and when the role expectations of one are incompatible with the role expectations of the other." [5] Similarly, Stouffer is concerned with situations in which a person ". . . has simultaneous roles in two or more groups such that simultaneous conformity to the norms of each of the groups is incompatible. . . ." [6] The role conflict analysis of Getzels and Guba[7] concerning the incompatible expectations to which air force instructors are exposed and Burchard's analysis[8] of role conflicts of military chaplains are based on the assumption that the individuals studied simultaneously occupied multiple positions. In the military study the subjects were confronted with dilemmas stemming from their roles as instructors and as officers. In the chaplain study "Questions were designed to bring the respondent face to face with the proposition that the role of military officer conflicts with that of minister of the gospel. . . ." [9]

In contrast to these multiple position formulations, other conceptions do not place this restriction on role conflict situations. Parsons' definition of role conflict cited earlier ignores the source of the "conflicting sets of legitimized role expectations." This allows the inclusion of situations in which an actor may be exposed to incompatible expectations as a consequence of his occupancy of a *single position*. A teacher, for example, may be involved in a conflict which is due to his perception that his principal and students hold contradictory expectations for his behavior. The source of the conflict arises from contradictory expectations held for the incumbent of a single position.

This wider conception is illustrated as well in Seeman's formulation of role conflict in which it is defined as "the exposure of the individual in a given position to incompatible behavioral expectations." [10] His empirical analysis is concerned with the variability in expectations held by a criterion group or groups for the behavior of the incumbents of a *single position,* the school administrator.

In this inquiry we will be concerned with incompatible expectations deriving from both single and multiple position occupancy. We will be interested in situations in which the expectations held for an actor in two positions (for example, husband and superintendent) are perceived as incompatible, and as well, in situations in which contradictory expectations devolve upon an actor as an incumbent of a single position (for example, a school superintendent's perception of expectations from teachers and school board members for his behavior as a superintendent).

Legitimate Expectations. Some authors in defining role conflict specify that the incompatible expectations be "legitimate," whereas others do not require this delimitation. Parsons, for example, restricts the concept of role conflict to an actor's exposure "to conflicting sets of legitimized role expectations. . . ." [11] He views "legitimate" expectations as "institutionalized role expectations. . . . The fact that both sides of the conflicting expectations are institutionalized means that there is the basis for a claim to legitimacy for both patterns." [12] Getzels and Guba apparently take a similar position. By legitimacy they mean "mutual acceptance" by ego and alter of expectations in a given situation.[13] Stouffer in his several role conflict inquiries[14] is concerned with role *obligations* and in one of them specifically with the universalistic and particularistic *institutionalized* obligations. In contrast to these formulations of role conflict, those of Sarbin, Seeman, and Jacobson and his collaborators do not require that the incompatible expectations be legitimate.[15]

Legitimacy, like exposure to incompatible expectations, may be viewed from the standpoint of the outside observer or of the actor who participates in social behavior. For a theoretical scheme the purpose of which is to provide a basis for the prediction of an actor's resolution of a role conflict it is maintained that the actor's perceptions of the legitimacy of the expectations are more relevant than the perceptions of the outside observer. Although Stouffer dealt with it explicitly, analysts of role conflict situations have generally neglected the actor's perceptions of the legitimacy of expectations. Perhaps this could partly account for Borgatta's finding[16] that the expected role conflict of the noncom was in actuality not a frequent occurrence. In our judgment, the perceived legitimacy of expectations is a crucial dimension for the explanation of an actor's behavior in the face of incompatible expectations.

This discussion has given us an opportunity to specify the general frame of reference of the subsequent analyses. First, our interest is in the perceptions of actors, rather than the observer. Second, we shall be concerned with incompatible expectations resulting from an actor's occupancy of single as well as of multiple positions; intrarole as well as inter-role conflicts will be within the focus of inquiry. Third, the analysis will not be restricted to incompatible expectations which are perceived as legitimate. Attention will be directed to situations involving both legitimate and illegitimate incompatible expectations.

MAJOR CONCEPTS

It is now appropriate to introduce the definitions of the concepts we shall use in the description and analysis of the incompatible expectations to which the superintendents perceive they are exposed.

A *role congruency* is a situation in which an incumbent of a focal position perceives that the same or highly similar expectations are held for him. A school superintendent who perceived that his teachers, principals, students, and school board alike expected him to handle a discipline problem in the same manner would be confronted with a role congruency.

There are situations, however, in which a position incumbent perceives that he is exposed to expectations which are incompatible. A school superintendent, for example, may think that teachers and parents hold conflicting expectations for his behavior in dealing with a truant child. Any situation in which the incumbent of a focal position perceives that he is confronted with incompatible expectations will be called a *role conflict*.

An expectation may be considered by the person for whom it is held to be *legitimate* or *illegitimate*. A legitimate expectation is one which the incumbent of a focal position feels others have a right to hold. An illegitimate expectation is one which he does not feel others have a right to hold. An expectation which is felt to be legitimate will be called a *perceived obligation*. One which is felt to be illegitimate will be called a *perceived pressure*.

Role conflict situations may also be differentiated on the basis of whether the incompatible expectations are felt by the incumbent to derive from his occupancy of one or more than one position. An individual is confronted with an *intrarole conflict* if he perceives that others hold different expectations for him as the incumbent of a single position. The school superintendent frequently faces situations of this kind. The teachers, he feels, expect him to be their spokesman and leader, to take their side on such matters as salary increases and instructional policy. On the other hand, he feels that the school board members expect him to represent them, to "sell" their views to the staff because he is the executive officer and the administrator of school board policies. Since these incompatible expectations devolve upon him as the occupant of a single position, it is an intrarole conflict situation.

In *inter-role conflict,* an individual perceives that others hold different expectations for him as the incumbent of two or more positions. For example, *as a husband and father* in the family social system a superintendent may think his wife and children expect him to spend most of his evenings with them. On the other hand, his school board and P.T.A. groups, he may feel, expect him, as their school superintendent, to spend most of his after-office hours on educational and civic activities (for example, P.T.A. meetings, high school plays and athletic contests, school board meetings, Red Cross, etc.). The superintendent usually cannot satisfy both of these incompatible expectations. He is faced with inter-role conflict because the source of the dilemma stems from his occupancy of more than one position.

Sanctions. A sanction, as we defined it earlier,[17] is a role behavior, the primary significance of which is gratificational-deprivational. For the purposes of role conflict analyses, we would suggest that two kinds of sanctions be distinguished: internal and external. An internal sanction is one applied by the actor whose gratification is being considered, that is, by the incumbent of a focal position, whereas an external sanction is one performed by other actors or incumbents of counter positions. An internal sanction is one which an individual applies to himself, whereas an external sanction is one which someone else applies to him.

For the analysis of incompatible expectation situations with which we will be concerned, *actual* external sanctions will not be of interest. Although in a study of ongoing sequences of acts, the actual sanctions would be of direct relevance, for the study of single acts, the sanctions the incumbent of a focal position *perceives* before the acts are considered of more relevance. Consequently, our analyses will be concerned with an individual's perceptions of the external sanctions others will apply to him, rather than with the sanctions they actually do apply. Whether or not the perceived and actual sanctions are the same in any given situation is an empirical problem which will not be relevant to these analyses.

METHODOLOGY

Our first attempt in trial interviews to determine the major kinds of role conflicts to which superintendents perceived they were exposed was with an open-ended, relatively "unstructured" question approach. It was hoped that from the superintendent's discussion of his dissatisfactions with his position, of the major strains and tensions resulting from his job, and of what the "community" expects of him, would emerge the major incompatible expectations to which he perceived he was exposed. Superintendents frequently mentioned the difficulty of securing adequate financial support for their schools. They described certain pressures to which they were exposed from different groups and individuals in their communities regarding the employment of school personnel, school athletics, and the letting of school contracts. They frequently cited the heavy time requirements of their position.

These data did not, however, provide reliable information with respect to incompatible expectations. They most frequently revealed troublesome situations from the superintendent's viewpoint, but they did not provide coders with an opportunity to reach reliable conclusions with respect to exactly what the incompatible expectations were or by whom they were held. It seemed apparent that our a priori notions about the usefulness of an essentially nondirective approach were to some degree in error.

We decided then to use a more directive approach in our next set of trial interviews in which questions like these were used:

"People in important community positions frequently find themselves caught in situations in which different individuals and groups expect them to behave differently. What situations of this kind do you face? What situations do you face in which you are exposed to conflicting expectations for your behavior?"

Questions like these also elicited situations in which the superintendent was in disagreement with groups or individuals in his community but not necessarily situations in which he perceived incompatible expectations from different people in the community or school system. Even when the dilemma of the foreman in industry was used as an example, as it was in one of the pretest interviews, the superintendent described some of his disagreement with his teachers but did not detail, for example, any expectations held for him by his teachers which were incompatible with expectations held for him by his school board.

It became apparent that the problem was to develop a technique by means of which the interviewer could ask, "To what incompatible expectations are you exposed as a superintendent?" perhaps without using the exact phrase of "incompatible expectations." In earlier pretests what the interviewer had been trying to do was to "teach" the respondent what was meant by "incompatible expectations" in order to find out with what incompatible expectations the respondent was faced.

These preliminary pretests suggested as well that the number of counter positions and the number of incumbents of each counter position could complicate what at first appeared to be a simple situation. An attractive situation for the analysis of incompatible expectations is the superintendent's recommendation for salary increases for the teachers in his school system. We had originally intended to determine whether the superintendent perceived incompatible expectations from the teachers and school board members, and, if he did, to try to predict his resolution of the conflict. During the pretests, however, we found that when the superintendents discussed the salary dilemma, they were concerned with expectations of persons other than teachers and school board members. Sometimes they mentioned the P.T.A., sometimes the town finance committee and the mayor or city council. People who were economically influential, local politicians, the press, service clubs, the chamber of commerce, old-line families, and sometimes their wives were others mentioned in the course of a discussion of this situation. It became apparent that incumbents of a number of counter positions were often perceived as important referents for superintendents in making a decision.

Restricting consideration arbitrarily to those whose expectations were "logically" related to the superintendent's resolution of the salary dilemma, in this case the school board and teachers, resulted in the placement in a residual category those who might be the most crucial for his decision. This suggested that for an analysis of how a position incumbent resolves a role conflict, it is necessary to determine which incumbents of what counter positions he perceives as relevant.

A second complexity recognized in the course of pretests was that different incumbents of a single counter position may hold or may be perceived as holding dissimilar expectations. A conflict frequently cited in the literature is that of the adolescent caught between the contradictory expectations of his parents and his peers. The assumption is that parents hold one set of expectations and peers hold another. Although this is indeed a real possibility, it does not exhaust the possibilities inherent in the situation. This assumption may be tenuous. The degree of consensus between the incumbents of two different positions (parent and peer) and among incumbents of the same position is always empirically problematic.

After considerable experimentation with various techniques, a procedure which tried to take these possible complexities into account was developed. Four situations involving problems with which all superintendents must deal, and which on the basis of the pretests were judged likely to give rise to incompatible expectations, were presented to the superintendent. They concern (1) hiring and promotion of teachers, (2) the superintendent's allocation of his after-office hours, (3) salary increases for teachers, and (4) the priority the superintendent gives financial or educational needs in drawing up the school budget. For each situation three alternative expectations were presented that incumbents of relevant counter positions might hold. For example, in the situation involving the hiring and promotion of teachers, these three expectations were used:

A. Expect me to recommend the hiring and promotion of teachers and other school employees on the basis of merit only.

B. Expect me to give special consideration to their preferences in recommending the hiring and promotion of teachers and other school employees.

C. Have no expectations either way regarding whom I should recommend for hiring or for promotion.

Eighteen potentially relevant groups or individuals were listed on the instrument. Each of the superintendents was asked to indicate which of the three statements most nearly represented what each of the groups or individuals expected the superintendent to do in the situation.

If he said that one or more individuals held expectation *A* and one or more held expectation *B*, he was reporting incompatible expectations from two or more incumbents of positions counter to his own or of groups with which the school system must maintain relationships.

After the superintendent had answered the instrument by giving his perceptions of the expectations others held for him and if incompatible expectations were among them, the interviewer said that he interpreted these responses to mean that the superintendent viewed the situation as one in which "different people or groups expect you to behave differently in this situation." Except in a few instances, the respondents confirmed the interviewer's interpretation of his responses.

In addition, the superintendents were asked to say whether or not they felt that the expectations they said were held by others were "legitimate" or not. Furthermore, if incompatible expectations were perceived by the superintendent, the interviewer proceeded to probe with open-ended questions for the existence and extent of anxiety created by the situation, for the manner in which it was resolved, and for the sanctions perceived as resulting from selecting one or the other of the incompatible alternatives. This additional information will be used in the succeeding chapters.

After these four situations had been explored, the interviewer then probed for other situations which did or were likely to give rise to incompatible expectations from incumbents of positions counter to the superintendent's. Since a considerable amount of time had been spent on the four structured situations, the respondent could be assumed to have at this point a reasonably clear idea of the frame of reference of this part of the interview. As a consequence of this better understanding of the interviewer's purpose, other situations in which they were exposed to incompatible expectations were described by superintendents.[18]

An example of a city superintendent's responses to one of the "structured" situations will illustrate the exact method of securing the data for this analysis. In Figure 15–1 are presented the responses of this superintendent to the question of which groups or individuals held expectations for him with respect to hiring teachers.

A number of observations may be made from his responses. It is clear that he perceives incompatible expectations. Some individuals and groups expect him to conform to the A and others expect him to conform to the B expectation. It can be seen from his responses that he perceives that some politicians, some church groups, business and commercial organizations, labor unions, the P.T.A. and parent groups, some teachers, some of his personal friends, the taxpayers association, individuals who are economically influential, the service clubs, some of the school board members, some town finance committee members, his family, the chamber of commerce, and some of the newspapers expect him to recommend, hire, and promote teachers on the basis of competence or merit alone. All the other groups or individuals he views as holding the contrary expectation, namely, that he should give special consideration to their preferences with the exception of "farm organizations" with which this city superintendent was not concerned in any way.

In five cases some members of the groups or some individuals of a particular category held one expectation, according to the superintendent, whereas others in the same group or category held the contrary expectation. School board members, politicians, church groups, teachers, the town finance committee, and the press are described by

---

I. HERE ARE THREE ATTITUDES WHICH VARIOUS GROUPS AND INDIVIDUALS IN YOUR COMMUNITY MIGHT TAKE:

 A. Expect me to recommend the hiring and promotion of teachers and other school employees on the basis of merit only.

 B. Expect me to give special consideration to their preferences in recommending the hiring and promotion of teachers and other school employees.

 C. Have no expectations either way regarding whom I should hire or recommend for promotions.

FOR EACH GROUP OR INDIVIDUAL LISTED BELOW PLEASE CHECK THE BOX WHICH MOST NEARLY REPRESENTS WHAT THEY THINK YOU SHOULD DO ABOUT THIS:

	A	B	C		A	B	C
1. Politicians	✓	✓		10. Individuals influential for economic reasons	✓		
2. Church or religious groups	✓	✓		11. Service clubs	✓		
3. Farm organizations				12. Fraternal organizations		✓	
4. Business or commercial organizations	✓			13. Veterans organizations		✓	
5. Labor unions	✓			14. Individual school committee members	✓	✓	
6. Parents (P.T.A.)	✓			15. Town finance committee or city council	✓	✓	
7. Teachers	✓	✓		16. My wife—family	✓		
8. Personal friends	✓			17. Chamber of commerce	✓		
9. Taxpayers association	✓			18. The press	✓	✓	
				19. Other		✓	

Figure 15–1. Example of one superintendent's responses to the question of which groups or individuals held expectations for him with respect to hiring teachers.

this superintendent as comprising individuals who hold incompatible expectations for him.

The expectations perceived by another superintendent, one who is in a suburban community, are presented in Figure 15–2.

Omitting labor unions and farm organizations because these groups do not exist in his community, this superintendent, with two exceptions, perceived that all the groups and individuals listed expect him

---

I. HERE ARE THREE ATTITUDES WHICH VARIOUS GROUPS AND INDIVIDUALS IN YOUR COMMUNITY MIGHT TAKE:

 A. Expect me to recommend the hiring and promotion of teachers and other school employees on the basis of merit only.

 B. Expect me to give special consideration to their preferences in hiring and recommending promotions for teachers and other school employees.

 C. Have no expectations either way regarding whom I should hire or recommend for promotions.

FOR EACH GROUP OR INDIVIDUAL LISTED BELOW PLEASE CHECK THE BOX WHICH MOST NEARLY REPRESENTS WHAT THEY THINK YOU SHOULD DO ABOUT THIS:

	A	B	C			A	B	C
1. Politicians			✓		10. Individuals influential for economic reasons	✓		
2. Church or religious groups	✓				11. Service clubs	✓		
3. Farm organizations					12. Fraternal organizations	✓		
4. Business or commercial organizations	✓				13. Veterans organizations			✓
5. Labor unions					14. Individual school committee members	✓		
6. Parents (P.T.A.)	✓				15. Town finance committee or city council	✓		
7. Teachers	✓				16. My wife—family	✓		
8. Personal friends	✓				17. Chamber of commerce	✓		
9. Taxpayers association	✓				18. The press	✓		
					19. Other			

Figure 15–2. Example of one superintendent's responses to the question of which groups or individuals held expectations for him with respect to hiring teachers.

to base his personnel recommendations on the criterion of merit only. The two exceptions, politicians and veterans organizations, this superintendent feels, have no expectations for him with respect to his personnel decisions.

These two illustrations are examples of superintendents who are in a sense exposed to extreme situations. The first superintendent whose responses were presented is confronted with a number of conflicting expectations from different groups and individuals, and in some cases from different individuals within the same group and from groups of the same kind. The second superintendent whose responses were considered is confronted with a role congruency, since, according to his responses, there is no one who expects him to make any personnel decisions on the basis of anything but merit.[19]

Notes and References for Chapter Fifteen

[1] Eugene Jacobson, W. W. Charters, Jr., and Seymour Lieberman, "The Use of the Role Concept in the Study of Complex Organizations," *Journal of Social Issues*, VII (1951), p. 22.

[2] Melvin Seeman, "Role Conflict and Ambivalence in Leadership," *American Sociological Review*, XVIII (1953), p. 373.

[3] Talcott Parsons, *The Social System* (Glencoe: The Free Press, 1951), p. 280.

[4] Samuel A. Stouffer, "An Analysis of Conflicting Social Norms," *American Sociological Review*, XIV (1949), pp. 707–717.

[5] Theodore R. Sarbin, "Role Theory," in Gardner Lindzey (Editor), *Handbook of Social Psychology*, I (Cambridge: Addison-Wesley Publishing Company, 1954), p. 228.

[6] Stouffer, *op. cit.*, p. 707.

[7] J. W. Getzels and E. G. Guba, "Role, Role Conflict, and Effectiveness," *American Sociological Review*, XIX (1954), pp. 164–175.

[8] Waldo W. Burchard, "Role Conflicts in Military Chaplains," *American Sociological Review*, XIX (1954), pp. 528–535.

[9] *Ibid.*, p. 529.

[10] Seeman, *op. cit.*, p. 373.

[11] Parsons, *op. cit.*, p. 280.

[12] *Ibid.*, p. 282.

[13] Getzels and Guba, *op. cit.*, p. 165.

[14] Stouffer, *loc. cit.*, and Samuel A. Stouffer and Jackson Toby, "Role Conflict and Personality," *American Journal of Sociology*, LVI (1951), pp. 395–406.

[15] Sarbin, *loc. cit.*; Seeman, *loc. cit.*; and Jacobson et al., *loc. cit.*

[16] Edgar F. Borgatta, "Attitudinal Concomitants to Military Statuses," *Social Forces*, XXXIII (1955), pp. 342–347.

[17] See Chapter Four, pp. 64–67.

[18] These will be reported in another book which will analyze the major occupa-

tional problems of the superintendency in a sociological and socio-psychological framework.

[19] Other empirical efforts to examine role conflicts may be found in W. F. Whyte and B. B. Gardner, "The Man in the Middle: Position and Problems of the Foreman," *Applied Anthropology*, IV (1945), pp. 1–28; Jerome Laulicht, "Role Conflict, The Pattern Variable Theory and Scalogram Analysis," *Social Forces*, XXXIII (1955), pp. 250–254; Bernard C. Rosen, "Conflicting Group Membership: A Study of Parent-Peer Group Cross-Pressures," *American Sociological Review*, XX (1955), pp. 155–161; and John T. Gullahorn, "Measuring Role Conflict," *American Journal of Sociology*, LXI (1956), pp. 229–303. In addition John P. Spiegel and Florence R. Kluckhohn are engaged in a research project, "The Influence of the Family and Cultural Values on the Mental Health and Illness of the Individual," which is centrally concerned with the resolution of role conflict within the family. See John P. Spiegel, "The Resolution of Role Conflict Within the Family," *Psychiatry*, XX (1957), pp. 1–16. For an extremely provocative discussion of the problem of role conflict and mechanisms that may come into play in dealing with it, see Robert K. Merton, *Social Theory and Social Structure* (Glencoe: The Free Press, 1957) pp. 370–380.

sixteen

The Incidence, Resolution, and Consequences of Four Role Conflicts

In the first part of this chapter we will describe the incidence of role conflict among superintendents in the four situations which were used, and present the methods by means of which those who were exposed to conflicts resolved them. This descriptive material will serve as a background to the theory of role conflict resolution which will be presented in the next chapter and provide the data with which an initial test can be made of it. Before this theory is presented and tested, however, it is important to ask whether or not exposure to role conflict has any consequences for the way superintendents experience their jobs. An attempt will be made at the end of this chapter to answer this question for the four situations.

INCIDENCE AND RESOLUTION

The Personnel Situation. Our pretest interviews revealed a fact, largely unrecognized outside the educational profession, regarding the school superintendency. In many communities the superintendent is the manager of one of the largest local organizations—the school system. Not only is he responsible for the financial management of this enterprise, he is also its chief personnel officer. It is one of his tasks to supervise a large body of personnel, and another to make recommendations for their selection and promotion. It is quite clear that most superintendents feel obligated to make personnel decisions on the basis of merit.

In responding to one of the items of the Superintendent's Performances Instrument (see Appendix Table A–1, item 1), 86 percent of them said that it was absolutely imperative that they make recommendations regarding personnel selection and promotion only on the basis of this criterion. This professional requirement may, however, be incompatible with the expectations of influential individuals in the community and with the interests of local organizations. A local politician or school board member whose word carries great weight at city hall or with the town finance committee may ask the superintendent for the "slight" favor of recommending a friend or relative for the local elementary principalship vacancy. A personal friend may expect the superintendent to give his daughter the recommendation for a vacant teaching job. Big taxpayers may feel that they have a right to expect that their preferences be taken into account in appointing teachers in a school in their section of town. Some school board members may feel that since their position requires an expenditure of a great deal of time and energy without remuneration, their preferences among job applicants should be given special consideration by the school executive in his recommendations. Such situations may result in difficult dilemmas for the superintendent. By conforming to his professional obligation he may endanger his new school building program or his next budget request. By not yielding to the unprofessional expectations of school board members and key influentials in the community he may be endangering his own position.

In addition, many groups in the community may be dissatisfied with him if he yields to the wishes of those who expect special consideration for "their candidate." They may hold the expectation that he behave as a "professional" educator. The P.T.A., the teachers, and many other groups whose interests are similar to the educational profession may feel that he is not conforming to their expectations if he does not base his recommendations solely on the competence criterion. That this area of decision-making is a fertile source for perceived role conflicts can be seen in Table 16–A.

TABLE 16–A. PERCENTAGE OF SUPERINTENDENTS WHO PERCEIVED THEIR EXPOSURE TO ROLE CONFLICT AND TO ROLE CONGRUENCY IN FOUR SITUATIONS

Situation	Role Conflict, %	Role Congruency, %	N
Personnel Hiring and Promotion	71	29	105
Time Allocation	53	47	105
Teacher Salary Recommendations	88	12	105
Budget Recommendations	91	9	105

Seventy-one percent of the superintendents perceived that they had been exposed to role conflict with respect to hiring and promoting teachers. Of the 30 superintendents (29 percent) who perceived role congruency in this area, 29 said they were exposed to only the "merit" expectation. The other superintendent, however, felt that all the groups and individuals listed who held an expectation, expected their candidates to be given special preference. It is of interest to observe, parenthetically, that this superintendent said he conformed to this "unprofessional" expectation and considered it legitimate. He remarked, "It's not my school system; it's theirs. That's why I give them what they want."

Table 16–B reports the proportion of superintendents who perceived that incumbents of each counter position held: (a) the expectation that he base his recommendations on the merit criterion; (b) the

TABLE 16–B. PERCENTAGE OF SUPERINTENDENTS WHO PERCEIVED PARTICULAR EXPECTATIONS FROM SPECIFIED GROUPS AND INDIVIDUALS WITH RESPECT TO HIS PERSONNEL RECOMMENDATIONS

Group or Individual	(a) Merit Expectation, %	(b) Special Preference Expectation, %	(c) Mixed Expectation, %	(d) No Expectation, %	N^*
1. Politicians	23.8	27.6	7.6	41.0	105
2. Church or religious groups	40.4	20.2	11.5	27.9	104
3. Farm organizations	30.6	0.0	1.6	67.8	62
4. Business or commercial organizations	42.0	2.9	0.0	55.1	105
5. Labor unions	26.4	7.5	0.0	66.1	53
6. Parents (P.T.A.)	88.6	6.6	3.8	1.0	105
7. Teachers	81.9	4.8	10.4	2.9	105
8. Personal friends	60.0	17.1	6.7	16.2	105
9. Taxpayers association	62.3	3.3	3.3	31.1	61
10. Individuals influential for economic reasons	39.9	21.0	2.9	36.2	105
11. Service clubs	65.6	5.7	0.0	28.7	87
12. Fraternal organizations	42.9	15.1	5.4	36.6	93
13. Veterans organizations	38.5	29.8	4.8	26.9	104
14. Individual school committee members	64.8	10.4	24.8	0.0	105
15. Town finance committee or city council	67.7	3.9	4.9	23.5	103
16. My wife—family	80.6	0.0	0.0	19.4	103
17. Chamber of commerce	58.4	6.2	0.0	35.4	65
18. The press	68.2	3.4	4.5	23.9	88

* When N is less than 105 it is usually because the group or individual did not exist in certain communities; the few *no answers* when the group or individual did exist are also excluded.

expectation that the superintendent give special consideration to their preferences; (c) mixed expectations (that is, some held the A expectation and others the B expectation); and (d) no expectations regarding the superintendent's personnel recommendations.

Table 16–B reveals in macroscopic perspective the sources of the inconsistencies in the expectations for their personnel decisions to which superintendents perceive they are exposed. The most consistent source of only the merit expectation is parents or parent groups (89 percent in column a), with teachers (82 percent), and his wife (81 percent) coming next. Veterans organizations are most likely to hold only the "preference" expectation (30 percent in column b), with local politicians (28 percent), economic influentials (21 percent), and church groups (20 percent) next. Interestingly, although the majority of superintendents perceive that their school board members hold only the "merit" expectation (65 percent in column a) this is the group among whose members incompatible expectations (both merit and preference) are most likely to be held (25 percent in column c), with church groups (12 percent), and teachers (10 percent) next in this category. In the next column it will be seen that farm organizations (68 percent in column d), labor unions (66 percent), and business organizations (55 percent) are groups which superintendents perceive as most likely to hold no expectations for their superintendents with respect to personnel decisions.

From these data it is possible to conclude not only that superintendents are frequently confronted with role conflicts with respect to their personnel decisions, but also that these incompatibilities may stem from different groups and individuals or from groups and individuals of the same kind. Sometimes what the school board expects conflicts with what the teachers expect. In other cases, some school board members expect one thing, and others expect the other. For the 71 percent of the superintendents who perceived that they were exposed to incompatible expectations, there is clearly a problem which must be resolved. What do superintendents do when they perceive that some groups or individuals expect them to make personnel decisions solely on the criterion of merit, whereas other groups or individuals expect the superintendent to give their candidates special preference?

When a superintendent had indicated that he was exposed to incompatible expectations he was asked how he resolved the dilemma implied by this condition. Of the 105 superintendents in the sample, 30, or 29 percent, did not perceive incompatible expectations, and in three of the remaining 75 cases the data are inadequate for a judgment regarding the resolution of the dilemma. Therefore, the discussion of the resolution techniques of superintendents when confronted with role conflicts with respect to their personnel decisions will be restricted to the remaining 72 superintendents.

Sixty-one of the 72 superintendents (85 percent) did not conform to the expectations of those who demanded preferential treatment for their candidates and can be said to have resolved the dilemma in terms of the "professional" expectation of basing their personnel decisions on the criterion of merit.

Seven of the 72 superintendents resolved the dilemma by conforming to the "unprofessional" expectation. When exposed to this incompatible expectation situation they allowed the preferences of certain groups and individuals in their communities to override the merit criterion. Some of these superintendents described their yielding to special preference expectations as one of the "practical parts of the job." Another said that it is inevitable that he yield to the school board members because they are his superordinates.

Four of the superintendents in trying to resolve this conflict made an attempt to engage in some form of compromise behavior. All four of these said that they were primarily motivated to conform to the professional expectation, but that it was necessary in their particular communities to give some consideration to the preferences of their school boards and, in one case, to the veterans organization. Their solution was, essentially, "other things being equal," to give preference to those candidates who were the choices of the board or the veterans organization, but if the preferred candidate were incompetent, not to give preference. One of these superintendents said:

> I compromise. It's a matter of the degree of differential between the two candidates. If the difference in competence is too wide, I operate on the professional criteria. If there is little difference, there's no harm in recommending on the basis of the school committee's preferences. If I do this the committee will help me on the big picture—it's for the greater good of the school system. If you can justify it as being for the greater good of the system, then it's all right.

When confronted with incompatible expectations with respect to their personnel decisions, we can say in summary that the majority of the superintendents in our sample (85 percent) conformed to what can be described as the "professional" expectation, that some superintendents (10 percent) conform to the "unprofessional" expectation, and the remaining 5 percent make some attempt to compromise between the "professional" and "unprofessional" courses of action.

Time Allocation Situation. Our preliminary exploratory activities suggested that the demands made upon incumbents of the school superintendency position, like those made on other executives who occupy important and highly visible positions in the community, may require them to make decisions regarding their time allocation in the face of incompatible expectations.   Many superintendents reported that they were expected to attend meetings and to participate in committees of professional associations.   Local organizations like the Rotary Club or chamber of commerce frequently expect their superintendent to be active in their programs.   These demands often conflict with the expectations his school board or staff hold for him regarding how he spends his time.   More frequently, the expectations held for him by his school board and local community groups may conflict with how his wife and children expect him to spend his after-office hours.

Over 90 percent of the superintendents in discussing the impact of their jobs on their families reported that their wives were concerned about the infinitesimal amount of time they were able to spend with their families.   Some of their wives, however, apparently recognized that the superintendency demands large family sacrifices and reluctantly accepted this unfortunate but "irremediable" state of affairs.   Others were quite insistent that their husbands stay home most evenings. Many superintendents also said that their children expect them to be at home "like other fathers."   On the other hand, his school board, P.T.A. groups, civic and welfare organizations may expect him to spend most of his after-office hours on educational and civic activities. The superintendent presumably cannot satisfy both sets of expectations.

For the time allocation problem, the superintendents were asked to say what expectations they thought others held for how they spent their after-office hours.   Fifty-three percent of the superintendents reported that they were exposed to role conflicts with respect to how they spent their time. (See Table 16–A, p. 259.)   In Table 16–A it can also be seen that although more than half the superintendents were exposed to role conflict with respect to their time allocation, fewer superintendents reported incompatible expectations for this than for any of the other three problems—personnel, salary, and financial decisions—dealt with in the structured part of this section of the interview.

In Table 16–C the superintendents who did *not* perceive incompatible expectations are classified into five types according to the expectations they felt their wives held for them and the expectations held by

other individuals and groups in their communities with respect to
how they spent their after-office hours. Twenty of the superintend-

TABLE 16–C. TYPES OF EXPECTATIONS REPORTED BY SUPERINTENDENTS
WHO PERCEIVED ROLE CONGRUENCY IN THE TIME ALLOCATION SITUATION

Type	Wife's Expectation*	Expectations* of Other Groups and Individuals	Behavior † of the Superintendent	N
1	A	A	a	11
2	B	B	b	9
3	B	B or C	a	9
4	C	A	a	14
5	C	B or C	b	6
Total				49

* Expectation A = Spend most evenings on school and community business.
Expectation B = Spend most evenings with family or friends. Expectation C =
No expectations held.

† Behavior a = conforms to expectation A. Behavior b = conforms to expectation B.

ents did not perceive incompatible expectations for their time allocation because they felt their wives held the same expectations as all of
the others (Types 1 and 2). Eleven of these superintendents (Type 1)
felt they were consistently expected to spend most of their evenings on
school and community business. The other nine (Type 2) felt they
were consistently expected to spend most of their evenings with their
family or friends. The Type 3 superintendents felt that their wives
expected them to spend most of their evenings with their family or
friends, but that other individuals and groups in the community
either held the same expectation or had no expectation. The type 4
and 5 superintendents felt that their wives held no expectation in this
respect, and consequently, whatever the expectations of the other
individuals in the community, they perceived no incompatibility between them and their wives' expectations.

In Table 16–D are summarized the responses of all superintendents
to the time allocation instrument. Parents and P.T.A. groups were
most frequently mentioned as expecting the superintendent to de-
vote his after-office hours to school affairs (53 percent in column a),
with school board members (37 percent), taxpayers associations (30
percent), and town finance committee members (26 percent) next. Of
those who expected their superintendent to spend most of his time
with his family or friends, the superintendents' wives, were, as might
have been anticipated, most frequently mentioned (66 percent in
column b) and personal friends (44 percent) next. From very few cate-

TABLE 16–D. PERCENTAGE OF SUPERINTENDENTS WHO PERCEIVED PAR-
TICULAR EXPECTATIONS FROM SPECIFIED GROUPS AND INDIVIDUALS WITH
RESPECT TO THEIR TIME ALLOCATION

	(a) School Affairs Expectation, %	(b) Family Expectation, %	(c) Mixed Expectation, %	(d) No Expectation, %	
Group or Individual					N*
1. Politicians	22.9	1.0	0.0	76.1	105
2. Church or religious groups	16.2	10.4	0.0	73.4	104
3. Farm organizations	4.8	1.6	0.0	93.6	62
4. Business or commercial organizations	5.7	2.9	0.0	91.4	105
5. Labor unions	5.7	5.7	0.0	88.6	53
6. Parents (P.T.A.)	53.3	12.4	2.9	31.4	105
7. Teachers	18.1	19.0	0.0	62.9	105
8. Personal friends	6.7	43.8	1.0	48.5	105
9. Taxpayers association	29.5	0.0	0.0	70.5	61
10. Individuals influential for economic reasons	9.5	4.8	1.0	84.7	105
11. Service clubs	26.4	6.9	0.0	66.7	87
12. Fraternal organizations	14.0	8.6	0.0	77.4	93
13. Veterans organizations	15.4	2.9	0.0	81.7	104
14. Individual school committee members	37.1	18.2	7.6	37.1	105
15. Town finance committee or city council	26.2	2.9	1.9	69.0	103
16. My wife—family	14.6	66.0	0.0	19.4	103
17. Chamber of commerce	12.3	0.0	1.5	86.2	65
18. The press	25.0	2.3	0.0	72.7	88

* When N is less than 105 it is usually because the group or individual did not exist in certain communities; the *no answers* when the group or individual did exist are also excluded.

gories of individuals and groups did superintendents perceive "mixed" expectations, the highest percentage in this column being 8 percent which is obtained by school board members. In the case of all but four kinds of individuals or groups, the majority of superintendents, however, perceived that "no expectation" is held for their time allocation. The four exceptions are the superintendent's wife, individual school board members, parents groups and P.T.A., and personal friends.

What do superintendents do when confronted with role conflicts for their after-office time allocation? It is interesting first to see what those superintendents do who perceive no incompatible expectations. In Table 16–C (p. 264) in which the superintendents who did not experience incompatible expectations were categorized into five types, their behaviors are also described. As would be expected, the 11 superintendents whose wives and others expect them to spend most of their spare time on school affairs (Type 1) do so. Similarly the 9 superintendents whose wives and others both expect them to spend most of their spare time with their family or friends (Type 2) say they do this. The 9 superintendents whose wives expect them to stay home and who think others either expect them to stay home or have no expectation with respect to their after-office time allocation (Type 3) spend most of their time, according to their responses, on school affairs even though this conflicts with their wives' expectations and is not required by the expectations they think others hold. We might infer that these 9 individuals hold the "school and community affairs" expectation for themselves and behave according to it even though it is incompatible with the expectations they think their wives expect. The 14 superintendents whose wives hold no expectation and who are expected by others to spend their spare time on school affairs conform to this expectation (Type 4), and the 6 superintendents whose wives hold no expectation and whom others either expect to stay home or hold no expectation do spend most of their time with their families or friends.

How did those superintendents who perceived that they *were* exposed to incompatible expectations for how they allocated their after-office hours resolve the dilemma implied by this perception? Since 4 of the superintendents were widowed or single and the data from another 2 are inadequate for purposes of classification, this discussion will be restricted to 50 cases.

Thirty-three of the 50 superintendents gave priority to the occupational expectation to participate in school and community affairs over the family expectation to spend most of their evenings with their family (or friends). One superintendent said he did this because it was part of his job, although he felt it to be unfair to his family. "The school board and the P.T.A.," he said, "would get sore if I didn't, and I'd worry too. I don't think I'd be able to do a good job as superintendent of schools if I didn't." Another superintendent described his decision to spend most of his free time on school affairs as a ". . . matter of conscience. I feel I have to be out at least four nights a week to sell and protect my program. If I didn't go to their meetings they'd feel I wasn't part of the system and the town. Some of my friends think I'm nuts."

Four of these 50 superintendents, however, gave greater priority to their families in contrast to their occupational positions. In 2 of these cases the superintendents reported that the reason they did not spend most evenings on school-community business was poor health. In one instance the superintendent was in the job for only one year on a temporary basis. Another of the superintendents used consistently the "white lie" technique to avoid most evening meetings. He told those who asked him to attend or address school or community groups that previous commitments precluded his acceptance. It is of interest that his school system was in a relatively large community where the possibility of "checking" his statement would be rather difficult.

The remaining 13 of the 50 superintendents tried to resolve this role conflict by compromising. One superintendent used the device of showing up just frequently enough at important meetings in the community to avoid the charge of not being interested in school and community affairs. Another said that his wife would "beef" so much if he did not stay home some of the time that he yielded to her expectations whenever he could despite the contrary expectations. In other instances, although some community groups expected them to spend most of their after-office hours on school and civic affairs, the superintendents said they felt secure enough in their jobs, or that the community in general was reasonable enough in its time demands so that they could to some extent meet their family obligations.

The remaining cases were superintendents who used the "stop-start" technique, depending primarily on the protestations of their wives. These men would spend most evenings out until their wives began to protest vigorously over the small amount of time they devoted to their families. When this occurred, they would drastically cut the number of evenings they were spending on school and community activities. As the pressures built up from the community for their attendance at meetings, they would gradually drift back into giving priority to the job expectation. They would fulfill their occupational expectation until their wives were once again aroused and a new cycle would begin.

When confronted with incompatible expectations with respect to their time allocation, we can say in summary that the majority of the superintendents (66 percent) conformed to the "occupational" expectation rather than to the "family" expectation, that 4 (8 percent) conformed to their "family" obligation, and that thirteen (26 percent) adopted some kind of compromise over their time allocation which to some extent satisfied both sets of expectations.

The Teacher Salary Recommendation. Another decision-making area which is likely to give rise to role conflict for the superintendent is the teacher salary issue. The local teachers association and certain groups in the community like the P.T.A. may expect their school executive to fight for maximum salary increases for his staff. The interviews with the superintendents revealed that most of them are acutely aware of and concerned about the relative lag in teacher salary increases as compared to those of other occupational groups. They mentioned particularly that married male teachers frequently must take outside jobs to provide their families with minimum living standards. Most superintendents are former teachers and know from first-hand experience the difficulties of maintaining a "middle class" standard of living on a "lower class" wage level. In this connection it is interesting that when superintendents were asked to describe their major dissatisfactions with their jobs the one most frequently mentioned was their own inadequate salaries.

In addition, many superintendents realize that unless they can raise their school salary schedule to a higher level, they will lose many of their best personnel or will not be able to attract the best new teachers. As in the business and the sports world, a regularized scouting procedure exists in the educational field. Those school systems that can offer the most attractive salaries usually secure the most capable personnel. Many superintendents reported that a three hundred- to five hundred-dollar salary differential makes a significant difference in the quality of the professional staff a school system can attract. Consequently, not only do many superintendents feel obligated to secure higher salaries for their personnel, but they also feel that unless their salary schedule is a reasonably competitive one, they will not be able to maintain a competent teaching staff.

Most superintendents are acutely aware of expectations teachers and others have for them to promote higher salaries for school personnel. They are also aware of the consequences for the morale of the staff and on the "quality" of the school system if this expectation is not fulfilled.

There are, however, many individuals and groups who may hold opposite expectations for the superintendent. These groups are primarily concerned with the mounting cost of local government and particularly with its impact on the local property tax. There is little doubt that a major cause of this increase is rising school costs, especially higher teacher salaries. Owners of substantial properties as well as individuals living on fixed incomes may look toward local town or city officials to curb this fiscal threat to their economic well-being. The local taxpayers association also exhibits a great deal of interest in teachers' salaries, usually the largest item in the budget.

In addition, mayors do not find the increasing tax rates helpful in their bids for re-election. All of these individuals and groups may look to the superintendent to "hold the line" or "be reasonable" in his salary or budget recommendations. Such situations may make superintendents perceive that they are in the unenviable spot of the man in the middle.

It is not surprising, therefore, to find, as Table 16–A shows, that the superintendents' decisions on the teacher salary issue are typically made in a climate of incompatible expectations. Eighty-eight percent of the superintendents perceived that they were exposed to role conflicts in this area.

The responses of all superintendents to the salary instrument about

TABLE 16–E. PERCENTAGE OF SUPERINTENDENTS WHO PERCEIVED PARTICULAR EXPECTATIONS FROM SPECIFIED GROUPS AND INDIVIDUALS WITH RESPECT TO THEIR SALARY RECOMMENDATIONS

Group or Individual	(a) High Salary Expectation, %	(b) Low Salary Expectation, %	(c) Mixed Expectation, %	(d) No Expectation, %	N*
1. Politicians	14.3	51.4	5.7	28.6	105
2. Church or religious groups	34.6	5.8	2.9	56.7	104
3. Farm organizations	12.9	17.7	1.6	67.8	62
4. Business or commercial organizations	15.2	34.3	3.8	46.7	105
5. Labor unions	64.1	1.9	1.9	32.1	53
6. Parents (P.T.A.)	77.1	1.0	9.5	12.4	105
7. Teachers	99.0	0.0	1.0	0.0	105
8. Personal friends	57.1	1.0	4.8	37.1	105
9. Taxpayers association	9.8	75.4	3.3	11.5	61
10. Individuals influential for economic reasons	11.4	44.8	6.7	37.1	105
11. Service clubs	35.6	6.9	6.9	50.6	87
12. Fraternal organizations	20.4	3.2	3.2	73.2	93
13. Veterans organizations	27.9	4.8	3.8	63.5	104
14. Individual school committee members	69.5	14.3	14.3	1.9	105
15. Town finance committee or city council	18.4	59.2	11.7	10.7	103
16. My wife—family	70.9	0.0	0.0	29.1	103
17. Chamber of commerce	20.0	26.2	6.2	47.6	65
18. The press	27.3	25.0	1.1	46.6	88

* When N is less than 105 it is usually because the group or individual did not exist in certain communities; the *no answers* when the group or individual did exist are also excluded.

the expectations held by individuals and groups in their communities are presented in Table 16–E, which suggest that there are striking differences among the incumbents of different counter positions. Whereas 99 percent of the superintendents perceived that their teachers expected them to recommend the highest salary increases possible (column a), 75 percent of those with taxpayers associations in their communities reported that these associations held the opposite expectation (column b). Similarly a majority of the superintendents said that their town finance committee or city council, and local politicians expected them to minimize salary increases for teachers. In addition to reporting that their teachers expected them to recommend the highest possible salary increases, a majority of the superintendents reported that labor organizations, parents and P.T.A., personal friends, individual school board members, and their wives held the same expectation. Relatively few superintendents, however, are confronted with the "mixed" expectation from members of the same group or category, school board members obtaining the highest percentage (14 percent in column c) and town finance committee members the next highest (12 percent in column c).

We have seen that when confronted with incompatible expectations for the personnel and time allocation problems, at least a majority of the superintendents conform to the professional or occupational expectation. Very few said that they adopted a compromise solution, 4 of 72 in the case of the personnel decision, and 13 of 50 in the case of the time allocation decision. How do these figures compare with what superintendents do in the case of the salary dilemma?

Of the 105 superintendents who completed this instrument, 13 perceived their exposure to role congruencies. Of the remaining 92 superintendents, 7 gave insufficient information to permit coding of their behavior. Fifty-four conformed to the expectation of recommending the highest possible salary increases (64 percent of 85), 8 recommended the lowest possible salary increases (9 percent of 85), and 23 of 85 adopted some kind of strategy which did not require them to make an unequivocal choice between the two incompatible alternatives. Since there is little ambiguity about a choice of one over another of the incompatible expectations, the remainder of this section will be concerned with an examination of the different resolution techniques of those 23 superintendents who did not make such a choice but developed some procedure whereby they could to some degree either satisfy (18, or 21 percent) or ignore (5, or 6 percent) both demands.

The 5 superintendents who avoided the situation felt that removing themselves as active participants in the salary situation was the most effective procedure to follow.   One of these superintendents, not yet on tenure, who perceived that his school board members, the town finance committee, the taxpayers association, and individuals who were economically influential expected him to recommend the lowest possible salary increases, whereas his teachers held the contrary expectation, described his situation in this way:

> I put it all in the hands of the school committee.   It's a hot potato so I let the school committee handle it.   The teachers feel I should represent them; the school committee feels I should represent them; I'd hang myself by getting involved.   But I go along with the school committee recommendation 100 percent, whatever they decide.

Four of the 18 superintendents who compromise assume the position of negotiator when confronted with this dilemma.   They apparently work on the assumption that although the expectations they face conflict, it is their duty to negotiate "a settlement" that will be most satisfactory to everyone.   One superintendent perceived that his teachers, school board, and the P.T.A. expected him to recommend high salary increases to hold and attract competent personnel, whereas the town finance committee and taxpayers association expected him to recommend the lowest increases, because they felt that the town was approaching a financial crisis.   This superintendent said that he tried to explain these different viewpoints to every group and ". . . to bring the extreme views together."

Another of these four superintendents views the situation in these terms: "I use the salesman's technique.   I tell the town, 'You don't want cheap teachers if you want a good school system.'   I tell the teachers they have to be reasonable, that there has to be a compromise . . . if I completely agreed with the teachers, I'd be out of a job."

Three of the superintendents who compromise when exposed to the salary dilemma rejected both sets of expectations and substituted a new criterion in making their recommendations.   They took the position that since they could not fully conform to both sets of expectations they would try to develop a defensible rationale for their recommendations which would be independent of the incompatible expectations of others.   One of the superintendents recommended that the salary increases be contingent on a cost of living index.   The others used as their criterion for their recommendation an increase that would keep their school system in a competitive position with those of comparable size and wealth.   One superintendent says he tries ". . . to do what's fair in light of what other communities are doing. I don't want my teachers to be at a disadvantage, but neither do I want our system to be a leader in the salaries we pay."

Ten of the 18 superintendents who compromise resolve the salary dilemma by trying to modify the expectations of one group so that they more nearly approximate the expectations of those with whom they had initially disagreed. This technique differs from that of the superintendents who tried to adopt the position of negotiator, in that no attempt is made by these 10 to modify both sets of expectations, and additionally, once one of the group's expectation has been modified, the superintendents give their clear support to it. One superintendent tells his teachers that if they give him ". . . a reasonable request, I'll fight for it. If it's unreasonable, I won't. Then I tell them what I think is reasonable according to the town's ability to pay. It's not a matter of concession. It's the realistic way to support the profession."

The remaining superintendent who compromises combines several of the previously described strategies. His primary objective is to obtain the maximum salary increases possible. However, according to his assessment, the realistic way to do this is a little at a time. This superintendent said that he works on this principle: "He who fights and runs away, lives to fight another day." He goes on to say that ". . . it's a give and take matter. If your goal isn't damned you haven't lost. I have friends operating for better salaries for teachers who are on the town finance committee. This is the effective way to get results over time, if done consistently. You have to make compromises, and get part of what you want one year and part the next. You can't move too fast. The idea is to make steady progress."

The Budget Situation. The fiscal problems facing American public education are common knowledge. Many communities lack adequate building space to house the growing school population. Outmoded buildings and inadequate facilities and equipment materially impair the kind of educational program that can be offered children. Thousands of school systems do not offer courses in physics and chemistry because the schools cannot compete for prospective teachers with the salaries offered by industry to college graduates in the physical sciences. There is little doubt that one of the major reasons for the shortage of teachers, especially male teachers, is the relatively low salaries of teachers compared to occupations requiring similar educational preparation.

At the local community level these fiscal difficulties confronting the American educational system pose continuing problems for the school board and the superintendent. They are most sharply delineated in the early months of the year when the school budget is being prepared. For the superintendent whose job it usually is to make the initial recommendations for the budget request of schools it may be presumed to pose a basic problem.

The fourth incompatible expectation situation was concerned with the superintendent's perception of the expectations of others regarding budget recommendations. Our preliminary field work activities suggested that this area of decision-making could give rise to a number of incompatible expectations. Many individuals and groups in the community may expect their superintendent to give greater priority to the financial resources of the community than to its educational needs in preparing his budget request.

TABLE 16–F. PERCENTAGE OF SUPERINTENDENTS WHO PERCEIVED PARTICULAR EXPECTATIONS FROM SPECIFIED GROUPS AND INDIVIDUALS WITH RESPECT TO THEIR BUDGET RECOMMENDATIONS

Group or Individual	(a) Priority to Education Expectation, %	(b) Priority to Finance Expectation, %	(c) Mixed Expectation, %	(d) No Expectation, %	N*
1. Politicians	8.6	75.2	2.9	13.3	105
2. Church or religious groups	57.7	1.0	1.9	39.4	104
3. Farm organizations	19.4	22.6	0.0	58.0	62
4. Business or commercial organizations	11.4	50.5	4.8	33.3	105
5. Labor unions	50.1	11.3	0.0	38.6	53
6. Parents (P.T.A.)	96.1	0.0	2.9	1.0	105
7. Teachers	98.0	0.0	1.0	1.0	105
8. Personal friends	65.7	0.0	3.8	30.5	105
9. Taxpayers association	4.9	88.5	3.3	3.3	61
10. Individuals influential for economic reasons	17.1	57.1	4.8	21.0	105
11. Service clubs	54.1	9.2	5.7	31.0	87
12. Fraternal organizations	29.0	3.2	2.2	65.6	93
13. Veterans organizations	41.3	3.8	3.8	51.0	104
14. Individual school committee members	72.3	6.7	20.0	1.0	105
15. Town finance committee or city council	23.3	68.0	6.8	1.9	103
16. My wife—family	73.8	1.0	0.0	25.2	103
17. Chamber of commerce	27.7	29.2	9.2	33.9	65
18. The press	31.8	25.0	9.1	34.1	88

* When N is less than 105 it is usually because the group or individual did not exist in certain communities; the *no answers* when the group or individual did exist are also excluded.

Of the four situations in Table 16–A, the budget situation resulted in the exposure of the greatest proportion of the 105 school executives to incompatible expectations. Nine out of 10 of the superintendents said that they were exposed to incompatible expectations in regard to their budget recommendations. The expectations of different categories of indivduals and groups are highly similar to those obtained for the teacher salary situation. Table 16–F shows that a majority of the superintendents perceived that the taxpayers association, local politicians, town finance committee or city council, and economic influentials in the community expected them to give greater weight to the financial resources of the town or city. On the other hand over 95 percent of the superintendents perceived that the opposite expectation was held by their P.T.A. and teacher groups. Interestingly enough, 72 percent perceived that their school boards also held the latter expectation, while 20 percent perceived incompatible expectations among their board members.

Essentially, the problem posed by incompatible expectations in the area of "budget recommendations" is the same as that posed by incompatible expectations with respect to recommendations for teachers' salaries. For this reason, the techniques by means of which superintendents resolved the dilemma implied by incompatible expectations in this area are practically identical with those used to resolve the dilemma implied by incompatible expectations with respect to teacher salary recommendations. The relative proportions of those who adopted each of the four alternatives are comparable as well: the behavior of 5 of the 95 superintendents who were exposed to role conflict could not be coded, 62 (or 69 percent) of the remaining 90 conformed to the "educational needs" expectation, 3 (or 3 percent) of the 90 conformed to the "financial resources" expectation, 24 (or 27 percent) adopted some form of compromise, and 1 (or 1 percent) resolved the conflict by avoiding the situation. There is consequently little point in repeating the description of these techniques here. Later, however, when an analysis is attempted of the differences between those who resolve these dilemmas in one way and those who resolve them in another, the differences between the resolutions used for these two situations will be compared.

CONSEQUENCES OF CONFLICT

Now that the responses of the superintendents to the four instruments used in this part of the study have been described, it is interesting to consider briefly some of the possible consequences of the perception of role conflict. If Table 16–A is re-examined, it will be seen that, whereas in the case of each situation the majority of superintendents perceived their exposure to incompatible expectations, there were nevertheless some who did not perceive this incompatibility in their environment. What differences might we expect as a result of this difference in perception?

Partly on the basis of the assumption that the gratification an actor derives from the incumbency of his position is a function of the sanctions to which he is exposed, an hypothesis was presented in Chapter Thirteen which stated that a relationship would exist between consensus on role expectations and satisfaction. A very similar hypothesis may be presented with respect to role conflict and the satisfaction position incumbents derive from the occupancy of their positions. If it is assumed that exposure to incompatible expectations implies probable exposure to negative sanctions for failure to conform to both sets of expectations, then it follows that position incumbents who perceive that they are exposed to role conflict will perceive their probable exposure to negative sanctions to a greater extent than will position incumbents who do not perceive that they are exposed to role conflict. Given the additional assumption that gratification is a function of the sanctions to which an actor is exposed, the hypothesis follows that:

Hypothesis 16–1: Position incumbents who perceive that they are exposed to role conflict will derive less gratification from the occupancy of their position than position incumbents who do not perceive they are exposed to role conflict.

This hypothesis leads to three specific predictions which can be tested in each of the four situations which have been described. First, superintendents who perceive that they are exposed to role conflict will feel less satisfied with their jobs; second, they will feel less satisfied with their careers; third, they will worry more than superintendents who do not perceive their exposure to incompatible expectations. These predictions assume that "job satisfaction," "career satisfaction," and "worry," as measured by the instruments of our study, are adequate indexes of the "gratification" superintendents derive from the occupancy of their positions. In the case of both the Job Satisfaction and Worry scales (see Appendix B–1b and B–1c) we feel that this assumption is justified, because the items which comprise both of these scales are descriptive of superintendents' feelings about the positions they were occupying at the time of the study. The Career Satisfaction scale is, however, comprised of items describing the superintendents' feelings about their careers in general rather than the specific positions they were occupying at the time of the study, and consequently this assumption may be questioned, perhaps, as it applies to this scale.

The tests of these predictions are presented in Tables 16–G, 16–H, and 16–I.

TABLE 16–G.　MEAN JOB SATISFACTION SCORES OF SUPERINTENDENTS WHO PERCEIVED ROLE CONFLICT (c) AND WHO DID NOT PERCEIVE ROLE CONFLICT (nc) IN FOUR SITUATIONS

Situation	N_c	$\overline{X}_c$	N_{nc}	$\overline{X}_{nc}$	D	C.R.	Probability Less than	Direction Predicted Correctly (+) or Incorrectly (−) According to Hypothesis 16–1
1. Personnel Hiring and Promotion	75	1.36	30	1.87	0.51	2.2	.05	+
2. Time Allocation	56	1.39	49	1.63	0.24	1.1	not sig.	+
3. Teacher Salary Recommendations	92	1.41	13	2.15	0.74	2.4	.01	+
4. Budget Recommendations	95	1.40	10	2.50	1.10	3.2	.001	+

In Table 16–G are reported the mean Job Satisfaction scale scores of the superintendents who perceived role conflicts and those who perceived role congruencies for each of the four situations. For each situation those who perceived role conflict obtained the lower mean Job Satisfaction score, which is according to the prediction. Three of these differences are significant at least at the .05 level and are consequently interpreted as providing support for the hypothesis. The fourth, for the time allocation situation, is not significant and therefore provides no support for the hypothesis.

In Table 16–H are presented the mean Career Satisfaction scores of those who did and those who did not perceive role conflict in each of the four situations. Although in each case the differences are in

TABLE 16–H.　MEAN CAREER SATISFACTION SCORES OF SUPERINTENDENTS WHO PERCEIVED ROLE CONFLICT (c) AND WHO DID NOT PERCEIVE ROLE CONFLICT (nc) IN FOUR SITUATIONS

Situation	N_c	$\overline{X}_c$	N_{nc}	$\overline{X}_{nc}$	D	C.R.	Probability Less than	Direction Predicted Correctly (+) or Incorrectly (−) According to Hypothesis 16–1
1. Personnel Hiring and Promotion	75	1.33	30	1.60	.27	1.2	not sig.	+
2. Time Allocation	56	1.32	49	1.51	.19	0.9	not sig.	+
3. Teacher Salary Recommendations	92	1.36	13	1.77	.41	1.3	not sig.	+
4. Budget Recommendations	95	1.37	10	1.80	.43	1.2	not sig.	+

the direction predicted on the basis of the hypothesis (that is, those who perceive role conflict are less satisfied), the differences are in no case significantly different from zero. The data with this scale cannot be interpreted as supporting the hypothesis.

In Table 16–I are presented the mean Worry scale scores of those who did and those who did not perceive role conflict in each of the four situations. The differences in each case are in the direction

TABLE 16–I. MEAN WORRY SCORES OF SUPERINTENDENTS WHO PERCEIVED ROLE CONFLICT (c) AND WHO DID NOT PERCEIVE ROLE CONFLICT (nc) IN FOUR SITUATIONS

Situation	N_c	$\overline{X}_c$	N_{nc}	$\overline{X}_{nc}$	D	C.R.	Probability Less than	Direction Predicted Correctly (+) or Incorrectly (−) According to Hypothesis 16–1
1. Personnel Hiring and Promotion	75	1.39	30	1.07	.32	1.4	not sig.	+
2. Time Allocation	56	1.50	49	1.06	.44	2.2	.05	+
3. Teacher Salary Recommendations	92	1.35	13	0.92	.43	1.5	not sig.	+
4. Budget Recommendations	95	1.36	10	0.70	.66	1.9	.05	+

predicted (those who perceive conflict worry more), but in only two situations are the differences significantly different from zero. Only these two instances can be interpreted as supporting the hypothesis. We may say that the hypothesis received a certain degree of support and conclude in addition that the perception of role conflict is not so likely to affect a superintendent's satisfaction with his career as it is to affect his satisfaction with and, to a lesser extent, worry over his current job.

To some extent differences have been demonstrated between superintendents who do and those who do not experience role conflict in different situations. Although it is true that these "conflicts" are perceptions of the superintendents themselves, they are nevertheless perceptions of relatively objective conditions under which they carry out their jobs, and we might reasonably expect them to have some consequences for the way in which superintendents do experience their jobs. It is additionally possible, however, for a particular conflict in a particular situation to have immediate psychological effects on the superintendent, among them, feelings of anxiety. If a superintendent says that he is anxious about a particular role conflict to which he is exposed, we might then infer that for him exposure to this conflict is more disturbing than for someone who does not feel anxious. It would seem to follow that for individuals who are anxious when exposed to role conflict, this exposure will have more serious consequences than for those who are not anxious.

We have already shown that for some situations, those who are exposed to role conflict are less satisfied with their jobs, and worry more in general. Now, on the basis of the above reasoning we will attempt to show that those who are anxious when exposed to role conflict are less satisfied and worry more in general than those who are not anxious, although exposed to role conflict; more pronounced consequences result from conflicts which produce anxiety than from conflicts which do not.

The differences in the mean Job Satisfaction scores of those who are anxious and those who are not anxious when exposed to role conflict in each of the four situations are presented in Table 16–J. In three situations the direction of the differences is as predicted, and these differences are significant. In the Time Allocation situation, the difference is in the wrong direction, though insignificant, which, taken with the significant differences, comprises findings which approximate those found in the analysis of differences between those who do and those who do not experience conflict.

TABLE 16–J. MEAN JOB SATISFACTION SCORES OF SUPERINTENDENTS WHO ARE ANXIOUS (a) AND WHO ARE NOT ANXIOUS (na) WHEN EXPOSED TO ROLE CONFLICT IN FOUR SITUATIONS

Situation	N_a	$\bar{X}_a$	N_{na}	$\bar{X}_{na}$	D	C.R.	Probability Less than	Direction Predicted Correctly (+) or Incorrectly (−) According to Hypothesis 16–1
1. Personnel Hiring and Promotion	21	0.91	54	1.54	.63	2.4	.01	+
2. Time Allocation	20	1.45	36	1.36	.09	0.3	not sig.	−
3. Teacher Salary Recommendations	26	1.04	66	1.56	.52	2.2	.05	+
4. Budget Recommendations	28	1.00	67	1.57	.57	2.4	.01	+

In Table 16–K are presented the mean "Career Satisfaction" scale scores of those who do and those who do not experience anxiety when exposed to conflict in the four situations. Although the differences are all in the predicted direction—those who are anxious are less satisfied—in only one situation, the budget, is this difference significant. One possible interpretation of this finding is that the budget situation is a more inclusive one, decisions with respect to it affecting all other areas of school administration. Perhaps for this reason superintendents who are anxious when exposed to conflict in this situation are significantly less satisfied with their careers than superintendents who are not anxious.

TABLE 16–K. MEAN CAREER SATISFACTION SCORES OF SUPERINTENDENTS WHO ARE ANXIOUS (a) AND WHO ARE NOT ANXIOUS (na) WHEN EXPOSED TO ROLE CONFLICT IN FOUR SITUATIONS

Situation	N_a	$\overline{X}_a$	N_{na}	$\overline{X}_{na}$	D	C.R.	Probability Less than	Direction Predicted Correctly (+) or Incorrectly (−) According to Hypothesis 16–1
1. Personnel Hiring and Promotion	21	1.05	54	1.44	.39	1.6	not sig.	+
2. Time Allocation	20	1.30	36	1.50	.20	0.7	not sig.	+
3. Teacher Salary Recommendations	26	1.19	66	1.42	.23	0.9	not sig.	+
4. Budget Recommendations	28	1.00	67	1.52	.52	2.2	.05	+

Finally, in Table 16–L are presented the mean Worry scale scores of those who do and those who do not experience anxiety in the four situations. This might be considered almost a test of validity, although it is still reasonable to ask whether superintendents who are anxious in particular situations worry more in general than those who are not anxious. One line of reasoning which suggests an affirmative answer to this question is that there are generally "anxious" people, or "worriers" as well as "nonworriers." Another would be that the presence of anxiety in a role conflict situation results in more serious consequences for the way superintendents experience their jobs in general, among which, as we have shown, is the extent to which they worry in general. In Table 16–L it can be seen that the prediction which would be made with either line of reasoning receives support in three of the four situations.

TABLE 16–L. MEAN WORRY SCORES OF SUPERINTENDENTS WHO ARE ANXIOUS (a) AND WHO ARE NOT ANXIOUS (na) WHEN EXPOSED TO ROLE CONFLICT IN FOUR SITUATIONS

Situation	N_a	$\overline{X}_a$	N_{na}	$\overline{X}_{na}$	D	C.R.	Probability Less than	Direction Predicted Correctly (+) or Incorrectly (−) According to Hypothesis 16–1
1. Personnel Hiring and Promotion	21	1.95	54	1.17	.78	3.0	.01	+
2. Time Allocation	20	1.50	36	1.50	.00	0.0	not sig.	−
3. Teacher Salary Recommendations	26	1.77	66	1.18	.59	2.5	.01	+
4. Budget Recommendations	28	1.93	67	1.12	.81	3.6	.001	+

In the three situations in which the findings are as predicted on the basis of this reasoning (that is, those who are anxious when exposed to role conflict in that situation obtain higher mean worry scale scores), all the differences are significant at least at the .01 level. In the fourth situation which is again the time allocation situation, there is no difference at all between the means of the two groups. This is another finding which suggests that there are significant differences between intra- and inter-role conflict, the time allocation situation being the only example of inter-role conflict which is included in this analysis.

In this chapter we have examined the superintendent's responses to the role conflict instruments and to some extent have shown that exposure to conflict has consequences for the way in which the superintendents experience their jobs. Additionally, we have demonstrated that for some situations, the presence of anxiety as a result of the conflict leads to more pronounced consequences than the absence of anxiety. All of these data and findings provide a background against which to develop a theory of role conflict resolution which will be undertaken in the next chapter. The concepts of "legitimacy" and "sanctions" which in this chapter have been largely bypassed, will be reintroduced as integral components of the theory, but the differentiation between those who do and those who do not experience anxiety as a result of exposure to role conflict will not be used, since it is essentially a consequence and intensification of the exposure to conflict which provides no hint about the resolution employed under conditions of its presence or absence. The main point of the theory is to try to explain why some people do one thing and others another when faced with role conflict situations.

seventeen

A Theory of Role Conflict Resolution

We have shown that when confronted with role conflict position incumbents adopt different resolution techniques. The question for which the theory to be presented and tested in this chapter attempts to provide an answer is why people adopt different resolutions. A number of suggestive explanations of these differences may be taken from the literature.

Parsons, for example, in his brief treatment of the resolution of role conflict, says that:

> . . . differences have to be adjusted by an ordering or allocation of the claims of the different role expectations to which the actor is subject. This ordering occurs by priority scales, by occasion, e.g., time and place, and by distribution among alters. . . .[1]

Toby has suggested, "Institutionalized techniques exist for preventing role conflicts from arising."[2] These include role obligation hierarchies (excuses), an actor's claim that his lack of fulfillment of an obligation is involuntary (unavoidable "accidents"), etiquette rituals, and "legitimate" deception like the white lie. When these techniques cannot be used Toby suggests that an actor has only a limited number of alternatives available to him. These include repudiation of his role in one group, playing off one group against the other, stalling, redefinition of the role (or roles), the "double life," escape from the field, and illness. He concludes his paper with the observation that "The problem for research is the conditions under which one solution is chosen over another."[3]

Getzels and Guba have suggested that the analysis "of the effective handling of role conflict might well be pushed forward within the three concepts involved in these conditions: the choice of major role, the congruence of needs and expectations, and the legitimacy of expectations within the situation." [4] A major role is the one to which the actor commits himself at the point of decision-making in a role conflict. They view the decision as a function of (1) the role "that is most compatible with his needs" (congruence of needs and expectations), and (2) the legitimacy of the expectations: "If the individual chooses as his major role the one that is also the legitimate role in the situation he is less likely to be affected by conflicts or the threat of sanctions than when he chooses some alternate role." [5]

Stouffer and Toby investigated the relationship between a personality dimension and the resolution of "role conflict." They asked college students to say what their behavior would be when exposed to a series of hypothetical situations in which they had to select between two conflicting obligations. The choice in each case was between an obligation to a friend and one to society. Their study showed that the students could be classified on a unidimensional scale according to their tendencies to resolve dilemmas in a universalistic or particularistic way, and they say, ". . . (that) the results encourage one to believe that we can develop good measures of individual predisposition to a bias in a universalistic or particularistic direction." [6]

The preceding study stimulated Mishler to investigate the hypothesis that a particularistic role orientation is positively related to the characteristics of the authoritarian personality. Whereas Stouffer and Toby viewed one's role orientation as a personality bias, Mishler viewed it as a kind of behavior to which he related personality measures. He concluded that,

> The present study has shown that tendencies towards engaging in the same social behavior may be found within a number of different personality structures. . . . Two types of particularistic persons were found. One is oriented towards satisfaction and security in *internal* goals and is *cynical* about other persons. The second is oriented toward satisfaction and security in *external* goals and is *rebellious* against authority and social rules. Correspondingly two types of universalistic persons were found. One is *internally* oriented and has a *benign* attitude toward others. The other is *externally* oriented and *conforms* to authority and social rules. [7]

These previous formulations suggest certain strategic variables that deserve consideration in an attempt to formulate a theory of role conflict resolution. Getzels and Guba stress that the legitimacy of expectations and the congruency between personalistic needs and expectations may be the crucial dimensions affecting the resolution of the dilemma, that is, which role is selected as the major one. The empirical findings of Stouffer and Toby suggest the advisability of focusing attention on the actor's *predisposition* to behave in certain ways when faced with a role conflict. In the role conflict situations studied some actors tended to have a particularistic while others had a universalistic orientation to the situation. It is of further interest that Mishler's findings indicated that individuals with different types of personality structures tended to resolve the role conflicts in similar ways. This, of course, still leaves open the question of the conditions under which actors with different personality structures act in similar and in different ways.

It is worthy of comment that these prior formulations have directed little explicit consideration to the dimension of sanctions as a factor that may have an important bearing on the resolution of role conflict. Although the dimension of sanctions is central to Stouffer's basic formulation of role conflict,[8] it does not enter into the Stouffer-Toby analyses of the resolution of role conflict. In the Getzels-Guba approach to the problem it does not enter as a central variable. We shall try to give it a more strategic position in our theoretical approach to the resolution of role conflict.

Although each of these students of role conflict analysis is aware that in addition to conforming to one role or another, there are other possibilities of resolving the role conflict, their theoretical approaches to the problem are based on an actor's conforming to one or the other of the incompatible expectations or choosing one or the other of the roles. Little or no theoretical consideration is given in these formulations to the conditions under which an actor will engage in a compromise or avoidance behavior. For example, Getzels and Guba say:

> Theoretically, an individual in a role conflict situation may resolve the conflict—always omitting the possibility of changing the situation or withdrawing from it entirely—either by compromise or exclusion. He may attempt to stand midway between the conflicting roles, giving equal due to both roles, shifting from one to another as he believes the occasion demands, or he may choose one role as his significant frame of reference and assimilate all other roles in the situation to it. In actual practice it would seem that the situation at Air University—and one may well wonder whether this is not general to most situations—establishes the latter alternative as the one more likely to find acceptance. There seems to be a *major role* to which one must commit himself in order to determine his action at choice points, despite contrary expectations attaching to other roles he may simultaneously occupy.[9]

A major limitation of this *conclusion* is that it discards too easily other alternatives available to an actor in a role conflict situation. It precludes consideration of compromise and avoidance behaviors.

Another characteristic of this formulation deserves emphasis. The Getzels-Guba approach assumes that role conflicts occur only when an actor simultaneously occupies multiple positions to which are attached conflicting expectations. It is not surprising then that the theory focuses on the factors involved in an actor's selecting one position as the major position.

For our purposes such a formulation is distinctly limited. This is the case because it will be recalled that we have recognized that an actor may be exposed to role conflict as a consequence of his occupancy of a single position (intrarole conflict). For example, teachers and school board members may be perceived as holding conflicting expectations for their superintendent, *as a superintendent*. A theory which requires that an actor choose a major position (or role) is of no utility for understanding intrarole conflict resolution.

In addition, the theoretical scheme we require must yield predictions from among four alternatives an actor may choose in resolving a role conflict. When an actor perceives his exposure to a role conflict situation in which there are two incompatible expectations, *A* and *B*, there are four alternative behaviors available by means of which he can resolve the conflict, in the sense of making a decision. The actor may: (1) conform to expectation *A*, (2) conform to expectation *B*, (3) perform some *compromise* behavior which represents an attempt to conform in part to both expectations, or (4) attempt to *avoid* conforming to either of the expectations.

In the salary situation considered in the previous chapter, for example, a superintendent could conform to the expectation held by his teachers that as their superintendent he should attempt to secure the highest possible increases in salary for them. On the other hand he could conform to the expectation held by his school board that he should try to minimize the salary increases for teachers. Or alternatively, he could compromise by attempting to negotiate a salary increase that would represent less than the teachers demanded and more than his school board originally wanted to give. Or finally, he could remove himself from the situation by taking the position that the school board should negotiate with the teachers directly, removing himself from his intermediate position between them in the social hierarchy of the school system. A theory of role conflict resolution must therefore provide a basis on which to make predictions concerning which of these four alternative resolutions an actor will adopt.

The starting point for this exploratory effort to develop such a theory is the actor's definition of the role conflict situation according to two elements, legitimacy and sanctions. The first is his feeling about the legitimacy or illegitimacy of each of the incompatible expectations that he perceives is held for him in the situation. The second is his perception of the sanctions to which he will be exposed for nonconformity to each of the incompatible expectations. A third element of the theory, his orientation to legitimacy and sanctions, will be introduced later. For the moment our concern will be with how the legitimacy and sanctions dimensions can affect decision-making. First, we shall examine the possible influence of each of these elements singly, and then how they operate in combination.

The Legitimacy Dimension. We shall assume that actors are predisposed to conform to expectations they perceive as legitimate, perceived obligations, and are predisposed to avoid conforming to expectations which they perceive as illegitimate, perceived pressures. That is, if an actor feels that an individual or group has a right to expect him to behave in conformity with a given expectation he will be predisposed to conform to it. An individual who defines an expectation held by others for his behavior as illegitimate will be predisposed not to conform to it since failure to grant the other individual a right to expect a particular behavior implies the actor's rejection of his responsibility to conform to it. The assumption we have made with respect to the response of position incumbents to "legitimate" expectations is based on the reasoning that failure to conform to an expectation which is perceived as legitimate will result in negative internal sanctions.

If an actor perceives his exposure to two incompatible expectations, A and B, then, using only the criterion of legitimacy there are four possible types into which the situation the actor perceives as con-

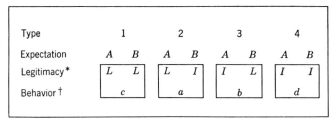

Figure 17–1. Behavior predicted for four types of role conflicts on the basis of the "legitimacy assumption."

* Legitimacy abbreviations: L = expectation perceived as legitimate; I = expectation perceived as illegitimate.

† Behavior abbreviations: a = conformity to expectation A; b = conformity to expectation B; c = compromise; d = avoidance.

fronting him may fall. These are: (1) *A* and *B* are both perceived as legitimate; (2) *A* is perceived as legitimate, and *B* is perceived as illegitimate; (3) *B* is perceived as legitimate, and *A* is perceived as illegitimate; (4) *A* and *B* are both perceived as illegitimate.

On the assumption that an actor is predisposed to conform only to legitimate expectations we would make the predictions presented in Figure 17–1.

In the second and third situations the prediction would be that the actor would conform to the legitimate expectation and reject or ignore the illegitimate one. In the first situation, since the actor desires to conform to both expectations even though they are incompatible, he would try to conform in part to both of them by adopting some form of compromise behavior. In the fourth case, since he considers both expectations illegitimate, he would be predisposed to conform to neither of them and therefore would engage in some type of avoidance behavior.

Given information only about an actor's perceptions of the legitimacy of the incompatible expectations we would emerge with this set of predictions. What would be predicted if we based our reasoning *only* on the sanctions dimension?

The Sanctions Dimension. We will assume that if an actor perceives that failure to conform to an expectation will result in the application of strong negative sanctions the actor will be predisposed to conform to it. This assumption is based on what Parsons has termed the "gratificational aspect of the need disposition" of the actor.[10] If an actor wants to maximize gratification from his interactions, he will be predisposed to behave in a manner that will minimize the negative sanctions (or maximize the positive ones) to which he perceives he might be exposed in his interactions. If he feels that nonconformity to an expectation will result in slight or no negative (or positive) sanctions, this element in his perception of the situation will have little or no effect on his behavior.

If an actor is exposed to two incompatible expectations, *A* and *B*, and we consider only his perception of the negative sanctions that will be applied by those who hold the *A* and *B* expectations for nonconformity to their expectations, and if we catgorize the negative sanctions into strong and weak, we secure the types of situations and predictions about behavior which are presented in Figure 17–2.

In the second and third situations he would conform to the expectation for nonconformity to which he perceived the greater negative sanctions. In the first, since nonconformity to either *A* or *B* would result in heavy negative sanctions he would try to compromise in order to minimize sanctions.   Such a decision would, we assume, maximize his gratification from the situation.   In the fourth case, we have no basis for prediction because he would not be predisposed to conform to either *A* or *B*.

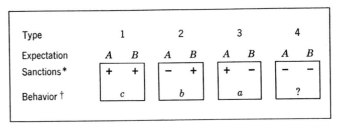

Figure 17–2. Behavior predicted for four types of role conflicts on the basis of the "sanctions assumption."

* Sanctions abbreviations: $+$ = strong negative sanctions applied for nonconformity to the expectation; $-$ = strong negative sanctions not applied for nonconformity to the expectation.

† Behavior abbreviations: a = conformity to expectation *A*; b = conformity to expectation *B*; c = compromise; d = avoidance; ? = no prediction possible.

Although for theoretical purposes we have examined each of the dimensions of legitimacy and sanctions separately, we assume that for any role conflict situation the actor perceives both of these dimensions and takes them into account in his decision-making.   What predictions could be made when both the legitimacy and sanctions dimensions are taken into account?   The sixteen combinations of the four types of legitimacy and four types of sanctions situations are presented in Figure 17–3.

On the basis of the assumptions made for the separate effects of the legitimacy and sanctions dimensions we could make predictions for behavior for these cells in Figure 17–3:

Cell 1: Compromise behavior, because both dimensions predispose compromise behavior.

Cell 4: Compromise behavior, because the legitimacy dimension predisposes to a compromise and the sanctions dimension has no effect.

Cell 7: Conformity to *A*, because both dimensions predispose conformity to *A*.

Cell 8: Conformity to *A*, because the legitimacy dimension predisposes conformity to *A* and the sanctions dimension has no effect.

Cell 10: Conformity to *B*, because both dimensions predispose conformity to *B*.

Cell 12: Conformity to *B* because the legitimacy dimension predisposes conformity to *B* and the sanctions dimension has no effect.

Cell 16: Avoidance behavior, because the legitimacy dimension predisposes avoidance of both *A* and *B* and the sanctions dimension has no effect.

However, for the other nine cells it is not possible with only these two assumptions to make predictions about behavior. This is the case because (1) the legitimacy and sanctions dimensions predispose

Type	1		2		3		4	
Expectation	A	B	A	B	A	B	A	B
Legitimacy	L	L	L	L	L	L	L	L
Sanctions	+	+	−	+	+	−	−	−
Behavior	c		?		?		c	

Type	5		6		7		8	
Expectation	A	B	A	B	A	B	A	B
Legitimacy	L	I	L	I	L	I	L	I
Sanctions	+	+	−	+	+	−	−	−
Behavior	?		?		a		a	

Type	9		10		11		12	
Expectation	A	B	A	B	A	B	A	B
Legitimacy	I	L	I	L	I	L	I	L
Sanctions	+	+	−	+	+	−	−	−
Behavior	?		b		?		b	

Type	13		14		15		16	
Expectation	A	B	A	B	A	B	A	B
Legitimacy	I	I	I	I	I	I	I	I
Sanctions	+	+	−	+	+	−	−	−
Behavior	?		?		?		d	

Figure 17–3. Behavior predicted for sixteen types of role conflicts on the basis of the "sanctions" and "legitimacy" assumptions.*

* The abbreviations used in this figure are as follows: legitimacy abbreviations: *L* = expectation perceived as legitimate, *I* = expectation perceived as illegitimate; sanctions abbreviations: + = strong negative sanctions applied for nonconformity to the expectation, − = strong negative sanctions not applied for nonconformity to the expectation; behavior abbreviations: *a* = conformity to expectation *A*, *b* = conformity to expectation *B*, *c* = compromise, *d* = avoidance, and ? = no prediction possible.

to conformity to opposite expectations (Cells 6 and 11), (2) one dimension predisposes a compromise behavior and the other conformity to one of the expectations (Cells 2, 3, 5, 9), (3) one dimension predisposes avoidance behavior and the other predisposes conformity to one of the expectations (Cells 14 and 15), and (4) one dimension predisposes avoidance behavior and the other a compromise behavior (Cell 13).

The two assumptions regarding the impact of legitimacy and sanctions on the resolution of role conflicts are inadequate in combination to provide a basis for predicting how an actor will behave in the majority of the logically possible situations in which they could occur. What is needed is a third element in the theory that will allow us to make predictions concerning how an actor will behave when he is confronted with all possible types of situations, rather than only a part of them.

Two factors were inadequate because assumptions about them provided no basis for predictions when an actor was exposed to a role conflict in which the legitimacy and sanctions elements predisposed him to undertake different behaviors. They provided no logical basis for predicting which of the behaviors he would select. This inadequacy suggests that a theory of role conflict resolution must make use not only of an actor's perceptions of the elements in the situation, but of his predisposition to give primacy to one or the other of them in his decision-making.

The starting point for such a theory is still an actor's definition of a role conflict situation. We assume that actors will have perceptions of the legitimacy or illegitimacy of the expectations and of the sanctions to which they will be exposed as a consequence of their nonconformity to each of them. We now introduce the additional assumption that individuals may be differentiated according to their primacy of orientation to the legitimacy or to the sanctions dimensions of the expectations in the situation. We shall posit three types of orientations to expectations, and for each of them we shall present a different set of predictions.

The first type characterizes the person who, when faced with a role conflict, gives primacy to the legitimacy dimension. His definition of the situations places stress on *the right* of others to hold the expectations he perceives they hold for him and de-emphasizes the sanctions he thinks will be applied to him for nonconformity to them. We shall characterize such a person as having a *moral* orientation to expectations. Since his concern is primarily with the legitimacy

of the expectations he will be predisposed to behave in a role conflict situation in such a manner that will allow him to fulfill legitimate expectations and to reject illegitimate ones. He will behave
according to the predictions presented earlier when we examined the
logical consequences of taking only the legitimacy dimension into
account in role conflict situations. If one of the incompatible expectations is viewed as legitimate and the other is not, he will be
predisposed to conform to the legitimate expectation. If both are
legitimate he will adopt a compromise behavior in order to conform,
at least in part, to both of them. If both are perceived as illegiti-

Type	1		2		3		4	
Expectation	A	B	A	B	A	B	A	B
Legitimacy	L	L	L	L	L	L	L	L
Sanctions	+	+	−	+	+	−	−	−
Behavior	c		c		c		c	

Type	5		6		7		8	
Expectation	A	B	A	B	A	B	A	B
Legitimacy	L	I	L	I	L	I	L	I
Sanctions	+	+	−	+	+	−	−	−
Behavior	a		a		a		a	

Type	9		10		11		12	
Expectation	A	B	A	B	A	B	A	B
Legitimacy	I	L	I	L	I	L	I	L
Sanctions	+	+	−	+	+	−	−	−
Behavior	b		b		b		b	

Type	13		14		15		16	
Expectation	A	B	A	B	A	B	A	B
Legitimacy	I	I	I	I	I	I	I	I
Sanctions	+	+	−	+	+	−	−	−
Behavior	d		d		d		d	

Figure 17–4. Behavior predicted for sixteen types of role conflicts for individuals with a "moral orientation." *

* The abbreviations used in this figure are as follows: legitimacy abbreviations: L = expectation perceived as legitimate, I = expectation perceived as illegitimate; sanctions abbreviations: $+$ = strong negative sanctions applied for nonconformity to the expectation, $-$ = strong negative sanctions not applied for nonconformity to the expectation; behavior abbreviations: a = conformity to expectation A, b = conformity to expectation B, c = compromise, and d = avoidance.

mate he will be predisposed to conform to neither of them and will adopt in consequence some type of avoidance behavior. In short, for an individual with such an orientation to expectations we can ignore his perceptions of the sanctions dimension in making predictions about his behavior. From his definition of the legitimacy of the expectations we can make predictions about his behavior. Thus, for the sixteen possible situations when the legitimacy and sanctions dimensions are combined we would make the predictions given in Figure 17–4.

The second type of primacy of orientation to expectations may be described as *expedient*. An individual who has this orientation is one who gives priority to the sanctions over the legitimacy dimension of the expectations perceived as held by others. Such a person is primarily concerned with minimizing the negative sanctions involved in the role conflict situation. His orientation is based on a desire to be self-protective, to provide the best defense for himself in view of the relative severity of the negative sanctions he feels others will apply to him for nonconformity to their expectations. Whether others have a right to hold certain expectations is irrelevant or of secondary importance to him. Such an individual will be predisposed to behave, when exposed to different types of sanctions situations, in the manner indicated in our earlier consideration of the logical behavioral consequences of taking into account only the sanctions dimension in resolving role conflicts.

When he perceives strong negative sanctions for nonconformity to one expectation and weaker negative sanctions for nonconformity to the other, he will conform to the expectation which would result in the stronger negative sanctions for nonconformity. If he perceives that equally strong negative sanctions result from both, he will compromise in order to minimize negative sanctions. If he perceives no negative sanctions for nonconformity to either of the expectations, the sanctions dimension will be of no value as a predictor of his behavior. In this instance the other factor in the model, the legitimacy dimension, would remain as the only basis for predicting his behavior. From the sixteen possible situations when the logical possibilities of the legitimacy and sanctions dimensions are combined, for expedients, we would make the predictions presented in Figure 17–5.

Since all the situations in the first column result in strong negative sanctions for nonconformity to expectations *A* and *B*, the actor will compromise in order to minimize both sets of negative sanctions. In columns 2 and 3 he selects the behavior dictated by minimizing negative sanctions.   In the first instance he conforms to expectation B and in the second to expectation A.   In the fourth column since he perceives no negative sanctions as operative he would base his decision on his perception of the legitimacy of the expectations and behave in accordance with the consequences that result from using the legitimacy criterion as the basis of decision-making.   In this instance his behavior is exactly like that of a moralist.

The theory has posited thus far that those individuals with a moral orientation will be predisposed to emphasize the legitimacy of expectations and those with an expedient orientation will be predis-

Type	1		2		3		4	
Expectation	A	B	A	B	A	B	A	B
Legitimacy	L	L	L	L	L	L	L	L
Sanctions	+	+	–	+	+	–	–	–
Behavior		c		b		a		c
Type	5		6		7		8	
Expectation	A	B	A	B	A	B	A	B
Legitimacy	L	I	L	I	L	I	L	I
Sanctions	+	+	–	+	+	–	–	–
Behavior		c		b		a		a
Type	9		10		11		12	
Expectation	A	B	A	B	A	B	A	B
Legitimacy	I	L	I	L	I	L	I	L
Sanctions	+	+	–	+	+	–	–	–
Behavior		c		b		a		b
Type	13		14		15		16	
Expectation	A	B	A	B	A	B	A	B
Legitimacy	I	I	I	I	I	I	I	I
Sanctions	+	+	–	+	+	–	–	–
Behavior		c		b		a		d

Figure 17–5. Behavior predicted for sixteen types of role conflicts for individuals with an "expedient orientation." *

* The abbreviations used in this figure are as follows: legitimacy abbreviations: L = expectation perceived as legitimate, I = expectation perceived as illegitimate; sanctions abbreviations: + = strong negative sanctions applied for nonconformity to the expectation, – = strong negative sanctions not applied for nonconformity to the expectation; behavior abbreviations: a = conformity to expectation A, b = conformity to expectation B, c = compromise, and d = avoidance.

posed to emphasize the sanctions they perceive for nonconformity to them.

We posit in addition a third type of orientation to expectations, the *moral-expedient* orientation.

A person who has this orientation does not give primacy to the legitimacy or sanctions dimensions, but takes both dimensions relatively equally into account and behaves in accordance with the perceived "net balance" of the two dimensions. Let us call such an orientation to expectations a moral-expedient or M-E orientation.

For some role conflict situations the decisions of an individual with an M-E orientation are relatively simple since both the legitimacy and sanctions elements lead him to the same behavior. If, for example, expectation *A* is perceived as legitimate and expectation *B* is viewed as illegitimate and if he perceives greater negative sanctions for nonconformity to expectation *A* than for nonconformity to *B*, he will conform to expectation *A*. In general, if using only the legitimacy dimension leads him to the same behavior as if he were using only the sanctions dimension, then there is no problem for him. Either criterion for behavior leads him to the same behavior.

By examining Figures 17–4 and 17–5 and observing which cell combinations of the legitimacy and sanctions dimensions lead to the same behavior we can easily isolate all the nonproblematic situations for him.

What is required is a basis for predicting his behavior in the other 9 cells.

A person with a M-E orientation is one who takes both the legitimacy and sanctions dimensions into account and is predisposed to adopt a behavior that emerges from a balancing of these two dimensions. Thus, if expectations *A* and *B* are both viewed as legitimate but he perceives greater negative sanctions for nonconformity to *A* than to *B*, then he will conform to expectation *A*. Weighing the two dimensions would result in clear cut resolutions of the role conflict in cells 2, 3, 5, 9, 14, and 15. In each of these instances on the basis of the sanctions and legitimacy dimensions there are two predispositions to one of the behaviors and only one to the other. For example, in cell 3 of Figure 17–6 both expectations are viewed as legitimate but there are heavier negative sanctions for nonconformity to the *A* than to the *B* expectation. Therefore, the M-E will conform to the *A* expectation. In cell 9 the sanctions dimension for both expectations is equivalent so the actor will base his decision on the legitimacy criterion and therefore conform to the perceived legitimate expectation, in this case *B*.

How would a M-E behave when the two dimensions would lead him to conform to opposite expectations, as in cells 6 and 11? In cell 6, the legitimacy dimension would require conformity to expectation A, but the sanctions dimension would lead to conformity to expectation B. Since the actor is a M-E he will engage in a compromise behavior because this seems to be the best balancing of the two dimensions when they lead to opposite behaviors; he is predisposed to do A on the basis of legitimacy, and B on the basis of sanctions, and therefore predisposed to both A and B, or to compromise. We are left with one additional cell in Figure 17–6, cell 13. In

Type	1		2		3		4	
Expectation	A	B	A	B	A	B	A	B
Legitimacy	L	L	L	L	L	L	L	L
Sanctions	+	+	−	+	+	−	−	−
Behavior		c		b		a		c

Type	5		6		7		8	
Expectation	A	B	A	B	A	B	A	B
Legitimacy	L	I	L	I	L	I	L	I
Sanctions	+	+	−	+	+	−	−	−
Behavior		a		c		a		a

Type	9		10		11		12	
Expectation	A	B	A	B	A	B	A	B
Legitimacy	I	L	I	L	I	L	I	L
Sanctions	+	+	−	+	+	−	−	−
Behavior		b		b		c		b

Type	13		14		15		16	
Expectation	A	B	A	B	A	B	A	B
Legitimacy	I	I	I	I	I	I	I	I
Sanctions	+	+	−	+	+	−	−	−
Behavior		c		b		a		d

Figure 17–6. Behavior predicted for sixteen types of role conflicts for individuals with a "moral-expedient" orientation.*

* The abbreviations used in this figure are as follows: legitimacy abbreviations: L = expectation perceived as legitimate, I = expectation perceived as illegitimate; sanctions abbreviations: $+$ = strong negative sanctions applied for nonconformity to the expectation, $-$ = strong negative sanctions not applied for nonconformity to the expectation; behavior abbreviations: a = conformity to expectation A, b = conformity to expectation B, c = compromise, and d = avoidance.

this instance neither of the expectations are viewed as legitimate but nonconformity to both is perceived as leading to strong negative sanctions. The moralistic dimension of his orientation leads him to an avoidance behavior and the sanctions dimension suggests a compromise. In this instance it is clear that he will not conform to expectation A or B. To minimize sanctions he would compromise or try to conform to both A and B, and to emphasize legitimacy he would avoid or fail to conform to both A and B. It is clear that an avoidance reaction does not conform at all to either A or B; but it is equally clear that a compromise fails to conform in part to both A and B, and therefore is in part, an avoidance. Consequently, the most probable resolution of situations of this kind by moral-expedients would be a compromise, which in part avoids and in part conforms to both expectations.

Figure 17–6 summarizes the predictions made on the basis of the three dimensions of legitimacy, sanctions and orientation for moral expedients, and Figures 17–4 and 17–5 together with 17–6 comprise the predictions made on the basis of the theory. The assumptions with respect to the legitimacy, sanctions, and orientation dimensions provide bases for the prediction of behavior under all forty-eight of the possible conditions under which position incumbents may be faced with role conflict. Given these conditions, it is possible to predict the behavior by means of which individuals will resolve the role conflicts with which they perceive they are faced.

Methodology. In Chapter Fifteen the methods employed to isolate the role conflicts to which the superintendent was exposed were described. The basic procedure was to present the respondent with four structured potential role conflict situations. For each situation three alternatives were given regarding the expectations that eighteen potentially relevant groups or individuals might hold. The superintendent was then asked to indicate which of the three statements most nearly represented the expectation he perceived each alter held for his behavior in the situation. If his responses revealed that contradictory expectations were held for his behavior and he validated our interpretation of them, we designated the situation as a role conflict.

After the respondent had indicated what expectations, if any, he perceived each of the eighteen listed groups and individuals held for him, the interviewer attempted to determine his feelings about the legitimacy of these expectations. The definition of legitimacy employed was the actor's perception of the right the others had to hold the expectation. If he perceived that the others had a right to hold the expectation, we will call it a perceived obligation or a *legitimate expectation*. If he perceived that the others did not have a right to hold it, we will call it a perceived pressure or an *illegitimate expectation*.

The respondent was asked to indicate for each group or individual whom he had said held a definite expectation for his behavior (responses in the *A* or *B* columns) whether "you think the individual or group named *has a right to expect you to do this."* He was asked to place a circle around the expectation of each individual or group which he believed to be a legitimate expectation. The superintendent's perception of the legitimacy of the expectations obtained through this procedure then allowed us to classify each role conflict situation into one of the four following types: expectations *A* and *B* both perceived as legitimate *(LL)*; expectation *A* perceived as legitimate and *B* as illegitimate *(LI)*; expectation *A* perceived as illegitimate and *B* as legitimate *(IL)*; and expectations *A* and *B* both perceived as illegitimate *(II)*.

After the legitimacy operation had been performed by the superintendent the interviewer began questioning the superintendent about his perception of the sanctions involved in the situation and about the way he resolved the role conflict. He also asked the superintendent to indicate the extent to which the situation "worried him" and why he undertook the particular course of action he reported to resolve the role conflict. He was asked to indicate how those who expected him to conform to expectation *A*, and then those who expected him to conform to expectation *B*, would react if he did not do what they expected of him. For 94 percent of the situations there was no disagreement between two coders on the classification of these sanctions. For those situations in which disagreement occurred the coders discussed in detail the reasons for the disagreement and finally developed a single judgment about a categorization of the role conflict on the basis of the sanctions.

The coding of the superintendent's resolution of the role conflict was derived from his response to the question, "What do you do in this situation?" There was 98 percent agreement between the coders on this operation and the disagreements were resolved in the same way as were those for the sanctions dimension.

The remaining element of the theory that requires consideration is the superintendent's orientation to expectations. That is, it was necessary to classify him as a moralist, expedient, or moral-expedient. The superintendent's responses to the Superintendent Performances Instrument described in Chapter Seven, p. 102 (see Appendix Table

A–1) provided the data used for this categorization. Each item in this instrument refers to expectations that could be applied to a superintendent. He was asked for the thirty-seven expectation items in this instrument, "As a school superintendent, what obligation do you feel that you have to do or not to do the following things." The response categories were: absolutely must, preferably should, may or may not, preferably should not, absolutely must not.

We reasoned that a person who would typically react to expectations that may be applied to him in terms of "it depends" is one who possesses an expedient orientation to expectations. He would be an individual who would tend to give heavy weight to sanctions in his interactions and slight weight to the legitimacy of expectations held for him. In operational terms he would respond to the expectation items with the preferably should, preferably should not, or may or may not response categories.

On the other hand a person whose typical response is not a contingent one, but is in terms of "I absolutely must" or "absolutely must not" carry out expectations, is one whose primacy of orientation is to their rectitude. He does not think in terms of factors in the situation that would lessen his obligations. Such a person would be predisposed "to honor" legitimate expectations regardless of the sanctions involved in the situation. Such a person would be a moralist.

One who shows neither of these patterns of responses to expecta-

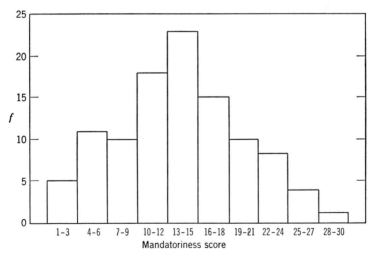

Figure 17–7. Frequency distribution of superintendents' mandatoriness scores on the superintendent performances instrument.

tions, but falls between the conditional and mandatory categories, would possess the characteristic required for the moral-expedient orientation. This orientation to expectations suggests that he is the type of person who would tend to take *both* the sanctions and legitimacy dimensions into account in reacting to perceived expectations.

This line of reasoning led to the following procedure. Each superintendent was given a score of 1 for each item in the Superintendent Performances Instrument for which he gave a mandatory response (absolutely must or absolutely must not). This provided a range of scores from 1 through 30 for the 37 items in the instrument. The distribution of mandatoriness scores can be seen in Figure 17–7. The estimated reliability of the scores is .884.[11] These scores were then split into the following three categories: 1–9, 10–18 and 19–30. On the reasoning outlined above those superintendents who fell into the low mandatoriness group (1–9) were defined as the expedients; those who fell into the high mandatoriness group (19–30) were considered moralists; and those who fell in the middle category (10–18) were categorized as moral-expedients.

A Test of the Theory. If we accept each of these operational indexes as adequately representing the variables and conditions described by the theory of role conflict resolution we can use them to perform an exploratory test. Superintendents who perceived their exposure to incompatible expectations in each of the four role conflict situations were categorized according to the perceived legitimacy of the expectations, the perceived sanctions to which they would be exposed for failure to conform to the expectations, and according to whether they were "moralists," "moral-expedients," or "expedients." The theory allows predictions of the behavior of superintendents of sixteen "legitimacy-sanctions" types for each of the orientation types. By comparing the behavior predicted on the basis of the theory for each of these forty-eight types with the actual behavior of superintendents who fell within these categories for each role conflict situation, we may say whether or not the theory has led in each case to the correct prediction.

In Table 17–A are presented the proportion of correct predictions for each of the forty-eight types for each role conflict situation. Although it would be possible to interpret the prediction for each of the forty-eight types separately as a testable hypothesis, this seemed indefensible on two counts. The first is that it seemed unlikely that there would be enough cases in many of the cells to allow for tests of the significance of the proportion correctly predicted. The second is that the theory can be considered implicative of only one general hypothesis, that the perceived legitimacy, perceived sanctions, and orientation are related to behavior in a particular though complex way, and that given particular conditions for each of these three phenomena a particular *prediction* can be made for behavior. It was felt that the theory as stated could be compared directly to a hypothesis describing how one or more predictor variables determines a criterion variable. For example, if it is hypothesized that height and weight are positively related to strength, then, if the hypothesis is quantitatively precise, given particular values of height and weight, *predictions* can be made of the particular value of strength. To interpret predictions for particular values of the predictor variables as hypotheses, and test them as such, suggests both a lack of confidence in the general theoretical description of the relationships among the variables of concern, and as well, a probably unjustified confidence in the extensity of the data available with which to make the tests.

On the basis of this reasoning it was decided to perform a single test of the theory of role conflict resolution for each situation, interpreting this theory as providing one general hypothesis about the ways in which the three predictors, legitimacy, sanctions, and orientation, are related among themselves, and how these in turn are related to the criterion, behavior. It is nevertheless important to present and to some extent discuss whatever differences may be apparent in the degrees of success with which the behavior of superintendents in different categories can be predicted.

As can be seen in Table 17–A, for 264 of the 291 role conflict cases (91 percent) the theory led to the correct prediction. Since, however, the four role conflict situations are not independent, in order to test the theory it is necessary to ask whether the proportion of correct predictions obtained for each situation could have occurred by chance. To answer this question, the number of correct and of incorrect predictions were compared with the number expected on the basis of two hypothetical "chance" models, the first we shall call the "chance expectancy" model, and the second and more stringent of the two, the "proportionate expectancy" model. The "chance expectancy" model assumes that each of the four alternative behaviors will occur by chance with equal frequency. With this assumption, the expected proportion of correct predictions is .25, and of incorrect, .75. Comparing the expected frequencies computed on the basis of this model with the frequencies obtained on the basis of the theory, results in the case of each situation in differences which are significant at the .01 level.

TABLE 17–A. THEORETICAL PREDICTIONS AND PROPORTION CORRECT IN A TEST OF A THEORY OF ROLE CONFLICT RESOLUTION

a. The Theoretical Predictions of Behavior for Moralists, Moral-Expedients, and Expedients in Sixteen Types of Role Conflicts*

Graphical grids showing, for each of the sixteen Types (1–16), the Expectation (A, B), Legitimacy, Sanctions, and Behavior predictions for Moralists, Moral-Expedients, and Expedients.

b. Proportion of Correct Predictions for Sixteen Types of Role Conflicts for Moralists (M), Moral-Expedients (M-E), and Expedients (E) in Four Situations†

Situation	M				M-E				E				Total of M, M-E and E			
Personnel hiring and promotion	0	0	9/9	0	0	0	31/31	0	0	0	12/12	0	0	0	52/52	0
	0	0/1	0	0	0	3/3	0	0	0	5/5	0	0	0	8/9	0	0
	0	4/5	0	0	0	0/1	0	0	0	0	0	0	0	4/6	0	1/1
	$N = 15$				$N = 36$				$N = 17$				$N = 68$			
	$P_{correct} = .87$				$P_{correct} = .97$				$P_{correct} = 1.00$				$P_{correct} = .96$			

Tables of observed data for sixteen-fold "legitimacy-sanctions" types, arranged by situation (rows: Time allocation; Teacher salary recommendations; Budget recommendations; Total of four situations) and by column blocks with values:

N = 48, P_correct = .79; N = 85, P_correct = .91; N = 90, P_correct = .93; Grand total N = 291, Grand total P_correct = .91

N = 10, P_correct = 1.00; N = 23, P_correct = .91; N = 22, P_correct = .96; N = 72, P_correct = .96

N = 28, P_correct = .82; N = 43, P_correct = .88; N = 50, P_correct = .96; N = 157, P_correct = .92

N = 10, P_correct = .50; N = 19, P_correct = .95; N = 18, P_correct = .83; N = 62, P_correct = .82

* The abbreviations used in the table of theoretical predictions are as follows: legitimacy abbreviations: $L =$ expectation perceived as legitimate, $I =$ expectation perceived as illegitimate; sanctions abbreviations: $+ =$ strong negative sanctions applied for nonconformity to the expectation, $- =$ strong negative sanctions not applied for nonconformity to the expectation; behavior abbreviations: $a =$ conformity to expectation A, $b =$ conformity to expectation B, $c =$ compromise, and $d =$ avoidance.

† The cells of each of the sixteen-fold tables correspond to the numbered "legitimacy-sanctions" types (1–16) of the table of theoretical predictions.

TABLE 17–B. A COMPARISON OF THE PROPORTION OF CORRECT PREDICTIONS
OBTAINED ON THE BASIS OF A "THEORY OF ROLE CONFLICT RESOLUTION"
WITH THE PROPORTION EXPECTED ON THE BASIS OF A "CHANCE EXPECTANCY
MODEL"

Situation	Number of Cases	Proportion of Correct Predictions by the "Theory"	Proportion of Correct Predictions Expected by "Chance"	t	Probability Less than
Personnel Hiring and Promotion	68	.96	.25	8.41	.01
Time Allocation	48	.79	.25	5.32	.01
Teacher Salary Recommendations	85	.91	.25	8.70	.01
Budget Recommendations	90	.93	.25	9.26	.01

This "chance expectancy" model is perhaps not realistic considering the actual frequencies of the four alternative behaviors, and is
certainly not the most stringent model with which the theory might
be compared. Since it is known that the four alternative behaviors
do not occur with equal frequency, a more stringent model would
attempt to take these disparities into account and would require that
each of the behaviors be selected "by chance" with the frequency
with which it is known to occur. In two of the situations, "Hiring"
and "Time Allocation," the fourth alternative, "avoidance," does not
occur at all, in the "Budget" situation it occurs only once, and in
the "Salary" only five times. A more extreme example will perhaps
clarify our reason for also using the "proportionate expectancy"
model with which to compare the theory. Suppose that it had been
possible to specify twenty alternative behaviors that could be selected
in each situation. Even though sixteen of them never occurred at
all, the proportion of correct predictions which would be expected
on the basis of "chance" would be 1/20, or .05. A comparison of the
theory with such a chance model, based on twenty alternative possible behaviors, would appear to be, if not a capitalization on chance,
at least a misrepresentation of realistic possibilities. With the assumption that each of the behaviors is selected "by chance" with
the frequency with which it is known to occur, the expected proportion of correct predictions for each of the four situations has been
computed on the basis of the data presented in Table 17–C. The
difference between the proportions expected in each situation according to the "proportionate expectancy" model and the proportions obtained on the basis of the theory is in each case significant
at the .01 level.

TABLE 17–C. A COMPARISON OF THE PROPORTION OF CORRECT PREDICTIONS
OBTAINED ON THE BASIS OF A "THEORY OF ROLE CONFLICT RESOLUTION"
WITH THE PROPORTION EXPECTED ON THE BASIS OF A "PROPORTIONATE-
EXPECTANCY MODEL"

Situation	Number of Cases	Proportion of Correct Predictions by the "Theory"	Proportion of Correct Predictions Expected by the "Model"*	t	Probability Less than
Personnel Hiring and Promotion	68	.96	.72	3.73	.01
Time Allocation	48	.79	.51	2.80	.01
Teacher Salary Recommendations	85	.91	.46	6.26	.01
Budget Recommendations	90	.93	.55	5.94	.01

* The definition of the proportion of correct predictions expected in each situation if the four alternative behaviors occur by chance with the frequency with which they actually occur is based on the following information:

Situation	Number of Cases	Proportions of Role Conflicts Resolved with Behaviors a, b, c, and d				Proportion Expected
		p_a	p_b	p_c	p_d	$(p_a^2 + p_b^2 + p_c^2 + p_d^2)$
Personnel Hiring and Promotion	68	.838	.103	.059	.000	.72
Time Allocation	48	.667	.083	.250	.000	.51
Teacher Salary Recommendations	85	.635	.094	.212	.059	.46
Budget Recommendations	90	.689	.033	.267	.011	.55

We are consequently led to the conclusion on the basis of the comparisons between the "chance" model and theory, as well as between the "proportionate" model and the theory, that the findings provide significant support for the theory in four role conflict situations.

Although evidence has been obtained which can be interpreted as supporting the general hypothesis based on the theory, there are several observations which can be made about Table 17–A suggesting limitations to the acceptability of this conclusion. The first is of the number of cells in which there are either very few or no cases. While it is true that an absence of cases in any cell is an interesting finding, it does not allow conclusions with respect to the validity of the theory for the whole range of types of role conflict situations for which predictions can be made. There are two cells in the "Grand Total" matrix which yield no cases, and nine others which yield seven or less. When these are broken down by situation and by orientation, there are many more cells which are inadequately or not at all represented. The most extreme case is found for "expedients" in the "Hiring" situation, where there are fourteen of the sixteen cells in which no cases occur.

Another possible limiting circumstance is the fact that there are interesting differences among the proportions of correct predictions for different categorizations of the data. For all four situations combined, for example, the proportion of correct predictions is highest for the "expedients" (.96), next highest for the "moral-expedients" (.92) and lowest for the "moralists" (.82). Differentiating the role conflicts by situation and combining superintendents of all three orientations, as we did in testing the theory, we find that the highest proportion of correct predictions is obtained in the "Hiring" situation (.96), the next highest in the "Budget" (.93), the next in the "Salary" (.91), and the lowest in the "Time Allocation" situation (.79). This last finding is perhaps interesting in that the "Time Allocation" situation is the only one of the four which involves expectations arising because of the superintendents' incumbency of two positions, or inter-role conflicts. The point of these observations is that there are differences within the data for which the theory can in no way account.

The general tests by means of which this theory of role conflict resolution has been empirically examined provide significant support for it. Nevertheless, since both the theory and the operations by means of which it has been tested are exploratory, it is important to ask, and as far as possible try to answer, first, whether there are significant factors in the determination of behavior in the face of incompatible expectation situations which this theory ignores, and second, whether or not the complexities involved in the theory are necessary to a successful prediction of behavior in these situations. The first of these questions is of the completeness of the theory; does it fail to take account of significant and relevant variables which could influence behavior in situations of this kind? The second question is of the parsimony of the theory; does it include factors which are unnecessary for an adequate understanding and prediction of behavior? Neither of these questions can be given a definitive answer, but both can and will be explored within the limitations of the data available.

In considering the first of these questions, of the completeness of the theory of role conflict resolution, it would seem appropriate to examine the cases for which the theory failed to provide a basis for a correct prediction. If some factor or factors have been left out of the theory which should be included, suggestions as to their nature are likely to be found in the responses of superintendents whose behavior was not correctly predicted on the basis of the theory. Since the prediction was incorrect, the behavior could not have been determined in the way the theory posits, and some other factors are likely to be relevant. This reasoning assumes, however, that the operations by means of which the theory has been tested are entirely adequate, which, when considering the exploratory nature of our analysis, is an assumption we do not feel justified in accepting. We feel that it is necessary to admit two possible sources of error in the tests which have been made: The first is the possible inadequacy of the theory, and the second the possible inadequacy of the operations by means of which it has been tested.

Of the 291 situations in which superintendents were exposed to incompatible expectations, the theory led to correct predictions in 264 cases. The remaining 27 were errors, and these 27 are the basis for this re-examination. Eight of these 27 errors arose in the "Salary" dilemma. The behavior of 5 of these 8 superintendents was coded as "avoidance" when, according to the theory, a "compromise" behavior was predicted. One of these superintendents said, "When the teachers make their demands I put it in the hands of the school committee. I just don't recommend. (Why do you do this?) The school committee has the authority and the responsibility. It's too hot for me; I let the school committee handle it." It might be suggested on the basis of this response that the theory as it was presented fails to recognize the possibility that negative sanctions may be minimized as much by avoidance as by compromise. Furthermore, if the formal definition of a position does not require incumbents to make certain decisions, as for example, decisions with respect to salary schedules, even though such incumbents recognize legitimate expectations with respect to these decisions, they may in the face of a dilemma resort to the formal definition as a justification for "avoiding" the obligations they recognize. It is interesting that all five of these superintendents have either an "expedient" or a "moral-expedient" orientation.

The six errors which were made in the "Budget" situation have nothing in common with one another, and although an interpretation could be offered of each one, the most likely explanation of their occurrence would appear to be the inadequacy of the operations.

Two of the three errors which were made in the "Hiring" situation suggest that there are limits to the strength of sanctions under which individuals with a "moral" orientation will continue to behave as moralists. In both of these cases, the superintendents perceived the "merit" expectation as legitimate, and the alternative as illegitimate. Since these superintendents were "moralists," the prediction was that they would conform to the "merit" alternative. This was incorrect; they conformed to the expectation they perceived as "illegitimate" and in both cases explained their behavior by reference to the strong negative sanctions which would result if they did not. In reviewing the interview protocols it became apparent that both of these superintendents were confronted with extreme sanctions and felt that it would serve no purpose for them to lose their jobs and be replaced by a superintendent who might not even recognize the legitimate expectation, let alone conform to it. Two suggestions might be made on the basis of these errors. The first is that there are limits to the strength of sanctions which individuals with a "moral" orientation can ignore. The second is more general. It might be suggested that the theory should be revised to allow for degrees of both "legitimacy" and "sanctions" and should make use of both of these factors as variables, rather than as dichotomies, in a prediction formula. That the theory does not do this must be recognized as an inadequacy, although it is one with which it would have been impossible to deal in this exploratory study. It would have been possible, of course, to develop the theory so as to take sanctions and legitimacy into account as variables, but with our data and operational procedures it would have been impossible to test it. In this sense it is recognized that not only the test, but the theory itself is exploratory.

The third error made for the "Hiring" situation can be accounted for by the inadequate operational procedures. This superintendent made a clear distinction between "professional" and "nonprofessional" staff. For the first group he said only the "merit" expectation was legitimate, and that strong negative sanctions would be applied only for failure to conform to this expectation, and he said he did conform to the "merit" expectation. For the "nonprofessionals" this superintendent recognized no legitimate expectations, perceived sanctions only for the "nonmerit" alternative, and he conformed to this "nonmerit" alternative. In order to include this superintendent in the analysis it was necessary to combine his separate responses for the two groups of employees he distinguished. The result was that his behavior was coded as "compromise" since he conformed to both expectations in part. This was incorrect since only one expectation, "merit," was perceived as legitimate, strong negative sanctions were perceived as resulting from failure to conform to both, and his orientation was "moral-expedient." More rigid operational definitions would have resulted in the exclusion of this superintendent from the analysis, but considering the latitude for interpretation which it was necessary to allow the coders, it did not seem justifiable to make this exclusion in the course of testing the theory.

The "Time Allocation" situation was the one on which the largest proportion of errors was made, 10 of the 48 cases being predicted incorrectly. Since this is the only situation in which the superintendent was exposed to inter-role conflict we may ask whether there is some other factor operating in this situation which did not enter in the other three situations and which the theory does not take into account. Two conclusions, which can perhaps be subsumed under one, are suggested by the responses of a number of these superintendents for whom the theory led to the incorrect prediction. Given incompatible expectations stemming from an individual's incumbency of two positions, some of our respondents invoked a "priority among positions" explanation of their behavior. Although according to their perceptions of the legitimacy and the sanctions and their orientation, the theory would lead to the prediction of a compromise, a number of superintendents said they "spent most evenings on school business," because, "It's my job." Other superintendents said "I feel I *should* be there," which suggests that they held an expectation for themselves to which they conformed irrespective of the other conditions in the situation. The theory takes into account neither the "priority among positions" nor the position incumbent's "own expectations." If an expectation for one position takes priority over an expectation for another position, it might be inferred that the incumbent perceives one as "more" legitimate than the other. Similarly, if a position incumbent does something because as he says in effect, "I expect this of myself," here too this might be inferred to be the "more" legitimate of the expectations to which he perceives he is exposed. These inferences return us to the suggestion that if the theory could have taken "legitimacy" and "sanctions" into account as variables rather than as dichotomies, it would have been a more precise theory in the sense of resulting in a larger proportion of correct predictions.

The conclusions which are suggested by this examination of the errors made in testing this theory of role conflict resolution may be summarized. First, it was suggested that the formal definition of a position with respect to a particular decision may influence the alternative behavior selected by a position incumbent. Second, the theory failed to recognize the possibility that negative sanctions *may* be minimized as much by avoidance as by compromise, depending on the particular situation, the nature of the sanctions, and the possibilities for "formal avoidance." Third, if it is operationally feasible to test such a revised theory, it can be suggested that the inclusion of perceived legitimacy and sanctions as variables rather than as dichotomies in a theory of role conflict resolution would be more accurately descriptive of the effects of these factors in determining behavior. Fourth, the expectations an individual holds for himself may not be congruent with the expectations he perceives and may influence his behavior independently of the perceived expectations and their legitimacy. And finally, in inter-role conflict situations, the expectations for one position may take priority over the expectations for the other, irrespective of the perceived legitimacy of either.

From an examination of the 27 instances in which the theory of role conflict resolution led to incorrect predictions, we were led to posit certain possible additional variables which might be relevant under certain circumstances. It remains true however, that in 264, or 91 percent, of the cases the theory led to the correct prediction, which suggests that the theory, as far as prediction is concerned, is reasonably adequate as it was presented. But on this criterion, of degree of successful prediction, it is possible that a model using only some of the factors involved in the theory would prove as adequate. This is the second question we shall ask about this theory of role conflict resolution: Is it a parsimonious theory, or does it include factors and assumptions which are unnecessary for the successful prediction of behavior?

In an attempt to answer this question three prediction models were developed each of which is based on some of the assumptions involved in the theory. Each of these prediction models will be presented and compared with the theory. Whether or not the theory allows us to make significantly more correct predictions in each of the four situations than each of the models will be considered the tests of whether or not the theory is more or less adequate on the criterion of successful prediction, which is, however, only one criterion against which the success of a theory can be evaluated. While we would be willing to defend the theory of role conflict resolution on logical grounds, we do not construe the findings to be presented as in any way supporting this defense. The theory is open to argument independently of the data and the findings, but the data and the findings can provide suggestions for its acceptance, revision, or rejection.

The first prediction model is based on the assumptions with respect to the perceived legitimacy of incompatible expectations. If position incumbents are predisposed to conform to legitimate expectations and predisposed not to conform to illegitimate expectations, it is possible to make predictions about a position incumbent's behavior in the face of two incompatible expectations of four types. The four types and the predicted behavior were presented on page 285 of this chapter and are summarized again in Table 17–D. Basing our predictions solely on this model, the results are presented in the second part of Table 17–D. Overall, this model provides 63 percent correct predictions.

The second model is based on the assumptions with respect to the perceived sanctions resulting from nonconformity to the incompatible expectations. If a position incumbent perceives that nonconformty to an expectation will result in strong negative sanctions, he will be predisposed to conform to it. If he perceives weak negative sanctions for nonconformity to a given expectation, he will not be predisposed either to conform or not to conform to it. On the basis of these assumptions it is possible to make predictions for three of the four possible types of situations in which there are two incompatible expectations to each of which an actor may perceive strong or weak negative sanctions for nonconformity. These types and the predictions based on these assumptions were presented on page 287 of this chapter and summarized again in Table 17–E. Since for the fourth type in which no sanctions are perceived, no prediction can be made, we must accept any cases falling in this category as errors as far as predicting behavior is concerned. The results of using this second prediction model are presented in the second part of Table 17–E. Overall, this second model provides 82 percent correct predictions.

A third model may be based on both these sets of assumptions with respect to legitimacy and sanctions, and as well, on the assumption that the predispositions derived from legitimacy and from sanctions combine equally in predisposing behavior. This model is equivalent to that part of the theory which defined the predictions for position incumbents with a "moral-expedient" orientation, which is presented on page 288 and is summarized again in Table 17–F. Basing our predictions solely on this model, the results are as presented in the second part of Table 17–F. Overall, this third model provides 83 percent correct predictions.

Having seen that each of these prediction models provides a sizable proportion of correct predictions, it is necessary to ask whether or not the theory is significantly better according to this prediction criterion. The comparisons between the number of correct predictions obtained on the basis of the "theory" and the number obtained on

TABLE 17–D.   THEORETICAL PREDICTIONS AND PROPORTION OF
CORRECT PREDICTIONS BASED ON A PREDICTION MODEL
USING THE "LEGITIMACY ASSUMPTION"

1. The Theoretical Predictions of Behavior in Four Types of Role Conflicts[*]

Type	1		2		3		4	
Expectation	A	B	A	B	A	B	A	B
Legitimacy	L	L	L	I	I	L	I	I
Behavior	c		a		b		d	

2. Proportion of Correct Predictions for Four Types of Role Conflict in Four Situations[†]

Situation	Type 1	Type 2	Type 3	Type 4	All types
Personnel hiring and promotion	$\dfrac{0}{0}$	$\dfrac{57}{68}$	$\dfrac{0}{0}$	$\dfrac{0}{0}$	$N = 68$ $p_{correct} = .84$
Time allocation	$\dfrac{5}{28}$	$\dfrac{5}{6}$	$\dfrac{3}{11}$	$\dfrac{0}{3}$	$N = 48$ $p_{correct} = .27$
Teacher salary recommendations	$\dfrac{9}{24}$	$\dfrac{46}{59}$	$\dfrac{0}{0}$	$\dfrac{0}{2}$	$N = 85$ $p_{correct} = .65$
Budget recommendations	$\dfrac{17}{38}$	$\dfrac{42}{52}$	$\dfrac{0}{0}$	$\dfrac{0}{0}$	$N = 90$ $p_{correct} = .66$
Total of four situations	$\dfrac{31}{90}$	$\dfrac{150}{185}$	$\dfrac{3}{11}$	$\dfrac{0}{5}$	$N = 291$ $p_{correct} = .63$

* The abbreviations used in the table of theoretical predictions are as follows: legitimacy abbreviations: L = expectation perceived as legitimate, I = expectation perceived as illegitimate; behavior abbreviations: a = conformity to expectation A, b = conformity to expectation B, c = compromise, d = avoidance.

† The four types of these tables correspond to the four "legitimacy" types of the table of theoretical predictions.

TABLE 17–E.   THEORETICAL PREDICTIONS AND PROPORTION OF
CORRECT PREDICTIONS BASED ON A PREDICTION MODEL
USING THE "SANCTIONS ASSUMPTION"

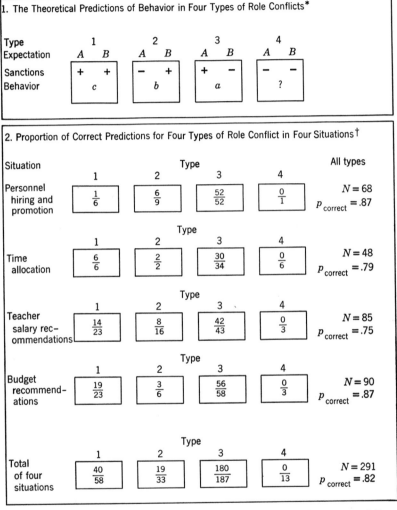

* The abbreviations used in the table of theoretical predictions are as follows: sanctions abbreviations: $+$ = strong negative sanctions applied for nonconformity to the expectation, $-$ = strong negative sanctions not applied for nonconformity to the expectation; behavior abbreviations: a = conformity to expectation A, b = conformity to expectation B, c = compromise, d = avoidance, and $?$ = no prediction possible.

† The four types of these tables correspond to the four "sanctions" types of the table of theoretical predictions.

TABLE 17–F.   THEORETICAL PREDICTIONS AND PROPORTION OF CORRECT PREDICTIONS BASED ON A PREDICTION MODEL USING THE "LEGITIMACY" AND "SANCTIONS" ASSUMPTIONS

1. The Theoretical Predictions of Behavior in Sixteen Types of Role Conflicts*

Type	1	2	3	4
Expectation	A B	A B	A B	A B
Legitimacy	L L	L L	L L	L L
Sanctions	+ +	− +	+ −	− −
Behavior	c	b	a	c

Type	5	6	7	8
Expectation	A B	A B	A B	A B
Legitimacy	L I	L I	L I	L I
Sanctions	+ +	− +	+ −	− −
Behavior	a	c	a	a

Type	9	10	11	12
Expectation	A B	A B	A B	A B
Legitimacy	I L	I L	I L	I L
Sanctions	+ +	− +	+ −	− −
Behavior	b	b	c	b

Type	13	14	15	16
Expectation	A B	A B	A B	A B
Legitimacy	I I	I I	I I	I I
Sanctions	+ +	− +	+ −	− −
Behavior	c	b	a	d

2. Proportion of Correct Predictions for Sixteen Types of Role Conflict in Four Situations †

Personnel hiring and promotion $N = 68$, $P_{correct} = .88$

0	0	0	0
$\frac{4}{6}$	$\frac{3}{9}$	$\frac{52}{52}$	$\frac{1}{1}$
0	0	0	0
0	0	0	0

Time allocation $N = 48$, $P_{correct} = .79$

$\frac{2}{2}$	$\frac{1}{1}$	$\frac{21}{23}$	$\frac{1}{2}$
0	0	$\frac{4}{4}$	$\frac{1}{2}$
$\frac{0}{3}$	$\frac{1}{1}$	$\frac{2}{5}$	$\frac{2}{2}$
$\frac{1}{1}$	0	$\frac{2}{2}$	0

Teacher salary recommendations $N = 85$, $P_{correct} = .77$

$\frac{8}{11}$	$\frac{4}{5}$	$\frac{8}{8}$	$\frac{0}{1}$
$\frac{6}{11}$	$\frac{2}{11}$	$\frac{33}{34}$	$\frac{2}{2}$
0	0	0	0
$\frac{1}{1}$	0	$\frac{1}{1}$	0

Budget recommendations $N = 90$, $P_{correct} = .87$

$\frac{14}{15}$	$\frac{1}{1}$	$\frac{19}{21}$	$\frac{1}{1}$
$\frac{3}{8}$	$\frac{2}{5}$	$\frac{37}{37}$	$\frac{1}{2}$
0	0	0	0
0	0	0	0

Total of four situations   Total $N = 291$, $P_{correct} = .83$

$\frac{24}{28}$	$\frac{6}{7}$	$\frac{48}{52}$	$\frac{2}{4}$
$\frac{13}{25}$	$\frac{7}{25}$	$\frac{126}{127}$	$\frac{5}{7}$
$\frac{0}{3}$	$\frac{1}{1}$	$\frac{2}{5}$	$\frac{2}{2}$
$\frac{2}{2}$	0	$\frac{3}{3}$	0

* The abbreviations used in the table of theoretical predictions are as follows: legitimacy abbreviations: $L =$ expectation perceived as legitimate, $I =$ expectation perceived as illegitimate; sanctions abbreviations: $+ =$ strong negative sanctions applied for nonconformity to the expectation, $- =$ strong negative sanctions not applied for nonconformity to the expectation; behavior abbreviations: $a =$ conformity to expectation A, $b =$ conformity to expectation B, $c =$ compromise, and $d =$ avoidance.

† The cells of each of the sixteen-fold tables correspond to the numbered "legitimacy-sanctions" types (1–16) of the table of theoretical predictions.

the basis of each of the "prediction models" for each of the four situations are presented in Table 17–G. We may conclude that the "theory" provides significantly more correct predictions than the "legitimacy model" in all four situations, but that only in the "Salary" situation does it provide significantly more correct predictions than do the "sanctions" and the "legitimacy-sanctions" models. Does this finding imply that the "sanctions" and "legitimacy-sanctions" models are as useful as the theory for predicting role conflict resolution? For the purpose of predicting the resolution of all role conflicts in three of the four situations, we would conclude that it does.

Another consideration, however, suggests a modification of this conclusion. The theory leads to exactly the same predictions as each of the models for a large proportion of the cases. Whether or not the theory is significantly better than each of the models consequently depends only on those cases for which the theory leads to a prediction different from that made on the basis of the models. When there are only a few such cases for any one comparison, it becomes much more difficult if not impossible for the theory to provide significantly more correct predictions. Although it would be inappropriate to apply a significance test to the difference between the number of correct predictions made on the basis of the theory and a model only in the cases for which the theory makes a *different* prediction from that made by a model, it is clearly relevant to compare them on this criterion using only these cases.

Table 17–H presents the number of correct and incorrect predictions made by the theory and by each of the three prediction models for each situation for *only those cases* in which the theory led to a prediction which differed from the one made on the basis of each of the models. For example, there were 8 cases in the "Hiring" situation for which the theory led to a prediction which differed from that made on the basis of the "legitimacy" model. In all 8 cases the theory led to the correct prediction and the model to the incorrect prediction. Comparing the theory with the "legitimacy" model for all four situations we may conclude that the theory is almost without exception more accurate. For 82 of the 84 role conflicts on which the theory and the "legitimacy" model led to different predictions in the four situations the theory was correct; in only 2 of the 84 cases did the "legitimacy" model lead to the correct prediction.

The comparisons between the theory and the other two models cannot be given quite so clear an interpretation, although it is only the "Time Allocation" situation in which the theory does not clearly lead to more correct predictions than does either the "sanctions" or the "legitimacy-sanctions" model. In the "Time Allocation" situation both prediction models lead to as many correct predictions as the theory (8 out of 19 in the case of the "sanctions" model and 4 out of 10 in the case of the "legitimacy-sanctions" model). In the remaining three situations, however, the theory consistently leads to more correct predictions than either model. Overall, in the 61 cases for which the theory led to a prediction different from that to which the "sanctions" model led, the theory led to the correct one in 39 cases and the model in only 14. In 8 cases neither of them led to the correct prediction. Of the 38 cases for which the theory and the "le-

TABLE 17–G. COMPARISONS OF THE PROPORTION OF CORRECT PREDICTIONS OBTAINED USING A "THEORY OF ROLE CONFLICT RESOLUTION" AND THE PROPORTION OBTAINED USING THREE "PREDICTION MODELS" IN FOUR SITUATIONS

Situation	Number of Cases	Proportion of Correct Predictions by the "Theory"	Proportion of Correct Predictions by the "Model"	χ^2*	Probability Less than
1. Comparison of the "Theory" and the "Legitimacy Model"					
Personnel Hiring and Promotion	68	.96	.84	6.12	.05
Time Allocation	48	.79	.27	23.04	.01
Teacher Salary Recommendations	85	.91	.65	18.38	.01
Budget Recommendations	90	.93	.66	21.33	.01
2. Comparison of the "Theory" and the "Sanctions Model"					
Personnel Hiring and Promotion	68	.96	.87	2.50	not sig.
Time Allocation	48	.79	.79	0.00	not sig.
Teacher Salary Recommendations	85	.91	.75	8.47	.01
Budget Recommendations	90	.93	.87	2.50	not sig.
3. Comparison of the "Theory" and the "Legitimacy-Sanctions Model"					
Personnel Hiring and Promotion	68	.96	.88	3.20	not sig.
Time Allocation	48	.79	.79	0.00	not sig.
Teacher Salary Recommendations	85	.91	.76	10.08	.01
Budget Recommendations	90	.93	.87	2.50	not sig.

* For comparing proportions obtained on the same individuals a chi-square different from that ordinarily used is required. For an appropriate treatment of this problem, see, for example, Helen M. Walker and Joseph Lev, *Statistical Inference* (New York: Henry Holt and Company, 1953), pp. 102–103.

gitimacy-sanctions" model differed, the theory led to the correct prediction in 29 and the model in 6. In 3 cases neither led to the correct prediction. These findings lead us to the conclusion that for those cases in which the theory led to a different prediction than we made on the basis of the models, the theory of role conflict resolution which we have examined leads to more correct predictions, in all but the single inter-role conflict situation ("Time Allocation"), than does any

TABLE 17–H. A COMPARISON OF THE NUMBER OF CORRECT PREDICTIONS OBTAINED USING A "THEORY OF ROLE CONFLICT RESOLUTION" AND THE NUMBER OBTAINED USING EACH OF THREE "PREDICTION MODELS" FOR CASES OF ROLE CONFLICT IN WHICH THE "THEORY" AND THE "MODEL" LED, TO DIFFERENT PREDICTIONS

Situation	Number of Cases for Which the Predictions of the "Model" and the "Theory" Differed	Number of Correct Predictions by the "Theory"	Number of Correct Predictions by the "Model"	Number of Cases for Which Neither the "Theory" nor the "Model" Was Correct
1. Comparison of the "Theory" and the "Legitimacy Model"				
Personnel Hiring and Promotion	8	8	0	0
Time Allocation	25	25	0	0
Teacher Salary Recommendations	24	23	1	0
Budget Recommendations	27	26	1	0
All Four Situations	84	82	2	0
2. Comparison of the "Theory" and the "Sanctions Model"				
Personnel Hiring and Promotion	11	8	2	1
Time Allocation	19	8	8	3
Teacher Salary Recommendations	19	15	2	2
Budget Recommendations	12	8	2	2
All Four Situations	61	39	14	8
3. Comparison of the "Theory" and the "Legitimacy-Sanctions Model"				
Personnel Hiring and Promotion	6	5	0	1
Time Allocation	10	4	4	2
Teacher Salary Recommendations	12	12	0	0
Budget Recommendations	10	8	2	0
All Four Situations	38	29	6	3

one of the three alternative "prediction models" with which it has been compared. To this extent, we may conclude that the theory satisfies the requirement of parsimony.

Summary. A theory of role conflict resolution has been presented which allows for the prediction of behavior, according to four alternative courses of action, when an individual is confronted with two incompatible expectations. The theory describes relationships among the perceived legitimacy of the expectations, the perceived sanctions resulting from nonconformity to them, the orientation of the individual to these legitimacy and sanctions dimensions, and his behavior. The accuracy of the predictions to which this theory led for school superintendents in four "incompatible expectation situations" was tested, and the evidence was interpreted as supporting the theory. In addition, an examination was made of the cases in which the theory led to an incorrect prediction, and suggestions made on the basis of this re-examination as to factors which were operative in these cases which the theory failed to take into account. Finally, the theory was compared with three prediction models, each of which was based on only some of the assumptions necessary for the theory. The conclusion was drawn that the theory was satisfactorily parsimonious relative to the success with which it allowed predictions of behavior.

Two relatively clear advantages may be claimed for this theory. The first is that it is concerned with and takes account of incompatible expectations stemming from an individual's incumbency of one or more positions. The basic phenomena with which the theory is concerned are incompatible expectation situations, and consequently both inter- and intrarole conflicts may be subsumed under it. The second advantage we would claim derives from the theory's concern with "expectations," whether legitimate or illegitimate, rather than "obligations" which may be considered to be legitimate expectations. Although illegitimate expectations are not obligations, their existence poses a dilemma for position incumbents for whom they are held. This theory of role conflict resolution takes account of and allows predictions about dilemmas of both kinds.

Although it is recognized that there are two limitations to this theory, both of these may, with appropriate modifications, be taken care of without changing the basic assumptions about relationships which the theory makes. The first, which has already been mentioned, is that both the legitimacy and the sanctions dimensions are dealt with as dichotomies, whereas a more precise theory would be based on their treatment as continuous variables. By elaborating the theory to take this into account and developing operational procedures by means of which to test the elaborated theory, it is felt that this limitation could be removed. Neither of these was practicable in the present study, since without the empirical test, it would be impossible to evaluate the necessity for or success of the theoretical elaboration. The second limitation which is recognized is that the theory as it has been presented can deal with incompatible expectation situations in which there are only two incongruent expectations. If there are three incompatible expectations for a position incumbent in one situation, the present theory would not serve as a basis for predicting his behavior. However, by simply extending the number of alternative behaviors (for example, to 8 in the case of 3 incompatible expectations) the theory would allow for the prediction of which of the 8 alternative courses of action an individual would take under different conditions of perceived legitimacy and sanctions (there would be 64 different conditions for which it would be necessary to make predictions for each of the 3 differently oriented types of individuals). The same assumptions would serve, and except in numerical detail, the theory would be unchanged.

More severe, perhaps, are the limitations we feel constrained to place on the test which has been presented of the theory. Aside from the possible inadequacy of the operational procedures we employed to define "perceived legitimacy," "perceived sanctions," "behavior," and "orientation," it must be pointed out that both the situations for which tests could be made and the position incumbents who were the respondents are quite restricted. For example, only one of the four situations was concerned with incompatible expectations stemming from superintendents' occupancy of two positions, or "inter-role conflict" situations, and in this case the theory provided the smallest proportion of correct predictions: only 79 percent as compared with 91 percent of all situations combined (see Table 17–A). The suggestion, based on an examination of those cases in which errors were made, that there may be in some cases a "priority among positions" points up the inadequacy of our test. It was impossible to examine this possibility in detail with our data, although it would seem necessary to do so before giving credence to the implication of the theory that it would apply to all incompatible expectation situations. Furthermore, the fact that superintendents are members of a "profession" would suggest that the "moral-expediency" dimension may be more cogent for their decisions than for the decisions of delinquents, for example.

Despite these possible inadequacies we would like to emphasize that a special point was made of using concepts in this theory which are widely applicable. The perceptions of incumbents of any position with respect to the expectations to which they are exposed, the legitimacy of the expectations, and the probable sanctions resulting from failure to conform to them are all concepts which are capable of operational definition under almost any conceivable condition. Furthermore, whether or not position incumbents are primarily oriented to the legitimacy or to the sanctions dimensions should be capable of operational specification no matter what the "absolute meaning" of legitimacy and sanctions may be for different incumbents of different positions. The isolation of these relatively serviceable conceptual elements of a theory of role conflict resolution may prove suggestive for further empirical explorations.

Notes and References for Chapter Seventeen

[1] Talcott Parsons, *The Social System* (Glencoe: The Free Press, 1951), p. 280.

[2] Jackson Toby, "Some Variables in Role Conflict Analysis," *Social Forces*, XXX (1952), p. 327.

[3] *Ibid.*, p. 327.

[4] J. W. Getzels and E. G. Guba, "Role, Role Conflict and Effectiveness," *American Sociological Review*, XIX (1954), p. 175.

[5] *Ibid.*, p. 174.

[6] Samuel A. Stouffer and Jackson Toby, "Role Conflict and Personality," *American Journal of Sociology*, LVI (1951), p. 400.

[7] Elliot G. Mishler, "Personality Characteristics and the Resolution of Role Conflicts," *Public Opinion Quarterly*, XVII (1953), pp. 134–135.

[8] Samuel A. Stouffer, "An Analysis of Conflicting Social Norms," *American Sociological Review*, XIV (1949), pp. 707–717.

[9] Getzels and Guba, *op. cit.*, pp. 173–174.

[10] Parsons, *op. cit.*

[11] In computing the reliability of these scores the total instrument was divided into separate halves. An attempt was made to insure parallel halves by matching on both proportion giving a mandatory response p and correlation with total scores r. Each item was represented by a point on a scatter diagram, the abscissa of which represented r and the ordinate p. A circle was drawn around the matched pairs and one member of each pair was randomly assigned to each half. The scores on the two halves were then correlated $(r_{AB} = .792)$, and finally the reliability estimated by the Spearman-Brown formula for double lengths $(r_{TT} = .884)$.

eighteen

Concluding Observations

The first part of this volume considered certain theoretical and operational problems of role analysis. These problems arose from our efforts to design the empirical studies reported in the second part of the volume which were concerned with propositions in which the expectations for and the behavior of position incumbents were involved. In this final chapter we will make some summary observations based on this research experience and consider certain of its possible implications for social science research involving "role analysis."

The role concept, in its present most frequent usage, focuses attention on ideas of central importance to the several social sciences. One of these is that human behavior is influenced to some degree by the expectations individuals hold for themselves or which other individuals hold for them. Another is that a person's locations or positions in social structures influence the kind of social relationships in which he is involved and the evaluative standards he or others apply to his behavior. Derivative from these is the basic proposition that human behavior is in part a function of the positions an individual occupies and the expectations held for incumbents of these positions. It is not surprising then that the role concept has found its way into models or conceptual schemes dealing with social behavior and that it is a central term in the writings of social scientists like Linton, Newcomb, and Parsons, in whose analyses attempts to cross the boundaries between the individual social science disciplines can be discerned.

But, as we and others who have examined the use of the role concept in the social science literature have observed, despite its increasing involvement in conceptual schemes for explaining social behavior and cultural and social systems, it has yielded few significant hypotheses of theoretical importance. If one judges the scientific utility of a concept by the degree to which it is involved in significant theoretical propositions that are capable of empirical examination, it must be said that in current formulations the role concept has not proved its worth.

To state that there has been little payoff in new knowledge from the role concept does not imply, however, that it has had no importance in the development of modern social science. Quite the contrary. The introduction of the role concept focused attention on phenomena that had been previously minimized or neglected in the individual social science disciplines. For psychologists the role concept emphasized that cultural and social structural dimensions need to be taken into account in analyses of *social* behavior. For cultural anthropologists it underscored that culture does not exist in a vacuum but is intimately linked to social structure. For sociologists it emphasized the need to bring evaluative standards and sanctions into analyses of social structure and social interaction.

As we have pointed out, however, the yield of theoretical hypotheses involving the role concept has been slight. Our research experience suggests certain factors which may account for this heuristically sterile condition.

First, research questions involving the phenomenon to which the role concept refers, whose examination might have yielded theoretically derived hypotheses, were ignored or by-passed because of postulates involved in the way the role concept had been formulated. We tried to show that involved in Linton's and many other definitions of role is the postulate of consensus on role definition.[1] The assumption of consensus precludes the use of the degree of consensus on role definition as a variable that may enter into theoretical hypotheses of relevance to a number of important social science problems. The empirical research reported in this book suggests that the questioning of this postulate permits the investigation of potentially significant questions of direct relevance to problems in formal organization theory and interaction theory. We have also considered its implications for the analysis of conformity-deviance and for a theory concerned with the behavior of actors when exposed to role conflict.

The abandonment of the postulate of consensus on role definition has other important theoretical consequences. One of these is concerned with the socialization process or the "acquisition of roles." In many treatments of this problem the assumption is made that there is a clearly defined and agreed upon set of expectations associated with a position, whether it is an age, sex, family, or occupational position. The empirical complexities of degrees of consensus on role definition that we have examined in this book make this assumption suspect. This suggests that the conditions under which expectations are learned or taught and who defines them may be quite variable. Data from our interviews with superintendents and school board members supports this contention. Consider these possibilities:

1. An incumbent of a focal position may define what most of his rights and obligations are and an incumbent of a counter position may accept his definitions.

2. Incumbents of counter positions may define most expectations and an incumbent of the focal position may accept them.

3. An incumbent of the focal position may define his rights while incumbents of the counter position may define his obligations (or their own rights) and both may accept each other's definitions of these role segments.

4. Neither the incumbent of the focal or of the counter position may have well-defined expectations for each other's behavior in their initial interaction and they may be eventually worked out through a trial and error process.

5. Some expectations may be learned prior to, and others during, position incumbency.

Our interviews with school administrators and their school board members revealed instances of each of these role definition and role-learning situations. The assumption that there is consensus on role definition on the basis of which socialization takes places is untenable for the occupational position we studied. We would suggest that it deserves to be challenged in most formulations of role acquisition, including even those concerned with the socialization of the child.

Another consequence of abandoning the postulate of consensus on role definition that deserves exploitation lies in the implications it has for explaining different behaviors of incumbents of the same position. Most students concerned with role phenomena, assuming consensus on role definition, have tried to account for variability in behavior by invoking such variables as different motivations, attitudes, or personality characteristics. Our research experience suggests that the different expectations held for incumbents' behavior and attributes are crucial for an understanding of their different behaviors and characteristics. Theoretical formulations which attempt to explain different behaviors of incumbents of the same position cannot be based on concepts in which the postulate of role consensus is involved.

Abandoning the postulate can also have consequences for a theory of social control. A model often posited is that incumbents of different positions in a social system agree on the rights and obligations associated with each other's position. If a member of the group does not conform to these standards, sanctions will be applied by other group members which will bring the deviant into line. If the sanctions do not have this consequence the deviant will be forced to leave the group. But when consensus on role definition is viewed as a variable these consequences may occur only under certain conditions of consensus. When group members hold variant role definitions of an actor's behavior, the same behavior may result in the application of negative sanctions by some members and positive sanctions by others. If one group member perceives that there is lack of consensus on the evaluative standards to be applied to another's behavior, he may not apply negative sanctions when the other's behavior deviates from his expectations because of the ambiguity in his own mind regarding the definition of his own role. Thus many school board members did not approve of certain behaviors of their superintendent, but as laymen dealing with a "professional" they were uncertain of their prerogatives to apply sanctions to the superintendent.

On the other hand, some superintendents, although acutely aware of the expectations their school board members held for them, did not conform to their standards and ignored negative sanctions to which they might be exposed. Some did not conform to these standards because they defined their roles differently from the way their superordinates did, and as moralists, they would conform only to legitimate expectations, regardless of the severity of the sanctions. In this case "internal sanctions" took priority over external ones. Others did not conform to some of the expectations of their superordinates because they perceived they would be exposed to greater negative sanctions from members of external systems (for example, P.T.A.) if they did. Similarly, some school board members who clearly deviated from the expectations other board members and their superintendent held for their behavior did not change their behavior or leave the group when negative sanctions were applied to them. The relevant sanctioning agent was outside, not inside, the school board conference room.

These empirical examples do not fit neatly into the usual treatment of social control, namely that the application or the threat of negative sanctions results in conforming behavior. They suggest that the important research question is the isolation of the conditions under which different consequences emerge from the application of sanctions.

There is another postulate involved in many formulations of the role concept that deserves critical examination. This is that although the same individual may be the incumbent of many positions at different times and therefore "plays many roles," or even *occupies* many positions simultaneously, he *activates* each role singly. For example, certain theories of role conflict resolution which we considered, while taking as the basis of conflict the simultaneous *incumbency* of two or more positions, assume that the conflict can be resolved only through the adoption or activation of *one* role. That is, an actor can activate only one role at any given moment of time. Linton[2] and others have introduced the concepts of active and latent statuses and roles to handle this assumption.

Some of our empirical analyses suggest that this may be a tenuous assumption. The empirical finding that regardless of the religion of the superintendent, the greater the proportion of Catholic school board members, the less the board conformed to professional expectations suggests that some members of the board may be activating multiple "roles." The additional fact that some superintendents in conversation tend to differentiate their members as male or female also suggests that in their interaction they perceive them as simultaneously activating multiple positions.

Implications of this empirical observation may be of major importance not only for a theory of role conflict but for a general theory of interaction. Thus, for many types of interaction, the behavior of an individual and the *anticipations* of his behaviors by other members of the group may be a function of multiple position occupancy. Students may hold different anticipations for the behavior of a teacher who is a male or female, who is young or old, married or unmarried. Husbands may hold different anticipations for wives who are and are not incumbents of occupational positions. The evaluative standards applied to a *person* by others and the anticipations for their behavior may be in part a resultant or function of the number of positions the person is perceived as simultaneously occupying.

This also suggests the need to examine the time dimension as related to *positional* and *personal* evaluative standards. When X and Y first interact they may hold expectations for each other based on their perceptions of each other's occupancy of a single position, for example, that of assemblyman in the workroom. As X and Y interact over time, *other* positions they occupy may enter into their perceptions of each other. X learns that Y is married, a father of three children, and a Catholic; and Y learns that X is a bachelor and does not belong to any church. As these further identifications become known they may influence the type and nature of interaction between X and Y and the evaluative standards they apply to each other's behavior. We are suggesting that over a given time period the evaluative standards one actor holds for another tend to shift from standards applied to an incumbent of a position to standards applied to a *person* with certain personality characteristics and performance capacities as the incumbent of multiple positions.

Another possible reason for the paucity of theoretical hypotheses capable of empirical examination deriving from existing role conceptions is the holistic manner in which the role concept has been defined. Our research experience suggests that when a more differentiated set of concepts are developed to denote subsidiary notions involved in the general conception of role, these microscopic terms may be fruitfully used in theoretical propositions. That is, the ideas to which role refers, if treated as a family of concepts instead of in a holistic manner, may be made available for theoretical hypotheses.

The concept of role sector allowed us to investigate theoretically derived hypotheses concerning different degrees of consensus on different role segments. The concept of expectation as an evaluative standard applied to an incumbent of a position by any specified role definer allowed the derivation and examination of hypotheses concerning different role definitions of different role definers. The concept of role behavior allowed us to make a distinction between the *actual* behavior of an incumbent of a position that could be referred to an evaluative standard and the evaluative standard itself. The conceptual distinction between expectations that are perceived as legitimate and those perceived as illegitimate had important implications for the development of a theory of role conflict resolution. The differentiation of intra- and inter-role conflict had consequences for rejecting certain theoretical explanations of the resolution of role conflict. And the definition of role as a set of expectations applied to an incumbent of a position by some role definer or definers, rather than as a set of expectations "ascribed by society," made it possible for the construct to take its place in a number of theoretical propositions. It may also have made it a more attractive concept for psychologists, who, although they may not be interested in what is "ascribed by society," can readily accept and deal with perceptions of individuals.

Still another possible reason for the heuristitc sterility of the role concept, closely related to those we have considered, lies in the difficulties involved in developing operational definitions for the nominal definitions it has most frequently received. It is not an easy matter to secure a measure of ". . . the sum total of culture patterns associated with a particular status"[3] or of ". . . attitudes, values, and behavior ascribed by society to any and all persons occupying this status. . . ."[4] Nor is it a simple operational matter to secure measurements on role defined as ". . . a sector of the total orientation system of an individual actor which is organized about expectations in relation to a particular interaction context, that is integrated with a particular set of value standards which govern interaction with one or more alters in the appropriate complementary roles."[5]

Such formulations may be useful for general theoretical models or speculative and descriptive analyses, but their utility for theoretically oriented research is problematic. Concepts that are quite difficult to define operationally are of limited use in the development of theoretical propositions that are capable of empirical verification or rejection.

In this research we have tried to define our theoretical terms operationally. Regardless of the theoretical adequacy of our concepts and the propositions in which they are involved, the hypotheses we developed were capable of empirical examination because their key terms were capable of operational definition. We have also emphasized the necessity for clear specifications of the subject population and the object population in any empirical role analysis. These basic specifications must be made if the limitations and generalizability of research findings are to be unambiguous.

One final point. There is a great need for concepts in social science that can be played "across the board," that is, concepts whose utility is not limited to a single discipline but which can be used by students of the several social science disciplines in conceptual formulations of certain of their strategic problems. Although we may have been unsuccessful, we have tried to conceptualize the basic notions involved in previous formulations of the role concept in such a manner that the same basic terms could be used in propositions that deal with problem areas traditionally viewed as the province of one or another of the individual social sciences. From one standpoint our treatment of macroscopic role consensus can be viewed as dealing with "the culture" of the superintendent-school board relationship. Our microscopic analyses are closely related to the kinds of problems with which students of the small group, both sociologists and social psychologists, have been concerned. The conformity-deviance problem is one in which students of different social sciences have displayed keen interest. The role conflict analysis dealt with a problem that has been of concern to both sociologists and psychologists. For all these problems it was possible to use the same set of basic concepts.

The inquiries reported in this book suggest that a family of role concepts may be useful for the analysis of problems at several different levels—at the level of individual behavior (for example, the resolution of role conflict), at the level of group behavior (for example, a group's conformity to a set of expectations), and at the cultural level (for example, consensus on role definitions). Furthermore, such concepts can be used in the analysis of problems that cut across different levels (for example, the impact of a *group's* conformity to a set of expectations on the gratifications of *individual* members of the group).

The fact that these concepts can take their place *along with other concepts* in a series of propositions and theoretically derived hypotheses concerned with the explanation of phenomena at the individual, social system and cultural levels suggests that it would be an unwise use of conceptual resources to limit their application to only one of the social science disciplines or to a selected problem area designated as "role theory." [6]

Concepts are needed in the social sciences that can be used in theoretical propositions concerning problems of interest to students of any social science discipline. A set of basic concepts like those we have used in the analyses undertaken in this book may constitute one means of crossing the terminological barriers separating the several social sciences and of facilitating closer relations among them. The implications of the theoretical and empirical analyses of one discipline for the others may be more clearly perceived if they make use of concepts that are theoretically relevant to and capable of operational definition at the different levels of analysis at which different social sciences at present operate.

That such concepts are needed is evidenced by the current trend in social psychology to reject ". . . the sterile dichotomy of isolated individual vs. disembodied group," in favor of "interactionism," [7] by the "culture and personality" studies in anthropology, and by the efforts of sociologists to develop a "general theory of social action." [8] Differentiated concepts that bring culture and social structure down to the level of the human organism and that allow perceptions of individuals to be viewed in cultural and social structural perspectives may accelerate these trends. The concepts that have evolved from our explorations in role analysis may be of service in this bridging operation. Whether or not they are, it is our conviction that efforts to develop such a "conceptual exchange" contribute to the emergence and development of a unified science of social man.

Notes and References for Chapter Eighteen

[1] It should be emphasized again that it is a matter of definition that the members of a social system must agree among themselves to *some extent* on some values or expectations. The point that has been continually stressed is that *the degree of consensus* on expectations is an empirical variable whose theoretical possibilities need to be exploited in social science inquiries.

[2] Ralph Linton, *The Cultural Background of Personality* (New York: D. Appleton-Century Co., 1945), pp. 77–79.

[3] *Ibid.*, p. 77.

[4] *Ibid.*, p. 77.

[5] Talcott Parsons, *The Social System* (Glencoe: The Free Press, 1951), pp. 38–39.

[6] For another viewpoint see Theodore R. Sarbin, "Role Theory," in Gardner Lindzey (Editor), *Handbook of Social Psychology*, Vol. I (Cambridge: Addison-Wesley Publishing Company, 1954).

[7] M. Brewster Smith, "Anthropology and Psychology," in John Gillin (Editor), *For a Science of Social Man* (New York: The Macmillan Company, 1954), pp. 64–65.

[8] Talcott Parsons and Edward A. Shils with the assistance of James Olds, "Values, Motives, and Systems of Action," in Talcott Parsons and Edward A. Shils (Editors), *Toward a General Theory of Action* (Cambridge: Harvard University Press, 1951), pp. 47–275.

appendix
a

Role Definition Instruments

The items used for each of the six role definition instruments and the superintendent and school board member responses to them, plus certain summary information, are presented in a series of tables in this appendix. The column headings used in these tables for the first five instruments are presented below. The column headings for the table presenting information pertaining to the Division of Labor Instrument (Appendix Table A–6) are presented immediately preceding the table.

COLUMN HEADINGS

(1) The item

(2) Size of superintendent (*S*) and school board member (*SB*) samples

(3)–(8) Expectation response categories:

(3) *AM*—Absolutely must

(4) *PS*—Preferably should

(5) *MMN*—May or may not

(6) *PSN*—Preferably should not

(7) *AMN*—Absolutely must not

(8) *NA*—No answer (or "does not apply" for the Participations and Friendships Instruments)

(9) Mean response of the superintendent and school board member samples for each expectation item (*AM* weighted as 1, *PS* as 2, *MMN* as 3, *PSN* as 4, and *AMN* as 5).

(10) Variance of the distribution of responses for each sample for each item.

(11) This column indicates whether the chi-square obtained for the comparison of the response distributions of the superintendent and school board member samples was significant at the .01 or .05 levels, or nonsignificant.

(12)–(14) For Instruments 1, 3, and 4 (Superintendent's Performances,
        Participations, and Friendships)
        Role behavior response categories to the questions:
        (Superintendent's question) Do you do this?
        (School board member's question) Does your superintendent
        do this?
        (12) *Y*—Yes
        (13) *N*—No
        (14) *NA*—Includes "don't know," not applicable, and no
        answer

(12)–(14) For Instrument 5 (School Board Members' Performances)
        Role behavior response categories to the question:
        (For both superintendents and school board members)
        Does your school committee do this?
        (12) *Y*—Yes
        (12a) *P*—Partly
        (13) *N*—No
        (14) *NA*—Includes "don't know," not applicable, and no
        answer

APPENDIX TABLE A–1.　EXPECTATIONS FOR SUPERINTENDENT'S PERFORMANCES

Superintendent's Question: "As a superintendent, what obligations do you feel that you have to do or not to do the following things?"; School Board Member Question: "As a school committee member, what obligations do you feel the superintendent has to do or not to do the following things?"

(1) Item	(2) Sample S (105) SB (508)	(3) AM	(4) PS	(5) MMN	(6) PSN	(7) AMN	(8) NA	(9) $\bar{X}$	(10) σ^2	(11) $P\chi^2$	(12) Y	(13) N	(14) NA
				Expectations							Behavior		
1. Make recommendations for the appointment, promotion, or dismissal of subordinates on the basis of merit alone.	S	90	15	0	0	0	0	1.14	0.141	.01	102	3	0
	SB	252	196	22	35	2	1	1.70	0.760		418	75	15
2. Urge people whom he respects to run for positions on the school committee.	S	3	14	32	32	24	0	3.57	1.140	not sig.	33	72	0
	SB	6	64	124	218	95	1	3.65	0.924		116	346	46
3. Carry out decisions of the school committee which he believes to be unsound.	S	52	27	9	13	4	0	1.95	1.416	.01	80	18	7
	SB	137	153	33	130	52	3	2.62	1.896		246	172	90
4. Favor local firms in the awarding of school contracts even though this may increase school expenses somewhat.	S	0	17	23	44	21	0	3.66	0.949	not sig.	39	65	1
	SB	6	112	75	186	115	14	3.59	1.234		155	314	39
5. Accept full responsibility for the decisions of his subordinates.	S	45	36	18	4	2	0	1.88	0.908	.01	91	14	0
	SB	142	261	51	49	4	1	2.04	0.837		396	89	23
6. Keep his office open to all community members at all times.	S	56	32	10	6	1	0	1.70	0.856	.01	94	11	0
	SB	167	294	24	20	1	2	1.80	0.514		453	47	8
7. Write articles for professional journals which will be of benefit to others in the profession.	S	4	68	33	0	0	0	2.28	0.276	not sig.	46	59	0
	SB	18	293	194	2	0	1	2.36	0.308		161	182	165
8. Keep a watchful eye on the personal life of his subordinates.	S	0	27	29	47	2	0	3.23	0.729	.01	41	63	1
	SB	59	274	88	75	10	2	2.41	0.891		315	131	62
9. Cooperate willingly with researchers who are attempting to advance knowledge in his field.	S	35	68	2	0	0	0	1.69	0.254	not sig.	105	0	0
	SB	170	327	10	0	0	1	1.68	0.255		428	11	15
10. Consult with staff members about filling vacant teaching positions.	S	21	65	18	1	0	0	1.99	0.409	.01	100	5	0
	SB	61	286	97	54	9	1	2.34	0.784		342	123	43

APPENDIX TABLE A-1 (Continued)

(1) Item	(2) Sample S (105) SB (508)	(3) AM	(4) PS	(5) MMN	(6) PSN	(7) AMN	(8) NA	(9) X̄	(10) σ²	(11) Pχ²	(12) Y	(13) N	(14) NA
				Expectations							Behavior		
11. Refuse to recommend the dismissal of a teacher the public wants dismissed if he feels that the public complaint is invalid.	S	63	32	3	2	5	0	1.61	0.981	.01	100	3	2
	SB	181	235	25	46	18	3	1.98	1.093		338	60	110
12. Speak to all major civic groups at least once a year.	S	5	57	42	1	0	0	2.37	0.348	not sig.	58	46	1
	SB	22	271	208	4	1	2	2.39	0.352		317	152	39
13. Have on paper a long range building plan.	S	34	64	7	0	0	0	1.74	0.324	not sig.	89	15	1
	SB	120	320	61	5	0	2	1.90	0.439		317	152	24
14. Seeks able people for open positions rather than considering only those who apply.	S	57	48	0	0	0	0	1.46	0.248	.05	103	2	0
	SB	219	278	8	1	1	1	1.59	0.308		446	50	12
15. Give consideration to local values or feelings regarding race, religion, national origin, in filling vacant teaching positions.	S	7	24	24	27	23	0	3.33	1.517	.01	60	45	0
	SB	20	189	72	154	72	1	3.14	1.384		242	232	34
16. Take directions from individual school board members.	S	1	0	11	33	60	0	4.44	0.570	.01	7	97	1
	SB	3	18	51	251	184	1	4.17	0.688		107	387	14
17. "Play up to" influential local citizens.	S	1	2	17	41	44	0	4.19	0.707	.05	8	97	0
	SB	2	10	34	261	200	1	4.28	0.500		72	412	24
18. Defend his teachers from attack when they try to present the pros and cons of various controversial social and political issues.	S	73	22	8	0	2	0	1.34	0.627	.01	100	3	2
	SB	145	252	62	40	6	3	2.03	0.833		346	63	99
19. Give a helping hand to school committee members who are coming up for re-election.	S	1	3	22	30	49	0	4.17	0.847	.05	21	84	0
	SB	5	20	83	216	183	1	4.09	0.763		90	377	41
20. Eliminate from his staff any political liberals who might be accused of being "pinks" or "reds."	S	17	31	31	12	13	1	2.74	1.556	.01	44	45	16
	SB	158	126	83	89	47	5	2.49	1.793		148	81	279

APPENDIX TABLE A–1 (Continued)

(1) Item	(2) Sample S (105) SB (508)	(3) AM	(4) PS	(5) MMN Expectations	(6) PSN	(7) AMN	(8) NA	(9) X̄	(10) σ²	(11) Px²	(12) Y	(13) N Behavior	(14) NA
21. Secure outside help from "experts" when curriculum changes are being considered.	S	10	69	26	0	0	0	2.15	0.320	not sig.	90	15	0
	SB	65	342	84	15	1	1	2.10	0.419		357	96	55
22. Establish regular channels of communication with local newspapers.	S	48	53	3	1	0	0	1.59	0.356	.01	97	8	0
	SB	75	333	82	15	1	2	2.08	0.440		401	88	19
23. Help his teachers to get higher salaries.	S	48	51	6	0	0	0	1.60	0.354	.01	105	0	0
	SB	38	287	145	34	2	2	2.36	0.538		436	59	13
24. Fight continuously against any local attacks on educational principles or methods which he knows are sound.	S	82	19	3	0	1	0	1.28	0.371	.01	101	1	3
	SB	257	218	15	14	3	1	1.60	0.537		427	25	56
25. Encourage the formation of local committees to cooperate with the school committee in studying school problems.	S	19	68	16	2	0	0	2.01	0.409	.05	92	13	0
	SB	62	303	97	36	8	2	2.26	0.674		328	144	36
26. Compile a list of the general characteristics desired in the teaching staff.	S	15	67	23	0	0	0	2.08	0.356	not sig.	74	31	0
	SB	88	337	75	6	1	1	2.00	0.387		314	140	54
27. Occasionally compromise with local pressure groups.	S	5	16	39	32	13	0	3.30	1.050	not sig.	52	50	3
	SB	5	64	163	177	96	3	3.58	0.936		191	236	81
28. Make no major curriculum changes without first seeking public support.	S	10	36	44	12	3	0	2.64	0.821	.01	64	41	0
	SB	10	122	153	174	47	2	3.25	0.974		140	307	61
29. Take a definite stand against any unreasonable demands which may come from local taxpayers.	S	70	34	0	0	1	0	1.36	0.345	.01	102	0	3
	SB	147	267	36	48	9	1	2.02	0.899		349	88	71
30. Make curriculum changes without consulting the teaching staff.	S	2	0	5	48	50	0	4.37	0.557	.01	19	86	0
	SB	5	23	53	326	99	2	3.97	0.570		72	400	36
31. Take a neutral stand on any issue on which the community is evenly split.	S	3	16	51	27	7	1	3.18	0.853	.01	37	65	3
	SB	30	175	161	124	17	1	2.85	0.937		244	163	101

APPENDIX TABLE A-1 (Continued)

(1) Item	(2) Sample S (105) SB (508)	(3) AM	(4) PS	(5) MMN	(6) Expectations PSN	(7) AMN	(8) NA	(9) $\bar{X}$	(10) σ^2	(11) $P\chi^2$	(12) Y	(13) Behavior N	(14) NA
32. Personally inspect all school plants at least once a year.	S	83	19	3	0	0	0	1.24	0.235	not sig.	101	4	0
	SB	401	103	3	0	0	1	1.21	0.181		495	8	5
33. Avoid involvement with factional groups in the community.	S	47	36	8	6	8	0	1.97	1.438	.01	90	15	0
	SB	200	251	19	24	12	2	1.81	0.799		449	41	18
34. Read most of the professional journals.	S	17	81	6	1	0	0	1.91	0.250	not sig.	89	16	0
	SB	79	364	62	2	0	1	1.97	0.293		399	14	95
35. Help the school committee resist demands by teachers for higher salaries.	S	0	2	38	39	26	0	3.85	0.662	.01	19	85	1
	SB	18	99	220	143	22	6	3.11	0.790		209	254	45
36. In drawing up the budget, cost factors are given greater consideration than educational needs.	S	1	7	6	48	43	0	4.19	0.783	.01	7	98	0
	SB	3	22	38	332	110	3	4.04	0.519		69	431	8
37. Work on committees sponsored by the state department of education and professional organizations.	S	11	87	6	1	0	0	1.95	0.199	.01	96	9	0
	SB	20	316	160	8	3	1	2.33	0.365		312	78	118

APPENDIX TABLE A-2. EXPECTATIONS FOR SUPERINTENDENT'S ATTRIBUTES

Superintendent's Question: "Suppose for the moment that you have accepted a job as Superintendent in another community. The school committee here asks you to recommend someone as your replacement. What kind of man would you recommend for the position?"; School Board Member's Question: "Suppose your school committee had the job of hiring a new Superintendent. Which of the following qualities do you feel are relevant to the job of school superintendent, and if relevant, how important do you think they are?"

(1) Item	(2) Sample S (105) SB (508)	(3) AM	(4) PS	(5) Expectations MMN	(6) PSN	(7) AMN	(8) NA	(9) $\overline{X}$	(10) σ^2	(11) $P\chi^2$
1. 50 to 59 years of age.	S	0	5	45	48	7	0	3.54	0.477	.01
	SB	2	46	288	150	22	0	3.28	0.494	
2. Married.	S	12	71	18	0	0	4	2.07	0.294	.01
	SB	15	106	342	42	3	0	2.83	0.403	
3. Outspoken.	S	4	38	33	29	1	0	2.86	0.808	not sig.
	SB	22	175	160	137	14	0	2.89	0.886	
4. Church member.	S	12	60	33	0	0	0	2.20	0.389	not sig.
	SB	94	287	126	1	0	0	2.07	0.436	
5. 60 years of age or over.	S	0	0	9	58	38	0	4.28	0.371	.05
	SB	0	1	99	265	143	0	4.08	0.477	
6. A good public speaker.	S	8	82	15	0	0	0	2.07	0.215	not sig.
	SB	57	368	81	2	0	0	2.06	0.284	
7. Well informed on modern educational practices.	S	85	18	2	0	0	0	1.21	0.204	not sig.
	SB	417	90	1	0	0	0	1.18	0.152	
8. Practical.	S	74	29	0	1	0	1	1.30	0.271	not sig.
	SB	334	170	4	0	0	0	1.35	0.243	
9. Democrat.	S	1	2	91	6	5	0	3.11	0.292	not sig.
	SB	0	2	477	12	17	0	3.09	0.154	
10. Have doctor's degree.	S	1	14	88	2	0	0	2.87	0.173	.01
	SB	23	175	303	7	0	0	2.58	0.362	
11. Fired for not yielding to political pressures in last position.	S	0	0	92	12	1	0	3.13	0.135	.01
	SB	32	65	339	45	23	4	2.92	0.649	

APPENDIX TABLE A–2 (Continued)

(1) Item	(2) Sample S (105) SB (508)	(3) AM	(4) PS	(5) MMN	(6) PSN	(7) AMN	(8) NA	(9) $\bar{X}$	(10) σ^2	(11) Px^2
				Expectations						
12. Personally ambitious.	S	8	77	14	6	0	0	2.17	0.409	not sig.
	SB	71	306	84	42	5	0	2.22	0.676	
13. Skilled in public relations.	S	41	64	0	0	0	0	1.61	0.238	.01
	SB	124	340	42	2	0	0	1.85	0.319	
14. Tactful.	S	71	31	0	0	0	3	1.30	0.212	.01
	SB	252	245	9	2	0	0	1.53	0.308	
15. Male.	S	49	51	5	0	0	0	1.58	0.339	.05
	SB	196	232	79	1	0	0	1.77	0.498	
16. White.	S	62	30	10	3	0	0	1.56	0.608	.01
	SB	182	223	103	0	0	0	1.84	0.537	
17. Able to express ideas clearly.	S	67	38	0	0	0	0	1.36	0.231	not sig.
	SB	311	194	2	1	0	0	1.40	0.259	
18. A man who believes in as little government as possible.	S	2	36	37	22	8	0	2.98	0.933	.01
	SB	17	114	124	148	98	7	3.39	1.287	
19. A man who believes in the welfare state.	S	1	1	20	51	32	0	4.07	0.615	.01
	SB	40	77	122	137	129	3	3.47	1.540	
20. Socialist.	S	0	0	11	43	51	0	4.38	0.445	not sig.
	SB	0	2	83	185	237	1	4.30	0.559	
21. Easy-going.	S	0	14	29	47	14	1	3.58	0.781	not sig.
	SB	2	63	135	217	89	2	3.65	0.853	
22. Man of vision.	S	55	47	3	0	0	0	1.50	0.307	not sig.
	SB	195	282	11	2	0	18	1.63	0.302	
23. Married with children.	S	2	53	49	0	0	1	2.45	0.286	.01
	SB	5	192	311	0	0	0	2.60	0.259	
24. Widower.	S	0	0	73	30	2	0	3.32	0.257	.01
	SB	0	1	459	46	2	0	3.10	0.099	
25. Previous success as an educational administrator.	S	46	54	5	0	0	0	1.61	0.333	.05
	SB	152	313	43	0	0	0	1.79	0.338	

APPENDIX TABLE A-2 (Continued)

(1) Item	(2) Sample S (105) SB (508)	(3) AM	(4) PS	(5) MMN	(6) Expectations PSN	(7) AMN	(8) NA	(9) X̄	(10) σ²	(11) Px²
26. Teetotaler.	S	2	24	76	3	0	0	2.76	0.277	not sig.
	SB	30	119	339	13	5	2	2.69	0.443	
27. Experienced teacher.	S	50	51	4	0	0	0	1.56	0.322	.01
	SB	163	293	51	0	0	1	1.78	0.373	
28. Have master's degree.	S	42	52	11	0	0	0	1.70	0.418	not sig.
	SB	195	234	77	0	0	2	1.77	0.483	
29. Conservative in dress.	S	2	75	27	1	0	0	2.26	0.248	.05
	SB	46	324	138	0	0	0	2.18	0.329	
30. Bachelor.	S	0	0	45	52	8	0	3.65	0.381	.01
	SB	3	2	383	106	14	0	3.25	0.285	
31. A man of intellectual brilliance.	S	0	35	60	5	1	4	2.71	0.359	.01
	SB	44	222	223	17	0	2	2.42	0.485	
32. Educationally "conservative."	S	0	31	39	29	6	0	3.10	0.791	.01
	SB	21	229	124	130	4	0	2.74	0.835	
33. Smoker.	S	0	0	103	2	0	0	3.02	0.019	not sig.
	SB	0	3	499	6	0	0	3.01	0.018	
34. Firm disciplinarian.	S	4	63	29	9	0	0	2.41	0.489	.01
	SB	80	316	79	29	3	1	2.13	0.579	
35. Jewish.	S	0	0	68	29	8	0	3.43	0.397	.01
	SB	0	0	435	62	11	0	3.17	0.181	
36. Educationally "progressive."	S	23	68	9	5	0	0	1.96	0.494	.05
	SB	159	315	21	12	1	0	1.78	0.419	
37. Protestant.	S	3	26	76	0	0	0	2.70	0.269	.01
	SB	2	42	463	0	1	0	2.91	0.099	
38. Persistent.	S	22	71	11	1	0	0	1.91	0.345	not sig.
	SB	84	357	57	9	1	0	1.99	0.366	
39. Under 30 years of age.	S	0	0	32	67	6	0	3.75	0.301	not sig.
	SB	0	4	181	285	38	0	3.70	0.374	

APPENDIX TABLE A-2 (Continued)

(1) Item	(2) Sample S (105) SB (508)	(3) AM	(4) PS	(5) MMN	(6) PSN	(7) AMN	(8) NA	(9) X̄	(10) σ²	(11) Pχ²
				Expectations						
40. 40 to 49 years of age.	S	1	40	62	2	0	0	2.62	0.293	not sig.
	SB	4	219	279	6	0	0	2.56	0.285	
41. Negro.	S	0	0	17	48	39	1	4.21	0.494	.01
	SB	1	1	182	221	103	0	3.83	0.559	
42. 30 to 39 years of age.	S	0	35	65	4	0	1	2.70	0.286	.01
	SB	2	72	351	79	4	0	3.02	0.344	
43. Catholic.	S	0	2	82	17	4	0	3.22	0.285	.01
	SB	0	1	462	39	6	0	3.10	0.116	
44. Female.	S	0	1	14	63	27	0	4.10	0.418	.01
	SB	1	2	145	282	78	0	3.85	0.451	
45. Sense of values.	S	79	26	0	0	0	0	1.25	0.186	.01
	SB	259	242	5	0	0	2	1.50	0.270	
46. Scholarly.	S	16	64	24	1	0	0	2.10	0.410	not sig.
	SB	106	314	85	2	0	1	1.97	0.391	
47. Dynamic leader.	S	16	81	8	0	0	0	1.92	0.223	.01
	SB	75	325	101	6	1	0	2.08	0.405	
48. Vigorous.	S	39	63	3	0	0	0	1.66	0.282	.01
	SB	81	387	38	0	0	2	1.92	0.228	
49. Republican.	S	0	15	88	1	1	0	2.89	0.177	.01
	SB	1	11	493	1	2	0	2.98	0.047	
50. Works well with other people.	S	83	22	0	0	0	0	1.21	0.166	.01
	SB	318	189	1	0	0	0	1.38	0.239	
51. Attractive personal appearance.	S	21	80	4	0	0	0	1.84	0.212	not sig.
	SB	78	387	43	0	0	0	1.93	0.233	
52. Divorced.	S	0	0	43	55	7	0	3.66	0.359	.01
	SB	0	3	294	186	25	0	3.46	0.359	
53. Businesslike in financial matters.	S	63	41	1	0	0	0	1.41	0.261	.01
	SB	220	274	14	0	0	0	1.59	0.296	
54. Promoted from within the local school system.	S	0	5	79	18	3	0	3.18	0.301	not sig.
	SB	3	61	357	76	10	1	3.06	0.370	

APPENDIX TABLE A–3. EXPECTATIONS FOR SUPERINTENDENT'S PARTICIPATIONS

Superintendent's and School Board Member's Question: "Would you please indicate how you feel about the following kinds of organizational memberships or activities of a Superintendent?"

(1) Item	(2) Sample S (105) SB (508)	(3) AM	(4) PS	(5) MMN	(6) PSN	(7) AMN	(8) NA	(9) $\bar{X}$	(10) σ^2	(11) $P\chi^2$	(12) Y	(13) N	(14) NA
				Expectations								Behavior	
1. Take an active part in local politics.	S	0	2	10	60	33	0	4.18	0.453	not sig.	9	96	0
	SB	1	15	70	249	171	2	4.14	0.595		50	434	24
2. Take an active part in church affairs.	S	4	62	36	3	0	0	2.36	0.364	not sig.	69	36	0
	SB	13	264	222	8	1	0	2.45	0.342		282	100	126
3. Take an active part in a local fraternal organization.	S	0	25	76	4	0	0	2.80	0.236	not sig.	32	59	14
	SB	2	141	335	26	0	4	2.76	0.291		209	150	149
4. Have his wife be active in the P.T.A.	S	0	25	58	18	4	0	3.01	0.562	not sig.	38	61	6
	SB	2	113	263	106	14	10	3.04	0.567		113	271	124
5. Join the taxpayers association.	S	1	12	60	29	3	0	3.20	0.511	not sig.	5	46	54
	SB	2	56	218	100	27	105	3.23	0.621		23	229	256
6. Take an active part in the local veterans' organization.	S	0	29	73	2	0	0	2.74	0.290	.05	17	53	35
	SB	1	90	368	33	5	11	2.90	0.292		84	282	142
7. Serve on several civic and welfare committees such as the Red Cross.	S	0	76	26	0	0	0	2.22	0.228	.01	84	21	0
	SB	10	261	215	20	1	1	2.49	0.380		305	128	75
8. Hold office in the town or city government, such as on the town finance committee.	S	0	1	13	48	42	1	4.26	0.758	not sig.	1	103	1
	SB	2	3	44	231	223	5	4.33	0.480		4	489	15
9. Participate in the affairs of the teachers' organization.	S	11	41	33	19	1	0	2.60	0.878	.05	69	35	1
	SB	25	227	112	121	17	6	2.76	0.969		297	164	48
10. Take an active part in a local service club (e.g., Rotary or Kiwanis).	S	4	75	25	1	0	0	2.22	0.280	.01	61	21	23
	SB	10	210	265	4	0	19	2.54	0.306		327	90	91
11. Take an active part in the local chamber of commerce.	S	1	45	57	1	0	1	2.56	0.285	.01	13	43	49
	SB	3	98	275	41	0	91	2.85	0.339		66	221	221

APPENDIX TABLE A–4. EXPECTATIONS FOR SUPERINTENDENT'S FRIENDSHIPS

Superintendent's and School Board Member's Question: "How do you feel about a Superintendent having an intimate friendship with . . . ?"

(1) Item	(2) Sample S (105) SB (508)	(3) AM	(4) PS	(5) MMN	(6) PSN	(7) AMN	(8) NA	(9) X̄	(10) σ^2	(11) $P\chi^2$	(12) Behavior Y	(13) Behavior N	(14) Behavior NA
1. A farm organization leader.	S	0	8	84	11	0	2	3.03	0.184	not sig.	14	58	33
	SB	1	33	313	26	7	128	3.01	0.239		37	232	239
2. A business organization leader.	S	0	10	80	14	1	0	3.06	0.268	not sig.	42	58	5
	SB	2	69	362	44	12	19	2.99	0.356		125	199	184
3. A labor organization leader.	S	0	4	70	26	4	1	3.29	0.359	not sig.	8	75	22
	SB	0	24	278	104	43	58	3.37	0.543		20	304	184
4. An individual school committee member.	S	0	1	47	50	7	0	3.60	0.393	.05	24	81	0
	SB	1	18	276	177	32	4	3.44	0.457		170	289	49
5. A newspaperman.	S	0	9	81	15	0	0	3.06	0.225	not sig.	19	85	1
	SB	0	59	352	75	8	14	3.06	0.332		97	308	103
6. A member of the town finance committee.	S	0	4	75	24	2	0	3.23	0.291	not sig.	28	77	0
	SB	1	40	330	94	30	13	3.22	0.470		67	331	110
7. A principal, teacher or other subordinate.	S	0	2	57	42	4	0	3.46	0.362	not sig.	35	70	0
	SB	0	28	274	171	31	4	3.41	0.475		139	273	96
8. A politician.	S	0	3	55	36	11	0	3.52	0.516	not sig.	15	89	1
	SB	1	10	234	180	72	11	3.63	0.588		74	334	100
9. A church leader.	S	0	9	83	13	0	0	3.04	0.208	.01	34	71	0
	SB	3	100	373	23	5	4	2.85	0.287		169	190	149
10. A leader of the local taxpayers association.	S	0	4	75	25	1	0	3.22	0.266	not sig.	6	62	37
	SB	1	19	252	100	22	114	3.31	0.438		23	266	219
11. A leader of a fraternal organization.	S	0	2	95	8	0	0	3.06	0.092	not sig.	30	72	3
	SB	0	30	427	32	10	9	3.05	0.202		94	221	193
12. A leader of the local veterans organization.	S	0	3	93	9	0	0	3.06	0.111	not sig.	18	85	2
	SB	0	32	428	34	7	7	3.03	0.187		72	263	173
13. A leader of the P.T.A.	S	1	11	83	10	0	0	2.97	0.237	.01	27	78	0
	SB	7	83	314	77	20	7	3.04	0.533		122	266	120
14. Individuals influential for economic reasons.	S	0	4	82	18	1	0	3.15	0.224	.05	27	78	0
	SB	1	32	326	112	28	9	3.27	0.449		68	286	154
15. A leader of a service club (e.g., Rotary or Kiwanis).	S	0	9	90	6	0	0	2.97	0.142	not sig.	40	57	8
	SB	1	74	383	23	6	21	2.92	0.250		161	183	164

APPENDIX TABLE A-5. EXPECTATIONS FOR SCHOOL BOARD MEMBERS' PERFORMANCES

Superintendent's and School Board Member's Question: "How do you feel about the school committee doing the following?"

(1) Item	(2) Sample S (105) SB (508)	(3) AM	(4) PS	(5) MMN	(6) PSN	(7) AMN	(8) NA	(9) $\bar{X}$	(10) σ^2	(11) Px^2	(12) Y	(12a) P	(13) N	(14) NA
				Expectations								Behavior		
1. Pay the necessary expenses to allow the Superintendent to attend meetings of professional organizations, visit other school systems, and do other things which will keep him up to date on educational developments.	S	55	50	0	0	0	0	1.48	0.249	.01	89	9	7	0
	SB	337	153	13	3	1	1	1.38	0.337		478	9	19	2
2. Allow the Superintendent to spend as much as a day a week away from his own school system engaging in professional activities not directly related to his job.	S	15	44	32	12	2	0	2.44	0.876	.01	44	26	35	0
	SB	36	83	144	176	66	3	3.30	1.229		153	4	336	15
3. Appoint only teachers nominated by the Superintendent.	S	53	50	2	0	0	0	1.51	0.288	.01	83	13	9	0
	SB	113	195	87	72	40	1	2.47	1.452		335	1	170	2
4. Concern itself with the personal life of the Superintendent.	S	2	17	41	38	7	0	3.30	0.780	.01	16	27	61	1
	SB	35	112	77	196	87	1	3.37	1.433		151	3	349	5
5. Concern itself with administrative problems.	S	4	14	19	47	21	0	3.64	1.126	.01	24	39	42	0
	SB	117	161	74	133	22	1	3.21	1.492		350	13	144	1
6. Protect the Superintendent from community pressures.	S	28	53	20	4	0	0	2.00	0.610	.01	48	32	25	0
	SB	224	216	41	22	4	1	1.75	0.705		390	6	83	39
7. Help "sell" good education to the community.	S	82	23	0	0	0	0	1.22	0.171	not sig.	72	26	7	0
	SB	376	125	3	1	1	2	1.27	0.246		450	5	48	5
8. Have a clear statement of the policies under which the school system should be operated.	S	73	30	2	0	0	0	1.32	0.257	not sig.	57	39	9	0
	SB	303	200	3	0	1	1	1.41	0.278		403	9	90	6
9. Take full responsibility for its decisions.	S	86	18	1	0	0	0	1.19	0.173	not sig.	79	23	3	0
	SB	421	84	1	1	0	1	1.18	0.161		492	1	13	2

APPENDIX TABLE A-5 (Continued)

(1) Item	(2) Sample S (105) SB (508)	(3) AM	(4) PS	(5) MMN	(6) PSN	(7) AMN	(8) NA	(9) $\bar{X}$	(10) σ^2	(11) $P\chi^2$	(12) Y	(12a) P	(13) N	(14) NA
				Expectations								Behavior		
10. Have a clear-cut statement of the division of responsibilities between the school committee and the Superintendent.	S	60	35	8	2	0	0	1.54	0.515	not sig.	57	34	14	0
	SB	237	216	35	19	0	1	1.68	0.582		351	6	148	2
11. Individual school committee members give directions to the Superintendent.	S	0	1	1	16	87	0	4.80	0.236	.01	7	14	84	0
	SB	9	14	41	213	230	1	4.26	0.735		126	8	367	7
12. Give directions directly to the Superintendent's subordinates.	S	1	1	0	7	96	0	4.86	0.287	.01	6	14	85	0
	SB	5	15	8	162	317	1	4.52	0.577		58	3	441	6
13. Keep the Superintendent informed of important matters that come to their attention.	S	59	42	2	2	0	0	1.50	0.402	.01	89	15	1	0
	SB	363	141	1	0	2	1	1.30	0.260		500	0	7	1
14. In deciding issues the members vote as representatives of important blocs or segments.	S	2	3	2	30	68	0	4.51	0.688	.01	10	18	77	0
	SB	7	29	38	218	215	1	4.19	1.642		99	13	393	1
15. Have open meetings.	S	17	45	31	10	1	1	2.35	0.806	.01	60	23	21	1
	SB	177	206	71	47	6	1	2.01	0.966		393	7	105	3
16. School committee members participate in community activities.	S	11	82	12	0	0	0	2.01	0.221	not sig.	89	15	1	0
	SB	102	349	56	0	0	1	1.91	0.303		484	16	6	2
17. "Every member of the committee imbued with the philosophy that schools exist only for the education of the future citizen."	S	44	51	5	5	0	0	1.72	0.581	not sig.	62	33	10	0
	SB	215	192	46	38	10	7	1.87	0.988		377	9	97	25
18. "A board which functions as a unit not as individuals."	S	76	20	5	2	2	0	1.42	0.682	.01	69	29	7	0
	SB	269	195	12	22	9	1	1.63	0.753		417	9	81	1
19. "Respect the judgment of the Superintendent on strictly educational matters."	S	53	50	1	1	0	0	1.52	0.326	not sig.	90	12	3	0
	SB	254	237	14	1	1	1	1.54	0.339		454	12	40	2
20. A committee not afraid to take stands regarding education in advance of community thinking.	S	47	53	3	1	1	0	1.63	0.462	not sig.	62	34	9	0
	SB	248	243	12	3	0	2	1.54	0.331		429	5	63	7

Notes for Appendix Table A-6

THE DIVISION OF LABOR INSTRUMENT

This instrument is different from the other role definition instruments in that each item has a separate set of response categories. The dimension involved in each set of response categories is the allocation of responsibility between the superintendent and school board.

First, the 13 items with the response categories used are presented. Then the superintendents' and school board members' responses to the items, plus certain summary information, are presented in Table A–6.

DIVISION OF LABOR ITEMS AND THEIR RESPONSE CATEGORIES

A. When a New Teacher Is to Be Hired.

(4) The school committee acts solely on the nomination of the Superintendent.

(3) The school committee usually acts on the nomination of the Superintendent, but sometimes takes a hand in interviewing candidates.

(2) The school committee or one of its subcommittees usually does the interviewing and selecting, although it gives some consideration to the recommendations of the Superintendent.

(1) The school committee or one of its subcommittees always interviews the candidates and selects the best one.

(X) Other.

(NA) No answer.

B. If a New Building Is Needed.

(4) The school committee expects the Superintendent to recommend a specific building program.

(3) The school committee expects the Superintendent to take the lead in drawing up a specific program in consultation with the school committee.

(2) The school committee would form its own building committee which would take the lead in drawing up a building program in consultation with the Superintendent.

(1) The school committee would form its own building committee to draw up a building program on its own.

(X) Other.

(NA) No answer.

C. When a New Textbook Is Needed.

(4) The school committee always accepts the recommendations of the Superintendent in choosing a textbook.

(3) The Superintendent takes the initiative in choosing textbooks, but the school committee also reads several textbooks and may sometimes choose one not recommended by the Superintendent.

(2) The school committee or one of its subcommittees takes the initiative, reading several different textbooks and selecting the best one in consultation with the Superintendent.

(1) The school committee or one of its subcommittees takes the initiative, reading several textbooks and selecting the best one on its own.

(X) Other.

(NA) No answer.

D. On the Budget.

(4) The Superintendent draws up a budget on his own.

(3) The Superintendent draws up a budget in consultation with the school committee or one of its subcommittees.

(2) The school committee or one of its subcommittees draws up a budget in consultation with the Superintendent.

(1) The school committee or one of its subcommittees draws up a budget on its own.

(X) Other.

(NA) No answer.

E. On Instructional Policy.

(4) The Superintendent makes all of the decisions on his own.

(3) The Superintendent makes recommendations in consultation with the school committee, and the school committee acts on them.

(2) The school committee formulates instructional policy in consultation with the Superintendent, and the Superintendent is directed to carry this out.

(1) The school committee formulates instructional policy on its own.

(X) Other.

(NA) No answer.

F. On Public Relations.

(4) The Superintendent is responsible for and administers the public relations program.

(3) The Superintendent formulates a public relations program in consultation with the school committee, and the Superintendent administers the program.

(2) The school committee formulates a public relations program and the Superintendent administers the program.

(1) The school committee is responsible for and administers the public relations program.

(X) Other.

(NA) No answer.

G. How Are Teachers' Grievances Handled?

(4) Teachers always bring their grievances to the school committee through the Superintendent.

(3) Teachers usually bring their grievances to the school committee through the Superintendent.

(2) Teachers usually bring their grievances directly to the school committee members.

(1) Teachers always bring their grievances directly to the school committee members.

(X) Other.

(NA) No answer.

H. Who Handles Relationships with Community Groups That Wish to Use Pupils for Their Own Purposes? (E.g. Use of school band, soliciting funds for charities, making posters, etc.)

(4) They are handled entirely by the Superintendent.

(3) They are handled largely by the Superintendent.

(2) They are handled largely by the school committee.

(1) They are handled entirely by the school committee.

(X) Other.

(NA) No answer.

I. When a Community Organization Wishes to Use School Property, the Request:

(4) Is handled at the Superintendent's discretion.

(3) Is acted upon by the Superintendent under policy approved by the school committee.

(2) Is usually presented to the school committee and acted upon by the school committee.

(1) Is always presented to the school committee and acted upon by the school committee.

(X) Other.

(NA) No answer.

J. Who Is Responsible for and Supervises the Maintenance Necessary to Keep the School Plant in Good Operating Condition?

(4) This is entirely the responsibility of the Superintendent.

(3) This is largely the responsibility of the Superintendent.

(2) This is largely the responsibility of the school committee.

(1) This is entirely the responsibility of the school committee.

(X) Other.

(NA) No answer.

K. Who Is Responsible for the Child Attendance Regulations?

(4) This is entirely the responsibility of the Superintendent.

(3) This is largely the responsibility of the Superintendent.

(2) This is largely the responsibility of the school committee.

(1) This is entirely the responsibility of the school committeee.

(X) Other.

(NA) No answer.

L. Who Makes Recommendations for Increases in Salaries of School System Employees?

(4) The Superintendent makes all such recommendations.

(3) The Superintendent makes most such recommendations.

(2) School committee members make most such recommendations.

(1) School committee members make all such recommendations.

(X) Other.

(NA) No answer.

M. Who Initiates Policy Matters?

(4) The Superintendent initiates all policy matters.

(3) The Superintendent initiates most policy matters.

(2) The school committee initiates most policy matters.

(1) The school committee initiates all policy matters.

(X) Other.

(NA) No answer.

COLUMN HEADINGS FOR APPENDIX TABLE A-6

(1) Item

(2) Size of Superintendent (S) and School Board Member (SB) samples.

(3)–(8) Expectation response categories for each item reported above. The responses indicate the way the superintendent or school board member answered the question: "What do you think, ideally, is the best way to do these things?"

(9) Variance of the distribution of responses for each sample for each item.

(10) Mean response of the superintendent and school board member samples for each expectation item.

(11) This column indicates whether the chi-square obtained for the comparison of the response distributions of the superintendent and school board member samples was significant at the .01 or .05 levels, or nonsignificant.

(12)–(17) The *actual* behavior response categories for each item reported above. The responses indicate how the superintendent or school board member answered the question: "How are these things *actually done* in your school system *now?*"

APPENDIX TABLE A–6. EXPECTATIONS FOR DIVISION OF LABOR

Superintendent and School Board Member Questions: "Different communities work out a different 'division of labor' between the school committee and the Superintendent. For the following activities please indicate: What do you think, ideally, is the best way to do these things? . . . How are things *actually done* in your school system *now*?"

(1) Item	(2) Sample S (105) SB (508)	(3) 1	(4) 2	(5) 3	(6) 4	(7) X	(8) NA	(9) σ^2	(10) $\bar{X}$	(11) P	(12) 1	(13) 2	(14) 3	(15) 4	(16) X	(17) NA
				Expectations									Behavior			
a. When a new teacher is to be hired.	S	0	0	30	74	0	1	0.320	3.71	.01	0	1	52	52	0	0
	SB	24	73	296	111	3	1	0.867	2.98		14	53	288	148	4	1
b. If a new building is needed.	S	0	19	64	19	2	1	0.583	3.00	.01	1	18	58	22	6	0
	SB	14	210	202	50	19	13	0.794	2.61		11	182	177	72	42	24
c. When a new textbook is needed.	S	0	4	7	92	0	2	0.316	3.85	.01	1	1	3	100	0	0
	SB	9	56	213	228	0	2	0.844	3.31		2	16	89	398	0	3
d. On the budget.	S	0	4	74	26	0	1	0.381	3.21	.01	0	3	68	34	0	0
	SB	2	70	409	25	0	2	0.303	2.90		1	53	395	58	0	1
e. On instructional policy.	S	0	9	76	19	0	1	0.406	3.10	.01	0	9	69	27	0	0
	SB	0	68	415	24	0	1	0.272	2.91		0	41	387	80	0	0
f. On public relations.	S	0	6	78	19	0	2	0.355	3.13	.01	2	3	67	33	0	0
	SB	20	82	364	35	0	7	0.567	2.83		22	56	302	105	0	23
g. How are teachers' grievances handled?	S	0	0	11	92	0	2	0.148	3.89	.01	0	2	55	48	0	0
	SB	10	17	193	284	0	4	0.681	3.49		5	47	302	149	0	5
h. Who handles relationships with community groups that wish to use pupils for their own purposes? (E.g., use of school band, soliciting funds for charities, making posters, etc.)	S	3	6	52	43	0	1	0.778	3.30	.01	2	11	60	32	0	0
	SB	102	111	225	62	0	8	1.416	2.49		97	111	228	60	0	12
i. When a community organization wishes to use school property, the request.	S	5	4	86	9	0	1	0.492	2.95	.01	8	18	71	8	0	0
	SB	107	133	245	19	0	4	1.136	2.35		102	156	229	15	1	5
j. Who is responsible for and supervises the maintenance necessary to keep the school plant in good operating condition?	S	0	6	46	52	0	1	0.566	3.44	.01	0	4	48	49	4	0
	SB	32	103	225	137	7	4	1.152	2.94		29	80	232	153	11	3
k. Who is responsible for the child attendance regulations?	S	2	4	16	82	0	1	0.622	3.71	.01	2	3	17	83	0	0
	SB	20	35	183	268	0	2	0.955	3.38		17	24	176	290	0	1
l. Who makes recommendations for increases in salaries of school system employees?	S	1	4	28	71	0	1	0.577	3.62	.01	1	4	38	62	0	0
	SB	38	70	237	158	0	5	1.180	3.02		28	77	222	177	0	4
m. Who initiates policy matters?	S	5	4	75	20	0	1	0.656	3.06	.01	3	3	87	12	0	0
	SB	44	122	287	54	0	1	0.938	2.69		35	105	308	60	0	0

Scales and Original Instruments

In this appendix are presented the Guttman scales used in this research and the items from which they were derived, and other instruments used in the analysis. The appendix is divided into four sections. The first (B–1) presents instruments, and scales derived from them, responded to by the superintendents' sample only; the second (B–2) presents an instrument (and a derived scale) responded to by the school board member sample only; the third section (B–3) presents instruments (and derived scales) responded to by both samples. Other instruments are presented in the fourth section, B–4. For the first three, the items for a given instrument together with the distribution of responses, are presented first, and then the scale based on these responses is described.

It will perhaps be helpful to go through one example in order to demonstrate the method of presenting the scales. Let us take the first scale in section 1, that on Level of Aspiration. This is a "three-item H-technique scale." This refers to the number of *contrived* items in the scale, not to the number of original items. Next, certain information on the reproducibility of the scale is shown. The reproducibility of this scale is 99.1, which is very high. However, since there are only three items in the scale it is possible to get high reproducibilities by chance. It is therefore desirable to calculate the chance or minimum reproducibility and compare it with the obtained reproducibility.[1]

The chance reproducibility of 92.7 obtained for the Level of Aspiration scale is quite high—higher in fact than Guttman's requirement of 90. Because of this feature of scale reproducibility with small numbers of items we adopted the arbitrary criterion of requiring an

---

[1] For a method of computing chance reproducibility see Matilda W. Riley, John W. Riley, Jr., and Jackson Toby, *Sociological Studies in Scale Analysis* (New Brunswick: Rutgers University Press, 1954), pp. 317–320.

obtained reproducibility of 95 (rounded) for all 3-item scales. In this case the obtained reproducibility of 99.1 is above both the chance reproducibility of 92.7 and the criterion of 95. Because the sampling distribution of the coefficient of reproducibility is unknown it is impossible to say whether it is significantly higher, however,

The error ratio is presented for each scale in an attempt to move toward the establishment of some standards of acceptability for scales with small numbers of items. It is defined here as:

$$\text{Error Ratio} = \frac{1 - \text{Obtained Reproducibility}}{1 - \text{Chance Reproducibility}}$$

This ratio was proposed by Borgatta, though his definition of it is in terms of errors rather than reproducibilities.[2] No criterion of acceptability is suggested, but it is hoped that experience with it will lead to some useful rule of thumb.

Ambiguous nonscale types (that is, those nonperfect patterns which could not be assigned a unique scale score by the criterion of minimum error) were scored by "middle class assignment," which assigns the score midway between the two most extreme scores which might be assigned according to the minimum error criterion.[3] This assignment violates the minimum error criterion. However, in counting the number of errors for the calculation of the reproducibility the assumption was made that this criterion had been followed. For example, on the Level of Aspiration Scale the pattern $+ - +$ was scored 2, for which the perfect type is $- + +$. One error was counted for the type since it could have been scored either 1 or 3 with only one error, and a half error was assigned to item a and a half to item b. This is not a conservative approach, but it seems a more accurate way to indicate the scalability of the set of items even though it overstates the reproducibility of the scale.

The section on the "definition of contrived items" should be read as

[2] Edgar F. Borgatta, "An Error Ratio for Scalogram Analysis," *Public Opinion Quarterly,* XIX (Spring, 1955), pp. 96–100. Borgatta defines the error ratio as the ratio of errors in the scale to the maximum number of errors for a scale of the same marginal frequencies. It can be shown that these two definitions of the error ratio are equivalent. Borgatta notes as advantages of the error ratio that it ". . . depends (it is not implied to be a linear dependence) on the amount of covariation among the items of the scale and is insensitive to effects of differences in marginal frequencies except as these place limits on covariation. Further, error ratios are directly comparable . . ." (p. 99).

[3] Edgar F. Borgatta and David G. Hays, "Some Limitations on the Arbitrary Classification of Non-Scale Response Patterns in a Guttman Scale," *Public Opinion Quarterly,* XVI (Fall, 1952) pp. 410–416.

follows, still taking the Level of Aspiration Scale as an example. Starting in the left-hand column and reading across, the table indicates that contrived item *a* is derived from original items 1, 13, and 5. Each of these original items had been scored positively if the response was either 4 ("I would very much like to") or 5 ("I am extremely anxious to"). Scored in this way these three original items had positive marginals of 23, 25, and 26 respectively. Respondents were scored positive on contrived item *a* if they had positive responses to at least two of the three original items. Under these definitions, contrived item *a* has a positive marginal of 25. The definitions of contrived items *b* and *c* can be read across in similar fashion. It will be noted that the definition of a positive response on the original items varies for the several contrived items.

APPENDIX TABLE B–1. SUPERINTENDENTS' SAMPLE ONLY
$(N = 105)$

a. LEVEL OF ASPIRATION

(1) THE INSTRUMENT

How Desirous Are You of Doing the Following Things? (Check one box to the right of each item below.)	I would not want to . . .	I am not especially anxious to . . .	I have some desire to . . .	I would very much like to . . .	I am extremely anxious to . . .
Response scored as →	(1)	(2)	(3)	(4)	(5)
1. Obtain a superintendency posisition in a larger school system.	18	42	22	17	6
2. Obtain a superintendency position which would carry more prestige.	23	40	28	12	2
3. Take every opportunity to advance my own career.	7	20	27	34	17
4. Obtain a superintendency position which would pay more money.	9	32	22	35	7
5. Obtain a superintendency position in a larger community.	12	39	28	20	6
6. Take a more important role in the activities of professional educational organizations.	4	26	47	22	6
7. Establish a good reputation among my professional colleagues.	2	6	12	49	36
8. Receive more recognition for my work from the citizens of my community.	2	19	37	37	10
9. Obtain a higher salary in my present position.	2	13	24	52	14
10. Eventually be superintendent in a city of a million or more.	78	23	3	1	0
11. Someday be president of the AASA.	61	37	3	4	0
12. Some day obtain a superintendency in a city of 300,000 or more.	55	38	9	2	1
13. Obtain a superintendency in a wealthy suburban community.	28	31	20	20	5

(1 = No answer)

(2) LEVEL OF ASPIRATION SCALE: A 3-item H-technique scale. A high score means high aspiration.

Reproducibility = 99.1
Chance Reproducibility = 92.7   Error Ratio = .12

The Scale						Definition of Contrived Items			
Scale Score	Frequency	Percent	Response Pattern			Frequency	Contrived Item	Original Item	Positive Response	Positive Marginal

Scale Score	Frequency	Percent	A	B	C	Frequency	Contrived Item	Original Item	Positive Response	Positive Marginal
3	22	21.0	+	+	+	22	$a =$ {1, 13, 5}	1	4, 5	23 }
								13	4, 5	25 } 2/3 pos. = 25
2	31	29.5	−	+	+	28		5	4, 5	26 }
			+	−	+	3	$b =$ {2, 11, 4}	2	3, 4, 5	42 }
1	30	28.6	−	−	+	30		11	2, 3, 4, 5	44 } 2/3 pos. = 50
0	22	21.0	−	−	−	22		4	3, 4, 5	64 }
							$c =$ {6, 3, 9}	6	3, 4, 5	75 }
								3	3, 4, 5	78 } 2/3 pos. = 83
								9	3, 4, 5	90 }

APPENDIX TABLE B–1 (Continued)

b. JOB SATISFACTION

(1) THE INSTRUMENT

Please check the box on the right which best indicates your satisfaction or dissatisfaction with the corresponding aspect of your *present job*.	Very well satisfied	Fairly well satisfied	Fairly dissatisfied	Very dissatisfied
Response scored as →	(4)	(3)	(2)	(1)
1. Are you satisfied that you have been given enough authority by your school committee to do your job well?	69	31	2	3
2. How satisfied are you with your present job when you compare it to similar superintendencies in the state?	52	47	4	2
3. Are you satisfied with the progress you are making toward the goals which you set for yourself in your present position?	18	79	7	1
4. Are you satisfied that the people of your community give proper recognition to your work as superintendent?	33	65	5	2
5. How satisfied are you with your present salary?	11	71	18	5
6. How satisfied are you with your school committee?	55	39	8	3
7. How satisfied are you with your staff?	28	75	2	0
8. How satisfied are you with the amount of time which you must devote to your job?	17	56	29	3
9. How satisfied are you with the amount of interest shown by the community in its school system?	22	59	20	4
10. On the whole, are you satisfied that the school committee accepts you as a professional expert to the degree to which you feel you are entitled by reason of your position, training, and experience?	55	41	7	2
11. How satisfied are you with your present job when you consider the expectations you had when you took the job?	47	48	8	2
12. How satisfied are you with your present job in the light of your career expectations?	31	63	11	0

(2) JOB SATISFACTION SCALE: A 3-item H-technique scale. A high score means high satisfaction.

Reproducibility $= 99.4$
Chance Reproducibility $= 92.1$ Error Ratio $= .08$

The Scale					Definition of Contrived Items			
Scale Score	Fre-quency	Percent	Response Pattern	Fre-quency	Con-trived Item	Original Item	Positive Response	Positive Marginal
			A B C					
3	25	23.8	+ + +	25	$a =$	7	4	28 ⎫
2	26	24.8	− + +	25		12	4	31 ⎬ 2/3 pos. = 26
			+ − +	1		4	4	33 ⎭
1	31	29.5	− − +	30	$b =$	11	4	47 ⎫
			− + −	1		2	4	52 ⎬ 2/3 pos. = 51
0	23	21.9	− − −	23		10	4	55 ⎭
					$c =$	1	4	69 ⎫
						9	3, 4	81 ⎬ 2/3 pos. = 81
						5	3, 4	82 ⎭

APPENDIX TABLE B–1 (Continued)

c. CAREER SATISFACTION
(1) THE INSTRUMENT

In answering the following questions please consider the *superintendency as a career* rather than your present job.

1. How much does the superintendency give you a chance to do the things at which you are best?

Code	Frequency	
4	52	A very good chance
3	42	A fairly good chance
2	10	Some chance
1	1	Very little

2. How does the superintendency compare with other types of work?

Code	Frequency	
4	6	It is the most satisfying career a man could follow.
3	66	It is one of the most satisfying careers.
2	32	It is as satisfying as most careers.
1	1	It is less satisfying than most careers.

3. Considering the superintendency as a whole, how well do you like it?

Code	Frequency	
4	83	I like it very much
3	20	I like it fairly well
2	2	I don't like it too well
1	0	I don't like it at all

4. Are there any features of the job of superintendent which you dislike?

Code	Frequency	
1	0	Very many
2	26	Quite a few
3	73	Only a couple
4	6	None

5. If you "had to do it over again" would you enter the field of the superintendency?

Code	Frequency	
4	45	Definitely yes
3	44	Probably yes
2	14	Probably no
1	2	Definitely no

6. Are you making progress toward the goals you had set for yourself in your occupational career?

Code	Frequency	
4	5	I have achieved my goals
3	75	I am making good progress toward my goals
2	24	I am making some progress toward my goals
1	0	I don't seem to be getting anywhere
0	1	No answer

7. Has the superintendency lived up to the expectations you had before you entered it?

Code	Frequency	
4	18	Yes, in all respects
3	83	In most ways
2	4	In only a few ways
1	0	Not at all

8. If a young friend of yours were entering the field of education would you advise him to aim for the superintendency?

Code	Frequency	
4	31	Definitely yes
3	62	Probably yes
2	10	Probably no
1	2	Definitely no

9. Do you feel that the work which you do as a superintendent is satisfying?

Code	Frequency	
4	64	Very satisfying
3	41	Fairly satisfying
2	0	Fairly dissatisfying
1	0	Very dissatisfying

10. How many features of the job of superintendent do you especially like?

Code	Frequency	
4	72	Very many
3	31	Quite a few
2	2	Some
1	0	Very few

APPENDIX TABLE B-1 (continued)

11. In general do you feel that superintendents are given adequate recognition when compared to that received by other professionals such as lawyers and doctors?

Code	Frequency	
4	8	Yes definitely
3	44	In most respects
2	48	In some respects
1	5	Not at all

12. How much opportunity does the superintendency give you to follow your leisure time interests?

Code	Frequency	
4	1	Very adequate
3	36	Adequate
2	52	Inadequate
1	15	Very inadequate
0	1	No answer

(2) CAREER SATISFACTION SCALE: A 3-item H-technique scale. A high score means high satisfaction.

Reproducibility = 98.4
Chance Reproducibility = 92.1   Error Ratio = .20

	The Scale					Definition of Contrived Items		
Scale Score	Frequency	Percent	Response Pattern	Frequency	Contrived Item	Original Item	Positive Response	Positive Marginal
			A B C					
3	19	18.1	+ + +	19	$a =$	7	4	18
						8	4	31 } 2/3 pos. = 22
2	31	29.5	− + +	28		12	3, 4	37
			+ − +	3				
1	29	27.6	− − +	27	$b =$	5	4	45
			− + −	2		1	4	52 } 2/3 pos. = 49
0	26	24.8	− − −	26		11	3, 4	52
					$c =$	10	4	72
						2	3, 4	72 } 2/3 pos. = 77
						6	3, 4	80

APPENDIX TABLE B–1 (Continued)

d. SUPERINTENDENT'S INITIATIVE:

(1) THE INSTRUMENT

Please indicate your agreement or disagreement with each of the following statements by checking the appropriate box to the right.	Response Categories*			
	1	2	3	4
1. A superintendent should use his own judgment in interpreting school committee rules in specific cases. (I)	3	7	73	22
2. A superintendent should not "stick his neck out" by taking a definite position when a controversy arises about the interpretation of school committee rules. (L)	9	29	60	7
3. The only way a superintendent can keep out of "hot water" is to stick strictly to the letter of the rules adopted by the school committee. (L)	9	25	66	5
4. It is more important for a superintendent to abide by the spirit of school committee rules, than to stick to the letter of such rules. (I)	0	8	72	25
5. In most cases school committee rules should be adhered to, but there are always some exceptional cases in which the superintendent should exercise his own judgment. (I)	1	20	60	24
6. In deciding whether to give a literal interpretation to school committee rules, the "burden of proof" to show why this should not be done is always on the superintendent. (L)	13	62	30	0
7. It cannot be expected that school committee rules will deal justly with all specific cases if given a literal interpretation; the superintendent must use his own judgment. (I)	0	12	73	20
8. The superintendent is the executive officer of the school committee and as such has no discretionary power. (L)	2	14	68	21
9. Although legal responsibility for adopting rules and regulations which govern a school system rests with the school committee, the superintendent has a responsibility to interpret those rules in a way in which his professional training indicates will be best for the School System. (I)	0	8	69	28
10. School committee rules are absolutely binding on the superintendent. (L)	8	56	40	1
11. If school committee rules are to be given any free interpretation, the committee itself must do it, not the superintendent. (L)	7	32	63	3
12. School committee rules are only a framework within which the superintendent operates; day to day administrative decisions always demand that the superintendent use his own discretion. (I)	2	8	70	25

* Items marked (I) are "initiative items" and are coded from 4 = strongly agree to 1 = strongly disagree; items marked (L) are "legalistic items" and are coded from 1 = strongly agree to 4 = strongly disagree.

(2) SUPERINTENDENT'S INITIATIVE SCALE: A 3-item H-technique scale. A high score means high initiative.

Reproducibility $= 98.4$
Chance Reproducibility $= 93.0$　　Error Ratio $= .23$

The Scale					Definition of Contrived Items			
Scale Score	Fre-quency	Percent	Response Pattern	Fre-quency	Con-trived Item	Original Item	Positive Response	Positive Marginal
			A B C					
3	15	14.3	+ + +	14	$a =$	7	4	20 ⎫
			+ + −	1		8	4	21 ⎬ 2/3 pos. = 19
						5	4	24 ⎭
2	12	11.4	− + +	10	$b =$	12	4	25 ⎫
			+ − +	2		9	4	28 ⎬ 2/3 pos. = 24
1	47	44.8	− − +	47		10	3, 4	41 ⎭
0	31	29.5	− − −	29	$c =$	11	3, 4	66 ⎫
			+ − −	2		2	3, 4	67 ⎬ 2/3 pos. = 73
						3	3, 4	71 ⎭

APPENDIX TABLE B–1 (Continued)

e. WORRY:

(1) THE INSTRUMENT

Please indicate your agreement or disagreement with each of the following statements by checking the appropriate box to the right.	Never	Occasionally	Fairly Often	Frequently
1. Do the problems associated with your job keep you awake at night?	27	72	4	2
2. Once you have made a decision do you find yourself worrying whether you made the right decision?	16	82	7	0
3. Are you nervous when you go to School Committee meetings?	53	46	4	2
4. Do you "take your job home with you" in the sense that you think about your job when you are doing other things?	7	61	26	11
5. Do you breathe a sigh of relief when you travel away from your community?	54	39	6	6
6. Do you worry about what an individual or group will do if you make a decision contrary to their wishes?	34	65	6	0

(2) WORRY SCALE: A 3-item H-technique scale. A high score means high worry.

Reproducibility = 95.9
Chance Reproducibility = 90.7   Error Ratio = .44

The Scale | | | | | Definition of Contrived Items

Scale Score	Frequency	Percent	Response Pattern			Frequency	Contrived Item	Original Item	Positive Response	Positive Marginal	
			A	B	C						
3	17	16.2	+	+	+	17	$a =$	4	3, 4	37	2/2 pos. = 27
								5	2, 3, 4	51	
2	27	25.7	−	+	+	20					
			+	−	+	7	$b =$	3	2, 3, 4	52	2/2 pos. = 40
								6	2, 3, 4	71	
1	31	29.5	−	−	+	28					
			−	+	−	3	$c =$	1	2, 3, 4	78	2/2 pos. = 72
								2	2, 3, 4	89	
0	30	28.6	−	−	−	27					
			+	−	−	3					

APPENDIX TABLE B–2. SCHOOL BOARD SAMPLE ONLY

$$(N = 508)$$

SCHOOL BOARD MEMBER SATISFACTION

(1) THE INSTRUMENT

The following statements refer to various aspects of the way groups function which we would like you to apply to your school committee. After each statement would you say which of the categories on the card best describes *your feeling* about the way your committee functions.	Very well satisfied	Fairly well satisfied	Fairly dissatisfied	Very dissatisfied	No Answer
Response scored as →	(4)	(3)	(2)	(1)	(0)
1. The way individual school committee members fulfill the responsibilities of their office.	289	169	35	15	—
2. Goals or guiding principles of your school committee.	255	209	34	10	—
3. Persistence of the committee in doing a job.	306	155	39	8	—
4. The leadership in your committee.	266	166	44	27	5
5. The way decisions are reached.	268	167	50	23	—
6. Interest shown by other members.	321	161	19	7	—
7. Attempts to understand different points of view.	270	170	47	21	—
8. My own position on this committee.	287	186	23	11	1
9. The level of information about the schools and educational practices.	194	233	62	18	1
10. The way school committee meetings are conducted.	319	136	37	16	—

(2) SCHOOL BOARD MEMBER SATISFACTION SCALE: A 3-item H-technique scale. A high score means high satisfaction.

Reproducibility   = 98.0
Chance Reproducibility = 91.2   Error Ratio = .23

		The Scale				Definition of Contrived Items			
Scale Score	Frequency	Percent	Response Pattern	Frequency	Contrived Item	Original Item	Positive Response*	Positive Marginal	
			A B C						
3	123	24.2	+ + +	120	$a =$	9	4	194	2/2 pos. = 141
			+ + −	3		2	4	255	
2	161	31.7	− + +	147	$b =$	4	4	266	
			+ − +	14		7	4	270	2/3 pos. = 279
1	107	21.1	− − +	98		8	4	287	
			− + −	9		10	4	319	
0	117	23.0	− − −	113	$c =$	6	4	321	2/3 pos. = 379
			+ − −	4		5	3, 4	435	

* 7 no answer responses coded as negative.

APPENDIX TABLE B–3. COMBINED SAMPLES
$(N = 613)$

a. IDEAL DIVISION OF LABOR: A 3-item *H*-technique scale. A high score means more responsibility for the superintendent. (The questions on which these scales are based are found in Appendix A.)

The Scale for Combined Samples

Scale Score	Frequency	Percent	Response Pattern A B C	Frequency
3	123	21.6	+ + +	114
			+ + −	9
2	180	31.6	− + +	164
			+ − +	16
1	191	33.5	− − −	143
			− + −	48
0	76	13.3	− − −	74
			+ − −	2
	570	100.0		
	43		No ans.	

Reprod. = 95.6
Ch. Reprod. = 92.0   E.R. = .55

Definition of Contrived Items

Contrived Item	Original Item	Positive Response	Positive Marginal
$a =$	8	4	146
	1	4	244 2/3 pos. = 141
	12	4	280
$b =$	3	4	389
	11	4	406 2/3 pos. = 335
	9	3, 4	442
$c =$	7	4	450
	13	3, 4	502 2/3 pos. = 437
	10	3, 4	536

Scale for Superintendent Sample Only

Scale Score	Frequency	Percent	Response Pattern A B C	Frequency
3	61	59.2	+ + +	61
2	37	35.9	− + +	34
			+ − +	3
1	5	4.9	− − +	3
			− + −	2
0	0	0.0	− − −	0
	103	100.0		
	2		No ans.	

Reprod. = 98.4
Ch. Reprod. = 98.2   E.R. = .89.

Scale for SB Sample Only

Scale Score	Frequency	Percent	Response Pattern A B C	Frequency
3	62	13.3	+ + +	53
			+ + −	9
2	143	30.6	− + +	130
			+ − +	13
1	186	39.8	− − +	140
			− + −	46
0	76	16.3	− − −	74
			+ − −	2
	467	100.0		
	41		No ans.	

Reprod. = 95.0
Ch. Reprod. = 92.5   E.R. = .67

b. RATING OF SUPERINTENDENT ON PERSONAL CHARACTERISTICS:
(1) THE INSTRUMENT

For each of the following characteristics would you please check the statement which most nearly applies to you (superintendent's version) applies to your superintendent (school board version).

1. Personal Appearance	S	SB	Code
A commanding personal appearance	3	66	5
An attractive personal appearance	33	217	4
About average in personal appearance	65	203	3
Do not make an especially good personal appearance	3	21	2
Make a poor personal appearance	0	1	1
No answer	1	0	0

2. Practicality	S	SB	Code
Exceptionally hard-headed and practical	2	40	5
Very practical	68	311	4
Fairly practical	35	142	3
Rather impractical	0	15	2
Very impractical	0	0	1

APPENDIX TABLE B-3 (Continued)

3. Clearness of Expression	S	SB	Code	4. Intelligence	S	SB	Code
Exceptional ability to express ideas clearly	6	125	5	A man of intellectual brilliance	1	39	5
Above average ability to express ideas clearly	59	206	4	A man of superior intelligence	44	272	4
Average ability to express ideas clearly	39	155	3	A man of average intelligence	59	184	3
Do not express ideas clearly	1	20	2	Usually intelligent, but not very bright in some things	1	12	2
Have great difficulty in expressing ideas clearly	0	2	1	Not very intelligent at all	0	0	1
				No answer	0	1	0

5. Level of Information	S	SB	Code	6. Working with Other People	S	SB	Code
Exceptionally well informed on modern educational practices	5	136	5	Work exceptionally well with other people	44	145	5
Very well informed on modern educational practices	62	280	4	Work very well with other people	51	196	4
Fairly well informed on modern educational practices	38	84	3	Get along with other people	10	84	3
Not very well informed on modern educational practices	0	7	2	Sometimes create friction when working with other people	0	80	2
Very poorly informed on modern educational practices	0	0	1	Do not seem to be able to work with other people at all well	0	3	1
No answer	0	1	0				

7. Tact	S	SB	Code	8. Business Sense	S	SB	Code
Shows unusual tact; always says just the right thing	1	37	5	Shows extremely good business sense in financial matters	13	115	5
Very tactful; rarely says the wrong thing	51	194	4	Excellent business sense in financial matters	46	178	4
Usually tactful, but occasionally blunt	53	195	3	Shows rather good business sense in financial matters	46	181	3
Shows tact, but sometimes offends others	0	71	2	Not especially businesslike in financial matters	0	26	2
Very blunt; constantly offending people	0	10	1	Shows poor business sense in financial matters	0	7	1
No answer	0	1	0	No answer	0	1	0

9. Persistence	S	SB	Code	10. Sense of Values	S	SB	Code
Exceedingly persistent; voluntarily bends every energy to finish task	24	111	5	Unfailingly keen insight in distinguishing the important from the unimportant	8	91	5
Unusually persistent; seldom deterred by difficulties	49	209	4	Generally distinguishes the important from the unimportant even when confusion might be easy	79	209	4
Fairly persistent, ordinarily finishes a task before leaving it	30	145	3	Distinguishes satisfactorily between the important and the unimportant	18	121	3
Tends to leave difficult tasks unfinished unless encouraged to continue	2	39	2	Occasionally confuses the important with the unimportant	0	36	2
Easily deterred by obstacles, often gives up even if encouraged to continue	0	4	1	Commonly neglects crucial issues through attention to the unimportant	0	6	1

APPENDIX TABLE B–3 (Continued)

(2) RATING SCALE FOR SUPERINTENDENT'S PERSONAL CHARACTERISTICS: A 3-item
H-technique scale. A high score means a high rating.

The Scale for Combined Samples | Definition of Contrived Items

Scale Score	Frequency	Percent	Response Pattern A B C	Frequency		Contrived Item	Original Item	Positive Response	Positive Marginal
3	150	24.5	+ + +	146			9	5	135
			+ + −	4		$a =$	6	5	189 } 2/3 pos. = 166
2	221	36.0	− + +	206			1	4, 5	319
			+ − +	15			8	4, 5	352
1	131	21.4	− − +	104		$b =$	4	4, 5	356 } 2/3 pos. = 383
			− + −	27			3	4, 5	396
0	111	18.1	− − −	110			2	4, 5	421
			+ − −	1		$c =$	10	4, 5	432 } 2/3 pos. = 471
							5	4, 5	483

Reprod.　　= 97.4　E.R. = .32
Ch. Reprod. = 91.8

Scale for Superintendent Sample Only

Scale Score	Frequency	Percent	Response Pattern A B C	Frequency
3	21	20.0	+ + +	19
			+ + −	2
2	42	40.0	− + +	35
			+ − +	7
1	20	19.0	− − +	16
			− + −	4
0	22	21.0	− − −	22

Reprod.　　= 95.9　E.R. = .46
Ch. Reprod. = 91.1

Scale for *SB* Sample Only

Scale Score	Frequency	Percent	Response Pattern A B C	Frequency
3	129	25.4	+ + +	127
			+ + −	2
2	179	35.2	− + +	171
			+ − +	8
1	111	21.9	− − +	88
			− + −	23
0	89	17.5	− − −	88
			+ − −	1

Reprod.　　= 97.8　E.R. = .28
Ch. Reprod. = 92.0

APPENDIX TABLE B–3 (Continued)

c. EDUCATIONAL PROGRESSIVISM

(1) THE INSTRUMENT

How do you feel about these policies or programs?	Sample	Answer Categories* 1	2	3	4	NA	Other
1. Pupils are separated into "bright" and "slow" classes. (T)	S	17	29	46	8	1	4
	SB	117	214	140	30	4	3
2. In the first six grades pupils must meet specified academic standards in order to be promoted. (T)	S	6	47	26	16	0	
	SB	176	253	66	10	3	
3. A maximum class size of twenty-five in elementary schools. (P)	S	2	0	28	75	0	
	SB	7	24	158	318	1	
4. Sex education in high schools. (P)	S	11	23	55	15	1	
	SB	39	122	254	85	8	
5. A great deal of emphasis on a program of extra-curricular activities. (P)	S	2	23	57	23	0	
	SB	13	157	228	109	1	
6. Some kind of psychological guidance facilities available to pupils through the schools. (P)	S	2	1	32	70	0	
	SB	1	9	229	267	1	
7. Numerical grading given on regular report cards in the first six grades. (T)	S	1	8	53	43	0	
	SB	80	188	189	40	11	
8. Different salaries for elementary and high school teachers. (T)	S	7	3	21	74	0	
	SB	39	121	235	111	2	
9. Teachers act as advisers in extracurricular activities. (P)	S	0	1	36	68	0	
	SB	1	11	265	229	2	
10. More emphasis is placed on developing individual interests of the pupils, rather than on teaching subject matter. (P)	S	2	10	48	44	1	
	SB	12	150	224	117	5	
11. More emphasis is placed on teaching subject matter, rather than on developing individual interests of the pupils. (T)	S	0	14	58	31	2	
	SB	12	155	223	113	5	
12. Teacher participation in policy formation. (P)	S	1	2	41	61	0	
	SB	6	53	279	169	1	
13. Pupils regularly form into lines on the way to and from classes. (T)	S	4	20	58	21	2	
	SB	96	250	131	24	7	
14. Use of schools as neighborhood centers. (P)	S	2	0	28	75	0	
	SB	8	37	210	252	1	
15. Extensive use of psychological and mental tests. (P)	S	1	3	56	44	1	
	SB	4	83	279	136	6	

* The original check list read: A = highly desirable, B = desirable, C = undesirable, D = highly undesirable.

The items were classified as "Progressive" or "Traditional" (indicated by P and T respectively following the items) on the basis of their categorization by five raters, faculty members at the Harvard Graduate School of Education. On the 75 categorizations (5×15 items) there was 96% agreement.

APPENDIX TABLE B–3 (Continued)

(2) EDUCATIONAL PROGRESSIVISM SCALE: A 3-item H-technique scale. A high score means high progressivism.

The Scale for Combined Samples

Scale Score	Frequency	Percent	Response Pattern A B C	Frequency
3	103	16.8	+ + +	102
			+ + −	1
2	164	26.8	− + +	142
			+ − +	22
1	224	36.5	− − +	202
			− + −	22
0	122	19.9	− − −	119
			+ − −	3

Reprod. = 97.4
Ch. Reprod. = 92.6 E.R. = .35

Definition of Contrived Items

Contrived Item	Original Item	Positive Response*	Positive Marginal
$a =$	9	3, 4	118 ⎫
	17	4	161 ⎬ 2/3 pos. = 128
	15	4	185 ⎭
$b =$	19	4	230 ⎫
	20	3, 4	234 ⎬ 2/3 pos. = 243
	21	4	327 ⎭
$c =$	14	3, 4	325 ⎫
	13	4	337 ⎪
	10	4	393 ⎬ 2/4 pos. = 463
	18	3, 4	425 ⎭

Scale for Superintendent Sample Only

Scale Score	Frequency	Percent	Response Pattern A B C	Frequency
3	50	47.6	+ + +	49
			+ + −	1
2	33	31.4	− + +	26
			+ − +	7
1	18	17.1	− − +	15
			− + −	3
0	4	3.8	− − −	3
			+ − −	1

Reprod. = 96.2
Ch. Reprod. = 93.5 E.R. = .58

Scale for SB Sample Only

Scale Score	Frequency	Percent	Response Pattern A B C	Frequency
3	53	10.4	+ + +	53
2	131	25.8	− + +	116
			+ − +	15
1	206	40.6	− − +	187
			− + −	19
0	118	23.2	− − −	116
			+ − −	2

Reprod. = 97.4
Ch. Reprod. = 93.8 E.R. = .42

* No answer coded negative (traditional).

APPENDIX TABLE B–4. OTHER INSTRUMENTS

a. Political-Economic Conservatism Scale*

Instructions for Superintendents and School Board Members: The best answer to each statement below is *your personal opinion.* We have tried to cover many different points of view. You may find yourself agreeing strongly with some of the statements, disagreeing just as strongly with others, and perhaps uncertain about others. Whether you agree or disagree with any statement, you can be sure that many other people feel just the same way that you do.

Mark each statement in the box at the right according to how much you agree or disagree with it. *Please mark every one.* Write in +1, +2, +3; or −1, −2, −3; depending on how you feel in each case.

+1: I agree a little   −1: I disagree a little
+2: I agree pretty much   −2: I disagree pretty much
+3: I agree very much   −3: I disagree very much

1. When private enterprise does not do the job, it is up to the government to step in and meet the public's need for housing, water power, and the like.

2. Men like Henry Ford or J. P. Morgan, who overcame all competition on the road to success, are models for all young people to admire and imitate.

3. The government should own and operate all public utilities (railroad, gas, electricity, etc.).

4. In general, full economic security is bad; most men wouldn't work if they didn't need the money for eating and living.

5. The only way to do away with poverty is to make basic changes in our political and economic system.

6. There should be some upper limit, such as $50,000 per year, on how much a person can earn.

7. At this time, powerful "big business" is a greater danger than powerful "big unions" to our national welfare.

8. We need more government controls over business practices and profits.

9. Labor unions in large corporations should be given a larger part in deciding company policy.

10. The government should develop a program of health insurance and medical care.

11. America may not be perfect, but the American way has brought us about as close as human beings can get to a perfect society.

12. Strong labor unions are necessary if the working man is to get greater security and a better standard of living.

* We are indebted to Dr. Daniel J. Levinson for making this short form of the PEC Scale available to us.

b. Rating Scale of Superintendent's Functions

Question for Superintendents: What kind of job do you think you are doing in each of the following activities associated with your job? (Response categories: Excellent, Good, Fair, Poor.)

Question for School Board Members: Could you indicate how you feel about how the superintendent is carrying out these parts of his job? (Response categories: Excellent, Good, Fair, Poor.)

Items

1. *Personnel Administration:* The selection of teachers and other school employees, salaries, assignments, promotions, and separations from service.
2. *Financial Administration:* Budgets, handling of funds, purchases, and accounting.
3. *School Plant Management:* Site selection, relations with architects and contractors, furniture and equipment, repairs, and custodial services.
4. *Instructional Direction:* Curriculum planning, methods of teaching, evaluation of activities, working with teachers, audio-visual materials, textbooks, and libraries.
5. *Pupil Services Supplementary to Instruction:* Transportation, health services, and school lunches.
6. *Public Relations:* Community contacts with organizations, newspapers, radio, reporting to the public.
7. *General Planning:* for the school program as a whole.

c. Motivation Categories

Question for the Superintendent: Could you indicate what you think are the chief reasons each member ran for election to the school committee?

Response Categories: He (or she):

1. Felt that someone had to see that school expenditures were increased.
2. Wanted certain friends to get in or to advance in the school system.
3. Felt that the school superintendent should be removed.
4. A certain group in the community felt that they should be represented on the school committee.
5. Felt that someone had to see that school expenditures were decreased.
6. Felt it to be his (her) civic duty.
7. Did not like the way his (her) children were being educated.
8. Disapproved of the way the schools were being run.
9. Was interested in getting some experience in politics.
10. Other (what?)

Impact of Size of School Board
and Number of Response Categories
on the V Measure
of Microscopic Role Consensus

In the analysis of microscopic role consensus one of the measures of consensus used was the variance within the school board, a small variance denoting high consensus. Two factors which might not be considered an intrinsic part of consensus but which nevertheless contribute directly to the magnitude of a particular consensus score, because of the computational method followed, are size of school board and number of categories to which the individual members may respond. Here we will show how size and number of categories are related to the V consensus score and how to eliminate their effect on variance.

When the variance is taken as $\Sigma x^2/n_{sb}$ (the V of our analysis), the chance or sampling distribution of the variance is a function of the number of respondents and the number of possible response choices. Since all the items used in the microscopic analysis were taken from instruments allowing five possible responses, we shall deal first of all with this situation. The procedure to follow is to find all possible arrangements wherein n_{sb} people may be assigned to 5 categories. In general, the numbers of arrangements is $5^{n_{sb}}$, and the problem is to find how many of these are distinct arrangements, the frequency, and the V score of each.

For $n_{sb} = 2$, the arrangements, their frequencies and variances are:

* This appendix was prepared by William Douglas Brooks.

Arrangement	f	V
2^i	5	0.000
$1^i, 1^{i+1}$	8	0.250
$1^i, 1^{i+2}$	6	1.000
$1^i, 1^{i+3}$	4	2.250
$1^i, 1^{i+4}$	2	4.000

and the mean of this distribution is 1.000. The superscript i can take on any of the values 1 to 5. Thus, with $i = 1$, it means that, for example, in the pattern $2^i,2$ people give a 1 response, or with $i = 2$, the pattern $1^i, 1^{i+3}$ means that one person responds 2 while the other gives a 5 response. This arrangement gives the same variance as 1 person responding 1 and the other 4.

For $n_{sb} = 3$, the arrangements, their frequencies, and variances are:

Arrangement	f	V
3^i	5	0.000
$2^i, 1^{i+1}$	24	0.222
$2^i, 1^{i+2}$	18	0.889
$2^i, 1^{i+3}$	12	2.000
$2^i, 1^{i+4}$	6	3.556
$1^i, 1^{i+1}, 1^{i+2}$	18	0.667
$1^i, 1^{i+1}, 1^{i+3}$	24	1.556
$1^i, 1^{i+1}, 1^{i+4}$	12	2.889
$1^i, 1^{i+2}, 1^{i+4}$	6	2.667

and the mean of this distribution is 1.333.

Likewise for $n_{sb} = 5$, the mean is 1.600, or in general, the mean of the sampling distribution is:

$$E(V) = \frac{n_{sb} - 1}{n_{sb}} \cdot \frac{n_c^2 - 1}{12}$$

where $E(V)$ is the expected value of V, n_{sb} is the number of school board members, and n_c is the number of categories. Furthermore, since:

$$V' = \frac{\sum x^2}{n_{sb} - 1} = \frac{n_{sb}}{n_{sb} - 1} V$$

the expected value of V',

$$E(V') = \frac{n_{sb}}{n_{sb} - 1} E(V)$$

or

$$E(V') = \frac{n_c^2 - 1}{12}$$

a quantity dependent solely on the number of categories, or one from which the size factor has been eliminated.

To correct for the number of categories (which was not necessary in our analysis, except when dealing with division of labor items) it is necessary to make another correction factor. To adjust V (or V') scores based on 4 categories to obtain an estimate of what the score would be based on 5 categories we multiply $V_{(4)}$ by 24/15, or in general,

$$V_{k(c)} = \frac{n^2 - 1}{k^2 - 1} V_k$$

where $V_{k(c)}$ is the corrected V score based on k categories, n is the desired number of categories and V_k is the original V score based on k categories.

Interrelationships among Three Microconsensus Measures, V, M, and D

In a method similar to the analysis of variance technique wherein an individual's deviation from the total mean is partitioned into two components, we may likewise partition an individual school board member's deviation from his superintendent's score. Thus, for a score in board i, we have

$$(X_{ij} - Y_i) = (X_{ij} - \bar{X}_i) + (\bar{X}_i - Y_i) \tag{1}$$

where X_{ij} equals score for member j of board i, $\bar{X}_i$ equals mean score for all members of board i, and Y_i equals score of superintendent i.

Equation (1) indicates that the variation can be broken down into two parts, the deviation of the school board member's score from the mean of his board and the variation of the mean school board response from the superintendent's response. Squaring both sides of (1) gives:

$$(X_{ij} - Y_i)^2 = (X_{ij} - \bar{X}_i)^2 + (\bar{X}_i - Y_i)^2 + 2(X_{ij} - \bar{X}_i)(\bar{X}_i - Y_i) \tag{2}$$

Equation (2) represents the squared deviation of member j (board i) from the superintendent's response. Within each board there will be n_i (= number of members of board i) of these deviations. Summing over all members within a particular board, we have

$$\sum_{i=1}^{n_i} (X_{ij} - Y_i)^2 = \sum_{j=1}^{n_i} (X_{ij} - \bar{X}_i)^2 + n_i(\bar{X}_i - Y_i)^2$$
$$+ 2(\bar{X}_i - Y_i) \sum_{j=1}^{n_i} (X_{ij} - \bar{X}_i) \tag{3}$$

* This appendix was prepared by William Douglas Brooks.

Since
$$\sum_{j=1}^{n_i} (X_{ij} - \bar{X}_i)$$

is the sum of deviations of all members of board i around its own mean, the final term of (3) becomes zero. We have finally,

$$\sum_{j=1}^{n_i} (X_{ij} - Y_i)^2 = \sum_{j=1}^{n_i} (X_{ij} - \bar{X}_i)^2 + n_i(\bar{X}_i - Y_i)^2$$

which corresponds to $n_iD = n_iV + n_iM$, or

$$D = V + M \tag{4}$$

Name Index

Subject Index

Anxiety in role conflict, 277–280
and career satisfaction, 279
and job satisfaction, 278
and the worry score, 279
Attitudes, educational, homogeneity of the school board on and consensus, 183–185
measurement of, 184
of school board and role consensus, 193–195

Behavioral variability, assumptions of Linton, 26
Bureaucracy, characteristics of a, 100

Career satisfaction of superintendent, and role conflict, 276–277, 278–279
and role consensus, 214
and school board conformity, 234
Community, characteristics of, related to role consensus, 207–210
related to school board conformity, 235–237
Conflict, see Role conflict
Conformity, school board, 222–243
and evaluation of superintendent, 240–241
and motivation of members for seeking their positions, 238–240
and role consensus, 217, 218–219, 237–238
and superintendent's career satisfaction, 232, 234
and superintendent's evaluation of board, 233

Conformity, school board, and superintendent's job satisfaction, 232, 234
and superintendent's worry scale, 234–235
operational definition of, 224–230
problems in analysis of, 222–224
specification of role definers in analysis of, 222–223
Consensus on role definition instruments, among members of a single school board, 167–169
between a superintendent and his school board, 169–174
between superintendents and school board members, 116–121
intercorrelations among consensus measures, 170–171
methodological problems in obtaining summary microscopic score for, 170–174
see also Role consensus
Culture, concept of, 15–30
and postulate of role consensus, 22–30
as a tool of anthropologists, 21–22
impact on psychology, 23
impact on sociology, 23
C. Kluckhohn's formulation of, 22, 27
Linton's formulation of, 24–26
operational problems, 27–29
pitfalls in its use, 24
Smith's observations on, 23, 29
variant definitions of, 22–23
Culture concepts of Linton, 24–26
Culture patterns, ideal, 26

Data processing, 91
Deviant behavior, see Conformity